THE INSIDERS' GUIDE
TO THE OUTER BANKS OF NORTH CAROLINA

by
St. Leger "Monty" Joynes
and
Dave Poyer

Published and Distributed by
Storie/McOwen Publishers, Inc.
Highway 64
P.O. Box 308
Manteo
North Carolina 27954
(919) 473-5881

REVISED EDITION

7th printing, revised 1986

Copyright ©1986 by Dave Poyer and Monty Joynes
Printed in the United States of America

All rights reserved. No part of this book may be reproduced in any form without permission, in writing, from the publisher, except by a reviewer who wishes to quote brief passages in connection with a review in a magazine or newspaper.

ISBN 0-912367-11-3

PREFACE

The Outer Banks of North Carolina used to be a vacation traveler's secret, perhaps in the same way Sanibel Island, Florida was before the world learned of its shelling grounds. Many Tar Heels and Virginians knew of its get-away, restorative pleasures, but invitations to Nags Head cottages were reserved only for special friends and family.

Today, although The Outer Banks attract over a million visitors each year, the pace and character of the barrier islands remain in contrast to the accustomed places of most people.

We have enjoyed brief visits and weeks of cottage living on The Outer Banks for over 30 years. In many respects, despite the bypass road, the new shopping centers, and the other commercial developments, the essence of The Banks is the same that we remember from our childhood.

It was with affection and genuine respect for The Outer Banks and its natives that we undertook this book in 1978. As experienced travel writers, we set out to cover the historical attractions, recreation amenities, hotels and motels, restaurants, and gift shops in an organized, comprehensive manner. We engaged the enthusiastic support of old and new friends from Corolla to Ocracoke. Through their eyes and from their life long experiences, we became "insiders" and were treated to a wealth of cultural treasures.

The orientation for this book is north to south. The first chapter starts at the north end of the islands and works milepost by milepost to Portsmouth Island. We've included strip maps that you can easily read and understand. Wherever possible, when we are profiling restaurants, motels, or attractions, the order of appearance will also run north to south.

Part of the practicality of the maps and their accompanying legends is not only showing you where you are, but also what is all around you. You will find that every map legend refers you to the page where the profile is printed, and every profile refers you to the map,notated by mileposts. If you are finishing up the Elizabethan Gardens around lunch time, your Insiders' map will show you the nearby restaurants. Just review the individual profiles and decide where your budget and appetites want to go.

Even if you are a frequent visitor to The Banks, there are many surprises and discovery experiences waiting for you. We thought we knew The Banks, too, until we made it our job to search out every opportunity. Each year there are new places to investigate and report in annual updates of our book.

For newcomers or infrequent visitors, **The Insiders' Guide** will give you the advantage of years of experience and lead you directly to where your interests and personal tastes want to go.

PREFACE

Take time to read our suggestions and to review our maps and you will avoid the two basic travel dilemmas: getting lost and going over the family budget.

We have also spent many days researching your practical questions. What if you needed a hospital emergency room? Where can you get your car or boat repaired on a Sunday? What local phone numbers, or 24-hour services might you need? What should you know in the event of a hurricane warning? We've answered these questions and more in our Directory sections.

Since the Insiders' Guide to the Outer Banks was first published in 1979, it has sold in excess of 90,000 copies. The people who have purahased and used the book in past editions will recognize that this edition has been completely rewritten.

The authors retraced their steps of previous research trips, and not only refreshed the profiles of restaurants, motels, and attractions with new information and changes, but also added new sections and additional depth throughout the book. The format of the new edition has been altered to include this additional material.

The authors wish to express their gratitude to the hundreds of readers who wrote to share their own Outer Banks experiences. Their comments and observations were given careful consideration in the rewriting of this book.

By eating in every restaurant and inspecting every hotel and motel in this book, by researching Banks history and lore, and experiencing the hundreds of attractions, recreation spots, and shops, we have come to enjoy the Outer Banks in a personally meaningful way. There are lessons to be learned and a unique human spirit to be acknowledged on these islands. That, perhaps, is the real secret of the Outer Banks. We've done everything that we know to help you discover it for yourself.

Monty and Dave

Acknowledgements: For their help during the updating of this edition, the authors and publishers would like to thank Gigi Rozelle, Darroll Midgette, Ellen Gaskill.

Staff and Credits: McOwen Advertising: C.J. Oakley, Bill LeSueur, Joyce Strasser, Rick Magyan, interior design, production, cover art.

Storie/McOwen Publishers: Beth Storie, copy editor; Allan Graham, advertising sales.

Photography: Courtesy of J. Foster Scott, a free lance photographer who may be contacted at P.O. Box 16, Nags Head; 473-3033.

Line Drawings: Courtesy of Jerry Miller, Raleigh, N.C.

ABOUT THE AUTHORS

St. Leger "Monty" Joynes is a native of Norfolk, Virginia and has had a 20-year career as a writer and editor. He was the founding editor of two regional magazine publications, and was the Associate Publisher of *Holiday*, the national magazine, before becoming a book author.

As a travel author, he has co-authored four best selling regional travel guides. Hundreds of his travel related feature magazine articles have been published, and he is the author of two novels.

Monty's special expertise is in the field of food and beverage service, and hospitality industry accommodations. He serves as a consultant in these areas, and has been a frequent guest speaker at meetings and conventions nationally.

Dave Poyer is a novelist, Naval Reserve officer, diver, sailor, and defense analyst. He settled in the mid-Atlantic after leaving the regular Navy ten years ago. Since then he has published on historical and recreational topics in nearly every local and regional publication and several national ones. His contributions to the historical, recreational, camping, and shopping sections of this book represent thousands of hours of effort over more than seven years of camping, diving, sailing, researching, and appreciating the Outer Banks, their lifestyle, and their people.

Along with his work on the Insiders series of guidebooks, almost half a million copies of his novels are in print, including *White Continent, The Shiloh Project,* and *Star Seed.* His last book, from St. Martin's Press, was *The Return of Philo T. McGiffin,* a novel about Annapolis. Two more will appear in 1987, *The Dead of Winter* (Tor) and *Stepfather Bank* (St. Martin's). He is now engaged in an ambitious sea trilogy, the first book of which will be *The Med.*

Cape Hatteras

Drawing by Jerry Miller

TABLE OF CONTENTS

PREFACE	3
ABOUT THE AUTHORS	5
INSIDE **THE OUTER BANKS**	13
GETTING AROUND	21
THE NORTHERN BANKS	23
INSIDE **SOUTHERN SHORES, DUCK, SANDERLING and COROLLA**	27
Attractions	32
Recreation	35
Developments	36
INSIDE **KITTY HAWK**	43
Attractions	45
Recreation	49
INSIDE **KILL DEVIL HILLS**	51
Attractions	58
Recreation	63
INSIDE **NAGS HEAD**	66
Attractions	68
Recreation	73
Hang Gliding	75
INSIDE **BODIE ISLAND**	86
Attractions	86
U-85	89
OUTER BANKS **ACCOMMODATIONS**	108
Southern Shores, Duck, Sanderling and Corolla	8
Kill Devil Hills	120
Nags Head North	131
Nags Head South	136
Roanoke Island	142
Hatteras Island	147
Ocracoke	155
RENTALS - Cottages, Condominium & Apartment	163
Rental Firms	169
CAMPGROUNDS	178
Beaches North of Oregon Inlet	178
Bodie Island	179
Roanoke Island	180
Hatteras Island	181
Ocracoke	186
OUTER BANKS **CONDOMINIUMS**	188
BUYING REAL ESTATE	192

GOLD & SILVER SEASONS	195
OUTER BANKS **RESTAURANTS**	198
Southern Shores, Duck, Sanderling and Corolla	205
Kitty Hawk	207
Kill Devil Hills	213
Nags Head North	225
Nags Head South	231
Roanoke Island	241
Hatteras Island	245
Ocracoke	252
NIGHTSPOTS	258
Southern Shores, Duck, Sanderling and Corolla	258
Kitty Hawk	259
Kill Devil Hills	261
Nags Head North	263
Nags Head South	265
Ocracoke	266
SHOPPING	267
Southern Shores, Duck, Sanderling and Corolla	268
Kitty Hawk, Kill Devil Hills, Nags Head	273
INSIDE **ROANOKE ISLAND**	283
Attractions	291
Downtown	303
Shopping	310
Recreation	312
INSIDE **HATTERAS ISLAND**	317
Attractions	322
Recreation	338
Shopping	351
INSIDE **OCRACOKE**	359
Attractions	363
Shopping	374
FERRY INFORMATION	347, 399
SCUBA DIVING on the Outer Banks	381
OUTER BANKS **FISHING GUIDE**	384
PORTSMOUTH ISLAND	396
SERVICE & INFORMATION **DIRECTORY**	400
Emergency Numbers	402
PLACES OF WORSHIP	415
ANNUAL EVENTS	417
NEARBY **ATTRACTIONS**	421
BE AN INSIDER	429
INDEX	431

DIRECTORY OF MAPS

ROUTES TO THE OUTER BANKS	10
MILEAGE TO THE OUTER BANKS	11
OUTER BANKS AREA	20
NORTHERN BANKS	30
KITTY HAWK	47
KILL DEVIL HILLS	57
WRIGHT BROTHERS NATIONAL MEMORIAL	59
NAGS HEAD NORTH	70
NAGS HEAD SOUTH	80
BODIE ISLAND	89
ROANOKE ISLAND	289
FORT RALEIGH NATIONAL HISTORIC SITE	294
DARE COUNTY REGIONAL AIRPORT	298
DOWNTOWN MANTEO	308
ELIZABETH II STATE HISTORIC SITE	309
PEA ISLAND WILDLIFE REFUGE	323
HATTERAS ISLAND NORTH	336
HATTERAS ISLAND SOUTH	344
HATTERAS VILLAGE	349
CAPE HATTERAS AREA	342
OCRACOKE ISLAND	358
OCRACOKE VILLAGE	373
PORTSMOUTH ISLAND	395
CAPE LOOKOUT NATIONAL PARK	420

10 — AREA MAP

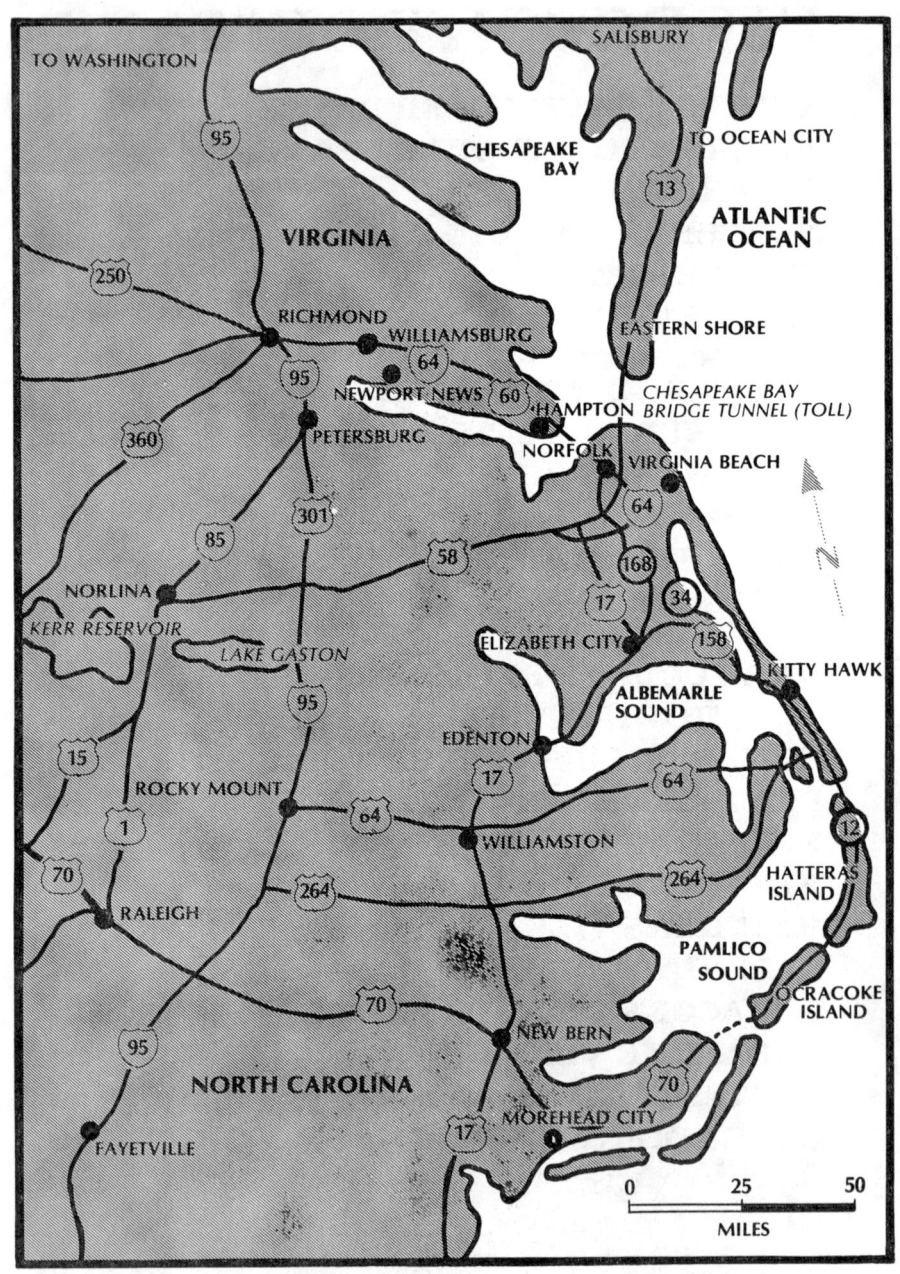

AREA MAP — 11

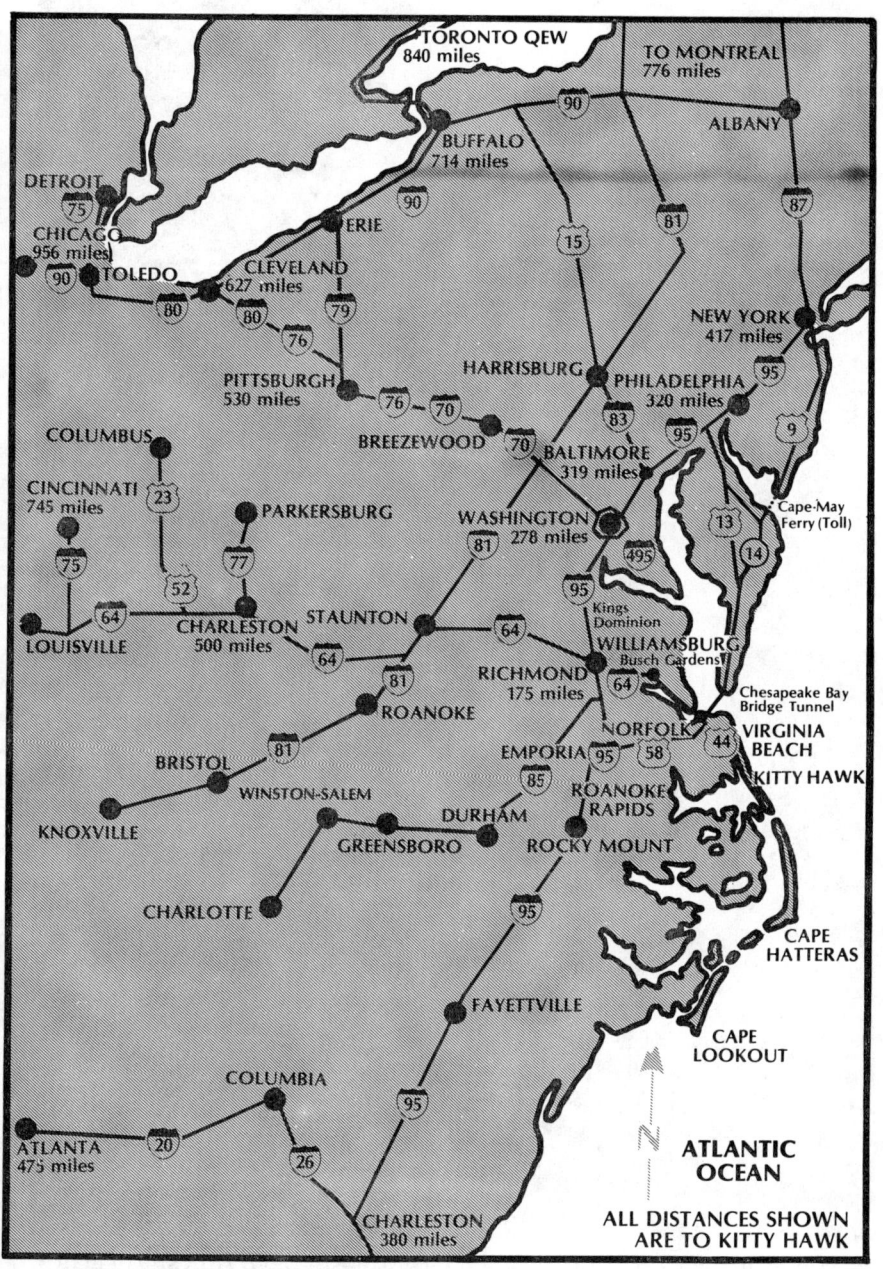

Wright Monument - A granite marker on top of Kill Devil Hill, site of man's first powered flight, honors the Wright brothers successful flight in 1903.

INSIDE
THE OUTER BANKS

What are the Outer Banks?

To the visitor, they are wind, sand, and fun.

To the artist, they are a thin line of beauty drawn at the edge of a blue, blue sea.

To the resident, whose family has lived there for generations, they are, quite simply, home.

How do you describe these lonely, remote, wind and seaswept barriers to the ancient sea?

Let's begin with the land: with geology.

Geologists call the Banks a prime example of the landform called the 'barrier island.' They are made entirely of sand, without the keel of rock that anchors most islands firmly to the earth. It is a fascinatingly evanescent phenomenon in geological terms, a landform so changeable and transient that changes are visible from year to year. A phenomenon that is, even now, in the process of passing forever out of existence.

As most people know, the level of the ocean has changed steadily throughout geological history, as a result of water released or stored up in the great polar icecaps. When, during the ice ages, great amounts of water are withdrawn from circulation, the consequent lowering of the sea extends coastlines far out into what is now the ocean.

This is, as most authorities now agree, how the Banks were formed. They are surprisingly recent. As the last great ice age, some 20,000 years ago, drew to an end, the sea was four hundred feet lower than it is now. The area we now call North Carolina extended some thirty miles farther out, to the edge of the North American Continental Shelf. The polar icecaps, warmed by some still mysterious climatic change, then began to melt, and the sea rose.

The Banks must have begun as dunes, at the very edge of that ancient shore. Rivers from inland contributed silt to build them up. But as the sea rose, the dunes were submerged, becoming sand bars.

Thousands of years passed. The waves kept rolling in, and the bars grew. They also moved, pushed westward and southward by the prevailing northeast winds and seas. The rising sea flooded the low land behind them, forming estuaries that we today call the sounds. The Banks grew, and broke to the surface once again.

A few thousand years later, the rise in the ocean slowed, though it continues even today at the rate of about one foot per century. The Banks had a breathing space. Life began to take root as rain leached the salt from the sand. Beach grass and other vegetation helped to keep sand in place, further slowing the rate of migration.

Today the Outer Banks seem, to our short-lived eyes, a permanent landform. We see today a string of narrow, low islands, about twelve feet above sea level, from a few thousand feet to three miles across, punctuated by narrow inlets. But they're not permanent; they are alive, and they are moving even now. Two examples:

1. Oregon Inlet. Note, as you drive across the Herbert Bonner Bridge, the expanse of low, flat land under the northern piers. This land was not there when the bridge was built in 1964. It's new land, more than a mile of it. Bodie Island is extending itself southward. *All the islands are moving south.*

2. If you know anything about shells, examine closely those you find at the surf line at Nags Head or Coquina Beach or Hatteras. You will notice many old fresh and brackish water snail and oyster shells. You may also see large flat chunks of what looks like dried horse manure. This is peat, formed in freshwater bogs. How did these materials get to the sea side of the islands? Answer: they didn't move. They stayed right where they were and the islands have migrated over them. *All the islands are moving west.*

Of course, it's all happening very slowly. Don't cancel your reservations; it will be thousands of years before the Banks rejoin the North Carolina mainland. But it's fascinating to understand how dynamic, moving, living the Banks are.

Within these living islands, five major natural communities have evolved in response to different conditions. The *Ocean Beach* habitat is between the surf line and the dune line. There is little vegetation in this area, but clams, ghost crabs, and a few other small marine animals exist or venture above the surf line. Primarily the Ocean Beach habitat belongs to the birds: willits, sanderlings, plovers, terns, and gulls. All are present, especially during the summer months.

The *Barrier Dune* habitat is man-made, but is a distinctive community nonetheless. The 14-ft. barrier dunes along the Eastern shore were stabilized with plantings of sea oats, beach grass, cordgrass, panic grasses, and such shrubs as wax myrtle, bayberry, and baccharis. These plants are all salt-resistant and have deep, extensive root systems that hold the sand against the wind and sea. Mice, rabbits, small harmless snakes live here, as well as toads, racerunner lizards, and again, many birds.

Behind and partially protected by the dunes is the *Herb-Shrub* habitat. This extends clear across most of the center of the islands, except where submerged by moving dunes. Characteristic plants are wax myrtle, bayberry, yaupon, live oak, cordgrass, and blackberry. Rabbits and mice are more common than amid the dunes, and larger animals (raccoons, foxes, mink) are seen along with toads, frogs, and lizards and their predatory snakes. Land birds live here, including marsh hawks and short-eared owls.

The *Tidal Marsh* habitat is found on the sound side of most of the islands. Its cordgrass, rushes, and other salt or brackish water plants nourish a vast variety of life: waterfowl, muskrats and nutria, falcons and hawks, ducks. Much of Pea Island, a wildlife refuge famous for its birds, is marsh. Amid the sheltering roots of the marsh plants grow many of the shrimp, crabs, mollusks, and fishes that later leave the marshes and enrich the sea.

The last habitat on the Banks, the *Maritime Forest*, is found at its widest points, where shelter from salt-carrying wind is best. Thick forests of live oak, loblolly pine, dogwood, and red bay alternate with freshwater ponds. Gray squirrel, opossum, and white-tailed deer live here, or have lived within these forests in historic times.

The Banks were like this — wild — when human beings arrived, and history, properly speaking, began.

The early movements of the Indians are shadowy; little of their lore crossed the gulf that separated their culture from that of the invading whites. Apparently North Carolina was settled between 500 and 1000 A.D. by Indians of Algonkian stock. By the late 1500's these had diversified into various tribes, speaking dialects of the original tongue. The Poteskeets were found around Currituck Sound; the Roanoaks, on Roanoke Island and the nearby mainland; the Croatoans, on what is now Hatteras. They ranged widely along the Banks, living on fish, shellfish, wildfowl, and deer; and cultivating maize, beans cucurbits (a gourdlike plant), and sunflowers.

The first European eye to rest on the Banks may have been Italian, for Giovanni Verrazzano sailed and mapped these coasts in 1524; or may have been Spanish, for Lucas Vasquez de Ayllon and others had learned to use Cape Hatteras as a shortcut from the West Indies back to Spain. But the Spanish, then

Pelican profile - The noble head of a brown pelican nesting in the Pamlico Sound forms a study in graphic design crafted in nature.

masters of the riches of the Inca and Aztec, had little interest in goldless forests and sand. They decided not to follow up their explorations and claims with colonies. It was left to the English, relative late-comers to exploration, to step in; and beginning in 1584, they did.

It was on Roanoke Island, where Fort Raleigh National Historic Site is now, that the first English colony in America was planted. It failed; the colony was lost (its complete story is told in the section, 'This is Roanoke Island'). But the English kept trying, and a few years later John Smith succeeded (at Jamestown Island) where John White had failed.

In many ways, residents of the Banks still look north to Virginia as their homes, almost as much as to Raleigh. This may reflect their ancestry, for the Banks were permanently settled by second-generation English who trickled down from Jamestown, Williamsburg, and Norfolk, leavened by fugitives from the King's justice and shipwrecked mariners. These early settlers were the direct ancestors of today's numerous Midgetts, Baums, Grays, Etheridges, Burruses, Tilletts, Manns, Twifords, and other old and famous families of the Banks. They settled at the islands' widest points, where forests offered shelter: Kitty Hawk, parts of Hatteras, and Ocracoke, as well as Roanoke and Colington Islands. It was not an easy life they led, as the section 'This is Kitty Hawk' makes clear; but it was a free one, and doubtless healthier than the cramped and plague-haunted cities of Olde England.

There was one part of the Banks that did flourish in those early days, though, and that was Ocracoke. The inlet, deeper then, was an important place of entry for oceangoing vessels. But Ocracoke was also attractive to another sort of seagoing entrepreneur: the pirate. 'This is Ocracoke' tells the story of the career and fall of old Occacock's most notorious citizen, Captain Edward 'Blackbeard' Teach.

The Bankers, independent in spirit then as they are now, sided firmly with the patriot side during the Revolution. Ocracoke was an important port of entry for French war supplies, and the inhabitants had several lively skirmishes with British would-be invaders. But the inlet silted up later, after Oregon Inlet opened in 1846, and in any case the large new steamers drew deeper water than the sounds and inlets of eastern North Carolina could provide. Ocracoke, and its sister village, Portsmouth, began to decline.

The War between the States brought several sharp battles early in the war. At Hatteras Inlet (August, 1861), Chicamacomico (October, 1861), and Roanoke Island (February, 1862), the Federals won their first victories of the war and established a control over the Banks that lasted throughout the conflict. The inhabitants, few of whom owned slaves, were not strongly atttached to the Southern cause, and many took the oath of allegiance to the United States.

As if to reward them, the postwar years saw a steady flow of Federal dollars to the Banks, and they were spared Reconstruction. Navigational improvements had become unavoidable, and three fine new lighthouses (Corolla, Bodie Island, and Hatteras) were built 1870-1875. These provided employment to locals as lighthouse keepers and assistants, and a flow of something new to these bare islands — cash. Seven stations of the U.S. Lifesaving Service were also built along the coast from the Virginia border to Cape Point, Hatteras.

Changes were taking place in the Banks' internal economy, as well. Nags Head was becoming the area's first and finest summer resort (see 'This is Nags Head'). Commercial fishing and wildfowl hunting replaced wrecking and whale oil as sources of income.

The twentieth century, destined finally to end the fabled isolation of these low, remote islands, began with a symbolic event: the arrival of the brothers Wright. The history of their failures and their final success, told in 'This is Kill Devil Hills,' is probably the best-known story of the Outer Banks, though the Lost Colony must run a close second.

The boom years began in 1930-31. The rest of the country was in a depression, true, but these years marked the completion of the first road accesses to the 'beach,' the Wright Memorial Bridge across Currituck Sound to Kitty Hawk and the Washington Baum Bridge from Roanoke Island to Nags Head. Paved roads down the islands followed, and development began.

Another milestone was passed in the late 30's, when the Federal Government decided to 'save' the Banks. Six Civilian Conservation Corps camps were established and millions of dollars were spent erecting sand fences and planting sand-binding vegetation along 115 miles of shoreline. The Cape Hatteras National Seashore was officially established in 1953, and now controls most of the land from Whalebone Junction down to Ocracoke Inlet, with exemptions for the villages of Rodanthe, Waves, Salvo, Avon, Buxton, Frisco, and Hatteras and Ocracoke Villages. The National Park Service also administers the other two most popular visitor attractions, the Wright Brothers National Memorial and Fort Raleigh.

The Second World War saw the Banks' isolation end — with explosions. In 1942 Hatteras abruptly became the war's front line as Hitler's U-boats struck at American merchant shipping. Scores of vessels went down, many in sight of the Beach's horrified residents; but the tide turned here, eventually, and the first U-boat sunk by Americans lies a few miles off the beach of Bodie Island.

The postwar period saw two concurrent booms; short-term visitors, attracted by the National Park Service facilities and the sea, and longer-term summer residents. The now-ubiquitous beach cottage, built on piers or posts in case of hurricane flooding, appeared first at Nags Head and has spread steadily north. Until recently, the permanent (winter) population of the area had not changed much since 1900. That population has grown significantly, however, in the past few years. These permanent residents, many of whom own, run, or work in seasonal retail establishments, now derive most of their income from services to visitors, though commercial fishing is still important in Hatteras and Wanchese.

These independent, clannish Bankers deeply love their home islands. It is for the visitor, though, that the Outer Banks seem to have been designed.

For camping, fishing, swimming, hang gliding, surfing; for tennis and golf; for beachcombing, birdwatching, and just lying on a fine sand beach in the sun. For vacationing, honeymooning, winding down, taking it easy, dropping out, goofing off. For learning a little American history first-hand. For getting to know the sea and wind again. That's what the Banks are really for.

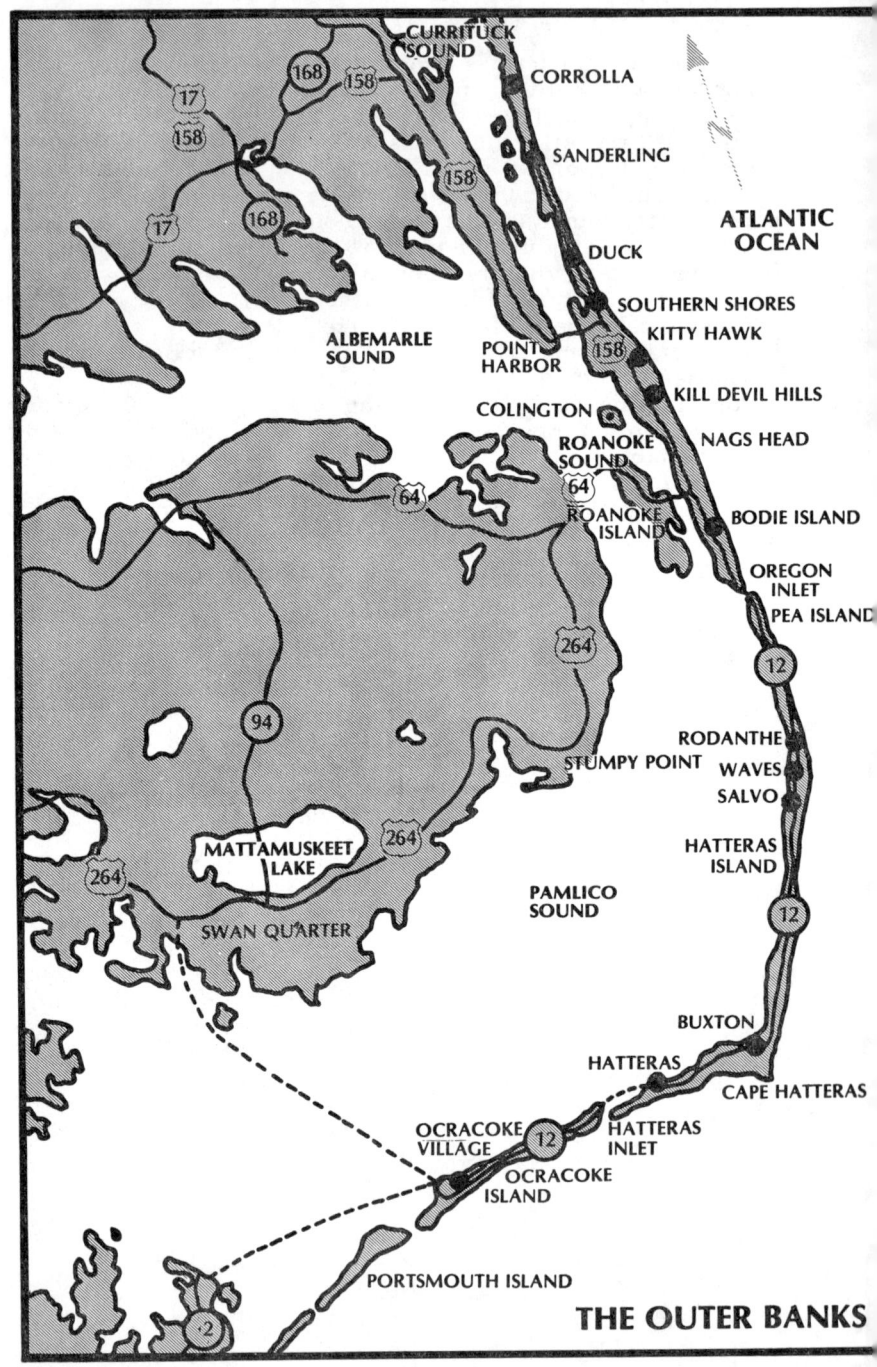

THE OUTER BANKS

GETTING AROUND

The new arrival to the Banks will come in one of three ways: by car, by light plane, or by boat. Most will arrive by private auto, from the north via Route 158, from the west via Routes 64 or 264, or from the south on Cedar Island or Swan Quarter Ferries. A few will fly in to the Dare County or First Flight airfields. And a few will cruise in on private boats, perhaps the most enjoyable way of all to arrive.

You have to have a car to really enjoy the Banks. There is, unfortunately, no real alternative to the automobile. You can walk around Manteo or Ocracoke Village, but you can't walk from Kitty Hawk to Salvo, unless you're tougher than the authors. There is no regular inter-island bus service, though charter busses are available (see 'Directory'). If you fly or sail into the Northern Banks you can rent a car (again, see 'Directory'). Bicycle? A nice idea, but you should be careful. Over the last few years, while the 158 Bypass has been resurfaced, an extra width has been added on each side of the road from Nags Head through Kitty Hawk to allow for bikers. This improvement has made cycling much safer on the Banks but with all the summer traffic you should still exercize caution. If you're going on the cheap, it may be possible to hitchhike, but you know the risks.

Roads on the Outer Banks have been greatly improved. The once narrow Rt. 158 Bypass has now been resurfaced and widened in Nags Head, Kill Devil Hills, and Kitty Hawk — up to five lanes in some places where traffic is heavy. Pavement extends all the way up to Corolla. From Whalebone Junction south Highway 12, a two-laner with some rough spots, leads all the way to Hatteras Village. Oregon Inlet is crossed by a modern concrete bridge which, incidentally, gives a beautiful view of the inlet. Hatteras Inlet is crossed by a free ferry; see Hatteras section for schedule. Continuing south, Highway 12 on Ocracoke is paved but ends at Ocracoke Village, where toll ferries connect to Swan Quarter and Cedar Island, N.C. See Ocracoke section for information on these ferries.

A note of caution: in storms, the beachfront roads and Highway 12 may be flooded or cut by overwash as heavy seas break through the barrier dunes. Ferry service is stopped during storms and even the bridges can't be called totally safe. Please read the section on 'storms' in the Directory.

Sea oats, sand and blue sky await beachcombers along miles of uninhabited beaches on the Outer Banks of North Carolina.

THE NORTHERN BANKS

The history of the Currituck County section of the Outer Banks is a repetition of two themes: hunting and government. Let's begin with the ducks.

One of the least known, least documented (except for the Currituck County Historical Society's excellent efforts) parts of the Banks' long history is the story of rich men, waterfowl, and hunting clubs.

After Currituck and Caffey Inlets closed late in the nineteenth century, the sound, till then salty like those further south, suddenly changed. Marine plants and animals were replaced by those that thrived best in brackish (slightly saline) waters and marshes. The marshes began to attract thousands of ducks, geese, and swans. As the century drew to its close, a few northern businessmen discovered the new sport and began shooting there on a regular basis. The trip down then, though, was far rougher than it is today — most of them came by boat — and once they were here, they found it hard to live the way the local North Carolinians did.

The solution? Hunting clubs — enormous, semipalatial clubhouses, fitted with fireplaces, carpets, Tiffany chandeliers, oil paintings. In the years between 1869 and 1922, several great clubs were built on the Northern Banks, forming perhaps the closest analog to the "Great Houses" of Britain that America offers. Monkey Island was the first. Narrows Island, Whalehead, and Swan Island quickly followed. All were remote, luxurious, rambling houses with great screened porches and plenty of bedrooms and fireplaces. And they are all still there, back on the islands that dot the bay, or sited grandly at the edge of the marshes, handy to the duckblinds and boatsheds. It was a setting worthy of a Fitzgerald novel.

Of them all, the grandest, in some ways the most typical, and the easiest to find is —Whalehead.

The Whalehead Club began in 1874, when the "Lighthouse Club" (its original name) was formed by a group of wealthy men from New York. They hunted and fished there quietly enough for some fifty years, employing local Bankers as superintendents

and guides.
In 1922 Edward Knight, a Philadelphia man with interests in sugar, oil, and publishing, bought the property. Norris Austin, the Corolla postmaster, whose family has lived here since 1891, told us the story of how Knight tried to get his wife, also an avid shootist, admitted into the hitherto males-only club. The other members wouldn't have her. So he bought the place, renamed it Whalehead, then tore it down and began building a far grander clubhouse, a few hundred yards southwest of Corolla Lighthouse.

This, the present building, was completed in 1925, at a cost of around $383,000. For that kind of money in those days you got a three-story mansion of thirty-six rooms, ten full and two half baths. You got a coppered roof, screened verandas, custom dredging, and arched wooden bridges to your own little island. Knight died eleven years later, and the immense soundfront house passed from owner to owner. In World War II it was leased to the Coast Guard and used as a barracks. After that it was a hunting lodge again, for a time, then a boy's school (Corolla Academy, still active in England), then headquarters for a rocket testing company. It is now owned by developers.

Whalehead stands deserted now, its plaster deteriorating, paint flaking, windows staring dimly out over the lawns that slope down to the marshy sound. Abandoned refrigerators lean on the verandahs like ancient guests. There's talk of restoring the old lodge as a clubhouse, once the area is subdivided; but for the moment it stands empty, a monument to days when the northern Banks were remote, unknown, a land of sky-thronging clouds of ducks, slow-spoken Bankers, and well-dressed millionaires 'roughing it.'

The second "theme" in the history of the northern Banks has been the U.S. Government; specifically, the Coast Guard (formerly the U.S. Lifesaving Service). The two lifesaving stations at Corolla and the three farther south in Currituck County provided employment for the local inhabitants and contact with the larger world outside. The Corolla Lighthouse is still a U.S. facility, beaming its light far out to sea, though most of today's larger ships stay well clear of the shoaling water off the beach.

Today Corolla, and all the northern Banks, are undergoing rapid change. Subdivision and development are replacing the old patterns of fishing and soundside dwelling, and displacing or overshadowing the people whose ancestors lived simply here for centuries. The 159 permanent residents of Corolla are still isolated, but not for the same reasons. The pattern of development north of the Dare County line seems to be avoiding the obvious commercialism that prevails farther south, but in the process it is becoming exclusive. Residential areas are intensely private. The roadless expanse of Back Bay National

25 — SOUTHERN SHORES, DUCK, SANDERLING AND COROLLA

WHALESHEAD LIGHTHOUSE

Drawing by Jerry Miller

Wildlife Refuge to the north further limits access. Only residents are granted permits for transit (Virginia Beach is only 11 miles away), and these too are limited; there's a midnight curfew, and only so many trips are permitted per day through the refuge. The result is still isolation, which avoids a lot of the problems that free access for tourists brings, but which also makes many of the old residents rather bitter. It is a conflict between tradition and change, a conflict that the Outer Banks knows all too well.

INSIDE

SOUTHERN SHORES, DUCK, SANDERLING and COROLLA

It used to be that visitors coming to The Banks thought of Kitty Hawk as the "beginning" of the beach area. This was, after all, where almost all the rental cottages began unless you were lucky enough to have friends who owned some of the exclusive, private property above Southern Shores. Well, the the last few years on the Outer Banks have seen some dramatic changes in this northern beaches area. And, though the age-old struggle of development versus non-development has certainly played out here, we must admit that we are pleased and impressed with the quality and respect for the natural surroundings that seems to have guided the hand of the growth that has occurred.

To investigate Southern Shores, Duck, Sanderling, and Corolla, you first find Route 1200, Duck Road. This winding, scenic two-laner leaves Rt.158 at the stoplight in front of the Tourist Bureau's Welcome Center, located on the northern edge of Kitty Hawk, and heads north from there.

Southern Shores, one of the oldest, planned real estate developments on the Banks, is the first area you'll be driving through. It's a year round and summer residential community and you'll see a lot of cottages, though there are more substantial year round homes nestled nearby in the soundside woods. In the last several years, residential neighborhoods with names like Tuckahoe, Nantucket, and Georgetown Sands have been developed and dot the road to Duck.

You're in for some beautiful scenery as you drive along this seaside route. The road winds along for miles, rising briefly for a look at flat, brackish Currituck Sound, then diving to shelter itself between dunes covered with low, scrub woods. An occasional private road leads off to the right, to expensive, tasteful oceanfront cottages.

Despite the growth, the feeling to this area still is uncluttered, making obvious the success of the strict building codes established by the original developer and maintained by the Southern Shores city council. It's worth your time for an afternoon drive to just meander through this community.

continuing on till you find yourself in Duck.

Duck is reminiscent of the small villages of Hatteras but with a touch more polish. Like them, it's insular and self-sufficient, with many of its old time residents still depending on fishing for their livelihood. Many of the other residents, however, make their living either owning or working in the many new retail shops, real estate agencies, sailing centers and sundry other stores that have sprung up over the past few years. Still, as with its neighbor to the south, Duck has managed to maintain a somewhat quaint visage, offering plenty of vacationer amenities but without the commercial feeling of the lower beaches.

The sea is quite close to Duck and worth a right turn when you reach the village. Park and walk over the dunes. Sea oats, wild beans and peas, and a variety of shore birds throng the seaside; loons, cormorants, gannet, the same birds one sees at Pea Island; and of course, terns and gulls, hordes of them. Climb to the top of a dune and look far out to see. See a stirring in the water, as if silver-blue wheels were rolling just beneath the surface? They're bottlenosed porpoises, Tursiops truncatus, common in these fish-rich waters.

Leaving Duck and heading north, you will pass signs for the U.S. Army Coastal Engineering Research Facility, an 1800-foot-long-reinforced-concrete coastal engineering research pier used by the Corps of Engineers to investigate the forces that create and destroy beaches. Casual visitors are not permitted on the pier.

Traveling even further north on Rt. 1200, you enter the truly impressive development of Sanderling. Lining the oceanfront and sound are some of the most consistently beautiful houses to be found on the Outer Banks, all built under the watchful eye - and codes - of the Sanderling owners and managers. Throughout the development, much attention has been put to creating and maintaining landscaped areas filled with flowers and greenery indigenous to the Outer Banks. There's also a community pool, tennis courts, and nature trails. Regular activities are planned for the community members, such as evening clambakes, Fourth of July fireworks, and Labor Day picnics.

Winding roads take you on a tour of well-planned lots and architecture. The whole development really could be held up as an example of how, in these authors opinions, any seaside development should be handled. The folks in charge of Sanderling describe it as "the peaceable kingdom," a well coined phrase in this instance.

Appointments to see the property may be made by calling 261-2181 between 9:00 a.m. and 5:00 p.m. The sales center is located on Quail Way; just follow the signs posted in the community.

In the summer of 1985, another shining star was added to the Sanderling development, The Sanderling Inn and Restaurant.

SOUTHERN SHORES, DUCK, SANDERLING AND COROLLA — 29

Though both are reviewed thoroughly in the chapters to follow, they deserve some special mention here due to their architectural and historical significance. The Inn, built with architectural details accurate to the old Nags Head style, is a bastion of the Southern charm and grace that characterized this area at the turn of the century. It is large and airy with wide porches that provide cool, afternoon spots for conversation or drinks. Cedar shake siding, natural wood interiors, and English country antiques complete the mood of quiet elegance.

The Sanderling Restaurant is noteworthy because it is housed in an Historic Landmark, Caffeys Inlet Station. Designated U.S. Lifesaving Station Number Five, it was built on its present site in 1899 when, along with other stations, such as two at Corolla, one at Ocean Sands, and others dotting the shore every seven miles, it served as a home to the men who regularly patrolled the beaches searching for signs of shipwreck. Though abandoned and deteriorating for a number of years, the Station was given a new lease on life when it was originally renovated to be used as the Main Office for Sanderling real estate. The restaurant took over the space in the fall of 1985.

Just north of Sanderling you will come to a sign that tells you that you've left Dare County and are entering Currituck County and The Pine Island Sanctuary. You're also entering an area that, until October of 1984, was closed to all but property owners, blocking curious visitors from exploring the vast beach to sound undeveloped expanses. Though the area is now open to all who would venture and the number of houses has dramatically increased in the last two years this tip of the Outer Banks area still maintains a close semblance to the way life was on these shores many years ago. The Currituck Lighthouse blinks its warning each night; wild horses and other wildlife roam the undeveloped dunes; ghost-like hunt clubs provide picturesque reminders of the regal life they once provided; and mile after mile of undeveloped beach still anchor the northern tip of the main community of Corolla.

Modern-day life has come to this area in the form of carefully planned and developed communities, most notably one called Corolla Light. Here the focus is on large, well-built beach homes and villas clustered around private recreational facilities such as indoor pools, racquetball, tennis, and jogging trails, all tied together by attractive landscaping.

It's certainly a new look for this area which for so long stood untouched by any large-scale development. But, as we said before, it is well done and, to date, mindful of the fragile coastal beauty that created its appeal in the first place.

30 — SOUTHERN SHORES, DUCK, SANDERLING AND COROLLA

NORTHERN BANKS

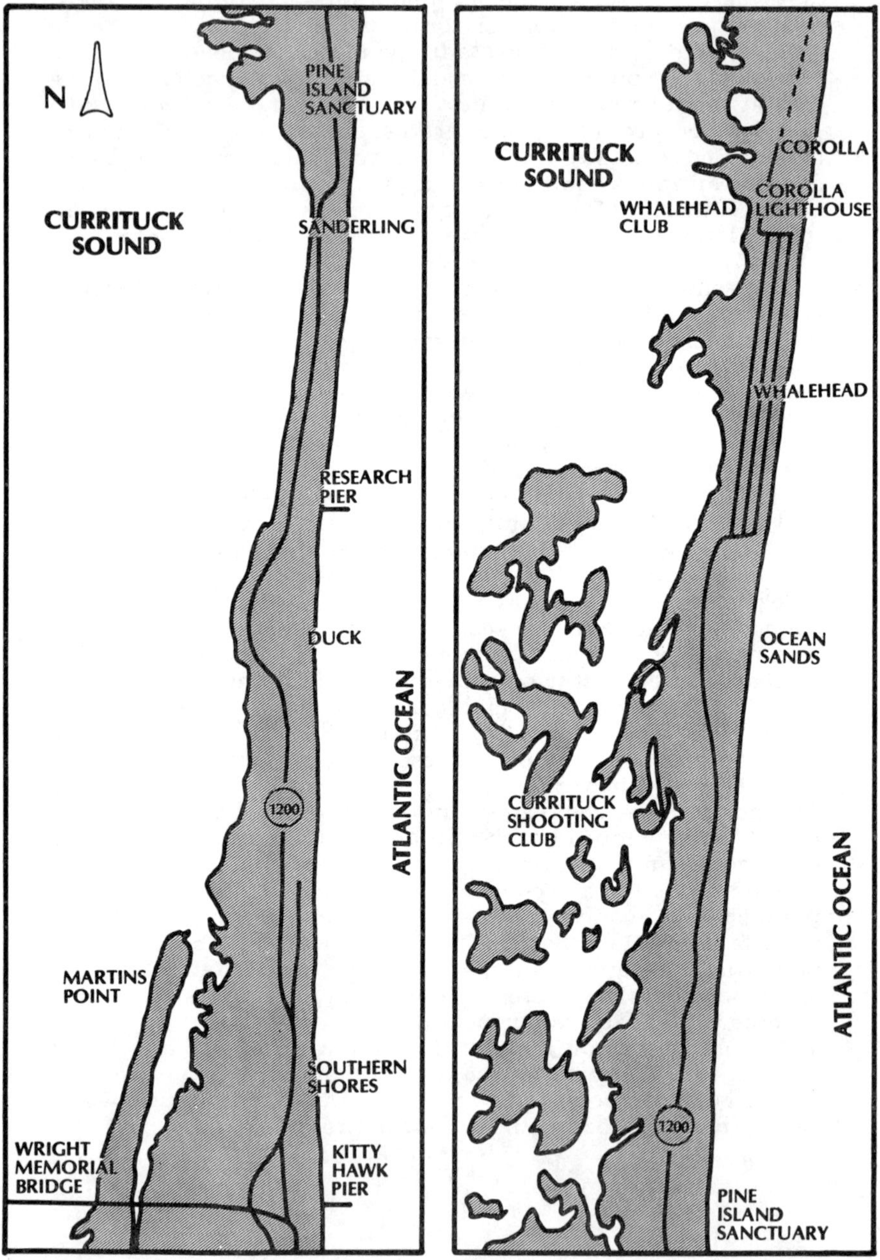

SOUTHERN SHORES, DUCK, SANDERLING, COROLLA

 ATTRACTIONS:
1. Pine Island Sanctuary, pg. 32
2. Corolla Lighthouse and Keeper's House, pg. 32

 RECREATION:
1. Barrier Island Sailing Center, pg. 35
2. Duck Landing Sailing, pg. 35

 HOTELS/MOTELS/CAMPGROUNDS:
1. The Sanderling Inn, pg. 118

RESTAURANTS:
1. Barrier Island Inn, pg. 204
2. The Sanderling Restaurant, pg. 205
3. Duck Deli, pg. 206
4. Osprey Landing Gourmet, pg. 206

SHOPPING:
1. Duck Blind Limited Art Gallery, pg. 272
2. Scarborough Faire, pg. 271
3. Osprey Landing, pg. 270
4. Loblolly Pines, pg. 269
5. Lucky Duck Gift Shop, pg. 269
6. Wee Winks, in Duck, pg. 269
7. Winks, in Corolla, pg. 268
8. Kellogg's True Value Home Center, pg. 268
9. Lion's Paw, pg. 270
10. The Farmer's Daughter, pg. 270

NIGHTSPOTS:
1. Barrier Island Inn, pg. 258

NORTHERN DEVELOPMENTS:
1. Northpoint, pg. 39
2. Ship's Watch, pg. 36
3. Ocean Pines, pg. 37
4. Barrier Island Station, pg. 36
5. Port Trinitie, pg. 39
6. Corolla Light, pg. 37

 SOUTHERN SHORES, DUCK SANDERLING, COROLLA
ATTRACTIONS

PINE ISLAND SANCTUARY

North of Sanderling   Map, pg. 30

   Just north of Sanderling as you pass the sign that tells you you're entering Currituck County, you come upon an area that is nothing but open beach to sound land as far as the eye can see. This is, for the most part, Pine Island Sanctuary. The property, which was donated to the Audubon Society by a local man with a deep respect for the coastal environment and the wildlife that lives there, is home to ducks, gulls, sanderlings and other sea birds, racoon, deer, rabbit, and many other animals. Audubon members can arrange with their local chapters to tour the Sanctuary. But for non-Audubon members, the rule is to stay off the property, for the protection of the dunes and the wildlife. Even driving through the Sanctuary, though, on SR 1200, is a pleasurable, relaxing experience and one we highly recommend.

COROLLA LIGHTHOUSE AND KEEPER'S HOUSE

Corolla Village   Map, pg. 30

   The northernmost of the four lighthouses of the Banks, Corolla was put in commission at what was then called Whales Head in 1875. Still active, still U.S. Government property, this

Chicamacomico Coast Guard Station - located in Rodanthe.

150-foot, 50,000-candlepower red brick tower dominates the small village of Corolla; but its surroundings of dunes and scrub brush seem to diminish it, unlike the Bodie Island and Hatteras lighthouses, which seem to stand out on the open spaces of the Southern Banks. The lighthouse is easily accessible from the nearby road.

The Keeper's house, located in the shadow of the lighthouse, has in the last several years been rescued from certain death by a local historical architect, John Wilson, IV. He and other concerned friends worked to get the house designated as an Historic Landmark, then went to work restoring the building to its original splendor. So far, the exterior surfaces and porches have been restored and work is proceeding on the interior. Though visitors are rarely allowed inside the building, a tour of the outside should be put on your "must do" list while you're on the Banks; the house is a beauty and a worthwhile lesson in the value of preserving our historic past.

SOUTHERN SHORES, DUCK SANDERLING, COROLLA
RECREATION

BARRIER ISLAND SAILING CENTER

North of Duck   261-7100
                    Map, pg. 30

Bill Miles and Joy Myers, both sailing and windsurfing enthusiasts, operate this sailing center, located at the end of the long pier behind Barrier Island Inn. Here you can rent sailboards, fun boards, super cats, and monohulls at hourly or half day rates. Bill and Joy also offer windsurfing and sailing lessons. One of the attractions about this spot, apart from its well-maintained equipment, is the breezy gazebo at the end of the pier where you not only rent your equipment but where you can also spend a lazy hour or so watching sailers, swinging in the hammock, or talking with other would-be water sports participants. The Inn is nearby too for respites of cold beer and snacks.

DUCK LANDING SAILING

Duck   261-7245
                    Map, pg. 30

There's no lack of places to sail in these parts! Duck Landing, located across the street from The Lucky Duck gift shop, offers lessons in both windsurfing and sailing. You can also rent windsurfing boards and sailboats if you're already a pro. Or, if you prefer to ride something that doesn't depend on the wind to move it, you can also rent jet skis.

Duck Landing is open from Memorial Day until early fall from 10:00 a.m. till 6:00 p.m.

SOUTHERN SHORES DUCK, SANDERLING, COROLLA

DEVELOPMENTS

SHIPS WATCH

SR Box 270 Y
Duck, NC 27949

261-2231
800-334-1295

Map, pg. 30

Ships Watch, a co-ownership development, is located just north of the Barrier Island Inn a mile or so above Duck village. Designed for ocean-to-sound enjoyment, the plans call for 53 individual homes to be built, all on about a half acre of land each. The homes are sturdily built and beautifully decorated, with open decks, screened porches, cathedral ceilings, and kitchens that probably are better equipped than most vacationers' kitchens. A wet bar, VCR, color television, and stereo cassette and radio are all provided. The master bedroom suite features a large Jacuzzi, king-size bed, and color television.

Amenities at Ships Watch include a large, solar heated pool, tennis courts, jogging trails, and a soundside pier.

The co-ownership program allows for complete or shared, deeded ownership.

BARRIER ISLAND STATION

BARRIER ISLAND STATION
Duck

261-3525

Map, pg. 30

Barrier Island Station is being developed in the Northmost part of the resort area, about a mile past the village of Duck. The resort offers an indoor pool, tennis, restaurant, and recreational amenities.

The designs for the six multi-level units are impressive. In addition to two-story, two and three bedroom apartments, there is an 1890 square feet three bedroom design which has four levels.

Private decks, fireplaces, cathedral ceilings, bay windows, thermal windows, lofts and juniper cabinets are a few of the design features.

Barrier Island Station is being offered as a time shared property.

OCEAN PINES

S.R. Box 297
Kitty Hawk, NC 27949

261-4181

Map, pg. 30

The Ocean Pines time-sharing property is located on an ocean-to-sound strip in the northern section of the Outer Banks at Duck. The land is in a residential area, and its seven separate buildings are spread out among the pines and the sand.

The one and two-bedroom cedar-sided units stand on the dunes in two-level balconied clusters. A large sliding glass door open onto each deck-like balcony. Interiors are contemporary, and the design includes a wood-burning fireplace, quarry-tile foyer and hearth, and an ultra-modern kitchen. Project amenities include the private ocean beach, access to the sound, covered and heated all-year swimming pool, jacuzzi, tennis courts, exercise room, and a bike and jogging track.

Ocean Pines is a member of the VHI Exchange Program and provides deeded ownership.

COROLLA LIGHT

Corolla
SR Box 328
Duck, NC 27949

261-4650

Map, pg. 30

Corolla Light is the first total community to be built in this northern Outer Banks area of Corolla. It's located right next to the lighthouse, on 215 acres of ocean to sound property. Over 100 of these acres have been set aside to remain in their natural state for the enjoyment of all owners. This non-cluttered approach to development seems to be the ruling one here.

Currently, individual oceanfront, soundfront and a few interior homes are being built. Later plans call for townhouses to be added.

Corolla Light centers around recreational amenities for year round use. There's a large indoor pavilion in the works that will

Come live your dream.

Live by the sea at Corolla Light, a resort village committed to excellence, dedicated to carefree living.

Be a part of this seaside community where your every need has been planned for and quietly assumed.

Where whatever the season, outstanding recreation facilities will complement your active lifestyle. Indoor swimming, tennis, racquetball... an oceanfront outdoor pool... bike paths and lighted tennis courts... All planned for you to enjoy.

Homesites ready for building. Luxurious Tennis Villas also available.

Let us show you Corolla Light.

Look for us by the historic Corolla Lighthouse, a 20 minute drive north of Duck. You'll see a side of the Outer Banks you won't find anywhere else.

Corolla Light
A RESORT VILLAGE

Corolla Light, P.O. Box 1025, Corolla, NC 27927 / 1-800-682-9899 / 919-453-3313
in North Carolina call toll free   other states call

contain a heated pool, two tennis courts, three racquetball courts, a health club and lounge and a spa. Outdoor facilities include jogging trails, lighted tennis courts, a competition-size pool, shuffleboard, basketball court, and a marina on Currituck Sound for sailing, surfcasting, or windsurfing.

By the time the community is completed, it will have on-site shops and restaurants as well. Central water and waste treatment facilities have been built to allow for this growth.

The setting for Corolla Light is one of the best on the Outer Banks, since it is bordered by Back Bay Wildlife Refuge on one side and sparsely developed, non-commercial beach communities on the other. Appointments to tour the community can be made by calling the number given above.

PORT TRINITIE

Duck 261-3922
SR Box 324
Duck, NC 27949

Map, pg. 30

Port Trinitie, located about 2 miles north of Duck, is a development based on co-ownership, fee simple deeds. Its 22 acres span from ocean to sound and include amenities such as maintained beaches, a pool, and tennis courts.

The co-ownership homes are offered in three floor plans of either 2, 3, or 4 bedrooms. Each home includes a master bedroom suite with its own private deck, a Jacuzzi, a living area that includes a woodburning fireplace and a built-in wet bar, and fully equipped kitchens and laundry rooms. The interior design is tasteful and subdued.

The property is carefully managed so that the homes and the grounds are always well maintained and attractive.

A Reception Center is open on the premises each day from 10:00 a.m. until 5:00 p.m.

NORTHPOINT

Duck Twiddy & Co., 261-3521
Professional Property, 261-7230
Managers

Map, pg. 30

Located in the village of Duck, Northpoint is another of the well built and planned co-ownership communities that are

The early shift - no doubt continuing a morning routine which includes walking the dog, this pair of early risers stroll the beach at North Carolina's Outer Banks while others try their hand at surfcasting into the sun.

prevalant in this northern beaches area. The development stretches from the ocean to the sound and provides amenities such as an enclosed year round swimmimg pool, two tennis courts, a basketball court, and a 100-foot pier extending into the Currituck Sound allowing for boating, fishing, and crabbing.

Northpoint homes, of which there currently are 15 with plans for a few more, are equipped with 4 bedrooms, 2½ baths — one with a large Jacuzzi, a fully equipped kitchen, washer/dryer, wet bar with an ice maker, telephones, fireplace, three color televisions, full stereo system,video disk player, fish cleaning table, gas barbecue grill, large decks, outdoor showers and screened porches.

Sharing in with the Wright brothers fascination with flying, these hang gliders soar above Jockey's Ridge, the east coast's largest sand dune.

INSIDE
KITTY HAWK

Kitty Hawk (the name is probably a corruption of the Poteskeet Indian 'Chickahauk') is the first commercialized part of the Outer Banks that visitors encounter (Southern Shores is actually the first township). It's a town, or an area, typical of the northern Banks — that is, a study in contrasts. There's a quaint old Kitty Hawk nestled far back alongside the sound. There's a more recent, but visibly aging, Kitty Hawk Beach, along the sea on Rt. 158 business. And there are booming new Kitty Hawks to the north, recently incorporated as Southern Shores, and Sanderling, and in the high dunes west of Route 158 bypass. There are long stretches of undeveloped dunes and near-impenetrable soundside woods, and there are miles of cheek-by-jowl summer cottages and glistening new shopping centers.

The Poteskeets moved out of the northern Banks about the time the Etheridges, Perrys, Baums, Gallops, Hills, and Twifords moved in from Virginia. There were not many of them. Living in mean dwellings on the sound side, amid forests and mosquitoes, they fished, raised a few scrawny cattle, and scratched in the sand to grow a few beans. It was a hard and squalid way to live and when, as sometimes happened, a shipful of rich merchandise like cloth, flour, rum, or logs blew ashore in a storm, there was a general stampede to the scene. When the government-appointed Wreck Commissioner arrived, if there was anything left, a *vendue* was held, auctioning off the remains for partial compensation of the vessel's owner. The wives' tales that the Kitty Hawkers used to tempt vessels ashore with lights are probably exaggerated. In 1700, however, it was reported that when "his Majesty's ship the Hady was drove a shore upon the sands between the Inlets of Roanoke and Currituck, the Inhabitants robed her and got some of her guns ashore and shot into her sides and disabled her from getting off." From time to time dead whales, too, were washed up, and trying (cooking) out their oil was another source of income.

Since the northern inlets (Currituck, Caffeys Inlet, and Roanoke, all now closed up) were shallow and treacherous, the northern Banks never developed the trade that Ocracoke and

Portsmouth did, and remained sparsely populated well into the twentieth century. Commercial duck hunting, shrimping, crabbing, eeling, and turtling supplemented the continued income from fishing, and some Kitty Hawkers went to work for the government after 1870, when the Life Saving stations and lighthouses were built.

Kitty Hawk's remoteness and isolation were probably among the reasons the Wrights decided to try out their new flying-machine designs there in 1900. Its steady, strong winds and soft sand were additional advantages. The story of their trials has been covered in 'Kill Devil Hills' section, as that area has since become a separate township.

With the easy access that the new bridges of '30 and '31 provided, the useless sandy stretches of Kitty Hawk suddenly became desirable real estate. By 1950 the old beach road, now Route 158 business, had become effectively choked, and a new bypass was built. Development now centers around this area, in the high sand hills overlooking the sound and Kitty Hawk is today primarily a permanent year round place of residence. But summer months find the area playing host to weekly and seasonal visitors also. It has the sun, sand, wind and ocean of the Outer Banks, but also most of the modern conveniences; shops, stores, golf courses, cable television — things the more remote and romantic section of the Beach lack. Obviously, it's a successful combination, and Kitty Hawk in the future can only grow.

 *KITTY HAWK*
ATTRACTIONS

DARE COUNTY CHAMBER OF COMMERCE INFORMATION CENTER

Rt. 158, MP ½   Map, pg. 47   261-3801

Half a mile east of the Wright Memorial (Currituck Sound) Bridge, you'll see a small red round building on a low rise to your right. This is the local Chamber of Commerce information center. Aside from information on member businesses, the Center operates as a clearinghouse for written or phoned-in inquiries, and can help you with hotel and motel reservations in advance (though they can't make them for you). Mailing address: P.O. Box 90-I, Kitty Hawk, N.C. 27949. Open 9:00 a.m. to 5 p.m. daily, year round.

THE WELCOME CENTER

Rt. 158 Bypass, Mp ¾
Map, pg. 47

Near the northern entrance to the Outer Banks, on a hill next to the Chamber of Commerce office, you'll see a new building designed to resemble the Banks' Life Saving stations of old. This is the new Welcome Center. Staffed by Dare County Tourist Bureau personnel, the Center offers tourist information and comfort facilities. Open from 9 a.m. till 5 p.m. during the off season, it extends its hours during spring, summer and fall to accommodate visitor needs.

KITTY HAWK:

 **ATTRACTIONS:**
1. Dare County Chamber of Commerce, pg. 45
2. Welcome Center, pg. 45

 RECREATION:
1. Duck Woods Golf Course, pg. 49
2. Kitty Hawk Fishing Pier, pg. 49
3. Sea Scape Golf Club, pg. 50
4. Colony House Cinema V & VI, pg. 50

HOTELS/MOTELS/CAMPGROUNDS:
1. Ocean Beach Campground, pg. 178
2. Kitty Hawk Camping Park, pg. 178

 RESTAURANTS:
1. R.V.'s, pg. 207
2. Ella's, pg. 208
3. Trade Winds, pg. 208
4. Station Six, pg. 209
5. Avalon Pier Restaurant, pg. 209
6. Newby's, pg. 211
7. Sportsman's Restaurant, pg. 211

 SHOPPING:
1. Ben Franklin's, pg. 273
2. The Dunes Shops, pg. 273

NIGHTSPOTS:
1. R.V.'s, pg. 259

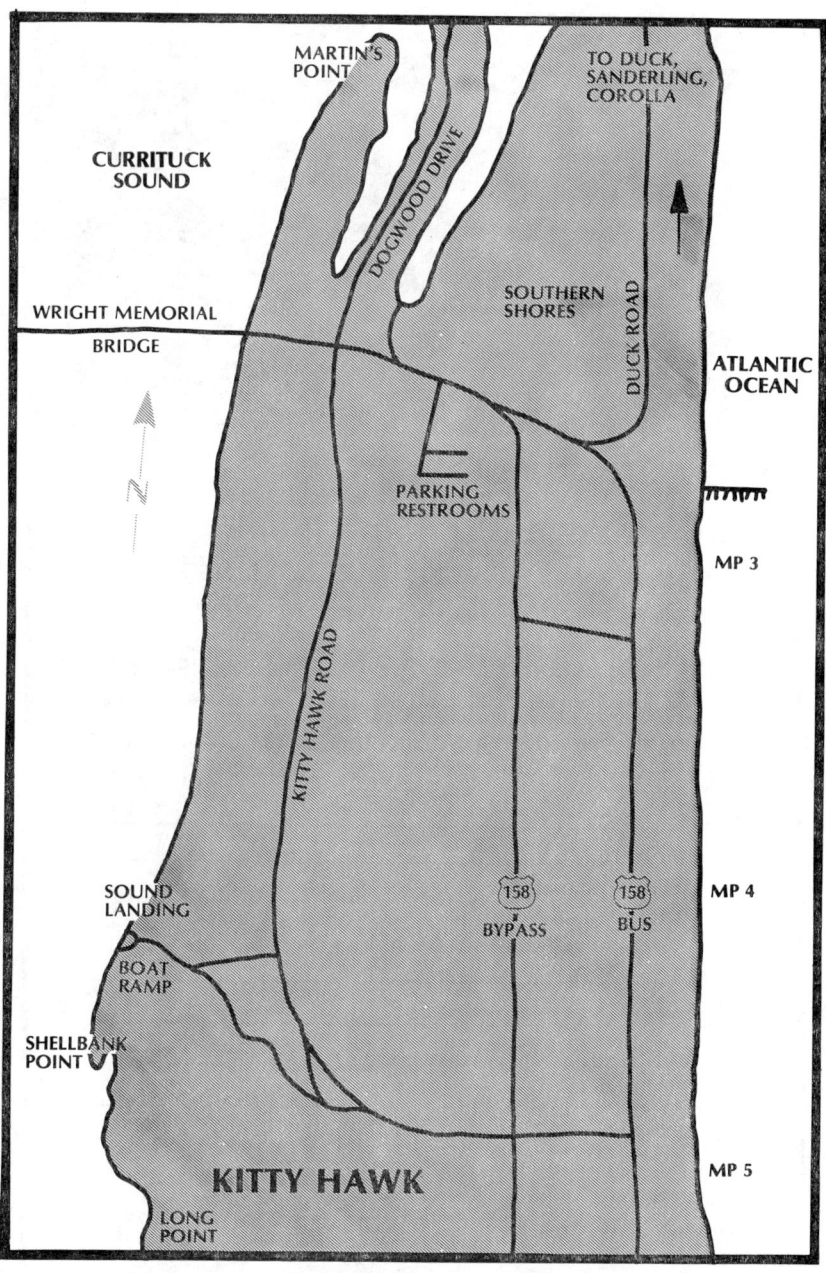

Subscribe and send no money now, or use your Visa or Master Card, or send a check — your choice!

Mail to: Outer Banks Current, P.O. Box 1836, Kill Devil Hills, NC 27948

- - - - - - - - - - - - - - - - - - - -

Please enter my subscription to the Outer Banks Current.
☐ Charge to _____ Visa _____ MasterCard
    # _____
    Exp. Date _____
☐ Enclosed is my check for $14 (Dare & Currituck Counties) *
☐ Please bill me.

Name _____
Address _____
City_____ State_____ Zip_____
Phone_____ Date_____
* Out of area — $17

Outer Banks CURRENT

919-441-3411

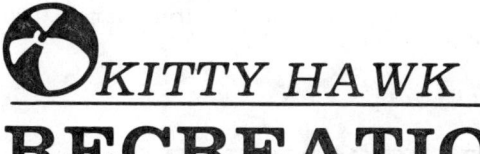
KITTY HAWK
RECREATION

DUCK WOODS GOLF COURSE

Rt. 158 Bypass, MP ¼   261-2744
Map, pg. 47

Duck Woods is the Banks' only private golf course, a green, well-sculpted marvel amid the sandy wastes of the beach. Located just east of the Wright Memorial Bridge, to the north of Rt. 158, Duck Woods has 18 holes, par 72, overall length 6,700 yards. There are the usual sidelines: a full service restaurant, serving beer and wine; a medium-sized pro shop; electric carts for rent; a driving range; a resident PGA professional and staff. Not so routine are two unlighted tennis courts and an outdoor pool. To join a private club like Duck Woods, contact the membership chairman through the number above and arrange for payment of initiation fee and dues. Duck Woods is open year round from 8 a.m. to nightfall.

KITTY HAWK FISHING PIER

Rt. 158 Business, MP 1   261-2772
Map, pg. 47

Owned by Kitty Hawk Piers, this is a privately owned establishment. Kitty Hawk Pier was built in 1954. It's 714 feet in length, lighted, and has a small restaurant, tackle shop, bait, ice, and rental tackle. The depth at the pier varies, since the sandbars just offshore are continually moving. Fishing is good here for all the inshore species normally caught off the Banks: bluefish, gray and speckled trout, flounder, spot, king mackerel, cobia, and channel bass. The state record stiped bass was taken here in 1969 and at one time the pier held the world record for bluefish (for state records and citation weights, along with a detailed discussion of fishing along the Outer Banks, see the Hatteras Island chapter). Kitty Hawk Pier is open April 1 to Thanksgiving. Admission: $2.50 a day, adult or child. Weekly pass $12.00. Seasonal pass, good also at Avalon Pier, $60.00. Handicapped in wheelchairs free.

SEA SCAPE GOLF CLUB

Rt. 158 Bypass, MP 3½   261-2158

Map, pg. 47

Located amid sandy hills on the sound side of Rt. 158 bypass, Sea Scape is an attractive course, though not as refreshingly green to the eye as mainland courses. The links are Scottish-type, without trees or water hazards — but what sand traps! The greens, the owner says, are among the smoothest and most level in the state. Sea Scape is an 18-hole course, par 71 (35 front, 36 back), 6200 yards long.

Amenities: sixty gasoline-powered carts for rent, grill, and Sea Scape Club 19th hole. Because of N.C. state law, if you want hard stuff you'll have to visit the ABC store one mile north and bring it in yourself; the club will provide setups.

Sea Scape is open from 7:00 a.m. till dark every day of the year. We recommend mosquito repellent in summer, especially after wet weather.

COLONY HOUSE CINEMA V & VI

158 Bypass, MP 4½   261-7949

Map, pg. 47

Two additions to the Colony House Cinemas are these two in Kitty Hawk. They provide family entertainment nightly. Check the local newspapers or their marquee for the current shows and times.

INSIDE
KILL DEVIL HILLS

THIS IS KILL DEVIL HILLS

The early history of Kill Devil Hills is indistinguishable from that of Nags Head and Kitty Hawk. In the old days they were all simply part of 'the beach.' The Kill Devil Hills themselves, a region of large, moving dunes, were unpopulated, though a small community known as Rosepock existed during the eighteenth century in the soundside woods north of Kill Devil Hill proper.

The name? There are almost as many explanations as there are sand hills. Some say that one happy day a cargo of New England 'Kill-Devil' rum came ashore and the Hill region was named in memory of it. Some say the name may be a corruption of 'Killdee' or 'killdeer,' a shore bird once common around the dunes. And there are the legends about bargains with the devil, and even more elaborate explanations undoubtedly made up after the fact in order to answer visitors, who persist in asking "why is it called Kill Devil Hills?"

At any rate, this patch of sand hills south of Kitty Hawk and north of Nags Head has been called Kill Devil since at least 1808, and the highest of them, naturally, was called Kill Devil Hill. But it was not until the dawn of the twentieth century that they found their niche in history.

This is the way it happened.

Way out in Ohio, along about 1899, two Yankee brothers, bicycle mechanics, took up building flying-machines as a hobby. No one in those days had yet flown a heavier-than-air machine, and therefore many of their neighbors thought their hobby odd.

In August of 1900, Wilbur and Orville Wright had completed and tested some flying models and were ready to build a man-carrying glider. Examining records of mean wind velocities from around the country, they found that according to the Weather Bureau a place called Kitty Hawk, in North Carolina, had strong, steady winds. They did a bit more research and found that it also had bare hills, made of nice soft sand, the better to crash-land into. Writing ahead to the Kitty Hawk weather station, they received assurances that the direction of the wind

This is the sign of experience.

Thirty years of it in the Outer Banks: development, sales and rentals. Years of getting to know about property values and growth. Years of helping people find just the right property.

- Over 500 rental cottages available.
- Free rental booklet.
- For rental reservations use our toll-free number: 1-800-334-6436.

**ROBERT A. YOUNG & ASSOCIATES • REALTORS
BOX 285, KILL DEVIL HILLS, N.C. 27948
SALES (919) 441-4816 • RENTALS 441-5544**

and the nature of the land answered their requirements. Captain Bill Tate, a prominent Kitty Hawker, wrote:

> If you decide to try your machine here & come I will take pleasure in doing all I can for your convenience & success & pleasure, & I assure you you will find a hospitable people when you come among us.

Wilbur arrived first, on September 13, after a miserable two-day schooner trip from Elizabeth City, and set up camp near Capt. Tate's home, about four miles north of Kill Devil Hill, in what is now Kitty Hawk. Orville arrived two weeks later and they soon had their first glider assembled, flying it for the first few trials with lines, like a kite. Later, they carried it four miles to the ninety-foot high sand hill and made about about a dozen long glides, taking turns piloting it. That ended the gliding season for 1900. Their time in the air had been short, but they had learned some important secrets. The lifting power of the wings was less than they had expected, but the wing warping system they had invented to enable them to turn the machine worked beautifully. They left for Dayton resolving to return the next year.

By summer, 1901, they had completed the second glider, a larger model with wings 22 feet wide and of 7 foot chord, with increased curvature to conform to Otto Lilienthal's aerodynamic tables. They arrived at Kill Devil Hill with it on July 10, and put in a few days building a 16x25 shed and drilling a well. Between July 27 and August 20 they made several dozen flights. They discovered that Lilienthal's figures were wrong. They decided that a vertical surface was needed at the tail. But in spite of that, they succeeded in gliding farther and more skillfully than anyone had before.

The next winter in Dayton passed swiftly. There was the bicycle business, of course, which was taking off; yet the Wrights found time to build the world's first wind tunnel and to carry out their own calculations of wing curvature versus lift. By September 19, 1902, they were back at Kill Devil Hill with a new glider, not much bigger than the old one, but designed now to their own growing knowledge of aerodynamics. And it had a tail.

Over a thousand flights in September and October of 1902 proved that they were very near the 'secret' of flight. The glider soared, remaining aloft for more than a minute and going over 600 feet. When they added a movable rudder to the vertical tail, the basic idea of the airplane was complete.

Satisfied with the glider itself, they went back to Dayton to buy an engine. No one would sell them one (what do they want it for? A *flying-machine?* Do they think we're crazy?). So they built one, a four-cylinder gasoline engine that delivered about 16 horsepower at 1200 rpm. Then they built a complete new plane. Finally they started on the propellers, discovered that no one really knew how to design one, and learned how themselves. Then they built them.

The final result did not look much like the planes of today, but all the elements were there. A 40-foot span double wing, with aileron control interacting with a movable rudder. Attitude was controlled with horizontal elevators. A gasoline engine, placed alongside the prone pilot on the lower wing, driving two counterrotating pusher props. And a launching system—a rail down which the plane could roll on a little dolly, which then dropped off.

They arrived at Kill Devil Hill for the fourth time in September, 1903. Completely ignored by the press, the outside world, and (by this time) by the Bankers themselves, they built another shed, repaired various breakdowns, and ground-tested the machine.

On December 14 they were ready to fly. Hoisting a signal flag brought several husky men trudging over the sand from the Kitty Hawk Lifesaving Station, some five miles away. The launch rail was set up near the top of the hill; Wilbur won the toss; the engine was warmed up, and the flying-machine slid down the rail. Wilbur, over-eager, brought the nose up too fast, stalled the plane, and dropped it into the sand at the foot of the hill.

After two days' work, repairs were completed. December 17 dawned cold and very windy, with 27 mph clocked at the government weather station nearby. The brothers dragged the machine out again and called the lifesavers. With the wind so strong, they decided to fly from a level track, and set the launching apparatus up near the sheds. At 10:35 Orville climbed aboard and started the engine. The propellers began to turn.

Facing a 27 mph wind, the machine started very slowly when Orville released the hold-down wire. Wilbur ran alongside. The flyer, in Orville's words later:

> ...lifted from the track just as it was entering on the fourth rail. Mr. Daniels took a picture just as it left the tracks. I found the control of the front rudder quite difficult on account of its being balanced too near the center and thus had a tendency to turn itself when started so that the rudder was turned too far on one side and then too far on the other. As a result the machine would rise suddenly to about 10 ft. and then as suddenly, on turning the rudder, dart for the ground. A sudden dart when out about 100 feet from the end of the tracks ended the flight.

He had been in the air only 12 seconds.

11:20 a.m.: second flight, Wilbur piloting. The wind dropped for a moment and the machine flew faster, going 175 feet in 11 seconds.

11:40 a.m.: third flight. Orville traveled 200 feet in 15 seconds.

12:00 noon: fourth and last flight. Getting the hang of it, Wilbur flew 852 feet in 59 seconds.

The brothers planned to go for distance on the next flight, perhaps as far as the lifesaving station, but a few minutes later, as the flyer was sitting on the sand, a gust of wind struck. The machine rolled over and over, destroying itself. The 1903 flying season was at an end.

That afternoon, after eating lunch and washing their dishes, the brothers walked to the Kitty Hawk weather station, which had a telegraph connection. Orville wrote the famous message:

> SUCCESS FOUR FLIGHTS THURSDAY MORNING ALL AGAINST TWENTY-ONE-MILE WIND STARTED FROM LEVEL WITH ENGINE POWER ALONE AVERAGE SPEED THROUGH AIR THIRTY-ONE MILES LONGEST 59 SECONDS INFORM PRESS HOME CHRISTMAS. ORVILLE WRIGHT.

In 1904 the Wrights shifted their experiments to a farmer's field near Dayton, extending their flights to 24 miles in 38 minutes by the end of 1905. Incredibly, they attracted little attention, even in Dayton. In 1908 they returned to Kill Devil Hill to test new aircraft, engines, and control arrangements, and there, belatedly, the press discovered them. The rest is history.

Kill Devil Hills' meagre population began to grow rapidly when Roanoke and Currituck sounds were bridged in 1920 and 1930. The hill itself, which Army engineers had stabilized with grass in 1928, was capped with the Wright monument in 1932. In 1938 the growing citizenry gained a post office, and in 1953 became an incorporated town...named, of course, Kill Devil Hills. Though it has a large permanent population, it is also one of the most popular resort communities, welcoming thousands of visitors and summer residents each year to enjoy sun, sand, sea, and wind.

Many of them—especially VIPs—come to Kill Devil Hills, appropriately enough, by air.

KILL DEVIL HILLS:

ATTRACTIONS:
1. Wright Brothers Memorial Visitor Center, pg. 58
2. Wright Brothers Memorial, pg. 60
3. First Flight Airstrip, pg. 59
4. Colington Island, pg. 62
5. Kitty Hawk Aero Tours, pg. 60
6. Wright Brothers Air Tours, pg. 62

RECREATION:
1. Avalon Fishing Pier, pg. 63
2. The Circus Tent, pg. 63
3. Sea Ranch Tennis Center, pg. 65

HOTELS/MOTELS/CAMPGROUNDS:
1. Bel-Air, pg. 120
2. Tan-A-Rama, pg. 120
3. The Mariner, pg. 122
4. Sea Ranch, pg. 122
5. Chart House, pg. 123
6. Tanglewood, pg. 125
7. Cavalier, pg. 125
8. Colony IV, pg. 126
9. Outer Banks Motor Lodge, pg. 126
10. Holiday Inn, pg. 127
11. Tanya's Ocean House, pg. 127
12. John Yancey, pg. 128
13. Econo Lodge, pg. 128
14. Ramada Inn, pg. 129

RESTAURANTS:
1. Krause's Steak House, pg. 213
2. Seafare III, pg. 213
3. Top of the Dune, pg. 214
4. Midgett's Barbeque, pg. 215
5. The Jolly Roger, pg. 215
6. Whaling Station, pg. 216
7. Papagayo's, pg. 216
8. Port O' Call, pg. 217
9. JK's, pg. 218
10. Stack 'Em High, pg. 219
11. Capt'n Dave's, pg. 219
12. Madeline's, pg. 220
13. Etheridge Seafood, pg. 220
14. Peppercorns, pg. 221
15. The Fish Market, pg. 221
16. Miller's Seafood and Steak House pg. 222
17. Starkey's Pizza, pg. 222
18. Evan's Crab House, pg. 223
19. Sands Family Restaurant, pg. 224

SHOPPING:
1. Seagate North, pg. 275
2. Sherli Shops, pg. 275
3. Oceanside Plaza, pg. 275
4. Seashore Shops, pg. 275
5. Sea Holly Square, pg. 276

NIGHTSPOTS:
1. Sea Ranch Lounge, pg. 261
2. Madeline's, pg. 261
3. Port O' Call Gaslight Saloon, pg. 262
4. Papagayo's, pg. 262

KILL DEVIL HILLS — 57

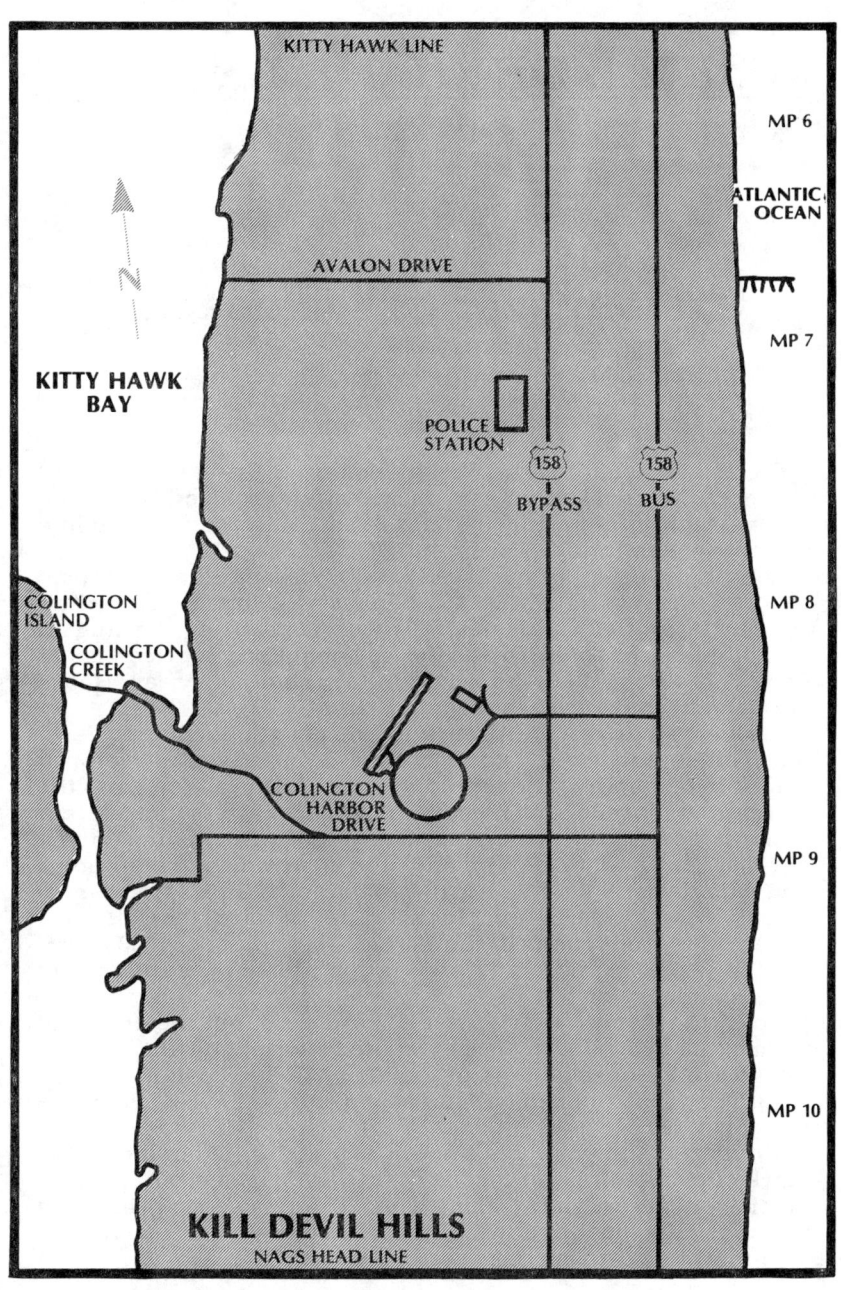

▙▟ KILL DEVIL HILLS
ATTRACTIONS

WRIGHT BROTHERS MEMORIAL

Rt. 158 Bypass, MP 8   441-7430

Map, pg. 57

    Eight miles south of the Wright Memorial Bridge, the Wright Brothers National Memorial is a complex of activities and reconstruction honoring the men who made flight possible—and those who followed them into the air.

    Looking at the map, you'll see that the first building you come to after turning off Route 158 bypass is a low, domed white structure on the right side of the access road. Parking is available in front of it. This is the National Park Service Visitor Center. It's open daily, and it definitely should be seen. Hours are variable with the season.

    It's well put together. Along with the usual information desk, restrooms, and book store, it has a very well-developed selection of displays and reproductions. The long struggle of the Wrights to fly is documented in a series of exhibits that explain at the same time the principles of powered flight. A wind tunnel, parts of the Wrights' motors and planes, samples of their notes and calculations lend an air of authenticity. In a large, light-filled room to the south, looking out toward the Hill, are fullscale reproductions of the 1902 glider and of the 1903 Flyer. On the walls are portraits of aviation pioneers, military and civilian, male and female.

    From the Center we suggest a short walk out the door and toward the two wooden sheds you see between you and the hill. These are reconstructions of the Wrights' 1903 camp, built in 1963. They're furnished with tools and equipment like those the Wrights used.

    Moving to the east, you'll see a large granite boulder. This marks the takeoff point for the flights of December 17. Looking north, you'll see signs marking where the first, second, third and fourth flights touched down. It doesn't look very far, and it isn't. You might say it was one small step for a man...

KILL DEVIL HILLS — 59

WRIGHT BROTHERS NATIONAL MEMORIAL

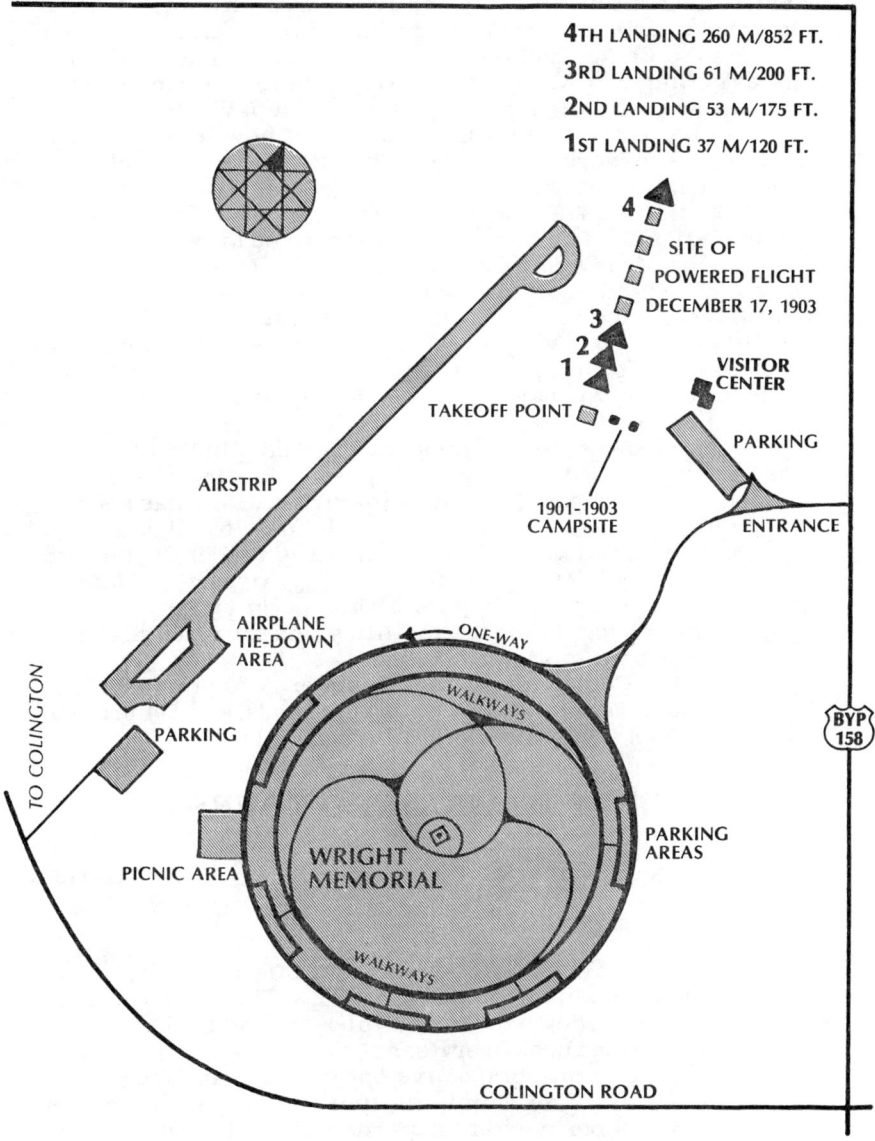

The Memorial itself is a good walk, and you may want to return to your car and drive around the circular access road (one way!) to the parking areas that ring Kill Devil Hill. We definitely recommend driving over if it has rained recently, for the area between the Center and the hill is low and you may find your ankles getting wet. No, you can't drive to the top on a motorcyle. And please stay on the paved paths going up. We thought this was another petty rule until we found out how hard the Park Service has to work to keep what is still just a big sand dune from blowing away.

Kill Devil Hill itself is ninety-one feet high. The granite pylon, rising sixty more feet into the air, was erected in 1932 under the supervision of the Army Corps of Engineers. Intended at first to be used as a lighthouse, the beacon was shut down when ships at sea confused it with the Bodie Island and Hatteras lights. Today, floodlit at night, it is visible from as far away as Duck, and from its base—there's a rampart to walk around on, and bronze busts of the brothers—you can see the sound, the sea, and most of the northern Banks.

You can also see light planes landing and taking off from a small strip in the woods to the northwest. This is the First Flight Airstrip. It is 3000 feet long, asphalt-surfaced, and has a small tie-down area (stay is limited to 24 hours). No lights, fuel, service, or navigational aids, other than a wind sock. If you need a fully-equipped airport see 'Dare County Airport' in Manteo, but this is a convenient strip for a short-term visit.

All National Park Service facilities and services are free. Grounds close promptly at 7:00 p.m.

The Visitor Center also offers summer programs and kite flying demonstrations at the Center, the sheds, and at the top of the hill. Ask at the Center desk for a schedule.

KITTY HAWK AERO TOURS

Wright Brothers Memorial   441-4460
                          Map, pg. 57

Captain Kitty Hawk (Jay Mankedick) offers several flying tours of the Banks in his six Cessna 172's. The local tour flies over ocean, shore, down to Oregon Inlet, around the lighthouse at Bodie Island, and back over Roanoke Island — very pretty and gives you a different perspective on how thin and fragile the Banks really are. The 25-minute tour is $13 per person for parties of 3; $16 per person for parties of 2. Mankedick offers other, longer tours north to Corolla and south to Ocracoke, as well as charter services. The Aero Tours operate from April 1 through December 1. You can make your reservations by going

KILL DEVIL HILLS — 61

Fisherboy - a string of flounder are kept fresh in the surf.

by their booth at the Wright Brothers Memorial in Kill Devil Hills or by calling.

WRIGHT BROTHERS AIR TOURS

Manteo Airport   Map, pg. 57   441-6235

Reservations for this air tour are made at Kite Kingdom shops. There is one in Sea Holly Square. The four-seater private aircraft will take two or three passengers for a full 30-minute overview of the Outer Banks from the Wright Brothers Memorial to the north of the airport on Roanoke Island to the Oregon Inlet Bridge in the south. Fees for the flight run about $15 per person.

COLINGTON ISLAND

Just south of the Wright monument, a narrow road leads off to the west from Route 158 bypass, near the 8½ mile marker. This is the road to Colington, or Colington Island, a little-known, seldom-visited part of the Banks that nonetheless deserves a footnote both for its history and for its gemlike beauty.

In Charles the Second's great divying up of North Carolina in 1660's, Sir John Colleton, an English gentlemen, was granted a small island in Roanoke sound, just west of present-day Kill Devil Hills. The flat, heavily-wooded island, protected by the dunes from salt spray and wind, had good soil, and was colonized in 1665 by a party under the leadership of Peter Carteret, making it the first permanent settlement in the Outer Banks. Since then the inhabitants have lived a happy and almost historyless existence, farming, raising livestock, and fishing.

The winding, five-mile drive today's visitor takes to and through Colington (the spelling has changed since Sir John's time) will pass small businesses—Colington Seafood, Joe and Kay's Campground, Billy's Seafood, Endurance Seafood, Cozy Cove, Colington Park Campground, Outer Banks Jewelers—roll over scenic old arched wooden bridges, twist and turn through forests of oak, holly, and pine. Several private, restricted-entry communities line the shores of the sound.

KILL DEVIL HILLS
RECREATION

AVALON FISHING PIER

Rt. 158 Business, MP 6   441-7494

Map, pg. 57

Avalon Pier, owned by Kitty Hawk Piers, Inc., was built in 1960 and is presently 650 feet long. The pier is lighted and has a restaurant, bait and tackle shop, ice, and gear for rent. Luther Jacobs tells us the catch includes bluefish, gray and speckled trout, flounder, spot, king mackerel, cobia, and channel bass, depending on the season (see Fishing section in Hatteras Island chapter). Avalon is closed Thanksgiving to April 1. Admission prices: $2.50 per day, adult or child. Weekly pass $12.00, season pass (good also at Kitty Hawk Pier) $60.00. Handicapped in wheelchairs admitted free.

THE CIRCUS TENT

Rt. 158 Bypass, MP 9

Map, pg. 57

More than 50,000 people a year visit a brightly striped tent in Kill Devil Hills, half a mile south of the Wright Brothers Memorial. That eye-catching structure houses a unique combination of Christian fellowship activities, special evening programs, a bookstore, and some delicious ice cream. it's staffed entirely by volunteers, mostly from North Carolina and Virginia. Everyone is welcome. The Tent is open from mid-June to late August. Stop by for the schedule of nightly shows and special summertime events, for some ice cream — a "Fat Lady Sundae" or a "Brown Bear" — or write to The Circus Tent, P.O. Box 1058, Kill Devil Hills, NC 27948.

SEA RANCH TENNIS CENTER

Rt. 158 Business   441-7126
Map, pg. 57

   The large building you see across the street from the Sea Ranch is the motel's tennis center and it IS open to the public. Open year round from 8:00 a.m. until 10:00 p.m. (hours are often extended in the summer), the Center provides two indoor courts and an observation lounge. Rackets are available for purchase as are balls, sweat bands, and other supplies. The pro, Rick Ostlund, also provides lessons by appointment.
   During the summer, and often even into the off seasons, reservations for court time are definitely required.

INSIDE
NAGS HEAD

Most everyone has heard the old story about how Nags Head got its name. How, as legend has it, the early inhabitants of the sandy banks were not above tying lanterns around horses' necks (or their tails, as one variation goes), and leading the animals up and down the beach. Merchant skippers at sea, seeing the bobbing lights, would take them for the anchor lights of ships safely in harbor, and would steer for them. When they ran aground, the Bankers salvaged the cargo to supplement their own meager belongings.

It seems more likely, all things considered, that this narrow section of the beach east of Roanoke Island was named by early settlers after geographically similar features of the English coast. But it *is* certain that some strange things used to take place off Nags Head. The story of Theodosia Burr Alston confirms that. Twenty-nine years old, daughter of adventurer, duellist, and former vice-president Aaron Burr, all trace of her was lost when her New York-bound ship, the *Patriot*, disappeared at sea in late 1812. Later in the century, deathbed confessions were reported of former pirates who said they had seized the ship and murdered all hands, setting the empty vessel to drift. In 1869 a portrait bearing a startling resemblance to Theodosia was turned up in a Nags Head cottage. Its owner, an old woman, said that it had been taken from a deserted schooner that had come ashore in early 1813....

Nags Head first became a resort in the early 1800's, when wealthy planters began the practice of taking ship for the Banks during summer months to escape the unhealthy climate farther inland. The first hotel was built in 1838, and did a good business; excess visitors were quartered in private residences. Summer cottages began appearing about this time, most of them near the sound rather than the sea side. Dancing, fishing, bowling, and sea-bathing occupied the visitors' time while native Bankers kept to themselves in their own soundside village in Nags Head Woods. In 1851 the hotel was enlarged and half a mile of muledrawn railway was laid to make the journey to the sea less wearisome.

In 1862 the Nags Head Hotel was burned by retreating Confederates. Rebuilt in the late 70's, it boomed anew as the popularity of the resort grew and transportation to it became more convenient.

One of the worst disasters in Banks history happened at Nags Head in 1877, when the 541-ton barkentine-rigged screw steamer USS *Huron* went aground in a November storm. The then-new Nags Head Lifesaving Station Number Seven was only two miles away, but Congress had been cutting costs, and it was unmanned. Local fishermen helped the men who made it ashore, but almost a hundred sailors were drowned or crushed as the fearful surf tore the iron ship to pieces. Today the *Huron* lies straight out between mile markers 11 and 12, even with the end of Nags Head Pier. Recent shifts have uncovered the wreck again, and local divers have recovered such artifacts as portholes, rifle rounds, cannonballs, fittings, etc. (see "SCUBA Diving" section).

More recent decades have seen the population of the area (incorporated as a town in 1961) increase slowly, but Nags Head still retains its individuality with respect to Roanoke Island, across the causeway and the Washington Baum Bridge, and the explosively growing communities farther north. A center of recreation (fishing, swimming, hang-gliding), art (the largest collection of studios and galleries on the Banks), and legend, Nags Head still holds to its old title as the premier resort spot of the North Carolina Coast.

 ## NAGS HEAD
ATTRACTIONS

REARVIEW MIRROR

Between the Highways, MP 11   441-4493
Next to Galleon Esplanade
Map, pg. 70

Think back to the first car you ever owned, the car you took on your honeymoon, the car you've seen in old movies and wished you had. These are the cars you'll see at the Rearview Mirror, a museum of automobiles that already is becoming nationally known and respected. There's a 1904 Caddy, a 1954 Corvette, a 1956 Thunderbird, and a 1914 Hupmobile, just to name a few in the collection. All told, eight generations of cars are on display with special features highlighted and information explaining the influence our society had on the cars, and vice versa. It's an intriguing place and one that every member of the family is apt to truly enjoy. Don't just wait for a rainy day to visit - it's worth your trip any day.

The museum is open daily year round. In season hours run from 10:00 a.m. until 9:00 p.m., Monday through Saturday and 11:00 a.m. until 5:00 p.m. on Sundays. Off season hours are 11:00 a.m. till 5:00 p.m., 7 days a week. Admission is $4.00 for adults, $1.50 for kids aged 6-12, and free for kids under 6 years old.

NAGS HEAD NORTH

 **ATTRACTIONS:**
1. Jockey's Ridge, pg. 71
2. Old Nags Head, pg. 70
3. Rearview Mirror, pg. 68
4. Huron Wreck, pg. 67

 RECREATION:
1. Colony House Cinemas 1 & II, pg. 73
2. Surf Slide, pg. 73
3. Deep Africa Mini-Golf, pg. 73
4. Dowdy's AMusement Park, pg. 74
5. Nags Head Fishing Pier, pg. 74
6. Footsball Palace, pg. 74
7. Forbes Candies and Carpet Golf, pg. 75
8. Go-Kart Grand Prix, pg. 75
9. Kitty Hawk Kites/Sports, pg. 77
10. Jockey's Ridge Mini-Golf, pg. 78

 HOTELS/MOTELS/CAMPGROUNDS:
1. Carolinian, pg. 131
2. Beacon Motor Lodge, pg. 131
3. Cabana East, pg. 132
4. Ocean Veranda, pg. 132
5. Olde London Inn, pg. 132
6. First Colony Inn, pg. 133
7. Sea Spray, pg. 135

 RESTAURANTS:
1. Sweetwaters, pg. 225
2. The Carolinian, pg. 225
3. Kelly's, pg. 226
4. Sinbad's, pg. 226
5. A Restaurant, By George, pg. 227
6. Plantation Restaurant, pg. 228
7. Fishtails, pg. 229
8. Gandalf & Co., pg. 229

NIGHTSPOTS:
1. Gandalf's, pg. 263
2. Fishtails, pg. 263
3. Atlantis, pg. 264
4. The Comedy Club, pg. 264

 SHOPPING:
1. Ben Franklin, pg. 273
2. The Beach Barn,pg. 276
3. Nags Head Hammocks, pg. 276
4. Gray's, pg. 277
5. Nags Head Station, pg. 277
6. Ye Olde Ham Shoppe, pg. 277
7. Galleon Esplanade, pg. 278
8. Surfside Plaza, pg. 278

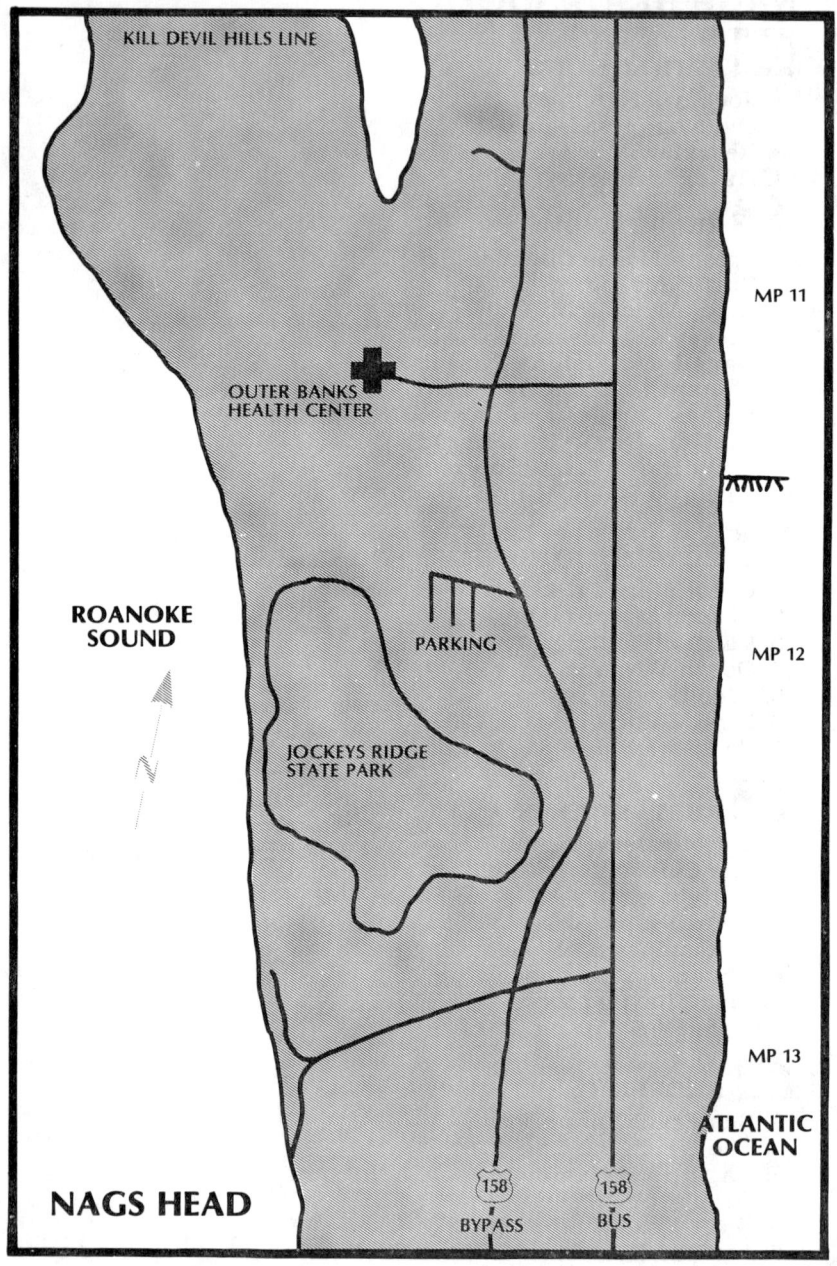

JOCKEY'S RIDGE STATE PARK

Rt. 158 Bypass, MP 12   Map, pg. 70

    One of the state's newest parks, Jockey's Ridge is unique both on the Banks and on the East Coast. It is the highest dune formation in the United States... and it is *strange*.

    These vast, blowing piles of fine white sand were not always here. In fact, the colonists made them, by destroying the natural cover of the banks with logging and stock grazing. Gradually, as vegetation disappeared, the wind began to pile the sand into great "walking dunes" that moved inexorably southwest, like gritty glaciers, covering houses and living trees. Jockey's Ridge was an attraction for tourists as early as 1851, when a Norfolk editor passed on the legend that "...the lady who may accompany you to its summit if not already a wife will shortly become yours." Today the Ridge is actually two great dunes, one lower to the east, parallel to Rt. 158, and the other, higher, beyond it. What do you do with a vast pile of sand? Well, we suggest a walk first of all. When we climbed it the day was foggy, and the dunes seemed an endless desert, somewhere unearthly— Mars, perhaps. When the wind blows, as it almost always does, long streamers of sand blow saharalike from the tops of the Dunes. You may see the hang-gliding confraternity in action above the ridges, hanging almost motionless or indulging in great kitelike swoops. From atop the dunes you can see both sea and sound, and far up and down the Banks; it's a great place for photographs, for walking around barefoot, for studying the strange patterns the wind sculpts in the sand.

    A parking lot has been constructed north of Jockey's Ridge, off Route 158 bypass, and Park authorities request you park there rather than directly opposite the dunes.

OLD NAGS HEAD

Rt. 158 Bypass, MP 12   Map, pg. 70

    Like most of the Banks towns, Nags Head was originally a small sound side community, and Old Nags Head is the remnant of that village. Just south of Jockey's Ridge you'll note a narrow road leading west. It's worth a short drive to follow its winding path back to the sound, a five-minute trip to see some classic old-style Banks homes. Some are even built on pilings out into the Bay.

Enjoy Beautiful, Sunset Dining From Our Panoramic Waterfront View

THE DOCK Restaurant

"Where Food and Friendship Are Offered in Abundance."

Less than 10 minutes from
The Lost Colony and The Christmas Shop

441-4077
Nags Head/Manteo Causeway

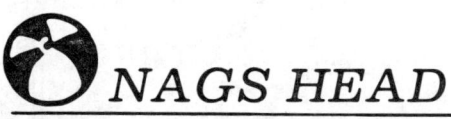

NAGS HEAD
RECREATION

COLONY HOUSE CINEMAS I, II

Rt. 158 Business, MP 10½ 441-5630

Map, pg. 70

Two of the seven Colony House Cinemas now located on the Outer Banks from Avon to Kitty Hawk, Cinemas I & II offer family entertainment year round.

SURF SLIDE

Rt. 158 Bypass, MP 11

Map, pg. 70

Just south of the Kill Devil Hills city limits, this is a big water slide with multiple curves. Restrooms, changing facilities, snack bar. Open summer only from 10 a.m. to midnight.

DEEP AFRICA MINI-GOLF

Rt. Business, MP 11½ 441-5875

Map, pg. 70

Another of the mini-golf spots that are very popular on the Banks in summer, Deep Africa has 36 lighted holes with an African motif. Open 10 a.m. to midnight during the season.

DOWDY'S AMUSEMENT PARK

Rt. 158 Bypass, MP 12 441-5151

Map, pg. 70

Dowdy's is a well-known fun spot just north of Jockey's Ridge, on the sea side of 158 bypass. Open during the summer season only, it offers amusement-park rides and games and has a circus-style snack bar.

NAGS HEAD FISHING PIER

MP 12, on the Atlantic 441-5141

Map, pg. 70

This privately owned pier is 750 feet long, and carries all the standard Outer Banks pier facilities of tackle shop, bait, and ice. The tackle is reasonable and the restrooms are newly overhauled and exceptionally clean. Blues, gray trout, spot, croaker, flounder, and, of course, channel bass are all taken off this pier, depending on season and the proclivities of the fish. The pier is lighted with sodium vapor lamps for night fishing.
 Monica Cremia, owner, Joe Justius' daughter, tells us that Nags Head is a "family pier," and that probably more women fish here than anywhere else along the Banks. She's especially proud of the pier's new restaurant, whose special fish of the day is yours ("You Catch 'em — We Cook 'em"). Nags Head Pier is open from April 1 through Thanksgiving, and twenty-four hours a day during the summer season

FOOTSBALL PALACE

Rt. 158 Business, MP 12 441-6158

Map, pg. 70

A popular spot with teens in the summer, the Palace offers plenty of diversions to take the edge off all that sun and sand. With over a hundred videos and pinballs, pool tables, footsballs, it's one of the primary game spots on the Beach. The roller rink is another big draw. Beer at the bar, bath house, public beach, and a snack bar round out the list of entertainments. In the summer the Footsball Palace is wall-to-wall. Open weekends all year; open all week from May to September 1, 9:30 a.m. to 1:30 a.m.

FORBES CANDIES AND CARPET GOLF

Rt. 158 Business, MP 12½   441-7293

Map, pg. 70

Forbes is a well-known regional candy chain operating out of Virginia Beach. Aside from what area people have come to expect from Forbes — a big, imaginative, mouth-watering display of fresh, quality candies — this outlet offers a good selection of Banks souvenirs, handmade candles, t-shirts, shell items, and jewelry. The store itself is open year round; the two eighteen-hole golf courses are open from May 1 to Labor Day, from 9 a.m. to 11 p.m.

GO-KART GRAND PRIX

Rt. 158 Bypass, MP 11½

Map, pg. 70

For a change of pace from everyday driving, there's nothing quite like screaming around a turn, the wind in your face, with other whining machines hot on your tail. Grand Prix offers a two-hundred-foot-long winding level course. Adults and kids are both welcome, but you must be ten or older to drive alone. Open from about 10 a.m. to 11 or 12 at night. Well lighted, of course!

HANG GLIDING

They swoop, they bank, they dart and dive; they hover, circle, ascend and descend with the easy grace of gulls. The brilliantly-colored wings flash and glow in the brilliant Banks sunlight. Wind, sand, and sun—that's hang gliding, one of the country's newest sports. And Jockey's Ridge, only a few miles from where men first flew at Kill Devil Hill, is its national center.

Hang gliding's roots go back beyond the Wrights — perhaps to Lilienthal, who was killed flying a glider not unlike these, or even farther back, to the first person who launched a kite. But its modern revival is a direct spinoff of the American space program. Francis M. Rogallo, a NASA engineer who now lives in Southern Shores, developed the flexible Rogallo Wing in order to bring down space capsules. Though the parachute finally won out, light mylar-and-aluminum-tubing gliders began to appear in the hands of sport fliers in the early 70's, and now the sport is booming.

"Basically, it's flying in its purest form," said John Harris, president of Kitty Hawk Kites. "It's as close as you can get to flying as the birds do. No noise, no engines, and the wind in your face." The novice hang glider begins with the basics, gliding down from a higher place to a lower, but soon learns to make use of the same thermals and ridge lift air currents that birds use in order to extend their powerless flights.

You can't learn to hang glide from a book, but to give you some idea of what the sport entails, here is a brief description of the sequence of events in beginning and controlling a glide.

The flier is attached at his or her waist to the center of gravity of the wing, at its midpoint. In front of him is a triangular metal control bar. The flight is begun downhill into the wind, with a good run to get up airspeed. The glider will begin to lift as it gains speed and will quickly leave the ground.

From here on, its attitude and direction is controlled by the pilot. Shifting the weight of one's body to the right dips the right wing and the glider will turn to the right. Moving the control bar forward or back with the hands causes the center of gravity to move and the kite's nose to pitch up or down. When the pilot runs out of hill or wind, and it's time for a landing, he comes in low into the wind and pushes the control bar out, causing the glider to stall; and, if he's skillful, drops neatly to his feet in a perfect standup landing.

It's a fairly safe sport, though less so than bowling; the most common injury is a broken arm. Accident rates are about three-tenths of one percent. One fatality has been recorded on Jockey's Ridge as a result of hang gliding. Crash helmets are recommended.

In the mid-seventies, a natural evolution of this form of flying took place when experimenters began attaching chainsaw engines to hang gliders. Today complete "ultralight aircraft," weighing two hundred pounds complete with specialized two-stroke-cycle engines, are available for advanced flyers. Still foot-launchable, these unlicensed flying machines are as yet unregulated by the FAA, and offer the same kinds of thrills Wilbur and Orville used to get.

According to Ralph Buxton, most hang gliding enthusiasts today tend to be in good physical shape, coming to the sport from sailing, bicycling, backpacking, surfing, parachuting, and other "risk sports." The students are more varied, but tend, he says, to be extroverts, and "a cut above average in intelligence, personality, and fitness." You can take a look or mingle with them year round in the lot back of Kitty Hawk Kites or aloft over Jockey's Ridge.

Season? There really isn't any; people fly here year round. But winter weather is less pleasant (although, as the Wrights found out, the winds are stronger). For that reason, the best weather is considered to be from mid-March to mid-November.

Who said that man will never fly?

KITTY HAWK KITES/KITTY HAWK SPORTS

Rt. 158 Bypass, MP 13   441-4124
Map, pg. 70

So far, at least, KHK is the only shop to service the hang gliding crowd, and its location across Rt. 158 from Jockey's Ridge makes it the center of activity. The present structure, with its dramatically soaring observation tower, was completed in 1979. KHK handles gliders, of course — Flight Designs, Wills Wing, and Moyes, new and used, from a few hundred dollars up to $2000 or more for an advanced new machine. The retail store handles kites, flying toys, art, harnesses and other gear, books, t-shirts, and other flying-related items.

The focus of activity at KHK, though, is on flying, and training others to fly. Hang gliding is self-regulated; you don't need any sort of a license or training or permit. But unless you're after a broken arm (or neck), it's the better part of valor to sign up for a KHK course. The beginning lesson is only $46, lasts for three hours, and gives you five flights. Advanced and Fledgling courses go farther, teaching you the techniques of flying higher, farther, and more skillfully. Call for reservations; the courses are given year round.

Next door to KHK is Kitty Hawk Sports. This shop concentrates on water and wind sports. Boogie boards, rafts, Prindle catamarans, windsurfers, and motorized gliders (Eipper Quicksilver and Flight Designs Trike) are on display, along with a top line of sportswear.

In July of 1986 a row of attractive, wooden shop between the two buildings opened, Kitty Hawk Connection. In these shops, all of which open onto a porch-like breezeway, you can find stores such as Nags Head Pro Dive Center, Montage, a print shop, Air Brush By Donna, an ice cream shop named How Sweet It Is, and Country Kettle Fudge.

A sailing center next to the Windmill Point restaurant on the Bypass offers lessons and rentals in windsurfing and sailing as well as jet ski rentals. Boards and other related items are sold in the check-in center.

The main KHK complex is open from 7:30 a.m. till 10:30 p.m. during the summer, more abbreviated hours during the off season. The KHSports shop is open from 8:30 a.m. till 10:30 p.m. in season, with shorter hours off season. The Connection shops will basically follow the hours of the two main shops. Hours for the sailing center run from 9:00 a.m. till 6:00 p.m. during the season.

JOCKEY'S RIDGE MINI-GOLF

Rt. 158 Bypass, MP 12   441-6810
Map, pg. 70

Don't be too surprised to see a green octopus and a sailing ship emerging from the southern end of Jockey's Ridge; they are props at two 18-hole mini-golf courses. The Ridge is slowly walking south—in a few years it may bury this location, and it's interesting to ponder the reactions of archaeologists centuries in the future when the green octopus and the fairy castle re-emerge. Lighted at night.

NAGS HEAD SOUTH

 ATTRACTIONS:
1. National Park Service Information Center, pg. 82

 RECREATION:
1. Jennette's Pier, pg. 83
2. Outer Banks Fishing Pier, pg. 82
3. Kitty Hawk Sports, pg. 82
4. Bayside Watersports, pg. 83
5. Colony House Cinema III & IV, pg. 83
6. Pirate's Cove Yacht Basin and Crystal Dawn, pg. 85

 HOTELS/MOTELS/CAMPGROUNDS:
1. Pebble Beach, pg. 136
2. Siver Sands, pg. 136
3. The Islander, pg. 137
4. Sea Oatel, pg. 137
5. Sea Foam, pg. 138
6. Owens' Motel, pg. 138
7. Surf Side, pg. 139
8. Best Western Armada, pg. 139
9. Sandpiper Court, pg. 141

 RESTAURANTS:
1. The Elegant Pelican, pg. 231
2. Dareolina Cove, pg. 232
3. Miller's Waterfront, pg. 232
4. The Dunes, pg. 233
5. Sam and Omie's, pg. 234
6. Owens', pg. 235
7. Windmill Point, pg. 236
8. R.V.'s, pg. 237
9. Tale of the Whale, pg. 237
10. Daniels, pg. 238
11. The Dock, pg. 239
12. Ship's Wheel, pg. 239

 SHOPPING:
1. Outer Banks Mall, pg. 278
2. The Chalet Gift Shop, pg. 279
3. Newman's, pg. 279
4. R.V. Cahoon's, pg. 281

NIGHTSPOTS:
1. Station Keeper's Lounge, pg. 265
2. Dareolina Cove, pg. 265
3. Outer Banks Coliseum, pg. 266

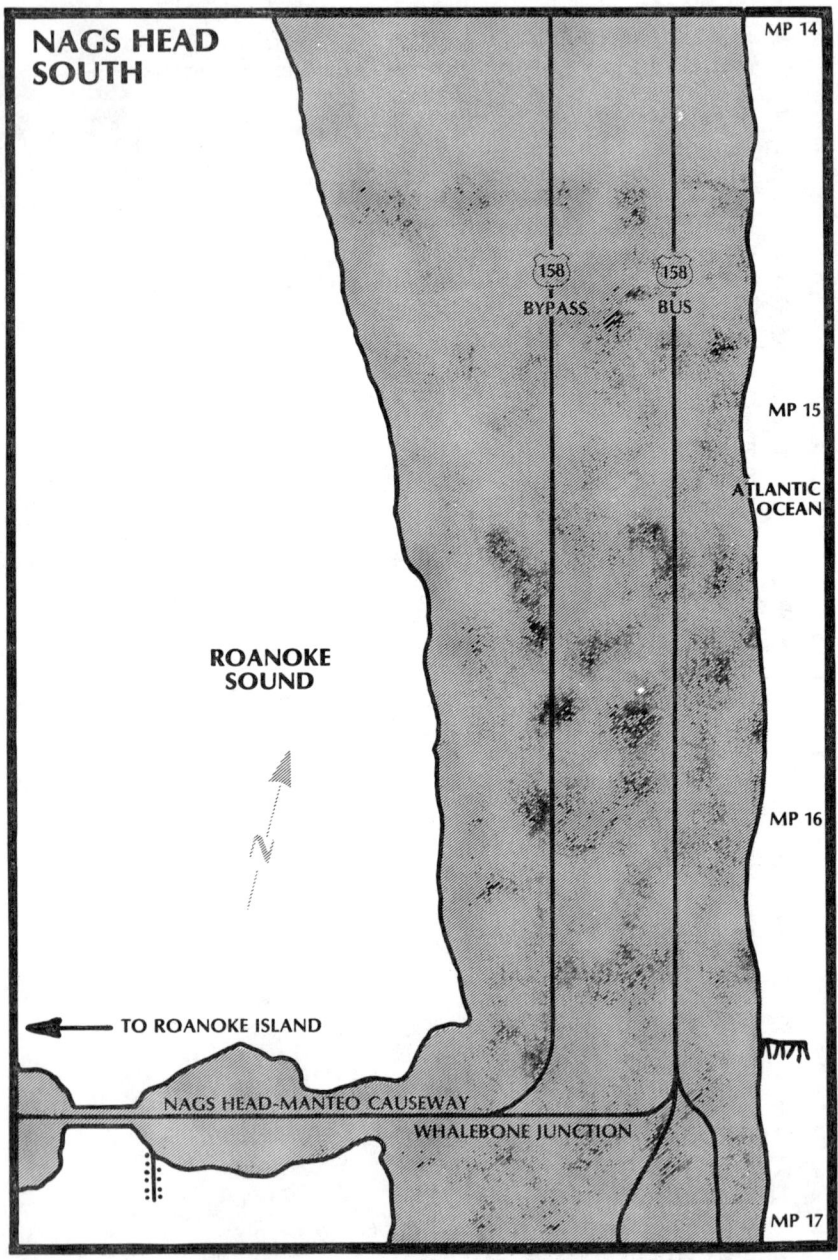

Shipwreck - the treacherous waters off Diamond Shoals have claimed hundreds of unlucky ships through the years. Known as the Graveyard of the Atlantic, this area still contains the remains of many old sailing vessels including this one which washed up on the beach in Nags Head.

OUTER BANKS FISHING PIER

S. Nags Head, MP 18½   441-5740
Map, pg. 80

Outer Banks Fishing Unlimited runs this seafront pier, 650 feet long, built in 1959. Lots of parking out front; lots of blues, gray trout, flounder, croaker, spot and channel bass out back. Pier is open 24 hours a day from early spring to late fall (lighted, of course), and provides rental tackle, fresh bait, snacks, and beverages. Admission $3 daily for fishing, $1 for sightseers. Season admission $50. Special rates for handicapped and groups.

NATIONAL PARK SERVICE INFORMATION CENTER

Whalebone Junction   441-6644
Map, pg. 80

On the right side of Highway 12 as you leave Nags Head going south, this booth offers information on NPS facilities and activities from the junction south to Hatteras Inlet.

KITTY HAWK SPORTS (WATER)

Rt. 158 Bypass, MP 16   441-4301
(located behind the Windmill)
Map, pg. 80

Kitty Hawk Kites and Sports runs this waterfront recreation business. From April through October, 9 a.m. till 6 p.m., water lovers can windsurf and sail in the sound under the watchful eye of qualified instructors. They also give lessons in both sports. Windsurfer boards and sailboats are available for sale and rental.

BAYSIDE WATERSPORTS

Rt. 158 Bypass, MP 16   441-4270

Map, pg. 80

Bayside Watersports provides Jet Skis, daysailers up to the Hobie 16, parasail rides and waterski towing for hourly, half day, or daily rentals. If you've the notion, you can rent a small sailboat for a week and they'll deliver it to your cottage. Everything that's for rent is also for sale. A good selection of used sailboats is usually in stock. Lessons are sometimes offered, so if you're interested in learning how to wind surf or sail, ask them if they're teaching.

COLONY HOUSE CINEMA III & IV

158 Bypass at the Outer Banks Mall   441-5630

Map, pg. 80

Adding to the list of cinemas on the Outer Banks are these two, located at the Outer Banks Mall. Family entertainment is offered, shows nightly.

JENNETTE'S PIER

Whalebone Junction   441-6116

Map, pg. 80

Nine hundred feet long, Jennette's is the longest pier north of Rodanthe. It has quite a history — first built in 1939, it's been repaired and rebuilt time after time since then. All the normal inshore species are available, as well as bait, ice, and tackle. The snack bar has beer on tap; the new game room has about thirty video games, plus pool tables. First opens mid-April; open twenty-four hours a day from mid-May to October; closes around the end of November. Rates are $3/day basic, $15/week, $65/season. This is the pier for shark and float fishing, which will cost you $2.00 a day extra.

Thirty motor court rooms and nine cottages are also available, convenient to the foot of the pier. Call 441-7245 for details and reservations.

84 — NAGS HEAD

MARINA PIRATE'S COVE MARINA

Conveniently located on the Nags Head Causeway.

- Gulf Stream fishing
- Inshore charter boats
- Head Boat—Crystal Dawn morning, noon fishing tours, evening cruises
- Boat tours to shipwrecks for diving or fishing
- Complete ship's shore
- Transient docking slips open all year
- Fish cleaning facilities
- New restaurant opening summer '86—breakfast, lunch, and dinner

PIRATE'S COVE YACHT BASIN AND *CRYSTAL DAWN*

Nags Head-Roanoke Causeway Pirate's Cove 473-3906
Crystal Dawn 473-5577
Map, pg. 80

A lot of changes have happened (and are still happening) at Pirate's Cove. This marina has about a hundred wet slips for 15 outboards to 75 yachts, with plans for more. (Depth in the channel is 12-15 feet.) Charter boats from 45 to 58 feet run Gulf Stream fishing trips out of here to where the big ones roam; cost is about $500 for six people. Other types of charters can be arranged individually.

Also changed at Pirate's Cove is the metamorphosis of Drafty's Tavern into the Ship's Store, a marine supply center serving almost any nautical need with a full products line.

But, perhaps the biggest difference that will begin showing up over the next couple of years is the development of townhomes and single family lots on the Roanoke Sound, behind the Yacht Basin. Plans call for a deep water canal with docks. Information can be obtained by writing P.O. Box 1997, Manteo, NC 27954.

There are still two familiar faces at Pirate's Cove. Nags Head Divers' 50 foot Sea Fox still operates from here taking divers out to off-shore wrecks (see the Scuba Diving on the Outer Banks section for more details). And Allan Foreman's head boat, the Crystal Dawn, still begins her popular run from this marina. Allan now books his cruises from a booth set up next to the boat, or you can call 473-5577. June through August he runs 2 trips a day: 7 a.m. to noon and 12:30 p.m. to 5:00. His Evening Cruise, complete with commentary on the Outer Banks and usually a spectacular sunset, begins at 6:30 p.m. For the small fee he charges for this pleasureable excursion — $5.00 adults, $2.00 children - you get more than your money's worth. During the off-season, he runs one trip a day from 8:00 a.m. till 1:00 p.m. All of these cruises can be enjoyed six days a week with Allan taking a break on Sundays.

INSIDE
BODIE ISLAND

Just south of Whalebone Junction, just south of the intersection of the Manteo-Nags Head Causeway with U.S. Highway 158, the town of Nags Head — indeed, all the commercial development of the Banks — comes to a sudden and complete halt, except for the narrow strip of beach houses along the sea side in South Nags Head. For here is Bodie Island, and the beginning of Cape Hatteras National Seashore.

Bodie (pronounced "body") Island is not an island now, though it was one at various times in recorded history. Hurricanes and storm seas opened and closed inlets repeatedly in the area where Whalebone Junction now is. Roanoke Inlet, south of Nags Head, closed last in the early 1800s. Faced with changing landforms, the Bankers have found it simpler to stay with island names even when formerly separate islands have merged. As on the other islands, stock was allowed to roam free on Bodie in the old days; later, with the commercial use of Oregon Inlet, it became important as the location of a lighthouse. The late 1800's saw several gun clubs built on the island to take advantage of the vast marshes and resultant clouds of waterfowl wintering over.

ATTRACTIONS

COQUINA BEACH

Bodie Island   441-7425

Map, pg. 103

This is one of the best swimming beaches on the whole Outer Banks coast—and, with the exception of a few picnic shelters, it's as wild as it was a century ago. Coquina is a sandy beach

A scene from The Lost Colony, a nightly ourdoor drama which unfolds the history of America's first English settlement on Roanoke Island.

about eight miles south of Whalebone Junction on Highway 12. It has new restrooms, bath houses, protected picnic tables, showers, and plenty of parking. Lifeguards are on duty from mid-June to Labor Day. "Coquinas" are the tiny shells you will find underfoot in the surf, like millions of tiny silver coins.

From this virtual isolation from the world, the seacoast of Bodie and Hatteras leapt into the headlines suddenly in 1942, when war — in the shape of Nazi U-boats—came to the East Coast. One of the pivotal battles of World War II was fought here, just a few miles off the beach, often in sight of the islanders; and the turning point of that battle took place just off Bodie Island. The relics lie there still.

After the war, Bodie Island, along with the rest of the Outer Banks, gained new life with the coming of highways and the tourist trade. Fortunately, this stretch of deserted, near-virgin shore was included when the National Seashore was established in 1953, and the wholesale development that has taken place further north will never touch the life-filled marshes and scrublands of Bodie Island.

LAURA A. BARNES

Coquina Beach   Map, pg. 103

After a certain length of time has passed, a wrecked ship is gradually transmuted from junk into something romantic and tragic; teredoed wood becomes the fabric of dreams. The *Laura A. Barnes* made that transition in only half a century. Built at Camden, Maine in 1918, she was one of the last coastal schooners built in America. In 1921, under sail from New York to South Carolina in ballast, the 120-foot ship ran into a nor'easter that drove her onto the beach, north of where she now lies (all her crew survived). In 1973 the National Park Service moved her bones to Coquina Beach for safekeeping, and she now lies, high and dry, at the southern end of the parking lot.

BODIE ISLAND LIGHTHOUSE AND VISITORS' CENTER

Bodie Island   441-5711
Map, pg. 103

Bodie Island Light, one of the four famous lighthouses of the Banks, is at the end of a turnoff to the west off Highway 12 some eight miles south of Whalebone Junction (opposite Coquina Beach).

The horizontally striped black and white lighthouse is still in operation under Coast Guard auspices. Built in 1872, the present 163-foot brick structure is the third lighthouse to stand at Oregon Inlet since it opened in a hurricane in 1846. The first, on the south side of the inlet, was destroyed by beach erosion, and the second was destroyed by the Confederates to confuse Federal shipping. Yes, the present lighthouse *is* rather far inland—in the nature of the Banks, time has built up the southern end of the island, and the inlet itself has "walked" south.

The Bodie Island Visitors' Center, also built in 1872, was formerly the lighthouse keeper's residence. Today it houses a Park Service information desk, small bookstore, restrooms, a series of displays on migratory waterfowl, duck hunting, and native shells.

Wandering back to the lighthouse (sorry, Coast Guard rules forbid climbing it), you'll notice the broad marshes behind it. A short walk back to them is not out of order if you're interested in life in the marsh. In the marshes you'll find cattails, yaupon, wax myrtle, bayberry, and Eastern baccharis. A short path and wooden platforms or overlooks are provided as vantage points.

The Visitors Center is open 9 a.m. to 6 p.m. daily during the summer and from 9 a.m. to 5 p.m. during the off season. Non-summer hours do sometimes vary, so it's best to call if you are going over and definitely want to tour the Center.

U-85

Off Bodie Island   Map, pg. 103

As you stand on Coquina Beach, the sun bright overhead, look straight out to sea. If you could take your car and drive outward for fifteen minutes, you would be over one of the strangest yet least known attractions of the Outer Banks. Only fifteen miles straight out, over a hundred feet beneath the glittering sea, the first Nazi submarine destroyed by Americans in World War II lies motionless in the murky waters of Hatteras.

Almost undamaged, except for rust and the encroaching coral, it lies on its side, bow planes jammed forever on hard dive. Its hatches gape open to the dark interior, where silt swirls slowly between dead gauges and twisted air lines. Its cannon points upward, toward the dim glow that is all that remains of the sun at eighteen fathoms. Its conning tower, flaked with corrosion, lies frozen in a roll to starboard that will last until its steel dissolves in the all-devouring sea.

Here, at 35° 55 N, 75° 18 W, it is still World War II. Here, and all along the coasts of the Outer Banks, dozens of wrecks lie half buried in the seabed. It is from here, from the silent hull of a 750-ton Type VIIb U-boat, that we can begin a journey back to the months when the Outer Banks was a battleline, when the German Navy patrolled and ruled our shores.

To Spring, 1942.

Adolf Hitler declared war on the United States on December 11, 1941, four days after Pearl Harbor.

In Europe the war was two and half years old. Deep in the Soviet Union, Nazi and Red forces churned the mud in a precarious balance outside the city of Moscow. In the West the British, in from the first, had come close to strangling in the noose the U-boats had drawn around their island. German submarines had sunk over a thousand ships, over a million tons of material and food; but as 1941 ended, quickly built escorts, ASDIC, and a convoy system were loosening the knot. In his operations room at Kerneval, Occupied France, Admiral Karl Doenitz wondered: where, now, would he find easy sinkings for his thinly stretched submarines?

On the eleventh of December, he knew.

Operation *Paukenschlag* (Drumroll) began on the eighteenth of January, when the Esso tanker *Allen Jackson* exploded a few miles off Diamond Shoals Light.

Within weeks, the entire East Coast was under siege, and it was almost defenseless. Most of our ships had been sent to the Pacific, or to the North Atlantic run, where two of them (*Reuben James* and *Kearny*) were torpedoed even before war officially began. Aircraft? Almost none. To defend the east coast of the United States in spring 1942, there was a total of ten World War I wooden subchasers, three converted yachts, four blimps, and six Army bombers.

When the U-boats arrived, it was slaughter. They struck on the surface, at night, often not even bothering to dive. The stretch of coast off the Banks was their favorite hunting ground. Armed with both deck guns and torpedoes, they would lie in wait at night, silhouette the passing coasters against the glow of lights ashore, and attack unseen by the men aboard. Ship after ship went down in January, February, and March. *Rochester; Ocean Venture; Norvana; Trepca; City of Atlanta; Oakmar; Tiger;* and scores of others. Oil and debris washed up on the beaches, and residents watched the night sky flame as tankers burned just over the horizon.

The "Arsenal of Democracy" was under blockade; and from the protected pens at Lorient and St. Nazaire more raiders, fresh from refit and training, sailed to attack a coast where in three months of war not one German submarine had yet been the target of an effective attack.

One of them was the U-85.

U-85 was a Type VIIb, specially modified for the Atlantic war. A little over seven hundred tons displacement, two hundred and twenty feet long, she was a little larger than a harbor tugboat, or the *Calypso*. She had been built in northern Germany in early 1941, the second year of the war. Her commander was Kapitanleutnant Eberhard Greger, Class of 1935.

Greger and U-85 spent her first summer working up in the deep fiords of occupied Norway. On August 28 she left Trondheim for her first wartime cruise. On September 10, the wolf tasted blood for the first time. Greger latched on to a Britain-bound convoy. U-85's first five torpedoes ran wild. Throughout that day and the next he ran eastward, staying with the convoy on the surface, just over the horizon. The diesels hammered as U-85 slashed through heavy seas. The convoy's escorts, American destroyers, tried repeatedly to drive her off with gunfire and depth charges. Each time, she submerged and evaded, then came back up and hammered ahead again, rolling viciously, but gradually drawing ahead to position for a new attack.

The next afternoon she reached it, and Greger sent U-85 dashing in on the surface. Boldness was rewarded: at 1642 he made a solid hit on a six-thousand-ton steamer, and, in the next half hour, struck at two more of the heavily laden merchantmen. Then the destroyers closed in for a close depth-charge counterattack. At a little past midnight, September 11, Greger brought her up slowly, and then crept toward home for repairs.

U-85's second war cruise was less dramatic. Battered by heavy weather off Newfoundland, shrouded by fog, she never made contact with her prey, and engine trouble eventually sent her back to St. Nazaire.

For her third war cruise, a new man came aboard. He sounds like a sailor Goebbels would have exulted over; young (26), tall (six feet), blond and well built; but this German must have been different from the Nazi stereotype. For one thing, he kept a diary; and it is thanks to Erich Degenkolb that we know as much as we do about his ship's last cruises.

According to Degenkolb—we can imagine him wedged into his cramped leather bunk, diary on his stomach, listening to the waves crash against the outside of the hull—U-85's third war cruise was her most rewarding, both to Doenitz and to her crew.

Operation Drumroll had begun, and U-85 was one of the first reliefs to be thrown into the battle. On the way across she sank a 10,000-ton steamer and took a near miss from a plane off Newfoundland. "Off New York," as Degenkolb wrote in his diary in February, she sank another steamer after a seven-hour surface chase. She chased convoys throughout the month, probably in the Western Atlantic approaches to New York, till her fuel tanks sloshed near-empty, and then set course for home, crossing the Bay of Biscay submerged and arriving in St. Nazaire again on the twenty-third of February.

A month's refit and leave, and it was time to sail again. At 1800 on March 21, 1942, with a brass band on the pier, with a blooded crew, a confident captain, and a well-tried ship, U-85 set out once more for "*Amerika.*"

The drumbeat of the U-boats had grown louder through February and March. No censorship could conceal the fact that ships were being lost. The explosions on the horizon, the oil on the beaches, the boatloads of huddled men being debarked at every seaport told the story too plainly for anyone to deny.

The Navy and Coast Guard, along with civilian authorities, were struggling with this new meaning of the once-remote war. Vice-Admiral Adolphus Andrews, directing the East Coast antisubmarine effort, found that aside from the lack of ships and planes, he had inadequate operational plans and even less clout. He couldn't even get the use of the destroyers and planes already in Norfolk assigned to the Atlantic Fleet.

One of the results of this unfortunate combination of censorship and unpreparedness was, typically, rumor. U-boats were refuelling, people whispered, in isolated inlets along the coast, and they had been seen in Chesapeake Bay itself. Citizens reported odd lights along the shore at night...obvious signals to someone out at sea.

One of the most persistent rumors concerned landings along the Outer Banks. German sailors, it was said, had actually slipped ashore, were mingling with the locals and even seeing movies, as ticket stubs supposedly recovered from sunken U-boats proved. Alas, a good story, but probably untrue. The Germans did land specially trained spies later in the war in

Quebec and at Narragansett, Long Island; but according to the Coast Guard, Navy, and FBI, that was it in World War II. No U-boat captain must have had much desire to hazard his craft close inshore, or risk losing a skilled *obermachinist* so that he could report on the latest Errol Flynn epic. All that **can** be proven is that where news does not exist, gossip and invention will swiftly take its place.

And in March and April 1942, reality was bad enough. Eight ships had gone down off North Carolina alone in January; two in February, as the first team of submarines headed back across the Atlantic; and then fourteen in March, as they were relieved. Once the "pipeline" of the eighteen-day cruise out of France was full, there would be eight boats on station all the time.
The Outer Banks were suddenly the focus of world war.
Cape Hatteras was dreaded by every merchant seaman on the East Coast. The "Graveyard of the Atlantic" was earning its name anew in the age of steam, and a new cognomen besides—"Torpedo Junction." On March 18, for example, the U-boats met an unescorted "convoy" of five tankers, and torpedoed three, plus a Greek freighter that stopped to rescue crewmen from a black sea filled with blazing oil.
This was how it was: in March 1942, three ships were going down every day, one every eight hours. But even worse was the closely guarded secret that the "exchange rate"—the magic number in antisubmarine warfare—was zero. Not one U-boat had yet been sunk off America.
It could not continue this way. Either the U-boats would be driven under, or all coastwise shipping would have to stop. America, the Allies, could not afford losses on this scale much longer.
It might not be too much to say, as Churchill later did, that it was the war itself that hung in the balance.

USS *Roper*, DD-147, was a fairly old ship in 1942, as warships go. At a little under 1200 tons, she wasn't all that much larger than U-85.
She had been born in Philadelphia, at William Cramp & Sons, in 1918. *Roper* evacuated refugees from Constantinople in 1919 and then spent a few years in the Pacific before being laid up in San Diego in 1922. Recommissioned in 1930, she spent the slow years of the Depression on reserve maneuvers and patrol duty in Hawaii, Panama, and the Caribbean. In 1937 she was transferred to the Atlantic Fleet.
When war began in Europe, the pace picked up. The old four-piper rolled from Key West to Yucatan, and then north in 1940 to the coast of New England. In early 1942, she ran a convoy to

Londonderry, passing the U-85, then on her third war patrol; they may have crossed each other's paths for the first time then, somewhere in the empty spaces of the North Atlantic.

In March, the rigorous glamor of convoy duty ended; she was ordered back to the coast for more patrol. Patrol—steaming endlessly through fog, storm, calm, night. Her crew carried out innumerable late-night actions: radar contact, a breakneck steam to intercept, the depth-charging that was always futile. Whales? Escaping U-boats? Her crew never knew. Perhaps some day, in a war that everyone knew now would last a long time, they would have their chance to fight. But for now, it was more of the same, everlasting patrol.

Kapitan-leutnant Eberhard Greger sailed U-85 on her fourth sortie on March 21, beginning the long transit submerged. In a few days, though, he was able to bring her up, and dieseled west through seas "as smooth as a table," as Degenkolb, relaxing belowdecks, jotted in his journal. They took some damage from a storm on March 30, but repaired it and continued the cruise.

At this stage of the war, Germany's submariners were confident men—especially off America.

By early April she was on station, ranging the coast from New York to Washington. On the tenth, Greger took his boat below to sink a steamer with a spread of two torpedoes. But targets were scarce.

He decided to head south, toward the easy pickings off the Outer Banks.

On the night of April 13, as U-85 hammered through calm seas at 16 knots, Degenkolb made his last entry: "American beacons and searchlights visible at night."

Lieutenant-commander Hamilton W. Howe, captain of the *Roper*, was tired. His crew was tired. The ship itself, twenty-four years old, was tired. But they were alert. The old four-piper did not yet have the new gear Allied scientists were racing to produce. But she had enough. A primitive radar and sonar. Depth charges. And plenty of guns—nice to have, if only a U-boat would play the game for once and surface, instead of skulking away underwater while the horizon crackled with flame from dying ships.

At midnight on the 13th, *Roper* was running southward off Bodie Island. The lighthouse, still operating, was plainly visible to starboard. The night was clear and starry, and at 18 knots the knife bow of the old DD pared phosphorescence from the smooth water. Most of her crew was asleep below.

On the bridge as Officer of the Deck, Ensign Ken Tebo was awake and alert. At six minutes past midnight, the radar suddenly showed a small pip a mile and a half ahead. The ship

The Oregon Inlet Bridge joins the northern beaches beyond Bodie Island with the Pea Island Wildlife Refuge.

had been plagued with these small contacts all night. Another small boat, Tebo thought; probably a Coast Guard craft, on the same mission as the destroyer—patrol. But he felt immediately that there was something strange, something different, about this one.

He ordered an eight degree change of course, to close slowly, and to present the smallest possible target—just in case. In seconds—the captain always slept in full uniform at sea—Howe was on the bridge.

Tebo explained the situation quickly. He still had that strange feeling. *Roper* was overhauling, but too slowly. At 2100 yards range the two men saw the wake of whatever it was up ahead. White, narrow, it glowed in the starlit seas. Howe ordered an increase in speed to 20 knots. It still might be a Coast Guard boat. But Howe made his decision. At the clang of General Quarters, seamen rolled from their bunks and ran to man their guns, the torpedo batteries, the depth charge racks astern, and the K-guns, weapons that threw the drums of explosive far out over the ship's side, widening the carpet of concussion that could crush the hull of any submerged enemy.

Aboard the speeding U-boat, most of the crew was asleep. Degenkolb had thrust his diary into his pocket and turned in. On the darkened conning tower, only a few feet above the sea, an officer and two lookouts stared ahead. They anticipated no trouble. A U-boat had a tiny silhouette, almost impossible to see from a ship's deck at night.

After a time, one of the lookouts turned 'round and tapped the officer on the shoulder. There seemed to be something astern. A target? The submarine's rudders swung, and she began to creep to the right.

Below, her men slept on.

Aboard the *Roper*, now only a few hundred yards astern, Lt. William Vanous, the executive officer, stood panting atop the flying bridge. Commander S.C. Norton was beside him. Below them the two men could hear the pounding of feet on metal as the bridge team manned up. The starlight showed more men on the forecastle, running toward the three-inch guns. Beside them, the searchlight operator was swinging his lamp around, and they heard the clang as BMC Jack Wright charged the No. 1. 50-caliber machine gun.

Vanous strained his eyes ahead. At the end of a white ribbon of wake a black object was slowly drawing into view. Could it really be a submarine? It was awfully small. He noted happily that the men on the bridge below were keeping the ship a trifle to the side of the wake; most U-boats carried torpedo tubes in their pointed sterns as well as in the bow.

Yes, thought the German officer ahead of him, there is something back there. And it was very close. He reached for the alarm toggle, and below him, under the waterline, Degenkolb suddenly awoke.

The two ships were turning. The submarine was slipping to starboard. In a few moments its stern tubes would point directly at its pursuer. Howe ordered the helm hard right, and called into the voice tube, "Illuminate!" Above him, with a sputtering hiss, the searchlight ignited. Vanous coached it out into the darkness, and caught his breath. The beam had swept across the conning tower of a submarine with five men running along the half-submerged deck toward her gun.

Someone shouted to Wright, and with an ear-battering roar the chief began firing. The machine gun tracers swept forward, hung over the black boat, then descended, dancing along the thin-skinned ballast tanks, then reaching up the deck toward the frantically working gun crew. Forward, a second machine gun opened up. The glare of the searchlight wavered, but held. In its weird light men began to fall.

At almost the same moment, crewmen along the destroyer's side pointed and shouted at a sparkling trail in the water: a torpedo!

Inside the hull of the *U-85*, other men heard the clang of machine gun bullets on metal. They ran for their stations, forty men in a hull no wider than a railway car. The ship shuddered as a torpedo went out astern. Erich Degenkolb swung a locker open and pulled out his yellow escape lung. Could Kapitan Greger submerge and escape? He hoped so, desperately. But from the sounds that came through the steel around him into what the U-boat men called the "iron coffin," it seemed that U-85's luck had finally run out.

On the *Roper's* bridge, Howe had no time for thoughts and no time for feelings. It was a U-boat, and it was **surfaced**. The ship was still shuddering around in her turn. "Open fire!" he shouted.

On the exposed forecastle, in the mounts on deck aft, the three-inchers began to fire. Their target was only 300 yards away now, almost point-blank range. But it seemed smaller. It was submerging. In a moment it would be gone.

The *Roper's* men saw their last round hit just at the base of the conning tower, where it joined the U-boat's pressure hull.

With the sound of a solid hit in their ears, the *Unterseeboot*-men knew their battle was lost. The ballast tanks were already filling, and the machine gun and shell fire must have holed them too. U-85 was on her last dive. There was only one way for her men to live now, and that was to get out of her narrow hull before it slipped forever under the icy sea.

Erich Degenkolb joined the crowd struggling under the ladder.

Seconds later he found himself topside. The deck was familiar, but fire was still drumming on the sinking boat. A blinding shaft of light picked out every splinter, every weldment of the hull. He stumbled from the blaze of fire and sound over the side. The water was freezing cold. Gasping, he came up, stuck the mouthpiece of the lung between his teeth, and tried to inflate it. His heavy clothes were dragging him down.

Suddenly the firing stopped. The light went out. He drifted, seemingly alone, for a few minutes, feeling the cold of the sea gnaw into his bare hands, into his face.

Then, all at once, a string of deeper detonations brought his attention up, into the night.

The last thing he saw was the American ship. Immense, black, blazing, it loomed over the sinking shell that had been his home, over the struggling men in the water who had been his friends. And from its sides, in brief bursts of reddish light, he saw the depth charges leap into the night and splash on either side, amid the waving, screaming men.

When the black ship slid under, Howe doused the light. He was suddenly conscious of how conspicuous he was. Lights, shooting...the killers, it was common talk among destroyermen, often operated in pairs.

A few minutes later, the sonar operator reported contact. The destroyer, darkened and silent now, wheeled and headed toward it.

"Prepare for depth charge attack," said Howe.

"Men in the water ahead, captain."

"All stop."

Her screws slowing, *Roper* coasted forward. From the bridge he could see them now. One of them was even shouting up at him... *"Heil Hitler."* But he was thinking. He held course. He knew they were there. But the contact was solid. It might be another sub.

"Fire depth charges," said Howe.

Astern, from the fantail, the launchers exploded. The charges arched out, hit, and sank, and seconds later 3300 pounds of TNT went off in the midst of forty swimming men.

Roper made no more attacks that night, but lingered in the area of the sinking, echo-ranging and with every lookout alert. At about six the sun rose, lighting the scene of recent battle. Oil slicked the low waves; life jackets and motionless bodies drifted in slow eddies as the destroyer nosed back and forth, sniffing for the vanished enemy. At 0850, obtaining a ping on a bottomed object, she made a straight run and dropped four more depth charges. A great gush of air and a little oil came up when the foam subsided astern. At 0957, Howe dropped two more depth charges over the largest bubbles. At last he concluded that it was over. The U-boat was still down there, but she was dead. Coached from aircraft from shore, still watching for that constantly-feared other sub, the *Roper* lowered a boat, and began dragging bodies aboard.

One of them, his face and body swollen and discolored from the depth charge that had killed him, was Erich Degenkolb.

The first U-boat! The news was electrifying. At long last one of them had been destroyed, by an American ship, and in the very area where for four months now the wolves had hunted with impunity. The story was immediately released to the press. But this was not the end. Roper continued south on her patrol, but the remains of U-85 were far too valuable to be left undisturbed.

Over the next weeks, divers explored the shattered boat. A hundred feet down, clumsily-suited Navymen clambered over torn metal, pried open hatches, traced fuel and air lines and manifolds, and tried unsuccessfully to raise the hull with compressed air. They were unable to get inside and it was impossible to raise the wreck without a major salvage effort — not an easy option off Cape Hatteras in April.

In the end, they left her there, possibly with some of her crew still inside the now-silent hull, under the canted conning tower, with its painted device of a wild boar, rampant, with a rose in its mouth. The divers, the ships were needed elsewhere. There were valuable cargoes to be recovered. And from now on, there would be casualties from the other side as well — U-352, sunk off Morehead City in May; U-576; U-701; dozens of others. And, last of all, U-548, sent down a hundred miles east of the Chesapeake Bay entrances three years later, in April, 1945.

The U-boat threat was anything but over, but on the Atlantic horizon more light was dawning than that of burning tankers. In the months after April, 1942, American strength increased steadily in our home waters. The threat was overcome, this time; the enemy was steadily shoved back, first to the center of the ocean, then to his home waters. Finally, with the loss of France in 1944, he could deploy only the few war-worn boats that could slip out from Germany itself past close blockade into the North Sea.

Lieutenant-commander Hamilton Howe retired as a rear admiral in 1956. He lives in Winston-Salem, North Carolina. Captain Kenneth Tebo retired in 1961, and lives in Falls Church, Virginia. Captain William Tanous died the same year in a naval hospital in Annapolis. Erich Degenkolb, N 11662/41, lies in Hampton, Virginia, in plot #694 of the National Cemetery.

Kapitan-leutnant Eberhard Greger's body was not recovered.

U-85 lies rusting on a white, sandy bottom, fifteen miles east of where Bodie Island light still glitters out over the troubled seas of Hatteras.

OREGON INLET FISHING CENTER

Bodie Island 441-6301
Map, pg. 103

Oregon Inlet is one of the centers of sport fishing activity on the Banks — especially of deep-sea Gulf Stream fishing. From this National Park Service-leased marina, dozens of charter boats operate, catching thousands of dolphin, wahoo, marlin, sailfish, and other sport fish every year.

Since they are concessionaires of the Park Service, the thirty-some charter boats that operate from here charge the same prices. You can reserve a full day offshore, including bait, tackle, and ice; full-day trips in the Inlet and the sound; and half-days in the sound (see THE OUTER BANKS FISHING GUIDE section for what you can expect to catch). You can make reservations at the Booking Desk (the number above) or with the captains themselves... and we recommend you make them well in advance during the summer, for Oregon Inlet is one of the busiest places in the Banks come June.

Don't feel quite up to an 1100-lb. blue marlin? A less demanding sport is head boat fishing, aboard Miss Oregon Inlet, a 65-ft. diesel boat out of Oregon Inlet Fishing Center. She carries up to 46 fisherpersons on half-day inlet and sound bottom fishing cruises, catching spot, croakers, gray trout, bluefish, mullet, sea bass, etc., etc. All bait, ice and tackle is included in the price. Schedule: Early spring and late fall, one trip daily, departing at 7:00 a.m. and returning at 11:30 a.m. During the season (Memorial to Labor Days) there will be two trips daily, 7:00 to 11:30 a.m. and 12:00 to 5:00 p.m. A non-fishing Twilight Cruise leaves on selected days at 5:30 p.m. If you've not fished the salt sea before, a head boat is a rewarding and much less expensive way to start.

Aside from charter and head boats, the Center also supplies a fish-cleaning service, restrooms, and three boat ramps into the sound. The marina restaurant is open from 5-9 a.m. for breakfast, and also offers a box lunch service. The tackle shop carries a complete line of surf and deep-sea fishing equipment, as well as basic snacks, drinks, and camping consumables.

Everything at Oregon Inlet is organized around the angler; the fish-cleaning service will take your fish right off the boat to a truck, and there are mounting services to do your lifetime trophy up proud. Don't miss the outdoor display of mounted deep sea game fish, including the World's Record 1,142 lb. Atlantic Blue Marlin caught off the Inlet in 1974.

The Oregon Inlet Fishing Center is nine miles south of Whalebone Junction, west of Highway 12 on the turnoff to the right just before the bridge.

BODIE ISLAND

 ATTRACTIONS:
1. National Park Service Information Center, pg. 82
2. Coquina Beach, pg. 86
3. Laura A. Barnes, pg. 88
4. Bodie Island Lighthouse and Visitor Center, pg. 88
5. U-85, pg. 89

 RECREATION:
1. Outer Banks Fishing Pier, pg. 82
2. Coquina Beach, pg. 86

 HOTELS/MOTELS/CAMPGROUNDS:
1. Oregon Inlet Campground, pg. 179

 RESTAURANTS:
1. Oregon Inlet Marina Restaurant, pg. 101

BODIE ISLAND — 103

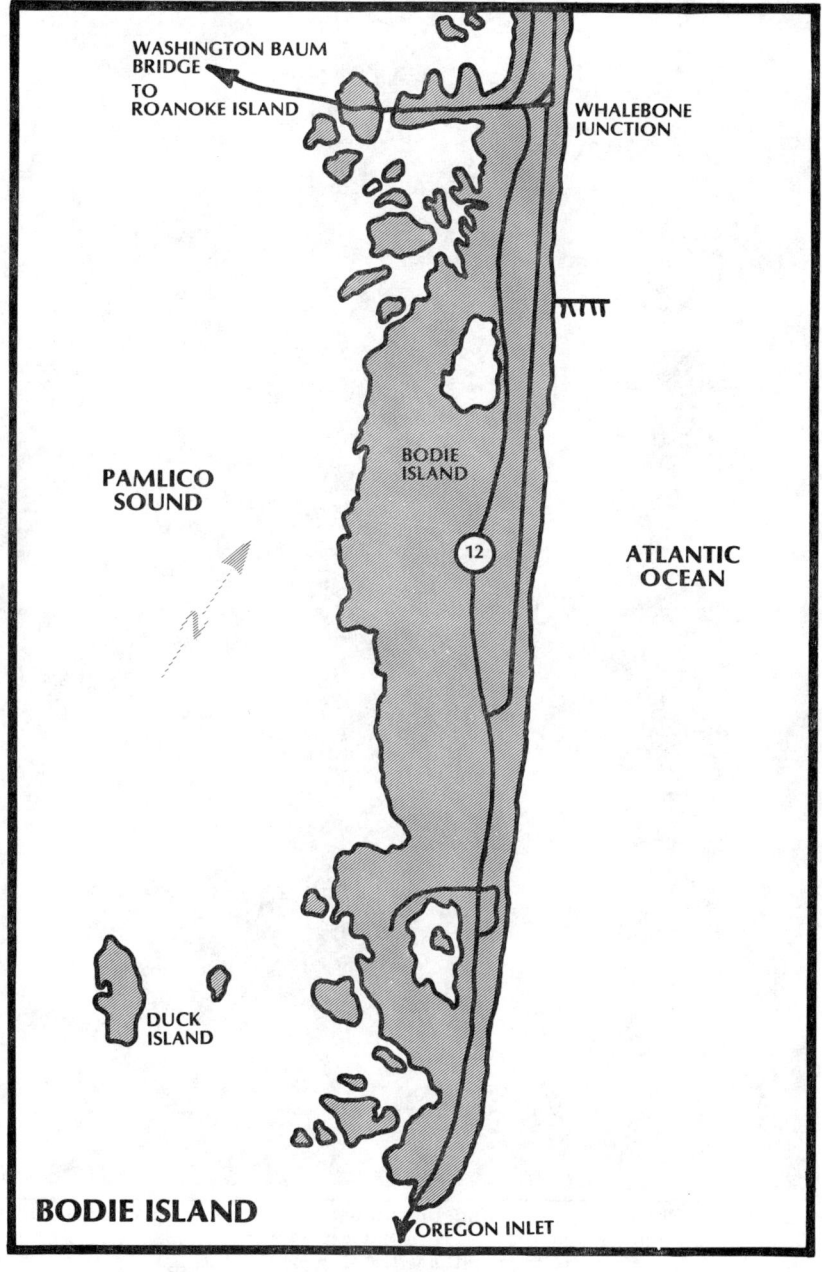

The Night Shift - Bodie Island lighthouse on the Outer Banks of North Carolina stands in sharp relief against an evening sky as a setting sun signals the beginning of the night shift. A powerful rotating beacon will soon appear, stretching nineteen miles out to sea warning mariners to steer clear of shoals which have claimed hundreds of ships over the years.

Billfish - A blue marlin at Oregon Inlet Marina is weighed.

OREGON INLET

Between Hatteras and Bodie Island   441-6301
Map, pg. 103

Driving south from Nags Head, through Bodie Island, you'll soon find yourself lifted skyward on an immense concrete bridge. From a hundred feet in the air you can see for miles — to seaward, over Atlantic swells; to soundward, over the vast calm sheet of the Pamlico.

This is Oregon Inlet, the Bank's major avenue for trade and fishing for over a hundred years.

Oregon Inlet opened during a hurricane in 1846, and was named, as was the custom in those days, after the first ship to make it through. Its opening brought shoaling to Ocracoke Inlet, and economic ruin to the once-flourishing town of Portsmouth.

Today it too is shoaling, and its consequences may be just as dramatic.

The Herbert C. Bonner Bridge, built in 1964 to provide access to the southern Banks, may have hastened this process by impeding the free tidal flow through the inlet. (Note, as you pass over it, the mile or more of new land under the bridge supports to the north.) But it is more likely that simple beach migration, the eons-long march of the Banks to the south and west, is the real cause. Whatever the causative factors, the inlet has required nearly round-the-clock dredging for the last few years, and now the silting is overtaking the Corps of Engineers ability to dredge.

The controversy over clearing or stabilizing the inlet, or whether it can be stabilized at all, has been going on for some years now. A long riprap jetty might keep the channel open, at great expense, but it too would have to be dredged, and there is no guarantee that it would work for more than a few years.

Meanwhile, the boatbuilders and trawling companies of Wanchese, have been hit with skyrocketing insurance rates. Many of them have moved south, to the Morehead City area. It is too soon to write Wanchese off as a fishing port, but there is no doubt that the situation there is serious.

The potential closing of the inlet also leads to the question: where will the next inlet be? Historically, the closing of an inlet has seemed to portend the opening of a new one somewhere else. All that water in the sounds has to go somewhere. We don't know, and no one can really predict, where an inlet will open. But it can happen pretty quickly, when those winter waves come crashing over the barrier dunes.

BODIE ISLAND LIGHTHOUSE

Drawing by Jerry Miller

OUTER BANKS ACCOMMODATIONS

There are over 120 motels and motor inns on the Outer Banks from Kitty Hawk to Ocracoke. Within these properties there are about 3,800 units, of which one-half or more are efficiencies with some facilities for cooking. Some of the accommodations qualify for the appellation "apartment," because they are fully equipped for housekeeping.

During the prime mid-June to September season, an estimated 85,000 visitors a week check into motels, cottages and campsites along the barrier island strip. The competition for the available rentals is keen. Do not expect to obtain lodging on the Outer Banks during the in-season unless you have a prior confirmed reservation.

If you make reservations between January and mid-March, you can generally get the accommodations you want. After mid-March and into April, you will have to compromise and take what is available. By May, better motel, cottage, and campsite properties have already been booked through the end of September.

THE MOTEL MARKET

There are, categorically speaking, few resort hotels on the Outer Banks, at least in the terms we think of Miami Beach, Atlantic City A.C. (After Casinos) or the Caribbean resort islands. Perhaps less than five properties offer room service, and in only a few are bell hops and tuxedoed restaurant captains to be seen. Although condominium construction is booming and the face of the islands has been changed by new elaborate restaurants, the resort area is still orientated to the vacationing family, and the oceanfront motel is its short term accommodation choice.

There are a few old style inns remaining in operation and a few

ACCOMMODATIONS

SANDERLING
1. Sanderling Inn

KILL DEVIL HILLS
2. Bel-Air Motel
3. Tan-A-Rama
4. The Mariner
5. Sea Ranch
6. Chart House
7. Tanglewood Motel
8. Cavalier
9. Colony IV
10. Outer Banks Motor Lodge
11. Holiday Inn
12. Tanya's Ocean House
13. John Yancey
14. Econo Lodge
15. Ramada Inn

NAGS HEAD NORTH
16. The Carolinian
17. Beacon Motor Lodge
18. Cabana East
19. Ocean Veranda
20. Olde London Inn
21. First Colony Inn
22. Sea Spray

NAGS HEAD SOUTH
23. Pebble Beach
24. Silver Sands
25. The Islander
26. Sea Oatel
27. Sea Foam
28. Owens'
29. Surf Side
30. Best Western Armada
31. Sandpiper Court

ROANOKE ISLAND
32. Elizabethan Inn
33. Dare Haven
34. Scarborough House Inn
35. Duke of Dare

HATTERAS ISLAND
36. Hatteras Island Motel
37. Ocean Aire
38. Avon Motel
39. Tower Circle
40. General Mitchell
41. Cape Hatteras
42. Cape Sandbox
43. Outer Banks
44. Lighthouse View
45. Falcon
46. Kona Kai
47. Durant Station
48. Sea Gull
49. Hatteras Harbor
50. Hatteras Marlin
51. Burrus Motor Court

OCRACOKE
52. Berkley Center
53. Bluff Shoal
54. Silver Lake
55. Island Inn
56. Pony Island
57. Oscar's House
59. Harborside
60. Sand Dollar
61. Ships Timbers
62. Crews Inn
63. Blackbeard's Lodge

large motel properties with good restaurants and live entertainment nightly on premises, but the majority of the properties are more or less on a par with the well-known interstate highway motel chains. The rooms have wall-to-wall carpet, color coordinated contemporary decor, tile shower/bath tub combinations, air conditioning, color TV, and perhaps a balcony.

Unless otherwise noted in the profiles, you can expect these standards in the properties we review. One exception on the Outer Banks is the room telephone. Many motels do not have phones in the room. If this is one of your requirements, be sure to ask about room phones at the time of reservation.

Of course there are older properties on the beach which do not have national motel chain standards. Most of these motels were built in the 1950s. Many have been modernized, but still show their age. Fishermen love these properties because they lend themselves to an informal, perhaps unshaven, vacation life style that doesn't like to worry about sand on the shag carpet.

These motels can still be comfortable and inviting. In fact, their porches and rocking chairs seem to promote old fashioned interaction among their guests. It seems easier to meet people somehow at these unpretentious spots. Generally they attract sportsmen and families on a budget. Almost all of these properties are in our economy rate class.

RATE GUIDELINES

Accommodations come in four basic categories: Economy, Moderate, Deluxe, and Luxury. The terms are specific more to room rates than they are to a definitive standard. Motels charging the same basic rates are not necessarily equal. There can be a great deal of qualitative difference between properties in each category. Factors such as location, age, up-keep, amenities, service, and even owner attitude come into play when you look beyond the numbers.

For your convenience, each motel property has been placed within a rate category. The rate range is based on the double occupancy of a standard room with two double beds in the prime season. The rate does not include the 7 1/2% state and local sales tax which is added to all bills.

Here are the definitions of the categories by rate:

$	$24 to $39
$$	$40 to $59
$$$	$60 to $79
$$$$	$80 and up

The spread in room rates not only represents properties within the category, but also individual rooms and efficiencies within the same motel. Size, location, and decor determine the price range of the same type of room within a property. If you want a room with access to the pool, or an oceanfront room with a private balcony overlooking the beach, make your request when you make your reservation. Often you can get a choice room simply by asking and exploring the possibilities with your reservations clerk. Look for tips on the perferred rooms in each property profile.

Motel profiles are arranged by mile posts, north to south, Sanderling to Ocracoke, along the Outer Banks. See the map reference for its relative location to restaurants and attractions.

RATING PERIODS

Most properties adjust their rates on the basis of three or four rating periods. Whenever we use the terms "in season," "prime season," or "peak season" we are essentially speaking about the period between Memorial Day weekend and Labor Day. Most properties get their top rate for the Memorial Day weekend, but may not demand it after those dates until the third or fourth week in June. Everyone agrees that the ten weeks from June leading to Labor Day in the first week of September are the most in demand, and their rates hit the high point.

Knowing the rating periods of the property you want is important if you are cost conscious. If a week or two difference in dates means a 30% saving, it is worth knowing.

The secondary rating periods are in the spring and fall months, and are called the "mid season" or "shoulder season." Rates for these periods are usually the same. Spring dates can start as early as April and run through mid-June. Fall dates usually begin after Labor Day and may run into October. Some properties which are open only on a seasonal basis combine the most desirable of these dates with the ends of the prime season dates to create another rating period. Rates during the mid season run 20% to 30% less than the prime rate.

The off season rates of most year round properties are in force during the months of Nov., Dec., Jan., Feb., and Mar. Seasonal properties may have an off season rate from opening through Memorial Day weekend, and from late September until Closing. Off seson rates are generally 40% to 50% less than prime.

Most properties have a rate chart displaying their rating periods and current rates. Request this information when considering reservations.

a rare find

New Oceanfront Hotel Nags Head Beach

A splendid new Ramada Inn is now open on the Outer Banks. There's no better place for your vacation. Come enjoy our excellent accommodations with a microwave and refrigerator in every room and an oceanfront heated pool and Jacuzzi. Peppercorns, a delicious seaside restaurant, awaits your dining pleasure. Our beautifully appointed hotel is a rare find, indeed.

Call today
919-441-2151

RAMADA INN
At Nags Head Beach

Kill Devil Hills

1701 S. Virginia Dare Trail • Kill Devil Hills, NC 27948

PETS

The North Carolina State law prohibits pets in motel and hotel rooms.

EXTRA PERSONS

There is no uniform standard concerning what constitutes an extra person. Children free in the parents' room could be under 18, under 12, under 6, or under 3 years of age. If you have children, be sure to ask about the specific policy at reservation time. Extra persons in a room add $3 to $8 per person to the daily room rate.

DEPOSITS

All hotels and motels require deposits to confirm vacation reservations. Policies vary, but average 25% to 33% of the total or one night's rate, whichever is greater. To cancel a reservation and get your deposit returned, some properties require 48 hours notice, some 72 hours, and a few up to two week's notice. Be sure you understand the cancellation policy when you make a reservation.

Deposits are usually due within three to seven days after making the reservation.

CHECK-IN, CHECK-OUT TIMES

Although there is no complete uniformity on check-in and check-out times, most properties use the 3 p.m. check-in, 11 a.m. check-out policy.

During the season, do not expect to get into a reserved room prior to the posted check-in time. House staffs are hard pressed to keep pace with room turnovers, and owners and managers do not like to issue a room key until the unit has been prepared and inspected.

For the same reasons, check-out times should be strictly observed. To encourage on time check-outs, many properties have provided post check-out dressing facilities for those who want a final morning by the ocean or pool

PAYING THE BILL

Many hotels and motels want the balance of the room reservation paid on arrival. Personal checks are seldom honored except for advance deposits. If the property does not accept credit cards, you had best be prepared to pay by travelers' checks or by a certified check issued by a bank prior to your trip. (Don't forget the taxes totaling 7 1/2% of your bill.)

Make sure that you are clear about the payment policy at your hotel or motel. No need starting off your holiday wth an unnecessary hassle. We do not encourage the carrying of large amounts of cash, not out of any specific fear, but just as a principle of traveler's common sense.

MINIMUM STAYS

To protect their prime season from one-nighters, most hotel and motel properties have established minimum stays. For example, Memorial Day and Labor Day weekends demand three day minimum stays in order to get a reservation. Some properties get a seven day minimum.

The minimum stay requirements will prevent an untimely attempt to cut off a day from the reservation. Unless dire circumstances exist, do not expect a refund for failure to honor the reserved minimum.

COTS AND CRIBS

Here is another non-standard policy on the beach. Infants are usually free, especially if you bring your own crib and linens. Some properties provide the crib free. Others provide the crib at a charge of about $6 a day. Cots, when available, usually get a rental fee of about $6.

If you have a baby, and some small ones who have to sleep by themselves, ask about cots and cribs at the time when you are considering reservations.

PARKING

All of the properties profiled in this guide have free parking facilities for at least one vehicle per guest room. If you have an oversized vehicle, and we're not talking about vintage Cadillacs, ask your hotel about parking prior to arrival.

Your hotel or motel can also advise you about transient docking for your boat, and ramp and parking areas for your boat trailer.

OFF SEASON PACKAGES

More and more Outer Banks properties are staying open all year. The advantages to the owner include keeping the house staff together, and generating revenue in additional off season months. The advantages to the consumers are in dollars saved.

An off season package will generally include room rates at half prices, or less, meals and beverages below menu prices, and free passes or discounts to almost anything that is open in the area i.e. golf course, miniature golf, movies, skating, etc.

Generally the rates quoted for a two nights, three days (weekend or weekdays) package will include a very low rate for additional days.

Off season visits to the Banks are not only cost saving retreats, but they also provide an excellent opportunity to inspect hotels, motels, and cottages for future consideration. The serious real estate or condominium buyer should also be interested in these packages.

Ask several places to put you on their off season package mailing list during your summer visit, or write for the off season flyers and brochures.

WEEKLY RATES

There is no way to average weekly motel rates and give a meaningful guideline. Most Outer Banks properties have a policy for weekly rentals, and usually there is a savings over the sum of the seven days. The savings could be nil, $2 a day, or a very favorable 10% or more. Ask about the weekly rate policy, and do a little simple arithmetic to see how the bottom line price compares with other places that you are considering.

If you are considering residence for a month, or for the season, some of the older, traditional properties quote rates for these periods at a considerable saving over their daily rates.

OCEANFRONT, OCEANVIEW

Any property that uses the term **oceanfront** must have rooms which have frontage on the ocean beach. The rooms may or may not have balconies, but they will afford direct access to the beach. Not all rooms of an **oceanfront** property have the **oceanfront** view.

Many properties advertise an **oceanview**. We take this term to mean that at least some of the rooms have a view of the ocean. For example, a building constructed on an angle to the ocean, but separated from the actual beach by another building, could still provide an **oceanview** from its ocean facing rooms, especially ones above the second story.

Our caveat is to approach the above terms with some reserve. Ask for a description of the view at reservation time. Be sure that you and the reservations clerk are talking the same language.

PERSONAL CHECK CASHING

Unless you have established prior credit, or have a local Outer Banks bank account, the general rule is that you will be unable to cash a personal check.

Wise vacation planners will use a combination of credit cards, travelers' checks, and cash.

GOLF AND TENNIS PRIVILEGES

Any property on the Outer Banks can advertise these two amenities because the local golf courses and the indoor tennis center welcome visiting players.

Some properties may have free passes and discount greens fee arrangements for their guests, but if you want to play, your only real problem is finding a playing partner.

GUARDED BEACHES

The Lifeguard Service on the major resort beaches is a private business which profits from the rental of beach chairs and umbrellas. Lifeguard stands are thus located in front of the larger motel properties where the swimming population congregates. The areas between the lifeguard stands are patrolled by a four wheel drive vehicle equipped for rescue.

Members of the Lifeguard Service are especially trained in ocean rescue and are equipped with surfboards and life rings. Some motel properties may also employ their own private lifeguards.

ACCOMMODATIONS — 117

Beach Apparatus Drill - members of the National Park Service, dressed in authentic costumes worn by the U.S. Life Saving service, recreate the Breeches Buoy drill once used on the Outer Banks of North Carolina to rescue ships stranded off the beach. The Keeper, Phil Noblett, is shown above (hat and tie) supervising a crew operating a beach cart which was used to haul the hawser line to the beach where it was then fired out to the stranded ship and used in rescuing people to safety.

SOUTHERN SHORES, DUCK, SANDERLING, COROLLA

ACCOMMODATIONS

THE SANDERLING INN

Sanderling, north of Duck 261-4111
$$$$
Map, pg. 30

When you want to get away for a luxurious, all-your-needs-taken-care-of vacation, this is the place for you. Opened in the summer of 1985, The Sanderling Inn offers prestigious accommodations in an area of the beach that knows no commercialization. Though the Inn itself is architecturally very pleasing, built in a true old Nags Head style with cedar shakes, dormers, and plenty of porches for beach gazing, it's the special touches provided in your room and elsewhere that really sold us. Touches like lounging robes, in-room baskets filled with Evelyn Crabtree toiletries, and a welcome basket of fruit and wine provided to you when you check in. During the high season, a Continental breakfast each morning and wine and hors d'oeuvres each afternoon are offered to guests, compliments of the management.

A library on the second floor Grand Gallery offers a large selection of current newspapers and magazines (they even have the New York Times and the Wall Street Journal — no small feat on the Outer Banks — and guests receive daily complimentary copies of USA Today) as well as video tapes, a very good selection of novels, and recorded music. There is also a book of original size Audubon prints that a collector — or anyone else in the know - would surely covet. All this quiet entertainment is surrounded by a room full of English country antiques, furniture and decorative pieces made by hand especially for the Inn, antique plates depicting Audubon scenes, and a porcelain collection valued in the six figures.

Downstairs in the Audubon Room, you see impressive nautical antiques, sculptors, and an attractive collection of porcelain fish. There's a comfortable lounging room with a bar and fireplace. The entranceway is enhanced by a cathedral ceiling from which hangs a brass chandelier that was handcrafted for the Inn in Louisiana.

Sanderling Inn offers 28 rooms, all tastefully decorated with well-equipped kitchens and privacy porches. Natural wood wainscotting in the rooms as well as throughout the Inn carry on the old Nags Head elegance. Four of the rooms offered are loft suites featuring living areas, kitchens, privacy porches, and half baths downstairs with upstairs bedrooms dressing areas and full baths. All the rooms provide exceptional sound or ocean views, with the corner rooms giving views of each.

A community pool, tennis courts, and nature trails, part of the Sanderling development, are available to all guests. And, being situated where it is on the border of the Pine Island Sanctuary, an Audubon Society property, there literally are miles and miles of totally undeveloped beach to walk.

Plans for 1986 include an addition of 30 more rooms and a facility for meetings. There's also a health spa in the works.

The management at the Sanderling Inn goes to any length to make sure their guests receive the attention they would expect to receive at a first-class inn. Our guess is that it will fast become one of "The" places to stay on the Outer Banks for those who can afford to be pampered.

Warm sand, soothing waves & friendly people. Vacationers keep coming back to our oceanfront efficiencies year after year. And for some very good reasons. Our rooms are family-sized and our comfort, location and friendly service are the best on the beach. You can count on it. Visit the Tan-a-Rama this year and just see if you don't plan on coming back again and again. Be sure to ask about our Mon.-Thurs. rates. Write or call for our free color brochure: P.O. Box 1350 • Kill Devil Hills, North Carolina 27948 • (919) 441-7315.

Tan-a-Rama

 ## KILL DEVIL HILLS
ACCOMMODATIONS

BEL-AIR MOTEL

Rt. 158 Business, MP 6½ 441-6132
$
Map, pg. 57

Harry and Nancy Powell's Bel-Air Motel is at the north end of the resort area, and offers a variety of accommodations for budget conscious families. The motel has an oceanfront building of one and two bedroom units with wind shielded porches opening directly on the ocean. Across the highway the motel has a pool, motel type units, and a string of two bedroom cottages on separate lots. All the efficiencies, suites (apartments) and cottages have TV and a kitchen for light housekeeping.

This is an older, but well-kept property which offers good value. The quiet residential beach, proximity to Avalon Pier, convenience stores, and restaurants make it a good choice for fishermen. There is even a fish cleaning station with running water in the cottage area.

Open from March through November.

TAN-A-RAMA

Rt. 158, MP 6½ 441-7315
$$-$$$
Map, pg. 57

Thirty-three of the units in this 35-unit oceanfront property are spacious efficiencies with fully equipped kitchens; five of these are 2 bedroom apartments with attractive decor, carpeting, wood paneling, color TV, and lounging area. Twenty-two of the one and two bedroom units are directly on the ocean.

The two story building has a guest deck on the beach from

The ever-changing ocean is a constant source of fascination to children of all ages.

which the patrons can watch the fishing at the nearby Avalon Pier. The large raised pool is located across the road adjacent to the offices of Young Realtors.

The cedar shake exterior and a new paint job keep the outside of this family-owned motel looking nice while regularly replaced drapes, upholstery, bedspreads and daily maid service keep the inside fresh.

The Tan-a-Rama also has a party room, the N'easter, which can be used for guest functions or as a game room on a rainy day.

THE MARINER

Rt. 158 Business, MP 7 441-7255
$$-$$$
Map, pg. 57

The Mariner is a 66 unit property with a definite resort flavor. The two-story and three-story main buildings form an "L" which shields the parking lot, large pool, walled patio, and recreation area from the highway. The drive-in entry is made through a passageway in the main building.

There are 29 motel rooms and 27 efficiency apartments with two and three bedrooms here. The accommodations are spacious, wood paneled, and have all the decor and comfort features befitting a modern motel.

Motel-type rooms are available on a daily basis in-season, but the deluxe apartments rent only on a weekly basis from mid-June thru the first week in September. A large oceanfront apartment, and units that will permit three-couple families to share a common kitchen-living area and still enjoy the privacy of separate bedrooms and baths, are seasonal favorites and are priced in the deluxe price range.

The recreation area has facilities for volleyball, shuffleboard, badminton, and horseshoes in addition to the large pool. There are beachside showers and a fish cleaning station, too. A raised gazebo sits atop the dunes for guests to enjoy views of the ocean and beach from its rail or seated on its long bench.

Guests who fly into the Wright Memorial air-strip just two miles from the Mariner will be provided complimentary ground transportation.

SEA RANCH HOTEL

Rt. 158 Business, MP 7 441-7126
$$$
Map, pg. 57

This is one of the showcase properties of the Outer Banks. Its overall accommodations, facilities, and amenities are hard to beat if you are looking for plush surroundings and resort night life.

The property consists of three buildings, a five-story oceanfront tower, a two-story section, and a new condominium section (Sea Ranch ll) which has 28 luxury suites sold in time shared ownership. It is our guess that a few of these suites will also be available for rental through the hotel.

Guest rooms in the Sea Ranch Oceanfront Tower area efficiencies with two double beds, and a private glass-enclosed balcony with an ocean view. Connecting rooms can form a suite. The main building guest rooms have balconies, and some units have a sitting room area, mini-refrigerator, and two double phones. A conference room can be provided for executive groups.

The Sea Ranch offers a modified or full American Plan (two or three meals a day) at a very attractive rate. There is also room service and complimentary coffee.

Facilities include owner Alice Sykes's stylish ladies fashion boutique, Alice's Looking Glass, the highly regarded Top of the Dunes Dining Room, and the Sea Ranch Lounge, a large double tiered, double dance floor, crystal chandeliered, long bar, big city show lounge with contemporary band entertainment nightly.

A glass-enclosed indoor pool with sundeck furniture, greenery, and restroom/shower area's is popular as is the Sea Ranch's indoor tennis center accross the highway.

Serious fitness patarons will enjoy the convenience and use of the Nautilus Center, located in the complex.

The Sea Ranch is one of the few deluxe, full-service properties on the Banks, yet its rates will be welcomed by the experienced beach resort traveler.

THE CHART HOUSE

Rt. 158 Business, MP 7　　　　　　　　　　　　　　　441-7418
$$　　　　　　　　　Map, pg. 57

David and Kristin Clark live in the large brick colonial oceanfront house, and host guests in the 18-unit modern two-story motel that sets perpendicular to the beach.

The motel rooms are spacious. The property dates from 1966 and has contemporary features such as extra sound-proofing, room refrigerators, and color TV. It is a clean and comfortable family accommodation.

There are also a few small rooms available in the oceanfront house. The rooms are pine paneled, and have more direct access

The Family Center for Fun on the Outer Banks!

On the Oceanfront
108 Rooms & fully equipped efficiencies
Pancake Shoppe • Pool • Color Cable TV
Children Under 12 Free

**Call toll free 800-228-5151
or direct 919-441-7727**

Quality Inn
John Yancey

Mile Post 10 • Box 422 • Kill Devil Hills, N.C.

to the beach than the motel units. A deck on the dune line provides a spot for oceanview relaxing.

The Chart House pool, not visible from the highway, has a patio area where guests can also relax in the sun.

The Sea Ranch with its restaurant, show lounge, and tennis center is adjacent to the Chart House which can be convenient for the smaller property's guests.

TANGLEWOOD MOTEL

Rt. 158 Business, MP 8   441-7208
$$

Map, pg. 57

It is hard to appreciate the design features of the Tanglewood from the highway. The two-story weathered wooden structure is shaped like a U. The pool and deck fill the verdant courtyard, and balcony which surrounds it. The open end of the U is shielded from the highway so that the courtyard, balcony, and lush greenery remind one of the new Orleans French Quarter.

Rooms here are small by modern motel standards, and the bathrooms are only equipped with showers. All of the 14 rooms however open onto the courtyard. Some of the units are two room efficiencies.

Guests appreciate the limited size of the Tanglewood and the unusual intimacy of the courtyard that brings people together.

CAVALIER

Rt. 158 Business, MP 8½   441-5584
$$

Map, pg. 57

The three single level wings of ths red brick and white columned motel border a large courtyard with pool, volleyball court, children's play area, and shuffleboard courts.

Parking is at the door of each unit, and the covered Colonial styled porch has furniture for guest relaxation. There is also a roof top observation deck atop the oceanfront units.

Accommodations here are varied. There are units with only shower bath facilities, pool side rooms with tub and shower and room refrigerators, oceanfront rooms with full baths, refrigerators, and picture windows, and oceanfront units with kitchenettes. Oceanfront rooms are raised above the parking lot and open onto a broad cement patio facing the surf.

This is a very attractive, well kept motel. It also rents two cottages. Mrs. Dot Wescott, the owner, lives across the highway from the motel. The highly rated Port O'Call Restaurant is opposite, and the Wright Memorial Monument is nearby of the Bypass road.

COLONY IV

Rt. 158 Business, MP 9   441-5581
$$
          Map, pg. 57

The Colony IV is a bright, bi-level modern 75-unit property owned by the Neal family. Rooms here equal the high standards of motel chains. Two double beds, room phones, picture windows, and balconies are the norm. Spacious, well-equipped efficiencies have eating areas and are good values for the family. Connections with adjacent rooms give options for additional sleeping space. Twelve units have direct access to the beach.

The two wings of the Colony IV converge at the raised swimming pool and patio. Guests can also relax at a shaded elevated platform on the dune line.

An additional 30 oceanfront units were added for the 1983 season. The motel also rents six large cottages, three of which are located across from the main property. Cottage guests have privileges at the motel pool and beach.

OUTER BANKS MOTOR LODGE

Rt. 158 Business, MP 9½   441-7404
$$
          Map, pg. 57

This attractive beige brick property consists of a single level strip of units connected by a breezeway to a two-story grouping of oceanfront rooms. The oceanfront accommodations are all efficiencies and open onto a wide beach-level porch. Second level units have a balcony complete with outdoor furniture for lounging.

There is a large raised swimming pool in the center of the parking area and a children's play area. Other amenities include a guest laundromat, and color cable TV.

All of the 38 units here are very spacious and attractively decorated and maintained. One and two bedroom efficiencies are offered, and connecting units are also available for large parties.

The Outer Banks Motor Lodge is located in the prime resort area convenient to restaurants and shopping. It is closed November through March.

HOLIDAY INN

Rt. 158 Business, MP 9.5   441-6333
$$$ (800) 238-8000
Map, pg. 57

This prime location property was completely renovated and refurbished in 1983. The makeover was not restricted to new carpets, bedspreads and drapes, it also included the creation of Madelines, a new restaurant and lounge in the spirit and decor of the 1920s. See our separate profiles under Restaurants, and Nightspots.

The Holiday Inn is a major Outer Banks hostelry which has always maintained a resort flair. More than half of the 105 rooms in the four-story hotel have balconies overlooking the ocean beach. There are also a few King Leisure rooms available at a premium price. The refurbish makes all the rooms fresh, bright, and attractive.

The Inn's beachfront is guarded in season and provides chair and umbrella rentals. Guests can also enjoy a large pool and patio with light food and beverage service.

The hotel's location within an easy walk to popular restaurants and the Sea Holly Square shopping complex help it to enjoy a high occupancy rate. The Wright Brothers Memorial is less than five minutes away. Meeting and banquet facilities are available for groups from 10 to 300 persons.

The Holiday Inn is open all year and provides live entertainment in the lounge Mon-Sat 9 p.m. to 2 a.m.

TANYA'S OCEAN HOUSE

Rt. 158 Business, MP 10   441-7328
$$$
Map, pg. 57

From the highway Tanya's may resemble the stereotype of many well-kept oceanfront motels. Two wings of single level brick units flank a two-story central building with rooms on the ocean. A green lawn leads to the raised pool and sun deck. The surprise, however, is inside. It is called the Tarheel Collection.

"Just for the fun of it," Tanya, the motel's past owner, and an interior designer friend custom decorated a theme room. It was a one-of-a-kind room which required historic research, extensive shopping for appropriate decorating materials and artifacts, and painstaking labor in the actual creation of a dream room from a stripped, bare motel space.

The results were so dramatic, and the sense of accomplishment so rewarding, that Tanya began the same process for other rooms in her 42-unit property. By 1979, seven rooms had been transformed. By 1983, the total was increased to 33.

Since each room is a unique environment, a separate story, only a few of their names can be listed here to tantalize the imagination. Imagine the fun of creating or just enjoying a Currituck Barn Loft, a Wright Brothers Camp, Jonathan Seagull's Nest, a High Hampton Mountain Cottage, or a Carolina Party Suite. Many rooms have waterbeds.

Each room has its own small refrigerator and TV, and opens onto the courtyard and pool. The ocean beach is just over the dune line.

Tanya's Ocean House's unique rooms & suites will be appreciated by the most discriminating traveler.

JOHN YANCEY MOTOR HOTEL

Rt. 158 Business, Mp 10 441-7727
$$$
Map, pg. 57

The recently remodeled John Yancey is a bright, cheery, full service motor hotel located directly on the water's edge. The casual, low-keyed atmosphere is further enhanced by the management and staff, who are especially accommodating and friendly. In addition to 320 feet of sandy beach for sunning, frolicking, and surf-fishing, there is a pool, and shuffleboard courts for you to enjoy.

The John Yancey features: rooms, efficiencies, family units, air-conditioning, cable TV, rental rollaways, and off season rates. Children under 12 are free and all rates are based upon double occupancy. MC, AMEX, Diners and Visa are accepted.

ECONO LODGE

Rt. 158 Bypass, MP 9 441-2503
$$ 1-800-446-6900
Map, pg. 57

Newly built in 1985, the Econo Lodge brings its familiar theme of "spending a night not a fortune" to the Outer Banks' vacationers. This lodge contains 40 rooms, all with either king size beds or two "Extra Length" double beds, color cable TV with free HBO, phones, air conditioning, and full size tubs/showers.

An enclosed pool is provided for year round enjoyment. The motel also offers an "Econo Traveler's Club" for frequent travelers: stay six nights and the seventh is free. Free coffee is always available in the lobby.

RAMADA INN

Rt. 158 Bypass, MP 9 1/2   441-2151
$$$$ 1-800-2RAMADA
Map, pg. 57

With the opening of the oceanfront Ramada Inn in 1985, the Outer Banks got its first real full-service hotel/convention center. The five story tower contains 173 rooms of which 89 have ocean views. All rooms have a balcony or patio, color television with HBO, air conditioning, and phones. And, unlike almost all other accommodations on the Banks, at the Ramada, room service, luggage assistance, laundry/valet service, and babysitting are available.

The hotel also offers a large swimming pool that will be enclosed and heated by the fall of 1986 and a Jacuzzi, surrounded by a large sunbathing deck. An oceanfront gazebo provides refreshments.

Meeting and convention facilities are housed in a three story commercial tower complete with a grand ballroom on the third floor overlooking the ocean, and several large executive meeting suites.

Peppercorns is the featured hotel restaurant, serving meals and light fare on the deck from 7:00 a.m. until 10:00 p.m.

NAGS HEAD NORTH ACCOMMODATIONS

THE CAROLINIAN

Rt. 158 Business, MP 10   441-7171
$$
Map, pg. 70

Bob and Leslynn, brother and sister, took on the job of restoring one of the Banks most enduring landmarks. The old hotel got a deserved facelift and its Southern charm is showing again.

The rooms and bathrooms have been scrubbed and repainted. New beds, bedspreads, curtains, and wall-to-wall carpets have been installed. Air conditioning has been added throughout, and a new oceanfront outdoor dining deck is the largest in the area.

Although rooms tend to be small here, the excellent mid-resort location, oceanfront views, and low rates make the Carolinian a good accommodations alternative.

The hotel has a pool and kiddie pool and offers both American and European plans for its guests.

Many, many families over the years called the Carolinian their vacation home. With the vitality and determination of its present owners, we hope that another successful era has begun for their storied oceanfront property.

The hotel also welcomes groups up to 300 people for meetings and banquets. Two houses, one four and the other eight bedrooms, are available for large families.

NAGS HEAD BEACON MOTOR LODGE

Rt. 158 Business, MP 11   441-5501
$$
Map, pg. 70

The Beacon is a large 48-unit property with many accommodation options. The three wings of the motor lodge contain large one room efficiencies, two and three room apartments, and motel-type rooms with various sleeping arrangements. Some rooms have a tile shower, no tub and others may be equipped with a small refrigerator.

The oceanfront rooms open onto a large walled beachfront terrace which is lit at night. There are areas with furniture on the terrace where all guests may take in the breezy view of the ocean. A raised deck at one end of the terrace has a picnic table.

In the center courtyard is the pool and recreation area which is cleverly screened from the highway. Amenities include a landscaped and lighted patio, large raised pool, two children's pools, playground, electronic game room, and guest laundromat.

Rooms here are tastefully decorated. Color TV is provided, as well as room phones. Parking is generally door front.

CABANA EAST

Rt. 158 Business, MP 11   441-7106
$$$
                      Map, pg. 70

The stylish facade and lobby decor of Cabana East compliment the Galleon Esplanade shopping complex across the street. Both were developed by George Crocker.

The two-story motel forms an "L" with one wing facing the highway. The pool, patio, barbeque picnic area, and sand volleyball court are concealed behind the building. Eighteen of the 38 units are on the pool with either small porches or balconies. Although there are technically no ocean views from the rooms, the beach is just over the dune line and the surf can be heard through an open window.

Refurbishing of rooms was continued in 1982 to maintain room standards. Home Box Office movies, room phones and small refrigerators are included in each unit. Guest rooms have two double beds and can be connected to efficiencies. There are both regular and large efficiencies, plus a deluxe Cabana Room.

OCEAN VERANDA

Rt. 158 Business, MP 11   441-5858
$$
                      Map, pg. 70

This accommodation was formerly called the Killdee Motel but the new owners made such extensive improvements, that it deserves to be considered a new property.

The large two-story rectangular building sets perpendicular

to the ocean with wide galleries running the full length of both sides. Outdoor furniture is placed on the galleries for guest convenience.

On the highway end of the building there is a very attractive raised pool and deck. Two poolside gazebos can be retreats from the sun or evening conversation nooks.

Rooms here are large and are very fresh as a result of the recent redecorating.

Efficiencies can connect with regular motel rooms to serve large families. All rooms have double beds and color TV. Free morning coffee is served in the motel office.

The location is in the heart of the resort area and has direct access to the beach. There are picnic tables near the beach, and an observation deck on the dunes for guest use.

OLDE LONDON INN

Rt. 158 Business, MP 12   441-7115
$
Map, pg. 70

Olde London Inn is a 70-unit property that has accommodations on the oceanfront, and in a two-story annex on the west side of the highway. It is owned by the John Yancey Corporation, and is their economy class option on the beach.

Although none of the single level rooms have an actual ocean view, the property is oceanfront. A large dune top sun and observation deck serves guests, and they have direct access to the private beach.

Room decor here is functional and seemingly identical room to room. There are both oceanside and westside efficiency units. Parking for the most part is at the door. All units have small refrigerators, and TV.

The Inn is just a short walk from the Nags Head Fishing Pier. Open May through September.

FIRST COLONY INN

Rt. 158 Business, MP 12   441-3666
$$
Map, pg. 70

Built in 1932, the three-story cedar shake, dormered roof giant of an oceanfront inn captures the style of an era prior to the advent of motels. Wide all-wood verandas wrap around the building on two levels. Connecting exterior corridors (or breezeways) give each room excellent ventilation from the

A "cat surfer" catches a wave for a thrilling ride to the beach.

natural cool of the ocean breezes.

Accommodations here are not plush, but comfortable. There is no air conditioning, TV or phones. Guests are encouraged by the environment to meet and talk. Outside, there is a wide beach level veranda where you might see ladies with hard-backed novels taking morning coffee in their housecoats. The Inn also has a front yard swimming pool.

There are rooms and efficiencies here for two, and two and three-room apartments for four. Two penthouse apartments with dormer windows also have private topside decks.

Jockey's Ridge and its hang glider adventurists are opposite the Inn across the Bypass.

The First Colony Inn offers a unique experience that is fast vanishing from the seaside resort scene. It is a look into the setting of an F. Scott Fitzgerald novel.

The Back Porch Restaurant, located within the Inn, offers excellent food and a cozy atmosphere. It's popular with locals as well as with hotel guests.

The 29 unit property is under new ownership and management.

SEA SPRAY

Rt. 158 Business, MP 12　　　　　　　　　　　　　　441-7270
$$

Map, pg. 70

Al and Kathy Otte are experienced motel managers who generate a friendly atmosphere at this 24-unit oceanfront property. The motel was greatly upgraded during the '82-'83 seasons, and its apartment-sized units and efficiencies, which accommodate two to four persons, are about as close to the ocean as you can get.

Each unit has Cable TV, HBO and air-conditioning. The cross ventilation from the oceanside through to the courtyard, however, may convince you to open the storm doors at either end of the unit and let the sea breezes and sounds of the surf into your room. Rooms offer the convenience of a small refrigerator, while apartments and efficiencies are equipped for light housekeeping.

The Sea Spray is a five-minute walk to the Nags Head Fishing Pier, and Jockey Ridge State Park is just West across the Bypass Highway.

This is an older property with no pool, but its comfortable accommodations, direct-ocean access, and proximity to restaurants and attractions make it a good choice for beach lovers.

 **NAGS HEAD SOUTH**

ACCOMMODATIONS

PEBBLE BEACH

Rt. 158 Business, MP 16 441-5111
$$$

Map, pg. 80

Pebble Beach is an attractive, active combination of motel, cottage, and apartment accommodations. There are 29 motel efficiency units, six two-room efficiency apartments, and four two bedroom apartments plus one, two, and three bedroom cottages at the oceanside location. Across the highway there are an additional four efficiencies and eight rooms.

Motel efficiency units are in a modern three-story building with balconies overlooking the large raised pool, and children's playground. The oceanfront apartments are two-story. All of the units are attractively furnished, and have modern conveniences including TV. Oceanfront rooms also offer free HBO.

Adjacent to the beach are picnic tables and a concrete half basketball court that sees a lot of pick-up action. It is so close to the ocean that it must be swept several times a day, and new basketballs soon become slick from the blowing sand. Pebble Beach owners must be basketball fans!

SILVER SANDS MOTEL

Rt. 158 Business, MP 14 441-7354
$

Map, pg. 80

The Silver Sands is one of the few motels not located on the oceanside of the beach road. It is a bit isolated in an area of Nags Head that has not been claimed for development. The path to the relatively pristine beach is across the highway via a public access. A few neighborhood cottages are the only competition for blanket space.

There are two separate sections to the motel. The older section is a strip of 16 red brick units which face a large raised swimming pool perpendicular to the ocean. The rooms are comfortable, well-kept, and have all the modern conveniences, including TV.

The adjacent two story, brown shingle and white stucco building is new and has ten units. The top level units have private balconies facing the ocean.

The Silver Sands has both rooms and efficiency units. All rooms have refrigerators. Jule Burrus owns and manages this attractive, quiet property.

THE ISLANDER MOTEL

Rt. 158 Business, MP 16   441-6229
$$

Map, pg. 80

Ed Thompson has made the Islander perhaps the most attractive and unusual small property on the resort strip. Although the buildings date from 1973, the extensive landscaping, attentive maintenance, and room redecorating program make this motel appear always new.

The two 3-story square buildings were constructed so as to meet at the apex of a respective corner. The unusual configuration gives every room a view and creates a number of semi-private patios which have been enhanced by landscaping, and furniture. The rooms on the second and third levels have glass enclosed balconies with large sliding windows.

Rooms here are large with space for a seating area. The coordinated decors and room accessories show good taste. A refrigerater is provided in all rooms. Kitchenettes are available in first floor accommodations. All units have two double beds.

A ramp at the rear of the property leads over the dunes to the ocean beach. The location is convenient to all the restaurants and attractions of South Nags Head.

THE SEA OATEL

Rt. 158 Business, MP 16   441-7191
$$$

Map, pg. 80

This Quality Inn has a prime location near good restaurants, recreational activities, and it is also convenient to the historical area. Its 111 units are divided between a three-story low-rise (with elevator), a two-story similar pink brick structure, a few drive-up one-story rooms adjacent to the pool and patio, and an across-the-street annex. The rooms in the main buildings (62 in all) have balconies on the oceanfront.

The Sea Oatel has 400 feet of ocean frontage, and there is a sheltered cabana on the beach which can be romantic for sun rises, or just a place to sit out of the sun with a cool drink to enjoy the view. This is a well-kept property with full hotel services, including a 24-hour desk. The lobby and its rooms are kept fresh and appealing with consistent painting and refurnishing. The room decors conform to the high Quality Inn standards and all have phones and HBO.

Snack and ice facilities are plentiful, and there is even a separate lounge area for card players. The "Oatel's" restaurant, the Dareolina Cove, can cater meetings and banquets.

SEA FOAM MOTEL

Rt. 158 Business, MP 16½   441-3831
$$

Map, pg. 80

Jackie O'Neal is very proud that her 30 motel-type guest rooms, 18 efficiencies, and two cottages attract so many repeat visitors each season.

The well-kept red brick, white railing and aqua blue trimmed Sea Foam has single and bi-level units with oceanfront and poolside views. Parking is around the center courtyard where a raised pool, sundeck, children's playground, and shuffleboard are available for recreation. There is a gazebo on the beach where guests can meet to enjoy the sea breezes.

Rooms here are tastefully furnished with all the modern conveniences except telephones. Oceanfront rooms have picture windows, and all units have balconies or porches equipped with outdoor furniture.

The location is within walking distance of several good restaurants, and the Nags Head Fishing Pier.

OWENS' MOTEL

Rt. 158 Busness, MP 16½   441-6361
$$

Map, pg. 80

The Owens' family has been in the same location for over 35 seasons with its restaurant and motel property. A new three-story oceanfront addition was added to the strip of single level oceanside motel units in 1981. An oceanfront pavillion and rocking chairs on an open platform are available for guest enjoyment.

All the oceanfront accommodations are efficiencies with private eight-foot deep balconies. Each room has two double beds, tile bath and shower, and electric kitchen. The oceanside rooms are also fresh and comfortable.

An additional ten motel units are located on the westside of the beach highway. The motel swimming pool is also in this area, next door to the well-known restaurant. The oceanfront motel is on a narrow strip of land in a prime location near the Nags Head Pier. The property totals 25 units including the westside accommodations.

SURF SIDE MOTEL

Rt. 158 Business, MP 16   441-2105
$$$

Map, pg. 80

The Surf Side Motel is a very attractive, new motel located right on the oceanfront. Its 60 rooms all feature private balconies with views of the ocean (some even have sound views too), phones, color TV, and air conditioning. There are special honeymoon suites, complete with champagne, as well as loft suites and meeting rooms. Each morning, complimentary coffee is served in the lobby and a social hour is held every night for guests.

The motel sports a large pool on the south side, providing both sound and ocean views. The beach is guarded. There are also several cottages for rent through the motel; ask at the desk or phone to make reservations. Surf Side is open year round.

THE BEST WESTERN ARMADA

Rt. 158 Business, MP 17   441-6315
$$$

Map, pg. 80

The Armada, at six stories, is a high-rise by comparison to other buildings on the Banks. It is visibly near Whalebone Junction, and convenient to the major restaurants and attractions of Nags Head. It is only 90 miles from Norfolk, and 197 miles from Raleigh.

The Armada was built as a resort property to attract families and meeting groups of up to 450 persons. It therefore has such

Surf Side Motel

Oceanfront

- Efficiencies and Cottages
- Pool
- Private Balconies

Charter Boat Available
"The Surf Side"
at Oregon Inlet Fishing Center

On the ocean at Milepost 16

P.O. Box 400
Nags Head, NC 27959
(919) 441-2105

amenities as a night club, childrens playground, game rooms, pool,2 restaurants, banquet facilities, and even a tennis court. The major attraction, of course, is the 200 ft. of beach frontage which has a lifeguard in season.

Rooms here are modern, and many of the 106 units have balconies which open to ocean views. One and two bedroom suites are available with a built-in kitchenette. All have phones. For group meetings, a convention center facility exceeding 5,000 sq. ft. can be arranged to complement its desired use.

SANDPIPER COURT

Rt. 158 Business, MP 19   441-6130
$

Map, pg. 80

After years of vacationing with their two sons on the Outer Banks, Katie and Lee Jones found a way to stay at the beach all summer: they bought a cottage court.

Now during June, July, and August, and weekends in April-May and Sept.-Oct., the Jones family hosts guests in their eleven cottages. There are one, two, and three bedroom accommodations. Each has a full bath and kitchen. All of the cottages have screened porches which extend the living area in good weather.

The cottages are clean and comfortably furnished for housekeeping with modern conveniences and fully equipped kitchens. Cable TV hook-ups are available for those who wish to bring their own TV.

The cottages are on the ocean and form a private street to the sand and surf. Fellow guests become happy neighbors as they meet on the way to the beach, and share the week's experiences. Renting at the Sandpiper Court is a very pleasant way for a family to enjoy the beach at a low relative cost. Many people prefer this style of vacationing over hotels and motels because of the relative privacy and convenience of cottage life.

Pre-season reservations can be made by calling (804) 489-3783 in Norfolk.

# ROANOKE ISLAND
ACCOMMODATIONS

ELIZABETHAN INN

Manteo 473-2101
$$-$$$

Map, pg. 289

The Manteo Motel Corporation has taken on a whole new look for the 1986 season with their brand new addition of a Nautics Hall fitness center and surrounding rooms. With the center, they join the leagues of a big city hotel in terms of amenities, and our guess is that lots of vacationers will opt to stay here, in this Manteo establishment, rather than on the beach because of the sports facilities offered. Four types of rooms are available here, all convenient to the Manteo waterfront, Christmas Shop, Lost Colony, and other local attractions.

The Highway Court is adjacent to the Inn's restaurant and provides a single level strip of units reserved primarily for business trade and stop-over visitors.

Behind the restaurant area, in a pine woods reached by an adjacent street, is the Elizabethan Manor. The Manor consists of 10 units designed to resemble a 16th century Tudor inn. The shaded pine wood setting and the off highway privacy has a romantic feel.

Nearby, but separate, is the two-story Center Court, a 20-unit modern, spacious motel with a broad veranda and balcony on all sides. A raised swimming pool and a shaded picnic area with tables are situated close to Center Court but easily accessable to all guests. A pathway leads to the Inn's restaurant.

The new Nautics Hall addition offers deluxe accommodations in rooms that surround the sports facility. Well constructed walls ensure that these rooms are well insulated from the happy noises that come from the activity in the 100 foot, heated pool, Nautilus workout room, racquetball court, whirlpool, aerobics room, and sauna. Guests are welcomed in all facilities, including the suntanning room (there is an extra charge for racquetball and tanning).

All rooms have phones, color TV with free HBO, and all but the Highway Court offer in-room refrigerators.

DARE HAVEN MOTEL

Manteo 473-2322
$

Map, pg. 289

The three wings of this single level red brick motel form a courtyard where you can park at your unit's door. A raised porch runs along the entire length of the buildings, and comfortable white wooden chairs are provided for guest convenience.

There are 26 well-kept units managed by Lib and George Pearce. Rooms are of average size, and designed to cater to families on a budget. The hospitality must be warm because Dare Haven has a lot of repeat guests.

The motel is open seasonally March to December. No pool. The property is across the highway from the Elizabethan Inn Restaurant, and convenient to all Roanoke Island attractions.

SCARBOROUGH HOUSE INN

Manteo 473-3979
$$

Map, pg. 289

Sally Scarborough had a dream for at least 15 years. Born in downtown Manteo, she carried the image of a country inn that she encountered in her childhood. It was not until her husband, Phil, a Wanchese native and Coast Guard officer, retired that she was able to hope that her dream might become a reality.

Today Scarborough House Inn is a reality on Hwy 64 across from the Christmas Shop, and architectually it is a period piece from a bygone era. Sally Scarborough, an accomplished furniture refinisher, has filled each of the guest rooms with collectables and antiques. Each item has a special story generally associated with Outer Banks history. Bathroom doors, for example, were saved from a decaying island church. Most of the bed frames are antiques. One once framed the birth bed of her mother. Some of the chests, chairs and dressing tables date from the mid 1800s and are in beautiful condition. Even the TV tables are old Singer Sewing Machine cabinets.

The rooms here are large and have all the modern conveniences including in-room refrigerators and a coffee pot. Sally will even place fruit and breakfast fare in the frig on request. Some rooms open to a porch where Carolina rockers have been placed for outdoor relaxing.

- 7 rooms with antique furnishings
- Private bath
- Color TV, refrigerator and telephone
- Moderately priced

FOR RESERVATIONS
WRITE OR CALL:
P.O. Box 1310
Highway 64-264
Manteo, NC 27954
(919) 473-3979

Hwy 64/264 - in Manteo
Clean, comfortable and reasonable rates
air conditioned - cable TV - phone (919) 473-2322

Scarborough House Inn is a charming accommodation that the discriminating traveler will appreciate. Room rates here are very low for all the care and attention provided. Opened for the 1984 season, this two story reproduction of a turn of the century inn is well placed for shopping, historical attractions, and restaurants.

DUKE OF DARE MOTOR LODGE

Manteo 473-2175
$

Map, pg. 289

The Duke of Dare is located off the main highway and is the closest motel to the Manteo harborfront and the Christmas Shop. The S & R Supermarket, Island Pharmacy, and Speed Wash (coin laundry) are located on the other side of a small pine woods.

The brick, bi-level, L-shaped motor lodge is trimmed in sky blue and yellow, and has all the standard modern motel features. There is a well-maintained raised swimming pool adjacent to the highway, and a children's swing set in a wooded area suitable for picnicking.

The motor lodge is open all year.

Hatteras Island Resort
AT RODANTHE

Located at Rodanthe, **Hatteras Island Resort** is just a short drive south of Oregon Inlet away from the crowds.

Within the resort complex you'll find a wide variety of comfortable, affordable accommodations for your family as well as first class amenities. Our motel rooms, efficiencies and cottages (2, 3 and 4 bedrooms) are all equipped with new color TV's, but most likely you'll be swimming in the surf or oceanside pools, fishing from our 1100' pier or visiting one of the many historic attractions in the area.

Cross Currents Restaurant is located on the oceanfront within Hatteras Island Resort. Come for a hardy breakfast overlooking the widest stretch of beach on the Outer Banks and for lunch at the longest pier on the East Coast. Our dinner menu includes the area's best steamed and broiled seafood as well as the biggest "Maryland Style" crab cakes on the beach! Or for a change of pace try one of our chicken, beef or pasta dishes. Regardless of the menu selection our prompt, attentive service and breathtaking view of the oceanfront panorama ensure a memorable dining experience.

To Reserve Accommodations:
LOCAL (919) 987-2345
IN STATE (800) 682-2289
OUT OF STATE (800) 331-6541
(EAST OF MISSISSIPPI)

Cross Currents Restaurant:
(919) 987-2721

 *HATTERAS ISLAND*
ACCOMMODATIONS

HATTERAS ISLAND MOTEL

Rodanthe 987-2345
$$

Map, pg. 289

    This 25-acre vacation complex on the oceanfront includes 32 motel-type rooms and efficiencies in a large double decked oceanside building (plus a few single level oceanfront units), and 35 two, three, and four bedroom cottages arranged in two clusters on the property. None of the units contain TV or telephones, but are comfortably furnished.
    The big attraction here is the Hatteras Island Fishing Pier at the head of the resort property. Guests have free sightseeing admission to the pier. There is also a large swimming pool, patio, recreation pavillion, and restaurant in the complex.

OCEAN AIRE MOTEL

Rodanthe 987-2244
$$

Map, pg. 289

    Lovie and Valton Midgett host guests at this small, 13-unit soundside property. The single level drive up motel has a prime location for fishermen. The Hatteras Island Fishing Pier is a few hundred yards opposite the motel on the oceanside. For fishing in the sound, the property has its own boat ramp and docking facilities in a private cove. A children's playground, picnic tables, a soundfront swimming area, and boats for rent make this a very desirable accommodation.
    Ocean Aire is open all year and attracts duck hunters, too, who stake out the nearby blinds. All rooms have cable TV, heat/AC

and are attractively furnished and well-maintained. The brick construction and white railed porches give this property an inviting appearance.

AVON MOTEL

Avon 995-5774
$

Map, pg. 344

This is a convenient oceanfront location only one-quarter mile from the Pamlico Sound, Avon Fishing Pier, and the only movie theatre The Cape Hatteras Lighthouse is about five miles away.

Earl and Daisy Younce own and manage this property. They cater to fishermen and families on a budget, so don't expect Holiday Inn frills. The rooms are clean, and comfortable, however.

There is a lot of activity around this motel and its guests appear to be having a good time. The beach is at the end of the long unpaved parking area that separates the two main motel buildings.

Compliments of

Tower Circle Motel

JACK STEWART GRAY
MARY LOUISE GRAY

P. O. BOX 88
BUXTON, N. C.
27920

PHONE 995-5353

TOWER CIRCLE MOTEL

Buxton 995-5353
$-$$

Map, pg. 342

This is a real fisherman's hide-a-way near the Cape Hatteras Light. Turn off Highway 12 onto Old Lighthouse Road and look for all the guests sitting on the porch swapping fish stories. A surf caster's paradise is just a short walk over the dune line.

There are 30 units here, 17 of which are efficiency apartments. This is an older property with functional rooms that predate the chain motel obsession for mock-plush. The juniper panelling, and the modest furnishings, however, are welcomed after a day on the beach. Restaurants and attractions are nearby.

GENERAL MITCHELL MOTEL

Hatteras 986-2444
$$

Map, pg. 349

The General Mitchell is typical of Hatteras accommodations which place function over style. The motel does not pretend to be a resort, it is rather a lodging for those who want to enjoy the access to exceptional fishing, hunting, and the beaches. However, it does offer a pool and heated spa - a rare and appreciated addition!

The two two-story motel wings run perpendicular to the beach. If it were not for the barrier dunes, you could see the ocean between them.

Fishermen seem to get priority here. They are provided with a lighted cleaning shed with running water, and freezer storage where they can store their catches.

Rooms and efficiencies to accommodate two to four persons are available. They are clean and well-kept, with air conditioning and cable TV.

The General Mitchell was named for "Billy" Mitchell, the young US Air Service colonel who directed the sinking of two retired battle ships off Hatteras to prove the potential of air power.

The motel is open all year. Call ahead and the management will give you a fishing report.

CAPE HATTERAS MOTEL

Buxton 995-5611
$$ Map, pg. 342

Carol and Dave Dawson have "literally renovated everything" on their popular, 30-year old oceanfront property. The 34 units provide many accommodation options on both sides of the highway.

All six of the two-story, two-bedroom duplex cottages have been rebuilt and completely redecorated. Modern efficiency units overlooking a lighted tennis court and the Pamlico Sound are also open. Several of these new units have king-sized beds. Yet another improvement was a new swimming pool, heated Jacuzzi, kiddie pool set in a patio area, and row boats.

The Cape Hatteras Motel provides many guest conveniences like beach umbrella and sun float rentals, lighted fish-cleaning stations on both ocean and sound sides, racquets and balls for the tennis court, and color cable TV in each unit.

The motel is open April through December. Prime weeks here are reserved early. There are also "winter fishing" rates for periods in April and November/December. Ask Dave Dawson for the latest fishing news.

CAPE SANDBOX

Buxton 995-5785
$$ Map, pg. 342

The Cape Sandbox is one of the newest motels on Hatteras Island. Its red brick construction, raised porches, and large, modern rooms make it very desirable.

The site is on Old Lighthouse Road within a quarter mile of the Lighthouse. The beach and excellent fishing grounds are just over the dunes. It is also convenient to restaurants and shops.

Facilities here include a lighted fish cleaning station and deep freezer storage, and hot/cold outdoor showers. Gae Zindel is the hostess at this well-kept property which is open from mid-March through mid-December. In addition to rooms and efficiencies, the Cape Sandbox rents a large two-bedroom apartment.

The sinage on the property can easily be missed, so follow directions.

OUTER BANKS MOTEL

Buxton   995-5601
               Map, pg. 342
$$

    Carol Dillon maintains a quality motel property that has ninety percent of her guests coming back year after year.
    Rooms here are pine paneled, carpeted, and show extra care in decor. Baths are tiled. There are efficiency units, and two and three-bedroom cottages and beachfront houses. The cottages and houses are restricted to weekly rentals in-season. All the units show high standards with air conditioning and satellite color TV.
    A raised pool with hot tub was added in 1984. A coin operated laundry is also available for guest use. There are a lot of extras here.
    This location on the beach is a very productive area for surf casting. A fish cleaning station is provided as well as a guest freezer for storage. Three rowboats on a southside creek across the highway are also available to guests for crabbing and fishing.
    The beach is especially wide in this area of Buxton, and the Outer Banks Motel is a very desirable location from which to enjoy it.

LIGHTHOUSE VIEW

Buxton   995-5680
               Map, pg. 342
$$

    The Hooper family operates this growing motel and cottage property. In recent years, two bedroom, two bath round shaped beachfront cottages have been added to the motel's rooms and one and two bedroom efficiencies.
    The 25-year Hooper hospitality brings many guests back each season for the excellent beach and surf fishing. Recently, one multi-unit building here was completely remodeled and redecorated. Most units have screened porches. No pool.
    The Lighthouse View is a good accommodation for fisherfolk and families on a budget.

FALCON

Buxton 995-5968
Map, pg. 342
$$

The Falcon Motel has 35 sand colored brick, single level units which stretch from the highway to a small creek on the sound. The wide paved drive provides parking at your door. Efficiency rooms and a two bedroom apartment rent weekly during the season.

A pool on the highway and the motel office are located opposite the string of units. Rooms are wood paneled and reflect a modern, functional, yet comfortable, approach to decor. Cable/satellite TV and a boat ramp are included amenities.

Fishing, restaurants, and attractions are convenient to this location near the Hatteras Light. The Falcon is Ike and Darrel owner-operated.

THE KONI KAI

Avon 995-4444
Map, pg. 344
$$$ (800) 845-6070

Koni Kai, also known as the Hatteras Beach Hotel and Racquet Club is the newest and most luxurious accommodation from Whalebone Junction south to Ocracoke. The five story oceanfront wing has 56 rooms and suites each with telephone, wet bar, refrigerator, fine furniture and lamps, beamed ceiling, and a large private balcony overlooking the ocean. From the top levels, you can also see the sound from the westside, Colonial lamp-lined exterior passageway. The hotel has perhaps the only elevators on the island.

The large attached building away from the beach houses a health spa and Nautilus equipment, an art gallery, and a full-service restaurant, lounge and raw bar. The connecting glass-enclosed structure covers an olympic-sized pool and indoor jacuzzi for year round use. The tennis courts are located in the sand flats adjacent to the hotel parking area.

Opened while still under construction during the 1984 season, the Hatteras Beach has been built to be a landmark on the Outer Banks. Perhaps it is the harbinger of highrise commercial development that will forever alter the character of these barrier islands. It certainly offers an accommodation alternative for those who are devoted to their big-city creature comforts.

DURANT STATION

Hatteras   986-2244
$$-$$$
Map, pg. 349

The Durant Station is on the site of the old Durant Coast Guard Station. In fact, the main building that was part of this Life Saving Station since 1878 is owned by the motel and can be rented to a large family group. Most of the rental units at the Durant, however, are in a long white frame two-story building with porches on both levels that is perpendicular to the ocean and its parallel highway. The ocean beach is just over the dunes at the end of the property.

Accommodations here appeal to fishermen who appreciate the Durant's position between Cape Hatteras and Hatteras Inlet, and families. Most of the units are family-style with kitchen facilities, and plenty of extra beds.

Bill Althans has made many recent improvements to the Durant. New decking, paneling, carpeting, kitchens and baths are part of the renovation. There's also a pool.

Six newly-remodeled three-bedroom condominiums located in a separate building on the property are an addition to the motel's rental offerings.

SEA GULL MOTEL

Hatteras   986-2550
$$
Map, pg. 349

This is an attractive red brick, modern property located oceanside near the National Park area. The 45 units are divided between single level and two-story buildings which form a courtyard around the fresh water swimming pool.

The rooms are pine paneled, attractively furnished, and have all the modern motel amenities. There are also efficiencies with fully equipped electric kitchens.

This is a well-kept motel. The ocean beach is just over the dunes in the backyard. The location is convenient to restaurants, the fishing pier, and the Billy Mitchell airport.

HATTERAS HARBOR MOTEL

Hattera Village   986-2565
$$
Map, pg. 349

Mark and Nadine Caldwell are the owners of this property

very near the entrance of the Hatteras sport fishing harbor and marina. The location is especially convenient for the off-shore fishing enthusiast.

Two single-level red brick buildings flank a two-story central structure. The resulting courtyard has a swimming pool. Painting, and other renovative activities were underway when the motel was last inspected.

There are four two-bedroom apartments in the central building, and both large and small efficiencies, plus non-cooking equipped rooms for daily or weekly rental. All of the 20 units have TV, heat/AC.

HATTERAS MARLIN MOTEL

Hatteras Village 986-2141
$$
Map, pg. 349

The Midgett family, a name well-known in Hatteras Life Saving Station lore, operates this two-story red brick motel in the center of activity at Hatteras Village. Five guest cottages are also rented through the motel.

The two-story building has white trim and balconies furnished with outdoor furniture. The location is within sight of the harbor fishing fleet, and village restaurants and shops. A driveway leads to a raised swimming pool and sun deck shielded from the highway, and additional motel units. Facilities are modern, and both one and two bedroom efficiencies may be rented. Rooms have cable TV and air conditioning and heat. Guests are allowed golf privilages.

BURRUS MOTOR COURT

Hatteras Village 986-2363
$$
Map, pg. 349

The village docks and marina are across the street from this comfortable red brick motel. The property appeals to sportsmen who frequent Hatteras for the fishing, and also to budget conscious families. Accommodations are neat, spacious, and have heat/AC, TV, and modern decor.

The three buildings form a "U" shape with the pool located behind the central structure, out of sight of the highway. There is a two bedroom duplex, rooms with two beds, and both large and small efficiencies in the accommodations mix totaling 34 units.

OCRACOKE ACCOMMODATIONS

BERKLEY CENTER

Ocracoke 928-5911
$$ Map, pg. 373

The Berkley Center is a beautifully landscaped three-acre estate on the Ocracoke Harbor directly adjacent to the Park Service and State ferry dock areas. The buildings date from the late 1950's, but the architecture and the cedar siding make them seem from an earlier period. The size of the Manor House with its broad rectangular tower has led passers-by to mistake it for a Lifesaving Station.

The master plan for the Berkley Center is to convert its three buildings and grounds into a small conference center and private corporate club. The Ranch House is being converted to guest lodging. The Meeting House will contain small meeting and seminar rooms equipped with modern audio-visual aids, reproduction machines, and a guest library.

The Manor House contains guest rooms, the dining room, a first floor bar and lounge, and a tower card room and bar with exceptional views of the island and harbor.

Amenities include fishing boats and equipment, vehicles for marsh and beach exploration, and hunting and fishing guides. A swimming pool and small marina are also in the plan.

Every morning, as part of your room charge, a wonderful breakfast is served for all guests in the Manor House, usually consisting of fresh breads, real butter and preserves, and hot coffee. It's a good chance for guests to mingle.

The property is operated by Ruth and Wesley W. Egan, Sr. Each room is individually furnished and decorated. Native Cypress, Juniper, and Fir paneling predominate.

The Berkley Center is certainly a relaxed and distinctive setting for an accommodation.

BLUFF SHOAL MOTEL

Ocracoke 928-4301
$$
Map, pg. 373

The seven units of this red brick property face the tree shaded main street on Silver Lake. The post office, community store,

Looking much as it did 150 years ago, the Ocracoke Lighthouse looms over the fishing village of Ocracoke.

and many of the village's shops are all within a short walk - several right next door. The Pelican Restaurant is right across the street. The gnarled trees out front must be very old.

The Bluff Shoal has a raised porch with comfortable wooden furniture for watching the Island traffic go by. Mike and Kay Riddick take pride in their property, and it shows in the care and the modern decor of the rooms. All the conveniences, including TV, are here. Open all year. No pool.

SILVER LAKE MOTEL

Ocracoke Village   928-5721
              Map, pg. 373
$-$$

The Wrobleski family built this two-story, 20-room motel on the Ocracoke Harbor in 1983. They moved a house, cleared the site, constructed the wooden double decked structure, paneled the rooms in California redwoods, and even built the upholstered redwood furniture and lamp tables.

Rooms here have an excellent view of Silver Lake. A second floor guest lounge with an open-air deck has an unobstructed view of the entire harbor.

The careful paneling, wallpapered bathrooms, louvered shutters and cafe curtains at the windows, pine flooring and oval braid rugs give the guest rooms appeal.

We appreciate the saving of the ancient scrub oak trees at the motel's entrance and the family hospitality extended by the Wrobleski's, especially the Mama. Air conditioning and quality color TV are standard in this new property.

ISLAND INN

Ocracoke   928-4351
$$
              Map, pg. 373

Built as an Odd Fellows Lodge in 1901, the Island Inn has briefly served as a school, a private residence, and a Naval officers quarter. It has been restored by Foy Shaw and Larry Williams to the point of being recognized in *Country Inns of the Old South*, and *Country Inns, Lodges, and Historic Hotels of the South*.

The Inn provides a variety of accommodations to suit many tastes. There are one-of-a-kind rooms in the old Inn itself, or

Hosts
FOY SHAW AND LARRY WILLIAMS
INVITE YOU TO

THE ISLAND INN AND DINING ROOM

Where we feature island seafood
and island cooking

An Inn with a flavor of yesterday
A dining room where waitresses care
A gallery of paintings,
watercolors and prints by JoKo

Island's Only Heated Swimming Pool

Ocracoke
North Carolina, 27960
(919) 928-4351

very modern motel rooms in the Stanley Wahab Wing, a 19 unit double decked structure with excellent views of the harbor. Two of the rooms were designed especially for honeymooners and have king sized beds and bay windows affording romantic sunset views.

In the main building, which also houses the Inn's popular dining room, the Crow's Nest demi-suites on the third floor may be some of the most sought after rooms on the Island. The large sitting area, the cypress cathedral ceiling, and the tasteful decor, plus the privacy are a couples delight.

The rockers on the wide porches, the Inn's card room which often produces spontaneous entertainment after dinner, and the careful detail of its restoration provide guests here a unique, relaxing experience. The Inn also rents a two bedroom cottage on the grounds. There's also the island's only heated pool in front of the Stanley Wahab Wing.

PONY ISLAND MOTEL

Ocracoke 928-4411
$$

Map, pg. 373

David and Jen Esham host guests at this long established Island accommodation. At 40 units (31 rooms and 9 efficiencies) it is still the largest motel on the Island.

The property has two modern design buildings on the highway just a short walk to Ocracoke Village. The rooms are spacious and have all the modern amenities.

There is a large lawn with picnic tables for family gatherings and recreation. The motel has a few bicycles for rent, too.

Reservations are necessary, and a three day minimum stay is requested from May through October. A ten percent discount is given for weekly rentals.

OSCAR'S HOUSE

Ocracoke 928-1311
$

Map, pg. 373

This bed and breakfast guest house, run by Ann Ehringhaus and Mike Hays, offers a fun alternative to motel lodgings. Built in 1940 by the Ocracoke lighthouse keeper, Oscar's House was actually first occupied by the World War II Naval Commander for the Ocracoke Naval Base. Oscar, for whom the house is named, lived here and worked for years on Ocracoke as a fisherman and hunting guide. Many stories have survived Oscar; he loved a good time. You'll have a good time at Oscar's House, too, since you'll be staying with some colorful locals.

They offer four air-conditioned bedrooms in this cozy house located one block from Silver Lake Harbor on N.C. Highway 12. Oscar's House is open in the warm weather months. You should call for reservations.

BOYETTE HOUSE

Ocracoke 928-4261
$$

Map, pg. 373

This attractive motel, opened in 1982, is named for a pioneer in Ocracoke hospitality who began to host guests as early as 1941.

The 12 unit, two-story natural wood structure has wide upper and lower decks. Rocking chairs are provided to promote the feeling of a small town inn.

The Boyette House provides modern comfortable rooms with two double beds, color TV, and a spacious lobby where guests can borrow from the bookshelves or pick up a continental breakfast at the coffee bar - opened early enough to make sure passengers for the early ferry get their java. There is even room service!

Guests can enjoy a sundeck for relaxing, and are within walking distance of Silver Lake and several restaurants. A seven nights stay earns a 10% discount. Open all year.

HARBORSIDE

Ocracoke 928-3111
$$

Map, pg. 373

This bi-level weathered blue motel sits perpendicular to the Silver Lake Harbor on the main street of Ocracoke Village. It is very convenient to the Swan Quarter and Cedar Island ferry docks.

The 18 pine paneled rooms are modern in decor and spacious. Four efficiencies are available.

The Harborside gift shop is across the narrow main street abd offers a wide assortment of gifts. The motel has a wide veranda with guest chairs where relaxing and watching the island happenings can be enjoyable.

SAND DOLLAR MOTEL

Ocracoke 928-5571
$$

Map, pg. 373

The Sand Dollar is a small, friendly motel located a little off the beaten trail near the Back Porch Restaurant. All the rooms are air conditioned and have cable TV. Efficiencies are also available along with several cottages.

Celia and Wayne Isbrecht, the owners, are sports enthusiasts too. They will gladly fill you in on the best fishing and hunting spots in the area as well as provide a 4-wheel drive service for surf fishermen. Their charter boat, the Sand Dollar, is available for trips.

SHIPS TIMBERS

Ocracoke 928-6141
$

Map, pg. 373

The Ships Timbers is a bed and breakfast that caters its hospitality to sailboard vacationers. Located in a 75 year old house built with lumber from the "Ida Lawrence," a ship that washed ashore on Ocracoke Beach in 1902, the b&b offers visitors who are especially hooked on windsurfing the chance to spend their vacation visiting with other enthusiasts and enjoying easy access to the water and B.W.'s Surf Shop, a sailboarder's outfitters shop. The residents of the house also give lessons to those who need them and plan special events and cookouts for their guests.

Rooms with single beds and double beds are available as are baby beds, roll aways and sleep sofas. Rooms have air conditioning, an outdoor grill is provided, and guests have limited kitchen privileges.

CREWS INN

Ocracoke 928-7011
$

Map, pg. 373

For vacationers who want to forego the hotel scene and settle into a nice, quiet place for the week, the Crews Inn just might be for them. Set in a turn of the century house in a residential area of the island, the Inn offers four rooms, two with private baths and two with shared baths. A continental breakfast is served every morning. Though the rooms are not air conditioned, they do have ceiling and window fans, and with the usual island breezes, the rooms are almost always comfortable even in the middle of the summer. Outside, a porch can be found on three sides of the house, providing rocking chairs and swings for lazy afternoons. The Back Porch Restaurant and shops are all within easy strolling distance.

One very colorful aspect of the house is the innkeeper, David Murrill, who can keep visitors fascinated for hours with his stories. He also is a walking directory of island happenings.

BLACKBEARD'S LODGE

Ocracoke 928-3421

Map, pg. 373

$-$$

Blackbeard's was actually built as a lodge and looks the part even after a new wing of efficiencies was added in 1979. Off the main road, back in a shaded woods, the weathered three story wooden structure is a maze of stairways, decks, and railings. It has been a fishermen's hide-a-way and family vacation spot for several generations.

The accommodations are not plush or modern by motel standards, but they are clean and comfortable like you might remember from a visit to your grandparents. The lobby is a period piece with a front desk made from the prow of a boat. A large ornate staircase leads to the upper level, and once a large dining room near the foot of the stairs fed the lodge's guests.

Ownership of the 35-unit Lodge changed hands in 1983, bringing an upgrading of the which includes color TV. Guests will also welcome the fact that the Back Porch Restaurant is located across from the Lodge.

All the rooms in the lodge are air conditioned and have private baths. There are 12 efficiencies, and special fishermen's quarters in the old section which sleep four to eight people in bunk beds at very low rates.

Blackbeard's is open April through October. A second-level sundeck for guests, and in-room instant coffee service are available.

COTTAGES, CONDOMINIUM AND APARTMENT

RENTALS

COTTAGES, CONDOMINIUMS AND APARTMENTS

There are more than 9,000 cottages, condominium units, and apartments in the Outer Banks seasonal rental pool. The variety of these accommodations represent every price range from economy to luxury, from remote beach shack to rich man's oceanfront villa.

Our first advice to the cottage seeker is to obtain a selection of rental booklets from real estate firms specializing in weekly rentals. If you are visiting Dare County, you can acquire many of the rental brochures at the Chamber of Commerce Information Center in Kitty Hawk, or from the Tourist Bureau Welcome Center, both east of the Wright Memorial Bridge on Rt. 158, or you can pick up individual booklets at the respective firms.

If you want to write for rental information directly, the names and addresses of firms offering rental booklets, and a brief description of the publication, are given at the end of this section.

The rental booklets generally include photographs of the individual properties plus a written description of sleeping accommodations, amenities, location, and seasonal rates. Most booklets include area maps. Some even pinpoint the exact locations of their rental properties. Generally there is also a calendar, and a reservation form to aid you in your vacation planning.

We have noted toll-free numbers where available. They are a cost saving way to determine availabilities of the rentals that interest you.

It is important to review carefully the policies and rental agreement rules imposed by the rental agency. With the respective booklet in hand, you can discuss the properties offered page-by-page with the rental agent and have a more meaningful communication.

Not every property represented by the real estate agency makes the booklet publication deadline, so if you are having problems getting exactly what you want on the dates you want, inquire about new listings.

Most rental properties are available for inspection during the off season. Consider a weekend trip to the Outer Banks to see the rental possibilities in person. Many motels which stay open all year offer very attractive winter (or off season) packages. Your inspection trip will not only be a welcome winter retreat, it will also give you peace of mind, and probably save you money on your summer vacation cottage selection.

If you intend to bring your boat, you must make slip and docking arrangements well in advance of your arrival. Trailers also require special parking considerations. Discuss your needs with the rental agent. See our profiles of marinas for alternatives.

The Outer Banks are hot in the prime summer months. Only a few properties are not equipped with air conditioning. An oceanfront cottage with cross ventilation may not need air conditioning, but what is quaint in the fall, can be hot and sticky at 90 degrees. Be sure you know what to expect.

RATES AND RATING PERIODS

Most weekly rentals have a two rate structure: in season or off season. Many properties, however, add two additional rating periods, the so-called shoulder, pre-season and post-season periods.

The prime season is generally considered to extend from the second week in June through the month of August. Since the Outer Banks is a family oriented resort, the prime periods follow the pattern of the childrens' summer vacation from school. Memorial Day and Labor Day weekends also demand prime season rates. The exact dates for when each realtor considers prime in season may vary. Be sure you are clear about this when making your reservation.

Many smart renters who have flexibility on vacation dates look to the shoulder seasons to get the lower rates. A cottage rented in May (or the first week of June) or in September may be $100 or more less expensive than the prime period although the difference in sun power is only one to four weeks.

A three bedroom cottage that rents for about $400 a week in season could drop to $250 off season. If the same property rated the shoulder seasons, the weekly rental might be in the $285 to $325 range.

It is difficult to generalize about both rates and rating periods. The rental market on the Outer Banks is highly competititve which means that you will pay basically the same rates for comparable properties. Personal taste not withstanding, the family that shops smartly, and does its homework in plenty of time to make reservations early, will be rewarded.

Our survey of the rental market leads us to suggest the following guidelines regarding rates. The rates quoted are for prime in season weeks, minimum accommodations for four or more. Oceanfront proximity, location to attractions and restaurants, condition of the property, decor, and amenities should be considered in evaluating the relative value of the specific rental.

ECONOMY	$299 and below
MODERATE	$300 to 599
DELUXE	$600-899
LUXURY	$900 and up

It is not uncommon for families and compatible couples to upgrade their cottage accommodations by planning their vacations together. To access relative value, carefully review the number of bedrooms, other sleeping options, and the maximum occupancy of rental properties. You may discover that by utilizing the full potential of a property, the cost-per-person, or per-couple, may enable the party to afford a deluxe or luxury class accommodation. An $900 luxury property that sleeps 10, for example, is cheaper per person than a $750 deluxe property that sleeps six.

LOCATIONS

These are the accepted terms for location categories on the Outer Banks:

Oceanfront - The distance from the ocean may vary, but there are no intervening houses or lots between the described property and the ocean.

Oceanside - Includes all properties on the ocean side of the beach road (US 158 Business in Nags Head, Kill Devil Hills and Kitty Hawk; Duck Road in Duck; Ocean Trail in Ocean Sands & Whalehead Beach; Rt. 12 on Hatteras and Ocracoke). Distance to the beach is usually specified in the cottage description. Access to the beach is by dedicated easements and/or private roads.

Between Highways - Applies to all properties between Rt. 158 Business (the ocean highway) and US Rt. 158 Bypass or NC Rt. 12 in South Nags Head.

Westside — All properties west of US Rt. 158 Bypass. Soundfront properties excluded.

Soundfront — The distance from the water varies, but none have intervening houses or lots between them and the sound.

RESERVATIONS AND DEPOSITS

Reservations begin to pour into rental firms as early as January. By February and March most of the annual clients have renewed their picks for the coming summer season. By April the choices are limited, and by May you will have to spend a lot of time trying to find an availability for your dates and needs.

In making reservations, give a lot of consideration to the bedding arrangements. Who in your family sleeps where? Privacy is the chief consideration. Make a floor plan of the unit and put names on the beds. Is the arrangement going to make you, the kids, and your mother-in-law happy? Talk to your rental agent about your personal needs. Maybe a rental folding bed will solve a potential problem.

Nearly all reservations require a 50% deposit of the total rental amount.

A rental contract (or lease) is sent for your review and signature after the property and rates have been determined. The lease and deposit, if mailed, generally must conform to deadlines established by the rental agent. The balance of rent, security deposits, pet fees, etc. are usually due at check-in time.

CANCELLATIONS

If you desire to transfer or cancel your reservation, you must be prepared to pay up to 20% in service fees. The amount will be taken from your deposit. In the event that the unit cannot be re-rented for the period of the cancelled reservation, the entire deposit may be forfeited.

PAYMENT

It is standard practice among Outer Banks rental agents to require the balance of the rental fee and taxes on arrival. Be prepared to pay when you pick up your key at the rental office.

The policy beach-wide is NO PERSONAL CHECKS. You should have cash, a certified check, or travelers checks for the balance due. Some firms are now requesting their clients not pay in cash due to security and insurance implications. Some accept credit cards.

PETS

Many rental firms do not permit pets in any of their properties. The tenant is subject to eviction with no refund of rent if a pet is found on the premises.

The properties that allow pets require a flea spraying fee ($20 to $30) which is collected at check-in.

CHECK-IN, CHECK-OUT TIMES

The policy in this area is uniform across the beach. Check-in time is 3 p.m. or 4 p.m. The time, however, means that you may arrive at the rental office after that hour to pay your balance and get your key. Since other renters want to hit the beach on their first afternoon, too, you may find a line of families waiting to process in.

Most agents are very firm about their check-in policy, and do not even begin to process check-ins until the appointed hour. Forget about getting your key early. Be patient, and let the family do some shopping while you are checking in. Remember, you expect your unit to be in excellent condition when you arrive. Well, you have to give the cleaning and maintenance crews those precious hours to get their jobs done.

By the same rationale, be prompt in vacating the unit when it is time to check out. You should vacate prior to the 10 a.m. or 11 a.m. stated policy.

RENTAL PERIODS

All rental properties require a minimum one-week contract.

The rental periods are either Saturday to Saturday, or Sunday to Sunday. The staggered schedule helps to avoid massed traffic at the key check-in and check-out hours.

WHAT TO BRING

Rental properties do not furnish linens, blankets, towels, radios, televisions, clothes hangers, or clocks. Unless a TV is provided, the mention of cable television (CATV) indicates that a cable antenna system with a quality signal is available. TV reception is very poor without cable.

COTTAGE CAPACITY

Most rental firms enforce the cottage capacity restriction noted in each property description. If a tenant exceeds the accommodation limit, he may be subject to eviction without refund.

FAMILY POLICY

Many rental firms rent only to families and responsible adults. The agent reserves the right to determine the qualifications of tenants under this policy, and can evict parties in violation of the agreement.

DEPOSITS

Some rental agents require key deposits and/or security deposits.

Cottage tenants are generally responsible for leaving the cottage in the condition in which they rented it. The hours before check-out are usually spent in cleaning. If basic cleaning requirements are not met, or if there is damage to the premises, all or part of the security deposit may be forfeited.

The property key must be returned to the rental office on check-out.

MAIL AND PHONE MESSAGES

Most rental firms will accept mail and phone messages, but they will not deliver anything other than dire emergency notifications.

Emergency calls at night should be directed to the local Sheriff's Office (See Directory). You should leave both your rental agents number and that of the local Sheriff with family members who may need to reach you.

Few rental properties on the Banks have telephones.

FULL SEASON RENTALS

Full season rentals are an important part of the rental market that may not be reflected in the real estate booklets. Thousands of summer employees need accommodations, and generally they are looking for two and three bedroom apartments that can sleep four to six roommates. Since young people with good jobs are willing to pay three to four thousand dollars for a summer pad, there are properties which cater to their needs.

If you are interested in a Memorial Day weekend to Labor Day rental, ask several agents to provide details on their listings.

RESORT RENTAL FIRMS

The following listing includes Outer Banks real estate firms with significant rental programs. Each firm has a booklet picturing rental listings that is available on request by mail or phone. We have noted the toll free numbers for your money-saving convenience. If your vacation plans include a weekly, or seasonal rental, we encourage you to examine several rental booklets.

Mention that you are familiar with the information regarding rentals within the **Insiders' Guide.** Knowing that you are familiar with the beach profiles will help your agent give you faster and more complete service.

ATLANTIC REALTY (800) 334-8401
P.O. Box 48-V 261-2154
Kitty Hawk, NC 27949

Atlantic Realty publishes a 40-page booklet showing nearly 80 rental properties. Each is specifically located on an area map. Contract conditions and other helpful information are included. Note the toll-free number.

AUSTIN REALTY CO. 987-2208
Salvo, NC 27972

Austin's booklet shows photos of 55 cottages in Rodanthe, Waves, and Salvo area. Photos are large. Includes a planning calendar, and environmental photos of the area.

170 — RENTALS

BRITT REAL ESTATE   261-3566
SR Box 272 Duck
Kitt* · Hawk, NC 27949

   Shows more than 100 properties in a 8½ by 11 inch format booklet of 35 pages. Includes calendar and general map.

CAPE ESCAPE   987-2336
P.O. Box 21
Salvo, NC 27972

   A 12-page folder shows eight cottages available in Rodanthe, Waves and Salvo.

COLONY REALTY
Box 250
Avon, NC 27915   995-5891

   Colony Realty is one of the largest real estate organization on Hatteras Island. It services rental properties in most areas. The colorful and informative 48-page rental booklet includes maps, attraction information, ferry schedules, and rental details. The booklet pictures about 160 cottages throughout Hatteras Island.

COVE REALTY   441-6391
P.O. Box 967
Nags Head, NC 27959

   There are about 60 properties pictured in their 30-page booklet. Within the colorful covers are included rental information, area maps, and a planning calendar.

DUCK'S REAL ESTATE   261-2224
SR 250, Duck
Kitty Hawk, NC 27949

   Duck's Real Estate provides a pretty, large format brochure showing their rental properties. All properties are in the Southern Shores and north area.

FIRST FLIGHT REALTY   (800) 334-8463
P.O. Box 1163   441-6311
Kill Devil Hills, NC 27948

   The photos are big in their small but informative rental booklet. More than twenty properties are shown.

RENTALS — 171

HUDGINS REAL ESTATE (800) 334-4749
P.O. Box 1332   261-4646
Kill Devil Hills, NC 27948

Hudgins is one of the newer companies on the beach and already has a good reputation. They offer 81 cottages from Corolla to South Nags Head.

JOE LAMB & ASSOCIATES   441-5541
P.O. Box 111   261-4444
Kitty Hawk, NC 27949

With two offices, one in Nags Head and one in Kitty Hawk, this well-established firm offers many cottages and condos from Corolla to South Nags Head.

KITTY DUNES REALTY   261-2171
P.O. Box 275   USA (800) 334-DUNE
Kitty Hawk, NC 27949   NC (800) 682-DUNE

Twenty plus years in business, this firm publishes an 80-page booklet picturing over 200 properties. Includes location maps, annual calendar and rental policies. Properties range from Corolla through the major resort areas to South Nags Head.

KITTY HAWK REALTY   441-7166
P.O. Box 69
Kill Devil HIlls, NC 27948

Its large booklet shows over 200 rental properties. Location maps, a calendar, and helpful information is included.

MIDGETT REALTY
P.O. Box 1066
Kill Devil Hills, NC 27948   441-6666
Hatteras Office   986-2141

Midgett is a famous name on the Outer Banks. Since 1876, seven Midgetts have been awarded the Gold Life Saving Award, and three others the Silver. Midgett Realty, a 20-year old firm, has several offices and publishes a very useful 65-page rental booklet with over 200 properties pictured.

NAGS HEAD REALTY (A Rich Company)   (800)222-1531
   441-4311
P.O. Box 130
Nags Head, NC 27959

This company offers rental cottages and condos from Duck to South Nags Head.

Outer Beaches Realty, Inc.

Invest A Little Get A Lot

LUXURIOUS OCEANFRONT and OCEANSIDE COTTAGES FOR RENT

On Beautiful Hatteras Island

- Fully furnished
- Weekly rentals
- Excellent fishing
- Free swimming pool for our guests
- Village shopping nearby

Write or Call for our Free Brochure

Outer Beaches Realty, Inc.
P.O. Box 280
Avon, NC 27915
(919) 995-5252

Sales • Property Management • Appraisals • Construction

OCEAN BAY REALTY 441-2101
P.O. Box 2676
Kill Devil Hills, NC 27948

This brand new company offers sales, construction, property management, commercial property, and appraisals.

OCRACOKE REALTY 928-6261
P.O. Box 238
Ocracoke, NC 27960

This new company, the first on Ocracoke to offer a large collection of rental properties on the island, presents a small format booklet containing 16 rental cottages. An overall map of the island, fact sheet, and reservation form also are included.

OUTER BANKS, LTD. 441-5000
P.O. Box 129
Nags Head, NC 27959

Shows its rental properties in a 64-page booklet with over 130 pictured. Includes good location maps, and some editorial content.

OUTER BEACHES REALTY, INC. 995-5252
P.O. Box 280
Avon, NC 27915

A 44-page booklet shows some 120 cottages in the Salvo, Rodanthe, Avon, and Buxton areas. The publication includes helpful sightseeing information and a map of Avon where most of the rentals are offered.

Seasonal rental clients may enter a Labor Day drawing and win a second, free fall or spring week's rental.

REAL ESCAPES
FROST MORRISON REALTY 261-3211
SR Box 232-Z, Duck
Kitty Hawk, NC 27949

Provides a 40-page booklet with pen and ink renderings of over 75 cottages. All of these properties are in the beach country above Duck. Cottages in Sanderling, Ocean Sands, and Whalehead are included.

SURF or SOUND

**RENTALS • SALES
PROPERTY MANAGEMENT**

CAPE HATTERAS

Oceanfront and Soundside Cottages all within walking distance of the Atlantic Ocean.

**WRITE OR CALL
FOR A FREE BROCHURE**

SURF OR SOUND, LTD.
P.O. Box 100-IG, Avon, N.C. 27915
919-995-5801

RENTALS — 175

ROBERT A. YOUNG & ASSOCIATES (800)334-6436
P.O. Box 285 Rentals 441-5544
Kill Devil Hills, NC 27948

The "Young People", in operation since 1950, offer a large format, magazine-size booklet with beautiful full color photos on all its cover pages. The pages show over 500 rental properties. The booklet also includes maps, a large planning calendar, church and attraction information and interesting black and white photographs.

ROLLASON & WOOD REALTY, INC. 441-5551
P.O. Box 326
Kill Devil Hills, NC 27948

Will send a 40-page rental brochure picturing over 120 properties.

SEAGULL REALTY 987-2258
P.O. Box 3566
Waves, NC 27982

This realty firm offers cottage rentals on Hatteras Island.

SOUTHERN SHORES REALTY 261-2111
P.O. Box 150 (800)334-1000
Kitty Hawk, NC 27949

Sends a big format, slick finish booklet that pictures nearly 340 cottages. Includes maps, color photography of the environment (including a double page ocean-to-Currituck Sound aerial view), calendar, and rental details. All of the properties offered are in Southern Shores and Duck.

SUN REALTY 441-7033
P.O. Box S (800) 334-4745
Kill Devil Hills, NC 27948
Kitty Hawk Office 261-3892 (Sales only)

Sun Realty represents over 350 rental properties. Its thick, four-color cover resort-rental booklet shows units from Corolla to South Nags Head in a large format. The publication includes maps, a calendar, house rules, and condo profiles.

SURF OR SOUND, LTD. 995-5801
P.O. Box 100
Avon, N.C. 27915

This 40-page booklet provides information on approximately 100 properties in the lower beaches area. Also included are ferry schedules and information on area attractions.

TANYA YOUNG & ASSOCIATES (800)334-7732
P.O. Box 608 441-1353
Nags Head, NC 27959

Tanya Young offers cottage and condo rentals as well as residential and commercial sales.

TODD REALTY, INC. 441-6306
P.O. Box 1955
Kill Devil Hills, NC 27948

A 20-page booklet shows 24 properties.

TWIDDY & COMPANY 261-3521
SR Box 232-C
Duck, NC 27949

Properties in this 73-page booklet are shown in brown ink line drawings. Most of the cottages shown are in the exclusive Duck to Corolla area. About 130 properties are profiled.

WRIGHT REALTY 261-2186
P.O. Box 166
Kitty Hawk, NC 27949

A 52-page booklet picturing about 100 properties gives details on location, amenities, policies, and rates.

A heron is a familiar sight along the western shores of the Outer Banks.

 *DUCK, KITTY HAWK, COLINGTON*

CAMPGROUNDS

OCEAN BEACH CAMPGROUND

Duck   261-2200
Map, pg. 30

Ocean Beach is the biggest campground in the north part of the Banks, and certainly is the one most off the beaten path. 245 sites right by the ocean, secluded, but fifteen minutes drive from Kitty Hawk stores. Most sites have full hookups and are pull-throughs. All have picnic tables and access to hot showers, toilets, electricity, dump station hot and cold water, laundry, grocery, gasoline, and beach rental equipment. For fun, there's a swimming pool (with jacuzzi), family rec room, gameroom, playground, and social activities during the summer — plus fishing and swimming in the ocean. Open April 1 through November 1. Rates vary according to season and closeness of site to ocean. To reach Ocean Beach drive north on Duck Road (Rt. 120) to Duck, turn right, and you'll be at the entrance.

KITTY HAWK TRAILER PARK

Rt. 158 Bypass, MP 3   261-2636
Map, pg. 47

Kitty Hawk is a moderate-sized park located on a sandy patch between Rt. 158 business and bypass. Entirely for full-hookup units (no facilities for tents or vans!), there are over a hundred and twenty permanent sites, and about twenty for seasonal transients. Small patios are provided for each location. Open year round.

COLINGTON PARK CAMPGROUND

Colington 441-6128
Map, pg. 57

One of the largest campgrounds on Colington Island, and the most suitable for short-term visitors. Unlike most Beach sites Colington is wooded, making it more pleasant in summer. 50 sites, all with water and power, and picnic tables. Hot showers, toilets, grocery, recreation room. Open April-Oct. 30.

COZY COVE CAMPGROUND

Colington Island 441-7886
Map, pg. 57

Cozy Cove, exactly 2.2 miles west of the Wright Brothers pylon, is a relatively new mobile home park and campground, with a lot of improvements in place and more coming. These include permanent sites with water, power, dump, and sewage; a boat ramp, pier, and slips on a bay that exits to Currituck Sound; and even pool and sound swimming facilities. For the summer transient trade, primitive tent spots are available along with RV spots with water and electric hookups. Mobile home sites in this wooded sound area go for less than $100 a month; nightly rates are $10 to $15 for RVs.

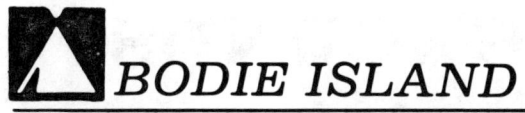

BODIE ISLAND CAMPGROUNDS

OREGON INLET CAMPGROUND

Bodie Island 441-6644
Map, pg. 103

The northernmost of the five National Park Service campgrounds on the Outer Banks, Oregon Inlet offers 120 delightfully primitive, flat, sandy, windswept, unshaded sites in the lee of the dunes at the south end of Bodie Island (to your left just before you start over the Oregon Inlet Bridge). No utility connections, but water, cold showers, toilets, picnic tables, and charcoal grills are available.

All the NPS campgrounds in the Banks operate under the same policy, charge the same fees, and use a common reservation system. We'll cover that here, then refer back to it in our later remarks on the other individual campgrounds.

Oregon Inlet, like all Park Service campgrounds, is open from mid-spring to mid-fall. For the early and late portions of this period it, like the other NPS facilities, are run without reservations; it's first come, first served. During the summer season, you may call 441-6644 for information on any of the NPS campgrounds, or write to Ticketron at the following address for reservations:

    Ticketron Reservations Office
    P.O. Box 2715
    San Francisco, CA 94126

You may also call the Ticketron office nearest you to make reservations. Basic charge for camping is $8.00; for reservations, another $3.50. Limit of stay is 14 days during the summer season. The Park Service recommends that persons camping on their grounds bring shading materials, mosquito netting, and long tent stakes (for the sandy ground).

ROANOKE ISLAND CAMPGROUNDS

SANDPIPER'S TRACE CAMPGROUND

Rt. 64, Manteo   473-3471

                    Map, pg. 289

Sandpiper's Trace, Bill Booker owner, is located four miles northwest of Manteo, on Route 64 — convenient to Fort Raleigh, the Lost Colony, and the Gardens. It has over 500 wooded campsites, making it one of the biggest campgrounds on the Banks — and there are lots of extras. There's a lighted fishing pier on the sound, with good bass, catfish, white perch, and bluegill fishing in summer. The grounds are outstanding: well-wooded, roomy, and stocked with quail, raccoon and flying squirrels. There's live music in the pavilion on Sunday evenings, and a recreation pavilion with game room, as well as the standard amenities—restrooms with hot shower, laundry, playground. This is a popular spot and we recommend reservations for the peak months, July and August, if you want a site.

HATTERAS ISLAND CAMPGROUNDS

Hatteras Island is the camping kingdom of the Outer Banks. There are literally dozens of campgrounds, many of them large, more of them small. Taken all together, they offer one of the finest areas for the tenter or the trailer camper to be found along the entire east coast of the United States.

The campgrounds covered here do not constitute a complete list of those operating on the island. As in all our listings in this book, we've tried to be selective, picking out for you the best places, and balancing this by looking for those that are different from the rest, offering distinctive camping experiences, locales, or services.

On Hatteras, for example, you'll find two basic kinds of campgrounds, surfside and soundside. The surfside campgrounds are located on the flat sand that is characteristic of most of Hatteras. There is usually little shade, plenty of wind and sun, and lots of sand. As we've noted elsewhere, for these you'll want to have sunscreens and long pegs to hold the tent down. The second kind is the soundside campground. These are located, for the most part, in the small forests of pine and live oak that line the sounds at the widest parts of Hatteras. They offer firmer ground, more shade, less wind; but, although the county is doing its best to control mosquitoes, they haunt the soundside woods in warm weather, especially in wet areas and after spells of rain (mosquitoes breed in fresh-water pools).

Whichever campground you choose, whether you camp in tent or trailer or even a mobile home, you'll find the kind of place you need on Hatteras. It's got variety, beauty, and closeness to nature — and isn't that what camping is all about?

PEA ISLAND RESORT

Rodanthe
Map, pg. 336 987-2337

Pea Island isn't really like the other campgrounds in that it's not really open to the public. You have to join to be able to use the facilities, but once that is accomplished, you have access to a myriad of recreational facilities as well as membership in other campgrounds and vacation spots all over the world. It shares some methods with time sharing in its marketing approach and the "exchange program" idea, but it's a totally separate operation.

This Rodanthe operation offers a heated indoor pool and Olympic-size outdoor pool, lighted tennis courts, miniature golf, basketball and shuffleboard courts, fresh water fishing ponds, a clubhouse where regular activities are planned by the full-time recreational director, a fishing dock and boat ramp, jet skis, jogging trails, and believe it or not, even more. The only thing you have to bring is your RV.

You can just drop in at the information center here to get information on the resort.

CAPE HATTERAS KOA

Rodanthe 987-2250
Map, pg. 336

Joan Berry, a friendly person, manages this large campground, located just south of Spur Road 1247, about fourteen miles south of the Oregon Inlet Bridge. It has 180 sites on the sea side of Highway 12, only a few hundred yards from the surf; in fact, you can hear it on the other side of the high Hatteras dunes from many of the sites, and a soothing sound it is by night. Most sites have water and power, and are located on flat sandy soil. Amenities include a dump station, laundry, pool, playground, game rooms, and there's a full-time activities director in the summer. The store is well-stocked. Of course there's salt-water fishing and swimming. You can also swim, snorkel, or fish in the sound, but it's mostly mud there... the sea's much better.

Rates range from $12 to $18.

KOA HOLIDAY CAMPGROUND

Rodanthe 987-2307
Map, pg. 336

Most of what was said above concerning the KOA Original also applies to KOA Holiday, which is just south of it. It has 250 sites with power and water, of which 41 also have sewer connections. Same amenities.

Rates here are the same as for the KOA above. An excellent service, we think, is trailer storage; you can store your trailer here year round if you wish, freeing you of the necessity of towing it down to Hatteras for each trip.

This site was formerly the Holiday Inn Trav-L-Park.

NORTH BEACH CAMPGROUND

Rodanthe 987-2378

Map, pg. 336

North Beach is right in Rodanthe and right on the ocean. What more can one ask from a campground? 110 sites, most with water and power. There's also hot showers, toilets, laundry, and a grocery. Just over the dunes are fishing and swimming. Open March till December. North Beach is just south of Chicamacomico Lifesaving Station, so if you're there during the summer, slip over and watch the Beach Apparatus Drill the Park Service puts on.

CAPE WOODS CAMPER PARK

Buxton 995-5850

Map, pg. 336

Located on the southern side of the Buxton "back road," Cape Woods is a good example of the soundside forest-type of camping. Over a hundred sites are laid out with wooded strips between, and many of the sites have shade. There are plenty of poplars, pine, and live oak. Another nice thing about Cape Woods is the two small freshwater lakes between which it lies; they're complete with bass and brim. Most of the sites have water, power, and picnic tables, and, of course, hot showers and flush toilets are available. Cape Woods is open year round, with prices ranging upward from a $10.00 base, depending on services.

BILL AND BARB'S CAMPER PARK

Buxton 995-5970

Map, pg. 336

This is one of the smaller campgrounds on Hatteras; because of its location in the Cape microforest, there are even some trees

— and in summer you'll appreciate their shade. About 20 campsites, all with city water and electricity and some with full hookups. Bathhouse with hot showers, flush toilets, and a picnic table at every site. The sign is easy to miss, so keep alert as you round the turn on Highway 12 on the outskirts of Buxton and head west on 1232. It'll be about four hundred yards on your left. Open year round except July and August. Rates for up to 2 people on one site are $9.00.

CAPE POINT CAMPGROUND (NPS)

Cape Hatteras   441-6644
                          Map, pg. 342

Cape Point is the biggest of the Park Service's five campgrounds on the Banks, and one of the wildest and nicest, too. Like the rest, there are no utility connections, but there are toilets, cold water showers, drinking water, charcoal grills, and picnic tables. Everything else you supply yourself. The 203-site campground is located just behind the dune line on the southwest face of the point, near Ramp 44, and is on flat, sandy ground. While checking it out we bogged down in what looked like firm sand, so take advantage of our mistakes and *stay on the road* unless you have four-wheel drive and oversized tires. Bring mosquito netting, awnings for shade, and long tent stakes for the sand. And bathing suits — it's a short walk to the ocean, and if you surf, the campground is located two miles away from the best surfing spot on the Atlantic coast. Cape Point, like the other NPS grounds, is open from mid-spring to mid-fall. In warm weather, outside of the peak season, it's open on a first come, first served basis. During the peak months, however, it is administered under the Park Service reservation system. (For details see "Oregon Inlet Campground" in the Bodie Island section.) Fee: $8.00 per night.

FRISCO WOODS CAMPGROUND, INC.

Frisco   995-5208
                          Map, pg. 344

We found Frisco Woods to be a standout campground. Ward and Betty Barnett, Hatteras natives, have developed its 14-acre soundside, part-forest, part-marsh location with care for nature and an eye for beauty. Frisco has 200 sites, many with full hookup, electricity and water. There are tables and hot showers, but otherwise the furnishings are spartan. The reason is that

Frisco caters to the naturally-oriented tent camper, rather than to the trailer crowd. The sites are all either in or beside virgin woods of pine, holly trees, and wild grapes. A naturalist's area on the Pamlico overlooks a wetland marsh habitat, and there's good crabbing and sound fishing. If you like semiwild, basic camping, this is the place. Open about March to December 1; basic fee $10.00 and up.

SURF AND SOUND CAMPGROUND

Frisco   986-2505

Map, pg. 344

Some 5 miles west of Buxton and ½ mile west of Frisco on Highway 12, Surf and Sound is an attractive large campground fronting both on the sea and the sound. 250 sites, about half with full hookups, the rest with water and power; all with picnic tables. Amenities include hot a well-stocked store, shower, toilets, laundry, and pool. Since the campground is on the ocean, you can swim, fish, or get your boat in the sound via their ramp. Open April to December.

FRISCO CAMPGROUND (NPS)

Frisco   441-6644

Map, pg. 344

Frisco is another National Park Service-run campground. On the southern side of the island, it's about four miles west of Buxton on Highway 12, then a left turn at the sign and drive to the beach. Frisco is open mid-spring till mid-fall, with 136 no-utilities sites. The location is well away from other activities and this is one of the more isolated campgrounds, so if you like it wild, Frisco's for you. 14 days limit of stay; fees $8.00 per night, payable at the entrance. This campground operates on a first come, first served basis all season. There are toilets, cold water outdoor showers, drinking water, charcoal grills, and picnic tables. See "Oregon Inlet Campground" for general information on all NPS campgrounds.

HATTERAS SANDS CAMPING RESORT
Hatteras   986-2422

Map, pg. 349

This is one of the largest, and best maintained, campgrounds on the Banks. Located very close to the ferry slips in Hatteras village, Hatteras Sands offers 105 sites with water and electricity. Sewage connections are available at some sites. Throughout the resort there are meticulously clean bath houses. Some pull-through sites also are available.

An Olympic-size pool is the feature of the amenities here, though there is also a nice gift shop and game room. A canal that runs through the resort provides for fun fishing and crabbing. The campground is also within easy walking distance to Hatteras village and its shops and restaurants.

The campground is open from March 1 until December 1. Discounts of 5% are given during off seasons. Nightly basic rates are within the $13 to $16 range.

OCRACOKE CAMPGROUNDS

OCRACOKE CAMPGROUND
(National Park Service)

Highway 12, east of town

Map, pg. 373

Operated by the National Park Service, Ocracoke Campground has 136 campsites just over the dunes from the ocean. No utilities, but there are cold showers, a dumping station, drinking water, charcoal grills, and flush toilets. Rates: $8.00 per night; reservations follow the system described earlier for the other Park Service campgrounds (see the write-up on Oregon Inlet Campground). Ocracoke is open mid-spring to mid-fall and a limit of stay of fourteen days is imposed.

As in other camping sites along the Beach proper, we suggest bringing awnings for shade, netting against mosquitoes, and longer than usual tent stakes for use in sandy soil with high winds from the sea. The campgrounds themselves are sandy and bare but rather pretty, and are only three miles from all the conveniences of Ocracoke Village. The beach is fine, but not lifeguarded except at the airstrip, up the beach a ways. Other than that, there's nothing around but beautiful emptiness.

Two private campgrounds presently operate on Ocracoke, Teeter's (near the British Cemetery) and George's Camp Plaza (on "the back road"; better ask a local resident just where). There are plans, we understand, for more.

CAMPGROUNDS — 187

The Ocracoke Lighthouse - one of the islands many attractions.

OUTER BANKS
CONDOMINIUMS

There has been a condominium construction boom going on since 1980 on the Outer Banks. Despite the then-high interest rates and uncertain national economy, condominium projects in Dare County led, and continue to lead, all other building categories, and what's more, they have been selling.

One reason for this phenomenon is a marketing concept known as Time Shared or Interval Ownership; another is a similar concept known as Co-ownership. You may have seen the promotions. If you qualify to inspect any of these properties, i.e. be married, tour with your spouse, have a verifiable income and be at least 23 years of age, you might be paid for your time plus be showered with gifts.

Gift certificates worth $25, in most cases, for touring various properties are available in restaurants and shops all over the beach most summers. A visit might also qualify you for a free vacation prize, gas grill, French wine glasses, a camera...the list goes on.

Be advised that your tour is actually a very professional sales presentation that many non-buyers before you have not been able to resist. Of course, that's why they will reward you for hearing the pitch! The basic tour takes about an hour; longer if you show interest in a particular unit and vacation time period.

It is gratifying to see that the Time Share and co-ownership methods of house or condominium ownership have been adopted in the real estate laws of most states. In 1975, as the Associate Publisher of **Holiday Magazine**, I developed the first national marketing campaign for the time share concept. The initial full page color spreads appeared in the **Saturday Evening Post, Holiday,** and **Country Gentleman** magazines. I believed that time share buying was the way to make resort condominiums accessible to the average resort vacationer, even in the times of a recession. Over 10,000 coupon responses resulted from the first exposure.

The Time Share concept means that you may purchase the ownership and use of a property for a specific period of time, generally one week or more. For example, you might actually purchase the use of the first two weeks in July. By deed, you actually own one twenty-sixth of the unit, and can sell, will, or otherwise convey this share as real property. You, of course, also bear your share of the taxes, maintenance, and condo association fees. The time share purchased price can be financed, and your unit comes fully furnished, including kitchen and serving essentials.

Co-ownership comes into play when a certain number of buyers purchase a large, well-built, and usually luxuriously decorated beach home. Each owner, usually around 10, then is able to use their share of the home for five week a year. Maintenance and other costs are shared, as in time sharing.

Time sharing seemed almost perfect. In 1975, deluxe condo units in some of the most desirable resorts in the United States were selling for under $9,000 for periods up to four weeks. But there was a flaw. Suppose you could not occupy your unit during the period you owned? Suppose the only weeks available were in February, and your property was a summer resort? Suppose you just wanted to go someplace different one year?

What was needed was a service to provide trading among time share owners. Jon DeHaun, trained in motel management, saw the potential of such a service and created Resort Condominiums International (RCI). Since Jon and I shared the podium at the American Land Development Association national convention in 1975, RCI has grown dramatically. Hundreds of resort properties in the US, Mexico, the Caribbean, and Europe, and thousands of time share owners have joined RCI. Members can put their units into the time share bank, and trade it for the use of another unit across the country. A rating system balances out the difference between a $95,000 unit on the Outer Banks and a $200,000 unit in Acapulco, and the difference is paid in cash. Even if your time period is not claimed for use during the year, you can still use its value for the use of another time share unit in the pool. Computers take care of the reservation details.

If you are serious about exploring time share properties on the Outer Banks, a property sales agent can more fully explain time share purchases, and membership in RCI or another trading service.

The following profiles include condominium developments recently on the market, and others which now are available for rent.

In case you're not reading this book from start to finish, please note that condominium and co-ownership developments in the Duck area are profiled in the beginning of this book under the heading of "Northern Developments."

SEA SCAPE
Beach and Golf Villas
P.O. Box 117
Kitty Hawk, NC 27949

261-3881

Sea Scape is located on Rt. 158 Bypass at the 2 mile marker. The spacious two bedroom, two bath villas are luxuriously equipped for house keeping.

Time Share property owners have all the privileges of the community complex which includes the golf course, tennis courts, swimming pool, and access to 600 ft. of restricted beach.

Sea Scape is a member of Escape Shares, one of the companies which arranges swaps between condo owners worldwide.

THE GOLDEN STRAND
P.O. Box 1715
Kill Devil Hills, NC 27948

441-4888

Located on the ocean at the 7½ mile marker in Kill Devil Hills, the Golden Strand offers two and three bedroom luxury apartments.

Every unit has a view of the ocean. Units include a fireplace, wet bar, HBO-TV, deluxe kitchen, sit down kitchen bar, and tasteful living room and dining area decor. Amenities include a pool, children's pool, and a gazebo at the dune line.

The Golden Strand is a member of Vacation Horizons International (VHI), a condo vacation exchange agency. It is a time shared property.

SEA RANCH II
Rt. 158 Business, MP 7
Kill Devil Hills, NC 27948

441-4445
(800) 334-4737

Sea Ranch II is a steel and concrete building on the oceanfront housing 28 luxury two bedroom suites. The property is adjacent to the Sea Ranch Hotel, a deluxe accommodation with indoor pool, restaurant, show lounge, shops, and other amenities which are available to Sea Ranch ll owners.

This property is being offered for interval ownership (time shared). The identical units include a king-sized bed and jacuzzi in the master bedroom/bath, a private glass enclosed balcony overlooking the ocean beach, gourmet kitchen, two color HBO-TV, washer/dryer and a second full bath.

OUTER BANKS BEACH CLUB
Rt. 158 Business, MP 9
Kill Devil Hills, NC 27948

(800) 441-7306
(800) 672-4795

The Outer Banks Beach Club was the first interval ownership property on the Outer Banks. Its round, three story buildings interconnected with balconies and decking are already a landmark on the oceanfront.

There is a choice of one or three bedroom units with either oceanfront, ocean view, or poolside views. Amenities include two swimming pools, steam bath, jacuzzi, HBO-TV, playground, cookout area, and beach cabanas.

The Beach Club is a member of RCI, the condo exchange company.

THE VILLAS　　　　　　　　　　　　　　　　　　　441-5981
King's Grant Realty
P.O. Box 596
Nags Head, NC 27959

The Villas was the first condominium development on the Outer Banks. It is a large complex built near Jockey's Ridge on the Roanoke Sound. There are 20 separate buildings and dozens of units available for rental. Two and three bedroom apartments, some with views of the sound, are priced in the moderate category.

The amenities include three tennis courts, two pools, a clubhouse, and soundside boating facilities for small boats. No pets.

THE WINDJAMMER　　　　　　　　　　　　　　441-4811
Rt. 158 Business, MP 15　　　　　　　　　　(800) 334-4743
Nags Head, NC 27959

This property has a prime location on the Nags Head oceanfront. Each of the Windjammer's buildings is angled for views of the ocean. All the units are designed as two bedroom, one and one half bath townhouses. There are upstairs bedrooms on the bi-level units, and private balconies. Furnishings are deluxe. Amenities include a large pool and sun deck.

The Windjammer is offered on an interval ownership basis, and includes first year membership in Resort Condominiums International.

HATTERAS COLONY　　　　　　　　　　　　　　995-5891
Beach & Fishing Club
P.O. Box 250
Avon, NC 27915

Colony Realty, the developer of Hatteras Colony Vacation Estates, has set aside some of its two-story newly constructed oceanfront homes in Hatteras Village for time sharing ownership.

The three bedroom, two and one-half bath home has 1660 square feet of living space plus more than 460 square feet of decking. Features include a wood burning fireplace, ultra modern kitchen, outside hot and cold shower, fish cleaning table with running water, plus TV, telephone, and everything necessary for housekeeping, including linens.

CAPE HATTERAS BEACH CLUB　　　　　(800) 334-8308
P.O. Box 550　　　　　　　　　　　　　　995-4115
Buxton, NC 27920

This development extends from the ocean to Pamlico Sound and is the closest private land to Cape Hatteras Point.

The two-bedroom, two-bath villas are offered for interval ownership. Steam, jacuzzi, and a private balcony are unit amenities. An indoor-outdoor pool, tennis court, and recreation area are in the master plan. The project is a member of RCI.

BUYING REAL ESTATE

After visiting the Outer Banks and experiencing its lifestyle, many families dream about having their own place here near the ocean.

The opportunities for interval ownership, or time sharing, have been discussed in another section, so let's turn attention to what you should know about purchasing your cottage in the sun.

The following check list is a compilation of caveats contributed by professional Real Estate Brokers who were interviewed for this section. If you are serious about buying a vacation or retirement home on the Outer Banks, here is what local insiders suggest that you investigate before closing on the property.

CHECK-LIST
ADVICE TO THE BUYER

1. Size of lot - if it's 50' x 100' or 60' x 100', (as many lots are) look for building restrictions that could create problems. How many bedrooms are allowed for that space? What is the overall building space you can have?
2. Does the lot front on an improved road? Will there be road maintenance?
3. Is the property damp? Make sure there is proper drainage.
4. Does the lot have beach access? If not, you may not be able to just pop over your neighbor's dune to get to the ocean - you may have to go way down the beach. If it **does** have access, your property value will be much higher.
5. Buying oceanfront? Check out erosion! Make sure you have enough space between the road & your setback from the beach. The state has published an erosion rate table - figure **30 times** the annual erosion rate and measure from the first **stable** line of vegetation. Exceptions can be made, but keep in mind that the usual setback is 60 ft. and that your septic tank must go on street side.
6. As it is possible to determine, what will your neighborhood look like in the future? Your lot should have a barrier dune.
7. Check out the insulation on any house. It has been only 6

years since houses started being fully insulated on the Banks.
8. Make sure you're familiar with the different tax rates for each town (KDH, Nags Head, etc.)
9. Any particular agreement made between you and your salesperson should be put in the contract.
10 Are you buying for a vacation home for personal use or for rentals? Retirement? Combination? Which is the most important to you? Choose the type of house and location accordingly.
11. **Where** do you want to be located (now and 10 years from now) — Oceanfront, oceanside, soundside, Manteo, neighborhood...?
12. Is your Real Estate Broker reputable? Do they know the area well - i.e. have they been here long enough to **really know** real estate here? Shop around - don't necessarily go with the first one you meet.
13. Building? Think about septic & building permits, contractors, efficiency of heat and special materials used for this area and climate.
14. Good contractor? Rely upon a good broker and the contractor's community reputation - insurance people, bankers, satisfied customers.
15. Be familiar with the Coastal Area Management Act.
16. Beware of the dangers of the ocean — Storms, erosion, hurricanes. Be appropriately insured,

Sunrise at the Outer Banks provides a quiet time for ocean surf fishing.

BIRDS, FISHING, AND A TOUCH OF SOLITUDE

GOLD & SILVER SEASONS

To every thing, says Ecclesiastes, there is a season. And to things on the Outer Banks, there are seasons too.

Not everything happens in the summer. As Insiders, some of our best times on the Banks haven't been in the three sun-and people-filled months of June, July, and August. We have fished the Stream offshore in the warm smoky days of late September and October; seen the snow geese and ducks whistle by overhead in long vees almost from horizon to horizon; slept in lonely cottages in the depth of winter, the gas stove hissing and the mad booming of the surf shaking the night; watched the spring come suddenly as a shot, turning the forests green almost in a day. There are times in January that are almost like April, and times in April that are almost like July.

We call them the "gold and silver" seasons of the year, and you too can drink their crisp sweetness long before and after the hectic heat of summer.

Many of the Outer Banks' most faithful lovers find fall the time they like best. Temperatures are actually more comfortable (considering the human physiological range of activity) in September and October than they are during the summer proper: highs in the upper sixties to mid-seventies, lows in the low sixties. These are air temperatures; the sea temperatures sound even better, for the ocean acts as a giant heat reservoir, storing up all those rays and keeping them well into the autumn. Water temperatures are still in the seventies through these months, though there is a slow decline as time goes on. It's all a question of how hardy you are.

But you don't have to be *in* the ocean to enjoy it. The fishermen know this, and that's why the autumn is their favorite time of all along Hatteras and offshore. Late September, October, November, and early December (see "The Outer Banks Fishing Guide") are the prime seasons for blue, trout, croaker, and king mackerel. Late October is the most exciting of these times, for

Surf Caster - Dawn finds a lone fisherman casting out to sea in some of the best fishing grounds on the East Coast.

this is the season of the blues. Fish like colder water than human beings, and as the sun wheels towards winter the sea off the Banks comes alive wth the small food fish these predators love. We've seen some fantastic blues blitzes on the crisp, high-ceilinged days when the gulls cry overhead and the wind has just a touch of bite....

And in the autumn the birds go by. Thousands, millions of them, heading south on the great flyways that stretch from Canada to South America. Snow geese, every variety of duck, pelicans — you can stand on the shore in northern Hatteras with binoculars and fill your sighting book. Take a look at our "Pea Island Wildlife Refuge" section, in the chapter on Hatteras Island, for a taste of what you can expect in the fall.

Winter in the Banks is usually snowless, but it gets cold, and windy as well. It seldom dips below freezing, though. We've used the cottages of Nags Head and Kitty Hawk to hole up during the winter and write, think, just get away. The amenities of restaurants, shops, and bars are hardly missed when you want to be alone — or alone with someone special. And if you just have to have company, there are plenty of friendly people (and open stores) on Roanoke Island all winter. They live there, and their welcome during the winter is just as warm — and even more personal — than during the more crowded months.

Spring comes early to the Outer Banks. We've been there on days in mid-January when the sun was warm and high and pine needles crunched underfoot in green grass, and all you wore was a sweater. By late March the temperature is already back up to the mid-sixties. Surf fishing begins, after a winter hiatus, with the arrival of the channel bass. April is the best spring month for these guys. Through March and April the pace slowly builds, and as May begins the whole tawny crescent of the barrier banks is once again ready for the summer.

To sum up, we think the term "Off Season," although descriptive, is not exactly accurate. There's really no "Off Season" for the Outer Banks the way there is for resort areas with wider swings in climate. If you choose to miss the hot months, or to make an additional visit outside of the most popular times, you can take advantage of lower rates, smaller crowds at your favorite diversions, and an entirely new range of enjoyments, recreations, and natural moods. In fact, we see (and predict) a lengthening of the active season on the Outer Banks. Already, in the last three years, the permanent population on the islands has doubled. More people are choosing to make this their year-round home, and as a direct consequence the occasional visitor will be able to take advantage of a longer, and in many ways a more enjoyable, season.

We call them the seasons of silver and gold. Maybe we've kept them to ourselves too long, but we've enjoyed them. You should too.

OUTER BANKS
RESTAURANTS

The food service traditions of the Outer Banks center around seafoods which are caught in local waters by the resident fishing fleet and then prepared by native cooks. The "fish-of-the-day" might be Bluefish, Speckled Trout, Croaker, Spanish Mackerel, Bluefin Tuna, or even Dolphin depending on the seasonal catch. Flounder, the flat fish with delicate taste, is plentiful and is featured in every seafood establishment. Filets fried whole in a light batter to a golden crispness, broiled with a lemon butter topping, or served fried with a crabmeat stuffing are the favored preparations. This species provides the most popular entrees on the beach.

Crabmeat entrees are also a staple on Outer Banks menus. The Blue crab's backfin meat is highly prized for flavor and recipe versatility. She-Crab Soup, praised by President George Washington in 1791, is a complex cream based soup with a hint of sherry. Not every chef attempts this gourmet's delight, so try it, if available.[1]

Crabmeat also appears in cocktail appetizers, or stuffed into mushrooms, but it is the entree list that gives it star billing. Crab Cakes are almost universally offered. (Ask for them broiled instead of fried for a purer crab taste). Soft shell crabs are more readily available since the advent of methods to "hold" the shell changng crustaceans. (Make sure your order is fresh, not frozen. They are subject to seasonal availability.) Sauteed Crabmeat and Crab Imperial (a specialty of the house in a few places) will also be seen.

True crab lovers, however, will want at least one trip to a family restaurant where the butcher paper is spread across the table and a few dozen steamed crabs are piled in the center for picking. The hot spicy crabs were alive and kickin' when the cooking started. Their shells turn red-orange and provide a bright contrast to the white succulent meat inside. Don't be afraid to order steamed crabs if you are a novice. The restaurant staff will show you how to open and extract the prized meat. A crab feast promotes family fellowship and is an evenings entertainment by itself.

---

[1] Crab Soup, a tomato based vegetable soup with bits of crab throughout is more likely to be offered.

The legendary bivalve, the oyster is next in the culinary list of Outer Banks restaurant treats. Under soups and appetizers, you will see them served as Oyster Stew (with or without milk), and on the half shell. Select oysters are usually served fried.

The clam is usually served on the Outer Banks in Clam Chowder, or French Fried Clam Strips, or in Clam Fritters. The ocean clams harvested here abouts are too large, and tough for eating on the half shell. You will see Cherrystone Clams on the half shell, steamed Hard Shell Clams, and Clams Casino in some places.

Scallops, however, are another matter. Beautiful scallops are brought to port almost everyday, and native cooks generally prepare them fried, sauteed in butter, or broiled.

More imaginative chefs will create a Coquille St. Jacques, Scallops en Brochette, or even a Scallop Creole. If you enjoy eating scallops, the Outer Banks is one of the best places we know to sample this meaty textured seafruit.

The final star on the seafood menu is the Shrimp. It appears in cocktail appetizers, in deep fried baskets, or steamed with spicy condiments. It is also welcomed in Shrimp Creole, on a Seafood Kebob, or simply sauteed or broiled. A few restaurants attempt the spicy Scampi.

The alternative to making an individual pick from this seafood bounty is to have it all on a combination platter. And that's what most people do, at least on their first restaurant night out.

OUTER BANKS STYLED CLAM CHOWDER

Every seafaring area takes its clam chowder seriously. Chowders come in three basic varieties. Manhattan Clam Chowder has a tomato base and may be on the spicy side with hints of tobasco, thyme, basil, and oregano. New England Clam Chowder is generally considered to have a milk base, and has salt pork, onion, and always potatoes added.

The Outer Banks variety (call it Hatteras style, Wanchese style or whatever) uses neither tomato or milk as a basic ingredient, but prefers to feature the clams in their own broth or liquor. Other ingredients may include diced potatoes, chopped onions, celery, parsley and the chef's choice of spices which enhance the clam flavor.

Chowder will sour very easily if it is not handled properly, especially if made in big batches. Chowder chefs agree that the cover on a pot of chowder should never be left on while it is cooling because the condensation will spoil it. A chowder should never go into the refrigerator until it has completely cooled to room temperature. Any skin that forms on the top of a cooled chowder should be carefully skimmed off. A chowder always tastes better on the second, or even third day if it doesn't ferment first!

Chowder is not easy to make and even harder to keep. It is little wonder that chowder chefs are so sensitive, and proud of their vulnerable creations.

It is very possible that no two Outer Banks clam chowders are the same. Perhaps they are not even the same at the same restaurant from one day to the next. It is the challenge and delight of the would-be chowder gourmet to sample the field and declare his own preferences.

HUSHPUPPIES

Nearly every seafood restaurant on the Outer Banks serves up a basket of hushpuppies with its entrees. Hushpuppies are a traditional Southern deep fried corn meal bread. The corn meal, flour, baking powder, salt, sugar, egg, and milk batter is dropped by the spoonful into deep hot fat and allowed to fry until it is golden brown.

Some Southern areas add finely chopped onion to their mix and like to fry the hushpuppy in the same oil used to fry the fish. But the Outer Banks hushpuppy cooks eschew the onion and the fishy hint to their creations in favor of a sweet, almost cake-like quality that is achieved by increasing the flour and sugar ratio and frying in oils reserved just for hushpuppies.

Hushpuppies can vary in diameter. Some cooks believe that the size of the round crispy breads is the secret to their texture and taste. Others guard their batter recipes in the conviction that they have discovered the perfect hushpuppy formula. Many restaurants on the Banks have loyal followers who are convinced that their hushpuppies are the best.

To tell the truth, few restaurants make hushpuppies from scratch anymore. There are excellent commercial mixes which get "doctored" so that the cook can claim it as his own. The quantitative and qualitative difference may actually be very small.

By legend, and this is perhaps a true one, hushpuppies got their name as southern cooks prepared the evening meal. Hungry hunting dogs would hang around the kitchen and bark for their share of the meal being prepared. The harried cooks, trying to get a meal completed for a waiting family, attempted to appease and quiet the dogs with bits of corn bread batter dropped into the hot frying fat. The little fried dough balls were thrown out the kitchen door with the admonishment, "hush puppy".

PLANNING & PRICING

For many years almost all seafoods served on the Banks were deep fried. Today, the broiler is just as popular, and there is a trend toward even further preparation diversity as chefs trained in other traditions come to cook on the Outer Banks.

The establishment of liquor by the drink on the main resort strip (Kill Devil Hills and Nags Head) in 1981 heralded a remarkable surge in new restaurant construction, renovation of established places, and rethinking all along the beach. The bar and lounge business has contributed to upgrading restaurant menus, decor, and service wherever it has been allowed. Mixed beverages, beer, and wine are now available in almost every restaurant within the legalized communities.

The restaurant competition on the Outer Banks is keen. The prime vacation months account for a large percentage of a restaurateur's income, so the good business person cannot afford to be outmaneuvered by menu pricing. Competitive enterprise seems to be working here to the consumer's benefit.

We experienced a basic uniformity of entree pricing for the most popular items. For example, a flounder filet stuffed with crab meat presented in restaurants of equal ambiance and kitchen quality will cost about the same price.

For our readers convenience we have established four categories as a guide to menu prices.

The cost guidelines are based on a meal for two persons which includes appetizers, entrees, two vegetables or side dishes, desserts, and coffee. The calculation for each restaurant was based on a la carte items at evening prices. Luncheon specials and other common sense factors can lower the basic check total just as cocktails, wine, and flaming tableside desserts can increase it.

Restaurateurs with pocket calculators can easily challenge our best intentions in offering menu price guidelines. A meal may be obtained in many places below the cost line especially at better places serving lunch. Inflation and menu changes will also come into play. But our dining-out attitude is to enjoy our favorite offerings on the menu and be prepared to pay the bill.

Here are the guidelines that are reflected in the restaurant profiles to follow:

$	A basic meal for two under $22.
$$	A check for two of $22 to $34.
$$$	Over $35 for two.
$$$$	Over $45 for two.

The guideline does not include the 4 1/2% NC sales tax, or the gratuity which should be at least 15% for good service.

Some restaurants in the primary resort area offer discounts and specials for early evening dining in order to encourage their patrons to avoid the peak dining hours. It is no secret that in-season, and on shoulder season weekends, the waiting lines at popular restaurants are long. Few restaurants will accept reservations except for large parties.

The restaurants profiled in this guide are arranged by mile marker, north to south, Corolla to Ocracoke. Each location is keyed to a detailed strip map for your further convenience. You should also pick up a copy of **Guide to Dining on the Outer Banks.** This inexpensive book ($2.95) gives you a wealth of details on the best of the area's restaurants with money saving coupons to boot.

RESTAURANTS

SOUTHERN SHORES, DUCK, SANDERLING,
1. Barrier Island Inn
2. Sanderling Restaurant
3. Duck Deli
4. Osprey Landing Gourmet

KITTY HAWK
5. R.V.'s
6. Ella's
7. Trade Winds
8. Station Six
9. Avalon Pier Restaurant
10. Newby's Sub Shop
11. Sportsman's

KILL DEVIL HILLS
12. Krause's Steak House
13. Seafare III
14. Top of the Dunes
15. Midgett's Barbeque
16. Jolly Roger
17. Whaling Station
18. Papagayo's
19. Port O' Call
20. JK's
21. Stack 'Em High
22. Capt'n Dave's
23. Madeline's
24. Etheridge Seafood
25. Peppercorns
26. Fish Market
27. Miller's Seafood & Steak House
28. Starkey's Pizza
29. Evan's Crab House
30. Sands Family Restaurant

NAGS HEAD NORTH
31. Sweetwaters
32. Carolinian
33. Kelly's
34. Sinbad's
35. A Restaurant, By George
36. Plantation Restaurant
37. Fishtails
38. Gandalf & Co.

ROANOKE ISLAND
51. Duchess of Dare
52. Cafe Rene
53. Elizabethan Restaurant
54. Queen Anne's Revenge
55. Fisherman's Wharf
56. Weeping Radish
57. Ship's Galley

NAGS HEAD SOUTH
39. Elegant Pelican
40. Dareolina Cove
41. Miller's Waterfront
42. The Dunes
43. Sam & Omie's
44. Owens'
45. Windmill Point
46. R.V.'s
47. Tale of the Whale
48. Daniels' Seafood
49. The Dock
50. Ship's Wheel

HATTERAS ISLAND
58. Emily's Soundside
59. Froggy Dog
60. Lighthouse
61. Orange Blossom Pastry Shop
62. Pilot House
63. Quarterdeck
64. Gingerbread House
65. Frisco Drive-In
66. Bubba's Bar-B-Q
67. Light Ship
68. Channel Bass

OCRACOKE
69. Back Porch
70. Island Inn Dining Room
71. Pelican
72. Howard's Pub
73. Cap't. Ben's
74. Pony Island Restaurant

SOUTHERN SHORES, DUCK, SANDERLING, COROLLA

RESTAURANTS

BARRIER ISLAND INN

Duck 261-3901
$$-$$$
Map, pg. 30

Barrier Island Station is one of the resort villages that has been swelling the affluent population north of Kitty Hawk. Located about six miles from the north end of Rt.158 Bypass in the village of Duck, the Barrier Island Inn is a surprising dining oasis in a sea of dune-top homes.

There are two places to dine in the Inn. The upper level, Duckside Tavern, serves informal luncheons and dinners from 11:30 a.m. to 10 p.m. daily. Take outs are available. The contemporary decor and windows overlooking a pier ornamented by small sailboats and crowned by a gazebo have a private country club feel. Sunsets over the Currituck are especially rewarding from this viewpoint.

Luncheons here are built around soups, sandwiches, and salads. Outer Banks clam chowder, and a blue crab bisque with a hint of sherry are complimented by a salad bar. Sandwiches include fancy burgers, crabcake, and barbecue. There is also barbecue ribs, steamed crabs and shrimp, and a variety of daily specials. Fresh steamed seafood with garlic butter was offered on our last visit.

The formal dining from 5:30 p.m. until 10 p.m. is taken downstairs and in a large room off the upstairs Tavern. The appointments again remind us of an affluent yacht or country club; relaxed, but with a touch of class. There are several raised alcoves for semiprivate parties.

In addition to traditional seafood preparations, the Inn offers seafood brochette, Long Point Island Duck (it should be their featured item) and char-grilled BBQ ribs. There is also beef, grilled marinated game fish and a nightly special worth investigating (e.g. Scampi, Live Lobster).

The Barrier Island Inn caters parties and offers a Sunday Brunch. The drive to Duck takes you past some of the most architecturally interesting houses on the Banks.

THE SANDERLING RESTAURANT

Sanderling, north of Duck 261-3021
$$$$

Map, pg. 30

One would expect any restaurant that was a part of the Sanderling complex to be excellent, and this one doesn't disappoint. Housed in the Historic Landmark, Caffeys Inlet Station, one of the many life saving stations that dotted the coastline during the early part of this century, the restaurant carries through a comfortable yet classy nautical theme in its five main rooms. The main dining room is in the Boat Room, the area in which the lifesaving boats were originally stored. Several large glass doors give the room a bright, airy feel and provide nice views, too. The Captain's Galley, a window-lined addition to the back of the building, provides an oceanfront area for morning dining. Upstairs, in the Life Saving Lounge, fine, imported premium wines can be enjoyed by the glass, along with imported beers. There's even a selection of wines under the Sanderling Inn label. And right off the lounge, an oceanfront deck offers a spectacular view of the ocean and lighted dune line where, in winter, deer can sometimes be spotted grazing.

And now for the food. From first sniff you figure you're in for something out of the ordinary since a wonderful aroma of hickory wood greets you at the front door. Executive Chef Craig Hartman works hard to continue that impression with unusual dishes like quail stuffed with crabmeat, hickory grilled lobster with tarragon butter, smoked Pine Island goose breast, and hickory grilled filet mignon with glazed wild mushrooms. Ingredients used are fresh and often imported, like the Belgian endive and the shiitake mushrooms. Baked goods are made fresh everyday as are desserts such as ice cream and sorbet. When possible, Chef Hartman searches out unusual meats such as venison to cook over the hickory. They're especially proud of their Currituck Sound Chowder which, they joke, "doesn't have a clam in it." Rather, it's filled with shrimp, oysters, crab, and game fish.

Lunch offers a variety of fresh fruits, salads, and grilled entrees along with hot and cold sandwiches served in freshly baked croissants. Breakfast features fruits, baked goods, and the expected eggs and meat, in addition to some unexpected dishes such as Carolina pecan griddle cakes, assorted yogurts, and cinnamon orange french toast.

Hours are 8:00 a.m. until 10:30 a.m. for breakfast; 10:30 a.m. until 2:00 p.m. for lunch; and, 6:00 p.m. until 10:00 p.m. for dinner. A Sunday brunch is served from 10:30 a.m. until 3:00 p.m. The restaurant is open year round and reservations are recommended at night.

DUCK DELI

Duck 261-3354
$

Map, pg. 30

The Duck Deli is almost always full of people — hungry people who know where to get great sandwiches and salads. Situated right in the middle of "beautiful downtown Duck," a friendly teasing phrase that locals use, the Deli is perfectly set to pick up business from the growing population of tourists who settle into this northern beach town for their vacations. Having once visited, they tend to come back day after day for the subs on freshly baked rolls, the umpteen number of deli sandwiches, the hamburgers, and the desserts — German chocolate being one of our favorites. They also offer beers and wine and you can call ahead for take-outs.

They've made it easy for you to remember their number too: just call 261-DELI.

OSPREY LANDING GOURMET

Duck 261-7133
$

Map, pg. 30

Nita and Latham Micas own and operate this well-stocked eatery, located in the Osprey Landing shopping center overlooking the sound. They offer a good variety of sandwiches as well as soups, salads, and fresh baked goods. One sandwich here called the Baby Boomlet Special, especially for kids under 10 years of age, is a "pbj" with crusts removed on request and containing "no sprouts, no onions, no strange gourmet mustards or mayo." They also carry natural sodas and juices, imported beers, and wines. Sandwiches may be eaten at tables placed on the deck with a close-up view of the sound and an almost always present breeze.

The restaurant is open from 10:00 a.m. until 9:00 p.m. in season Mondays through Saturdays; 10:00 a.m. until 6:00 p.m. on Sundays. Off season hours vary, so call before you go over.

 **KITTY HAWK**
RESTAURANTS

R.V.'S

Rt. 158 Bypass, Kitty Hawk Traffic Light   261-7377
Map, pg. 47
$$

R.V. Owens expanded his restaurant interests in 1984 to this striking Kitty Hawk landmark. The original R.V.'s, still operating in Nags Head near the Manteo Causeway, is now the little brother to the showcase restaurant at the north end of the Banks.

R.V.'s is one of the closest full-service restaurants to the rapidly developing areas of Duck and Southern Shores. When it opened, its nearest competitor was four miles away. R.V. has joined the commercial development trend north by building a large, 200-seat restaurant and lounge. The building rises above the dunes on stilts for a view of the ocean although it is on the Bypass road. Lattic work concealing the underpinning and a glassed-in deck enhance the architectural effect. In good weather, sections of the glass slide away to give diners a sense of the out-of-doors. A candy-striped canvas awning goes all around.

Interior details include 165 feet of brass rail, tongue and groove juniper siding, beveled glass, lots of Tiffany-styled lamps, and brass ceiling fans. The large bar will seat 30.

The fare at R.V.'s reflects the casual atmosphere. For lunch or dinner light items such as nachos, chicken fingers, cheese balls, potato skins, fried veggies, burgers, and special sandwiches are available. Up to this point, the menu resembles a Friday's. But look further for the native seafoods broiled, fried, or sauteed. R.V.'s knows what to do with shrimp, fish, and oysters. There are also homemade desserts.

R.V.'s is located at a growing crossroads that includes a Ben Franklin, a cinema, and a shopping center. The land is very narrow here from ocean to sound. It makes a good spot for a sundown rendezvous. Service daily from 11:30 a.m. until 2 a.m.

ELLA'S

Rt. 158 Bypass, MP 4 1/2   261-7331
                          Map, pg. 47
$$

The unusual building on the bypass in Kitty Hawk is the home of Ella's Restaurant and Lounge. Opened in 1985, the restaurant serves several dishes that vacationers used to something other than "true southern cooking" will be glad to find, like real deli sandwiches, kosher franks, and bagels and lox. They also serve a large variety of seafood, poultry and beef dishes. But, in our opinion, the best find here are the soups: Vichyssoise, Gazpacho, Ratatouille, She-Crab, Cream of Broccoli, and some Black Bean soup that brought us back several times. They also serve falafel, something that's not found many - if any - other places on the Banks.

Early bird specials are offered from 5 to 6 p.m. and a children's menu is available. Ella's is opened from 11:30 a.m. until 10:00 p.m., April through October.

TRADE WINDS

Rt. 158 Bypass, MP 4½   261-3052
                          Map, pg. 47
$

This is one of three Chinese restaurants on the **Outer Banks**. The Chef's Suggestions include Beef with Peking Sauce, Mu Shu Pork, Crispy Chicken, and a Chinese Vegetarian's Delight. The large menu has 13 shrimp and prawn dishes including hot and spicy Mandarin Shrimp, and Kung Pao Shrimp; 13 chicken preparations including Curry Chicken; 12 beef entrees such as Ginger Beef and Mongolian Beef; five pork dishes, plus five Lo Mein selections, six soups, Shrimp Toast and other appetizers, five Chow Meins, and five Fried Rice combinations. All the items are authentic in preparation and presentation, and the low prices for these excellent dinners will be appreciated.

A selection of beers and house wines are available. Look for this small restaurant in the Dunes Shops. Take-out orders are given special care. Open all year, daily 11 a.m. to 10 p.m.

STATION SIX RESTAURANT

Rt. 158 Business, MP 4½   261-7337

Map, pg. 47

$$

This restaurant offers one of the prettiest ocean views of any on the Banks, and it's also attracting some pretty good reviews on its food. One of their specialties is veal — they have a nightly veal special. But they also feature fresh, local seafood, steaks, homemade soups and desserts, and salads.

One of the main attractions of this restaurant is its atmosphere. As its name implies, the Station Six Restaurant is located in a building that was once an old Coast Guard Station, built in the early 1900s. (The Wright Brothers sent their historic flight message from here.) The building has been totally renovated, adding on a large deck overlooking the ocean and creating a delightfully inviting interior. The mood here is quiet and nice, punctuated by vases of flowers and low lights.

In addition to the main dining, a bar and lounge services diners and those who just want to enjoy a drink in a calm atmosphere. Open 7 days a week during the season, Station Six serves lunch from 11:30 - 3:00 and dinner from 5:00 - 10:00.

AVALON PIER RESTAURANT

Rt. 158 Business, MP 6   441-3311

Map, pg. 47

$

You might not expect a pier restaurant to be one that would garner praise, but this one is different. Don't let the unpretentious setting fool you; it's not fancy but the food is fine. And, it has another claim to fame as well: it's open 24 hours a day, the only restaurant on the Outer Banks to do so.

Breakfast serves plenty of eggs, meat and toasts, but several items stand out. The freshly baked blueberry muffins and the large fresh fruit bowl are great ways to start the day. And the hash browns they offer are made with green peppers and onions — really tasty. Dinner features absolutely fresh seafood since they are about as close to just-caught fish as you can get. The specialty here is there "ownmade" crabcakes.

Apart from the food, another nice thing is the friendliness and courtesy of the waitpeople. You can tell they really are glad you came to their restaurant, and that does make a difference.

NEWBY'S SUB SHOP

Rt. 158 Bypass, MP 6   441-7277
$

Map, pg. 57

Newby's is a bright, cheerful place where young people dressed in bathing suits feel comfortable and rock 'n roll background music rules the day.

The menu centers around subs, sandwiches and pizza, all well prepared with fresh ingredients. There's a good selection of domestic and imported beers, and they seem to do a brisk business with their soft, frozen yogurt.

The late night hours — open 11 a.m. to 1 a.m. in season — keep Newby's a popular spot long after other restaurants have closed.

SPORTSMAN'S RESTAURANT

Rt. 158 Bypass, MP4   261-4600

Map, pg. 47

$

Al Van Curen "invented" the 99-cent breakfast and the all-you-can-eat entree concept on the Outer Banks resort strip. His past successes have been Miller's and the Dune's. Now Van Curen has beat the trend toward the north end of the beach with Sportsman's, a family-styled restaurant.

The design and exterior of the Sportsman's is like Van Curen's other mass feeding stations where function supersedes flash. You will forgive all, however, when you see the low prices.

Breakfast here starts at 5:45 a.m. for the fisherfolk. It's a complete menu with specials to enhance its appeal until 2 p.m.

Lunch features homemade soups and salads and an all-you-can-eat salad bar. Soft shelled crab and fish filet sandwiches, plus burgers are also offered.

For dinner there are build your own combination seafood platters, steaks, fried chicken, and locally available seafood prepared under the broiler.

The all-you-can-eat entrees are generally fried seafoods with the exception of the Steamed Spiced Shrimp. They include the salad bar and are served with hushpuppies and choice of potato.

Wine, beer and cocktails are available. No credit cards, but personal checks (even out of town ones) will be accepted with appropriate ID. Service until 9 p.m. Child's menu.

 *KILL DEVIL HILLS*

RESTAURANTS

KRAUSE'S STEAK HOUSE

Rt. 158 Bypass, MP 5   261-3132
                                 Map, pg. 57
$$

    This restaurant with its three flags flying sits astride the dividing line between Kitty Hawk and Kill Devil Hills and is thus convenient to the northend cottages. The family owned and operated business serves breakfast and dinner in a simple, home-like decor.
    The breakfast menu is complete and includes Poached Eggs, Steak & Eggs, and a "special" for about a dollar.
    The evening menu's main feature is a buffet with loads of seafood. There is also the traditional seafood fare plus grilled calf's liver, choice steaks, and chicken. A salad bar, and children's menu are also available. Dinner is served from 5:00 to 10:00, with late nighters able to order until 11:00 or so.
    House desserts made daily include apple and cherry pie, and Strawberry Short Cake in season.

SEAFARE III

158 Bypass, MP 5½   441-5554
                                 Map, pg. 57
$$

    Located within the Seagate North Shopping Center, the Seafare III has matured from a restaurant which catered to shoppers into a full service establishment.
    A Hot Luncheon Buffet is served daily from 11 a.m. until 2 p.m. and is a real value. Seafood entrees, sandwiches, and a salad bar are also available during these hours.
    Beginning at 5 p.m. the Seafare III reopens to offer a complete seafood, steak, and chicken menu. There are 14 seafood

specialties and six cuts of beef. Children under six are served free from 5 to 6 p.m.

There are 10 dessert specialties. The fresh apple, peach, and cherry pies rate being served hot with cheese. Cocktails and Almaden wines by the glass or carafe are from the Trophy Lounge. Dinners served until 10 p.m. in season. Lounge open until 2 a.m.

TOP OF THE DUNES

Rt. 158 Business, MP 6   441-7126

Map, pg. 57

$$

The Sea Ranch, although it is a Quality Inn, has always been more than just another motel. With a classy ladies boutique (Alice's Looking Glass), formal night club, indoor tennis center, and indoor pool, you might expect its restaurant to be something out of the ordinary, too. And the Top of the Dunes is!

The smart decor of the Top of the Dunes is more New York than Kill Devil Hills. Papered and mirrored walls, carpeting, and table settings reflect owner Alice Sykes' good taste. There are window tables with the ocean dunes just beyond, and two raised black leatherette booths at the back of the room that might be sought for intimate dining privacy.

The menu is snazzy, too. Escargots Bourginonne is among the appetizers, and Chateaubriand for two, or a Flaming Shish Kabob can be impressive. The traditional Outer Banks seafood is listed plus African Lobster Tail, Frog Legs Provencale, Seafood Kabob, and Surf and Turf combinations. The Fisherman's Dinner Salad with fresh steamed shrimp and backfin lump crabmeat is also popular.

There is a well chosen wine list in the moderate price range, plus a few bottles of Dom Perignon for big spenders. Bar service is from the large lounge located on a lower level.

Top of the Dunes continues to be very popular with local people for some reasons that make good "cents" to visitors as well. The elegant evening environment and service can be enjoyed at moderate menu prices. There are always evening entree specials to please the budget conscious. For lunch, Top of the Dunes has been able to keep its attractive specials in the $3 range. This policy wins friends and keeps them coming back.

Service begins early at Top of the Dunes with breakfast and continues throughout the day until the final dinners at 10 p.m. Open all year.

MIDGETT'S BARBEQUE

Rt. 158 Bypass, MP 6   441-5636

Map, pg. 57

$

While dining at the Mark Hopkins' Nob Hill Restaurant with all of San Francisco's great wine and cuisine on the table, our host suddenly reflected and said, "There is only one food in the world to equal this: North Carolina barbeque."

On the Outer Banks, one of the places for Carolina barbecue is at the sign of the pink pig in Kill Devil Hills. Carl and Edith Midgett have made this spot famous with locals for over ten years. There are only 36 seats, but that's okay because the take-out business is so active. Catering is also available.

Barbecue is carved or minced right off the smoke pork shoulder and served as a sandwich, a sub, or on a plate with cole slaw and beans. Save room for a slice of Edith's fresh made pie of the day.

Midgett's has a daily special hot plate that may be the best meal bargain on the Banks. Entrees like Roast Pork, Salisbury Steak, Lasagna, and Roast Beef are served with two side dishes. There are also about a dozen sub and sandwich items on the menu.

Hours here are 7 a.m. to 4:30 p.m. in-season. Till 3:30 off-season. Closed Sunday. No credit cards.

THE JOLLY ROGER

Rt. 158 Business, MP 7   441-6530

Map, pg. 57

$$

This small seaside spot has the look of an old fashioned tavern where guests arrive to share the fireplace and the company of their host. If the host were ever a pirate, he must have been an Italian one because that is the menu emphasis. The decor here is clever, and sometimes humorous. Outside, for example, a lobster in a trap sits on the roof with a gull perched on top. Inside, a bearded life-sized pirate guards the entrance to one of the two small dining rooms from his seat in a barber's chair.

The Italian specialties served at the Jolly Roger include Spaghetti with either meatsauce, meatballs, white clam sauce, or vegetarian sauce; Eggplant Parmesan, Veal Parmesan, Lasagna, Italian Sausage, and Pizza with five topping choices.

Garlic Bread can be ordered on the side.

Seafood is also served. Shrimp can be ordered fried, sauteed, or spiced, and Crab Imperial is the seafood specialty. Fried or broiled platters, fish, oysters, soft shell crabs (also available in a sub), crab, and scallops are on the menu. Two Delmonico beef cuts are served from the broiler. Childrens menu and take-outs, plus complete bar service with glass and carafe wines. For dieters, there is an all you can eat salad.

Open 5 p.m. to 10 p.m.

WHALING STATION

Rt. 158 Business, MP 7¼   441-6001
Map, pg. 57
$$

The Whaling Station gets a lot of local people into its 82-seat restaurant. The fare is traditional Outer Banks seafood with Fried Chicken, Chicken Livers, and New York Strips added for diversity.

There is a small separate bar area for friends who drop in. The simple, home style decor makes for a relaxing environment.

The owner welcomes families, provides a children's menu, and takes a personal interest in everything that comes out of his kitchen. When the big name places have long waiting lines, try the Whaling Station as a pleasant alternative. Dinner only except for Brunch on Sunday.

PAPAGAYO'S

Rt. 158 Business, MP 7½   441-7232
Map, pg. 57
$$

The Croatan Inn is a charming old Kill Devil Hills landmark that still provides oceanfront accommodations. It is a real surprise to discover Mexican decor and cuisine in this venerable old setting. Nevertheless, the basket covered lamps, festive table cloths and wall decorations, pine beamed ceiling, and the lighted beach beyond the windows remind one of the Baja coast of Mexico, rather than the Outer Banks.

The food does not disappoint. Mexican favorites like

Enchiladas, Tacos, Burritos, and Tostadas have fresh ingredients and are served with style. The Tortilla Chips and Guacamole are made fresh daily. There are both hot and mild Mexican dishes, plus traditional Outer Banks seafood.

The La Cantina oceanfront bar and deck features frozen drinks, Margaritas and Sangria by the glass or pitcher and excellent Mexican beers. The coffee selection and desserts (Key Lime Pie, Bunuelo Relleno, and Sopaipillar) also show flare.

This is a fun place with a lot of color. The original Papagayo is in Chapel Hill, and the experience shows in the operation of the location here. Service begins at 5:30 p.m.; meals until 10 p.m.; bar service until 2 a.m.

PORT O'CALL

Rt. 158 Business, MP 8½   441-7484
            Map, pg. 57
$$$

If you have gourmet tastes, you will welcome an introduction to the Port O'Call. For 20 years this restaurant has been a Banks favorite, and since the mid 1970's Frank Gajar's skilled management has set the pace for sophisticated dining in the area. The Mobil Travel Guide rates Port O' Call at three stars.

This is a large, 250 seat, elegantly decorated restaurant where greenery, candlelight, tablewear, and nappery set the stage for the cuisine which arrives from the kitchen. Many tables in the cathedral ceiling main dining room look out to a formal garden.

In 1982, a major addition was added to the entrance area of the restaurant. Now patrons can enjoy three galleries filled with framed art, glass, and brass artifacts before and after dinner.

Another major addition was completed in 1983. It is the 150-seat, two-story Gaslight Saloon. The Victorian styled lounge features live music for dancing daily in-season.

The Port O' Call menu reflects a continental cuisine influence. Coquille St. Jacques, Trout Meuniere, Seafood Crepes Veronique, Bouillabaisse, Roast Duck a L'Orange, Veal Oscar, and Veal and Eggplant Piccata are examples. The soups (including an inspired real French Onion soup) the salads (artfully prepared and enhanced with an excellent house dressing) and the appetizers (Clams Casino, Oysters Rockefeller) all demonstrate the concern of this kitchen for excellence. The service staff stays together season after season and their good training shows, too.

Earlybird Specials are offered between 5:30 p.m. and 6:30 to encourage non peak hour dining. The Sunday Brunch Buffet (9:30 a.m. to 1:30 p.m.) serves up Eggs Benedict and whole table of savory delicacies.

The adult bar specializes in frozen Daiquiris and Coladas, and also mixes up imaginative non-alcoholic cocktails like the Space Shuttle Sling, the Dreamsicle, and the Virgin Colada for kids who want a change from Shirley Temples. Piano entertainment for dining background is provided five nights a week.

Dinner from 5 to 10 p.m. Reservations only for large parties.

JK'S

Rt. 158 Bypass, MP 8.5   441-3021

Map, pg. 57

$$-$$$

Grilling seafood, chicken, beef, and lamb over a mesquite wood fire is the national restaurant trend of the 1980s. J.K. Norfleet has captured the attention, and taste buds, of Outer Banks diners, offering mesquite cooking in a simple, relaxed 80-seat restaurant.

Everything, except side dishes like sauteed mushrooms and the fresh vegetable of the day, is done on the mesquite grill. A long, narrow window allows patrons to witness the cooking without feeling the heat, or absorbing the smoke.

It's the Texas grown mesquite wood smoke that imparts the unique flavor to meats as diverse as pork loin, steaks, lamb, ribs (pork or veal) and chicken. J.K.'s also grills salmon, swordfish, grouper, shrimp, and other seafoods locally available. The grilled Fresh Fish of the Day is always a good bet. The clam chowder they serve for an appetiser is some of the best we've tasted anywhere.

J.K.'s has a full service bar and a very attractive covered porch that make waiting for a table or lounging before dinner a treat. The wine list is worth seeing. Whoever put it together has an eclectic palate for small California wineries, and a sense for what compliments the mesquite. Plates for children and take out are also available.

Until all the mesquite in Texas is gone, the taste for this bit of cooking magic will sweep the country. Get it while it's hot!

STACK 'EM HIGH

158 Bypass, MP 9　　　　　　　　　　　　　　　　441-7064
$
　　　　　　　　　　Map, pg. 57

The official name of this breakfast spot is Stack 'Em High, Pancakes and So Forth. It was begun in June of 1981 by Kiki and Perry Kiousis, and you will note that the Greek national flag flies alongside the stars and stripes at the head of the ample parking lot.

Service begins at 7 a.m. as patrons move along a cafeteria-like line to pick up juices, fruits, beverages and utencils. Food orders are given, a numbered placque placed on your tray, and the hot food delivered to your table. Extra refills of coffee are free.

Special recipe Buttermilk Pancakes are the specialty: Short Stacks of three, and High Stacks of five. Short Stacks can also be ordered in other varieties such as blueberry, strawberry, pecan, apple, etc. Bagels, Blueberry Muffins, English Muffins, Danish, and Cereals are also available, as are the traditional eggs as you

CAPT'N DAVE'S

Rt. 158 Bypass, MP 9　　　　　　　　　　　　　　441-7303
　　　　　　　　　　Map, pg. 57
$$

Capt'n Dave's has been popular with families since 1977. It is a casual, cheerful, nautical theme restaurant where you can eat-in or take-out breakfast and dinner seven days a week in season.

A full service breakfast menu is available from 7 a.m. Dinners are served from 5 to 9 p.m.

The selections range from burgers and hot dogs to chicken, crab cakes, fried clams, shrimp, and steaks. Appetizers include soup n' salad, and steamed shrimp. Dessert Specialties are Key Lime Pie and fresh fruit cobblers.

Portions at Capt'n Dave's are generous, and special care is given to packaging the take-outs.

MADELINE'S

Rt. 158 Business, MP 9.5   441-6333

Map, pg. 57

$$

   Madeline's is the restaurant and lounge at the Holiday Inn. The 80-seat restaurant and 70-seat lounge came into being in the complete refurbishment of the Inn in 1983.

   The theme of Madeline's is a recreation of the 1920s in spirit and decor. The pass word, they say, at this speakeasy, is "fun." The truly hip will recognize the Tin Lizzie, the Black Bottom, and waistcoats.

   In the restaurant area, Madeline's has two moods. On the lighter side, she is Chicken Sticks, Potato Skins, Nachos, Steamed Shrimp, Beach Burgers, Monte Cristos, French Dips, and Original NC B.B.Q. The spiritual side of this mood (pardon the pun) is advertised as "better than bathtub gin." It includes nine specialty drinks with such names as 1st Flight Fruit Fantasia, Jockey Ridge Sling, Lost Colony, and Duck Blind. In reality they are a collection of untamed daiquiri and colada creations.

   For more serious appetitic moods, Madeline's has Sirloin, Steak and Seafood Kabobs, Beef Ribs, and traditional Outer Banks seafoods like Shrimp, Scallops, Fried Oysters, and Fresh Catch of the Day. There are also serious soups (She Crab, Clam Chowder), salads (Spinach in particular), and desserts (Fried Ice Cream, Hot Fudge Chocolate Cookie).

   After a ten-year flight as a themeless, unimaginative eatery and bar, the Holiday Inn has rocketed into a new age with Madeline's. The creative menu and decor is welcomed and appreciated Madeline's has live entertainment for dancing from 9 p.m. to 1 a.m. Mon-Sat.

ETHERIDGE SEAFOOD RESTAURANT

Rt. 158 Bypass, MP 9½   441-2645

$$ Map, pg. 57

   The Etheridge family name has been associated with good, fresh seafood on the Banks for just about as long as there have been people coming here. Now, to everyone's good luck, they've opened a restaurant to show off some of that seafood they get off their boats. The menu here offers a large variety of seafood dishes, all named after someone who works there or a family member; dishes like Mama Etheridge's Famous Fish Cakes and

Mermaid Jen's Seafood Shish Kebob. There are over 25 main seafood meals offered, not to mention the appetisers and beef dishes. They offer a good sized children's menu with non-seafood meals for the finicky eaters. And, after you've eaten yourself silly on the seafood, they even offer you low-cal desserts.

This really is a good restaurant and a welcomed addition to the 1986 dining out choices. During season, lunch is served from noon to 3:00 p.m. Dinner is served from 4:00 to 11:00.

PEPPERCORNS

Rt. 158 Business, MP 9 1/2   441-2151
Map, pg. 57
$$$

Peppercorns is located in the new Ramada Inn on the second floor. The decor is quiet and tasteful, decorated in deep greens, mauves, and pinks with lots of greenery and large windows that give it an open airy feeling. One of the most spectacular things about the restaurant is the panoramic ocean view you can enjoy while dining. The dune line is lighted and the view is so clear you feel as if your table is right on the beach.

Breakfast, lunch, and dinner are served and you can enjoy light fare - Continental breakfasts in the morning and burgers, sandwiches, and salads for lunch and dinner - on the spacious, oceanfront deck.

The dinner menu includes specialties such as Seabreeze Scallops, sauteed scallops with a hint of rósemary served on top of spinach fettuccine, Sauteed Ginger Chicken and Steak au Poivre. The ingredients used are obviously fresh and the meals are presented well, with obvious care taken in their preparation. A wine list with a nice assortment of imports is available.

Peppercorns is open year round from 7:00 a.m. until 10:00 p.m.

THE FISH MARKET

Rt. 158 Bypass, MP 9½   441-7889
Map, pg. 57
$$

This neat spot has a lot of vitality and became immediately popular after it opened in the 1981 season. The focus of the room is the oyster bar where a pretty young woman with a glove and oyster knife may be opening the bivalves like a pro. Clams and steamed shrimp also get passed over this bar as well as mixed drinks, wine and cold beer served in frosted mugs.

The menu is small and has a seafood emphasis. There are also daily luncheon specials, good soups, and sandwiches. All are well prepared and are good values. The Clam Chowder is highly regarded.

Open all year from 11:30 a.m. till 9 p.m. for meals.

MILLER'S SEAFOOD & STEAK HOUSE

Rt. 158 Business, MP 9½   441-7674
Map, pg. 57
$$

Eddie and Lou Miller remodeled, enlarged and otherwise transformed this location across from the Holiday Inn into a modern, successful 310 seat restaurant in 1981. They have positioned themselves for the family trade, and their Every Day Specials of Ham Steak, Beef tips, Ground Round, and Fried Chicken have scored with folks on a budget. A children's menu is also moderately priced.

Miller's offers complete bar service, and its broiled, fried, and sauteed seafood selections are always fresh and plentiful. A cheese crock, salad, choice of potato, and house breads come with all entrees.

Clam Strips and Fried Fish of the Day are offered as "all you can eat" items. Among the beef selections are two cuts of Prime Rib, or Delmonicos, a Filet Mignon, a Beef Kabob, and a Surf & Turf Combination.

Desserts here are made in the house. Try the Strawberry Supreme in season.

Miller's has a large parking lot and is adjacent to the Sea Holly Square Shopping Center.

STARKEY'S PIZZA

158 Bypass, MP 9.7   441-5070
Outer Banks Mall   441-3511
Map, pg. 57
$

This regional chain began as Milton's Pizza. As Starkey's (the new owner's name), the decor has changed a bit, but the pizza is as good, or better, than before in this 60-seat spot in the center of the resort strip.

But Starkey's is more than pizza. There is Spaghetti, Lasagna, Manicotti, Ravioli, Stuffed Shells, Subs, Sandwiches, Garlic Bread, and a salad bar. The taste may not be the equal of your favorite Italian restaurant at home, but the food quality is good and the price is even better. It's one of the places that we like to feed the family when our wallet needs a break.

For kids 12 and under, there is a special menu. A selection of beers and carafe wines are ready for the adults. Call ahead for carry-out service. Plenty of parking, and a waiting area out of the sun are other reasons why we like Starkey's.

EVANS' CRAB HOUSE

Rt. 158 Bypass, MP 10   441-5994
$-$$ Map, pg. 57

It is very easy to be enthusiastic about family dining at Evans' Crabhouse. The menu is varied, the preparations fresh and skillful, the portions generous, the service efficient and warm, and the prices excellent in value. The two large dining rooms seat 275 persons. Parties up to ten can be seated at family-sized tables. The fact that Cashar Evans has 15 highchairs available says something about the welcome he extends to children. There are even crayons for the little ones to color the white butcher paper that covers your table. Your server will sign his or her own name on the table as a way of welcome and introduction.

Everything on the menu at Evans' can be prepared for take-out. There is a side door and counter to keep this trade from disturbing the diners. Many entrees are available in child's portions. You can even buy a single steamed crab for the little one who wants a discovery experience.

Now, about the food. Try either of the Crab Soups. One has a spicy vegetable base, and the other is creamy rich. Both are full of beautiful crab meat. The Hot Spiced Steamed Crabs are a specialty. Spread 'em on the paper tabletop and have a feast. Your server will show you the techniques if you are a novice. Don't be afraid to become a crabpicker. It's food and therapy at the same time.

Crabs, of course, can be had as Crab Cakes, as Soft Shells, lump meat as a Cocktail, in a Crab Salad, and even sauteed with

Country Ham (another specialty). If you love that fiesty pinching crustation, Evans' is your crab heaven.

The Evans' menu is a large one. Clams on the half shell, or steamed, Jumbo Steamed Spiced Shrimp, Fried Chicken, and nearly 25 platters are offered. There are also steaks and sandwiches, and homemade desserts. Try anything that Evans' does with strawberries in season and you won't be disappointed. Beers, and a wine list that compliments the menu complete the meal.

The Evans' family enjoys a proud restaurant tradition. Their Fenwick Crab House in Fenwick Island, Delaware adjacent to the lighthouse, and the Mason-Dixon Line, is also highly rated. The Kill Devil Hills restaurant is generally open only for dinner during the resort season. To keep prices low, no credit cards are accepted.

SANDS FAMILY RESTAURANT

Rt. 158 Bypass, Mp 10½   441-1649
Map, pg. 57
$$

The name of this restaurant is descriptive of its offerings: it's a family oriented spot where little ones and corresponding parents can feel comfortable. Meals are simple with lots of fried seafood dishes. There are also selections such as liver with onions, barbeque, and fried chicken. Steaks round out the menu for the adults. The children's menu includes fried chicken, hamburger and fish.

Breakfast and lunch are also offered here with service starting at 7:00 a.m. and continuing until 10:00 p.m.

NAGS HEAD NORTH
RESTAURANTS

SWEETWATERS

Rt. 158 Bypass, MP 10   441-3020

Map, pg. 70

$$

A mixture of polished wood, brass, stained glass and plants helps to create the inviting atmosphere of this restaurant/nightspot in Nags Head.

Lunch at Sweetwaters features gourmet burgers, large deli sandwiches, and specials such as quiche. Dinner offers fresh seafood and steaks. There's also a full-service bar featuring every drink you can think of (and probably a few you can't!)

The mood here is casual and fun. The doors open at 11:30 a.m. and close at 1:30 a.m.

THE CAROLINIAN

Rt. 158 Business, MP 10.5   441-3615

Map, pg. 70

$$

Milton Warren, of Ice House fame in Virginia Beach, is at the helm of the Carolinian Restaurant now. The 70-seat room has always been charming enough with knotted pine paneling, oil lamps, and unusual hand-hune wooden chairs, and now, with Warren's experience, it's expected that the food will be equally appealing.

There's variety on the menu to please most any diners. Fresh seafood is, of course, a mainstay, but rack of lamb, veal, and beef entrees are also popular. All meals were served with fresh vegetables. Though we were too full to try them, the freshly made desserts looked very well prepared. Dinner is served at the Carolinian from 5 p.m. until 11 p.m. each evening. Mr. Warren does recommend that you make reservations during the busy summer season.

KELLY'S RESTAURANT AND TAVERN

Rt. 158 Bypass, MP 10½   441-4116

Map, pg. 70

$$

Anyone who has spent much time on the Outer Banks probably will recognize the name Mike Kelly. He's well-known in these parts for his expertise in the food business and that certainly shows in this "new" place of his. Kelly took over the building that once housed Munde's restaurant with its unusual interior, and did a rather extensive refurbishing of the interior. Now, as you enter the building, you're greeted by an attractive combination of wood, brass, greenery, and stained glass. Dinner is served either in the main dining room or upstairs in one of the several balcony like areas.

The food is as attractive as the building, and nicely varied. Kelly's offers plenty of well-prepared seafood dishes, but also includes chicken, beef, and pasta meals. There's also a raw bar selection of steamed or raw oysters, clams or mussels.

The large lounge at Kelly's is popular with the singles set. The huge horseshoe shaped bar, the big screen TV, and the multi leveled live entertainment area packs them in on weekends and on Monday night for the football games.

Dinner is served from 5 to 10 p.m. and entertainment and drink service until 2 a.m.

SINBAD'S

Rt. 158 Business, Mp 11   441-6727

Map, pg. 70

$$

Unless you are shopping at the Galleon Esplanade at mealtime, you might miss this chic spot off its main courtyard. Like all the shops in the Galleon, its restaurant shows a flair for design. The decor and lush plantings transport patrons to a setting which seems appropriate for the film Casablanca.

Soups are a specialty of the house, and are served in a 10 oz. mug. A blackboard announces the two daily selections which change from an inspired list of 24. Black Bean, Peanut, Asparagus, Gazpacho, Cucumber, and Pumpkin are on the list.

Salads here also get major billing. The Chicken Salad Madras with cashews, pineapple, green grapes, and a touch of curried mayonnaise, the Tabouli, and the Avocado stuffed with seasoned crabmeat or shrimp, all wake up the taste buds, and are delightfully presented.

As you might expect, the sandwiches are imaginative too. Four pocket bread selections, including a vegetarian Garden Sandwich, and two interesting open-faced sandwiches, a Turkey, Swiss & Avocado, and a Crabacado (crabmeat, avocado, and tomato slices on a vienna roll) illustrate the point. Special entrees, beverages, sandwiches, salads, and desserts not listed on the menu appear on the blackboard. The kitchen is always looking for new taste treats utilizing natural seasonal ingredients.

Sandwiches and salads are served daily from 11 a.m. to 5 p.m., and then again from 9 p.m. to midnight. Dinner specialties are offered from 5 p.m. to 9. The luncheon menu is available for take-out. Full bar service. Reservations accepted.

A RESTAURANT, BY GEORGE

Rt. 158 Business, MP 11   441-4821
                      Map, pg. 70

$$$

By its architectural design, exotic decor and appointments, service and menu, A Restaurant, By George remains one of the class dining spots on the Banks.

Adjacent to The Galleon Esplanade the restuarant is worthy of a tour as an attraction on its own merit.

Although the atmosphere is relaxed, the quality stemware, china, plush carpeting, fanback chairs, patch Madras table cloths, waiters in full safari gear, and individual, uniquely designed dining areas speak of style and elegance.

The lounge area was greatly expanded by new construction when liquor by the drink came to Nags Head, and is a most ambient watering hole. Living room styled conversation areas, special lighting effects, and lush greenery add to the total environment. A polished wooden staircase leads to a second lounge level where nooks for intimate tete-a-tete abound. And then on a third level is a unique lounging cupola with an exciting star burst lighting fixture. Take a peek at this! There is often entertainment on the beautiful grand piano in the lounge.

The dining rooms at A Restaurant, By George have names like The Windmill Room, The Cave, The Knitch, and The Celebrity Room. Each has its own personality and patrons. Total seating is about 175. Look for items on the menu that change with the availability of fresh foods or the chef's preference. These usually distinctive offerings are explained by your waiter. A relish bowl presentation, tempting breads, and a gourmet's wine list are also proffered.

A Restaurant, By George shows its flair in almost every one of its entrees. It does not attempt an exhaustive list, but carefully selects beef, fowl, and fresh seafood items that can consistently please its patrons. The filet Mignon Bearnaise, Steak Marchand De Vin, and the Bay Mornay (selected seafoods in a mild cheese and beer sauce) are examples of the continental style of the kitchen. Elaborate desserts, and special coffees brewed at the table in a Cona glass device add to the dramatic close of your candlelight dinner here. In season, dinners are served as late as midnight.

PLANTATION RESTAURANT

Rt. 158 Bypass, MP 11   441-5917
$$ Map, pg. 70

The two-story Colonial styled building resembles a plantation great house. The interior, divided into two dining rooms on the first floor, has the feel of a country inn. The restaurant is actually small despite its imposing facade. The second level of the building provides a residence for its owners.

Breakfast and dinner are served in the informal atmosphere of the Plantation. The emphasis is on "country cooking." Breakfast is served from eight until noon on the weekends; dinner from 5 to 9 p.m. daily.

Dinner here might begin with the Blue Crab Soup, or the Clam Chowder. Cajun Shrimp, marinated and broiled in a house herb sauce, and the Plantation Special of sauteed shrimp and scallops are very appealing. The seafood menu is not extensive, but will please most appetites.

The "country cooking" selections include Country Style Steak, Fried Chicken, Breaded Veal Cutlets, and daily specials. All these items are in the economy price range. Rib Eye steaks, fresh vegetables, three children's selections, ice cream sundaes, and house breads and desserts complete the fare.

The Plantation is proud of its own recipe Bloody Mary, and suggests a Cocoa-Mint (hot cocoa and peppermint schnapps) for after dinner.

FISHTAILS

Rt. 158 Bypass, MP 11.5   441-3001
                        Map, pg. 70
$$

The tattered lighthouse at the Pirate's Quay shopping center is Fishtails, which opened for the 1984 season. Don't let the trendy decor and the singles rush to its popular upstairs disco mislead you; satisfying food is served here.

Conch, usually seen around the Florida Keys, is offered here in fritters and in chowder. It is perhaps the only concession to the freezer. Everything else appears fresh and well prepared.

Salads show variety and care, and there are daily specials which are always a good value. The Seafood Quiche is well conceived and satisfies as a main meal. The menu may be limited in number, but the offerings among the sandwiches, burgers, seafood, steaks, and a Hawaiian Chicken are balanced. Fresh Broccoli, Marinated Mushrooms, and Fried Zucchini can be added from the a la carte section.

Fishtails has about 65 seats in a comtemporary decor of hardwood paneling, mirrors, and bay windows. Walls are accented with large nautical prints. The central oblong bar has six specialty drinks of the Fog Cutter variety, plus "mocktails" for those who like the flavor without the kick. Service from noon to 10 p.m.

GANDALF & CO.

Rt. 158 Business, MP 11.5   441-4773
                        Map, pg. 70
$-$$

Bob and Jan Kannry took a page out of Tolkien's fantasy in creating their seashore cafe. The 40-seat cool and cozy interior, and the screened porch, offer real food plus what a cafe is all about: interaction with the owners-operators. Here's a place where conversation is encouraged, where jazz for listening plays in the background, and where good wines by the glass are poured from the bottle.

The menu is filled with creative soups, salads, and sandwiches as well as pasta dishes, fresh seafood, and nightly specials. Regulars will recommend the Italian Wedding Soup, Fresh Dolphin Salad, as well as the classic Monte Cristo sandwich. Quiches are special here and change almost daily. The coffee is fresh ground.

All the sandwiches and char-broiled burgers are served with fresh fruit and a choice of fresh breads and cheeses.

Gandalf's is a happy gathering place for the artsy-craftsy as well as for people who want to feed their children something nutritious and appealing.

Oh, don't forget the desserts. They change daily. And when Jan or Bob make a Chocolate Mousse, or anything else, you can count on it being a made-from-scratch original.

Opened in April of 1984, Bob and Jan are already making Gandalf smile. Breakfast, lunch and dinner service from 7 a.m. to around midnight.

# NAGS HEAD SOUTH
RESTAURANTS

THE ELEGANT PELICAN

Rt. 158 Business, MP 16 441-2637
Map, pg. 80
$$-$$$

For vacationers who feel they have a truly refined palate, we suggest you try this new Nags Head restaurant at least once while you're in the area. It specializes in Continental cuisine made with a flair that only comes from a chef who is very sure of himself in the kitchen. In this case that's Arthur Sturges, also known as Capt. Cheesecake (one guess what their prized dessert is). He is one of only 10 chefs in the country to have earned the "Chaine des Rotisseur" rating.

You won't find fried fish on this menu. But, what you will find are dishes that make your mouth water in their uniqueness: Tournedoes of Beef Oscar, Pork Dijon, Baked Stuffed Shrimp, Crispy Roast Duck, Veal Marsala... see what we mean? It's all very well prepared and presented. Appetizers, too, are special. They serve Oysters Rockefeller, Escargot, Pate Maison (a blend of pork, veal, and duck liver, laced with cognac and served with a cumberland sauce.

Sauces are highlighted here, as are fresh herbs and other fresh ingredients. Capt. Cheesecake learned a lot of his expertise from the famous Chef Tell.

A beaded board atmosphere is elegant yet very comfortable and every table has a panoramic view of the sound. The bar area contains interesting old paintings as well as an antique fish from the 9th Street Fish Market in New York City. Throughout the restaurant, collections of dolls, handmade toys, and shells create interesting conversation pieces.

The Elegant Pelican is open March to mid December and serves from 5:30 p.m. until 10:00 p.m.

DAREOLINA COVE RESTAURANT

Rt. 158 Business, MP 16 441-7477
$$ Map, pg. 80

The nautical decor of this well-appointed restaurant adjacent to the Sea Oatel takes you aboard a ship of the line. Huge wood beams in the Galleon Room make you feel as if you are below decks. The larger Harbour Room has an unobstructed six window view of the beach and the ocean beyond. A separate cocktail lounge off the entrance is a pleasant distraction while you await your table.

Breakfast, lunch, and dinner are served by an efficient, friendly staff. The breakfast (7-11:30) menu is complete with a Carolina accent which includes biscuits, grits, redeye gravy, and a pot of coffee for each table.

Lunch (11-4) is a soup, hot sandwich, all-you-can-eat 40-item salad bar, and inexpensive fried seafood platter affair. Lunch here amid the rich atmosphere adds to the menu bargains.

For dinner, the Cove remains a moderately priced place to dine, and the candlelight gives the rooms new character. The menu is varied enough for everyone. The children are remembered with a special list. Prime Rib is a specialty, and the steaks are also recommended. Five Shore Dinners are popular with families on a budget, and include Ham Steak, Southern Fried Chicken, and Turkey.

Ernest's Outer Banks Clam Chowder is the clear broth soup so prized by Nags Head natives. The She Crab Soup is a delicacy which is special to crab lovers. The hot seafood entrees can be fried or broiled, and come with a cheese crock, choice of potato, the extensive salad bar, home baked bread, and hushpuppies. Crabmeat Norfolk over rice, and the Stuffed Flounder Almondine are presented with style.

The Dareolina Cove is near Whalebone Junction amid a concentration of restaurants and other resort attractions. Although it has a large parking lot, its popularity dictates that you dine early or late to avoid the crowds.

MILLER'S WATERFRONT RESTAURANT

Rt. 158 Bypass, MP 16 441-5161
$$ Map, pg. 80

This soundside restaurant was established during the 1981 season, and has a loyal following. The frame building stands alone amid the sea grass which grows to the edge of Roanoke Sound. An outdoor wooden deck has two levels and is screened in to allow for enjoyable outdoor dining or drinks. The westward view of sunsets is both romantic and memorable.

The tasteful interior is done in dark woods, and nautical accents prevail. A rowboat serves as a Raw Bar and displays a boatload of fresh spiced steamed shrimp, as well as oysters and clams on the half shell. Note the huge Blue Marlin mounted behind the rowboat.

Dinner entrees at the Miller's Waterfront Restaurant feature native fish, crab, shrimp, and lobster. Variety plates offer combinations of your favorite seafoods broiled, stuffed, and even on Kabob. The kitchen is under the personal supervision of Eddie Miller, the owner, who is very consciencious in maintaining quality standards. The work of another owner, photographer Paul Underwood, can be seen on the walls, and in an evening slide show which animates the bar and lounge with images of the Outer Banks.

For beef eaters, there is Prime Rib. A Steak and Lobster entree covers the undecided. There is also a childrens menu.

THE DUNES

Rt. 158 Bypass, MP 16½   441-9953
$ Map, pg. 80

This attractive, modern restaurant not far from Whalebone Junction specializes in breakfast and brunch service. Early risers can arrive at 5 a.m. in season, 6 a.m. off season, and find the coffee hot and the cooks ready. Eggs the way you like them are served with plenty of hash browned potatoes, or grits, and hot cakes or toast. Bacon, sausage, or ham can be placed on the side. Prices for an abundant breakfast served on a huge rectangular white plate are reasonable.

Specials include Steak and Eggs, Fish Row and Eggs, and Country Ham and Eggs, all served with the trimmings. Omelettes are well made, and you can make combinations of your choice from seven ingredients. There is also a special crab omelette. Of course there are cereals, french toast, fruits, and other traditional breakfast foods.

The large dining rooms are modern in decor, and are sun bright from the many windows. There is plenty of on-site parking.

Meals here come out quick, hot, and done to order. Portions are generous, so you won't go away hungry. Food service ends at 2 p.m. in season, and at 1 p.m. off season.

234 — RESTAURANTS

An Outer Banks Tradition For 40 Years

At Sam & Omies, you'll find all-year-long specials like:

Breakfast Special (includes coffee!) $1.50
Tuesday Nights...all the Spaghetti you can eat $3.75
Thursday Nights...Prime Rib $6.95
Every Weekend...a Seafood Special .... Ask For Details

But our everyday fare is pretty special too!

Come find out for yourself why we're the local's favorite restaurant.

Never closed except Christmas week and Thanksgiving

SAM & OMIE'S

Rt. 158 Bypass at Whalebone Junction   441-7366
$-$$

Map, pg. 80

Sam & Omie's has been a Nags Head institution for over 30 years. Although the originators of this weather-beaten retreat have been long gone, no one would dare to change the name. Fishermen from the pier across the highway and locals still consider Sam & Omie's their place to hangout for year round breakfasts, lunches and dinners.

The inside is a large L-shaped room built around a full service bar. There are four booths along the walls and about eight tables for service away from the bar. The light pine walls, and the cane back chairs soften the bar room atmosphere.

The food here is good and plentiful. Salads have variety, sandwiches have substance, and the seafood fare is priced below fancier nearby places.

Two sisters, Judy and Jakey Waits have carried on the Sam & Omie's tradition for over 15 years. The 125 seat restaurant is open 7 a.m. to 11 p.m. year round, though hours sometimes wind up a little earlier in the winter.

Many patrons here are in jeans and shorts, and the conversations are animated with laughter. The official Sam & Omie's T-shirt says it all: "Everyone should believe in something. I believe I'll go fishing."

OWENS'

Rt. 158 Business, MP 16½   441-7309
$$$

Map, pg. 80

Established in 1946, and at the same location for over 30 years, Owens' has been the most consistant quality restaurant in Outer Banks history. Many patrons return year after year, and have seen succeeding generations of Owens family members take their turns as host.

Owens' took advantage of the coming of liquor-by-the-drink in 1981 to completely remodel their existing establishment, and to add new construction. The "new" included a swank second floor Station Keepers Lounge which has the look of polished light woods, brass, and Tiffany styled glass. The entrance to the restaurant is through the Life Saving Station off the well lighted parking lot. A large staircase leads to the lounge which serves frozen specialties, mixed drinks, beer, and wine until midnight. Entertainment is provided by a performer on a baby grand piano.

The Owens' reputation is built on its seafood preparations. Its fried or broiled Seafood Platter has set the standard for this entree up and down the Outer Banks. The house specialties are Crabmeat Remick, lump crabmeat in a special sauce topped with cheese and served in a true scallop shell, Seafood Lobster Bisque, lobster chunks in a sauce of butter, sherry, tomatoes, and lump crabmeat, and Seafood Gumbo, a New Orleans style dish with four seafruits and fresh vegetables.

All the dinner entrees here are served with a cheese crock, salad, choice of potato, daily fresh vegetable, cornmeal hushpuppies, house baked bread loaf, and tea or coffee. There are many combinations to be made from the fresh seafoods and they can be prepared either fried or broiled. Children's dinners are also served.

Owens' also offers prime beef in five cuts, plus a **Flaming Kabob**. A Chicken Cordon Bleu, Ham Steak, Fried Chicken (Miss O's Golden Fried Boneless Breast of Chicken), and Lobster Tail are served for variety. Dinner hours are 5 to 10 p.m.

WINDMILL POINT

Rt. 158 Bypass, MP 16 1/2 441-1535

$$

Map, pg. 80

The Windmill Point Restaurant is found right on the sound in an area where nothing spoils the incredible view of the water. Along with the view, the atmosphere of the restaurant, built around artifacts and memorabilia from the S.S. United States, makes you feel that you could be on a luxury liner enjoying a fine meal.

The password here seems to be variety. Seafood items abound, but so do dishes like Cordon Bleu, Outer Banks Bar-B-Que Ribs, Seafood Quiche, and Canneloni Florentine. There literally is something to satisfy everyone, no matter what they're in the mood for. Most meals are served with salads, red potatoes, vegetables, and rolls. The restaurant also serves a seafood buffet that is very popular.

Upstairs, in the lounge area, several interesting artifacts from the S.S. United States stand out. The most prominent is the kidney-shaped bar that was found on the Promenade deck of the luxury ocean liner. Specialty drinks, Rum Runner, Nutty Irishman, and Bay Breeze among them, are featured.

Lunch is served as well and features lots of sandwiches, served with chips, and Italian dishes.

Service begins at 11:30 and continues until 10:00 p.m., Sunday through Thursday. On Friday and Saturday, meals are served from 11 a.m. until 11 p.m.

R.V.'S

Roanoke Island Causeway 441-4963
$-$$

Map, pg. 80

R.V. Owens, of the Owens Restaurant family, is the host and owner of this very popular restaurant.

R.V.'s is a soundside watering hole built high on stilts. Its handicap ramp looks long enough to be the flume ride line at Disney World. The style of R.V.'s is contemporary. Inside service is at the long bar, or in two raised areas with tables. Meals and drinks can also be taken on the screened back deck where the sound sunsets are on majestic evening display.

Popular with locals and singles, R.V.'s can be packed on the weekends with a noisy crew of charter boat people, sports fans, and visiting singles attracted by the action.

Lunch fare here includes Spinach Salad, Crabcake and Softshell Crab sandwiches, Potato Skins, Quiche, homemade Shrimp Salad, and Nachos. Desserts are delivered from a home kitchen. Try the Milky Way Cake if available.

R.V's has daily specials. If the Bar-be-cue Ribs are offered, order them! Other specials include Popcorn Shrimp, and seasonal fish catches, like Dolphin, that are supplied by R.V.'s charter boat friends.

Lunch begins at 11:30 a.m.; dinner at 5 p.m.; drinks until.

TALE OF THE WHALE

Roanoke Island Causeway 441-7332
$$

Map, pg. 80

Don and Carole Bibey host this popular causeway restaurant that overlooks the Roanoke Sound. An outside deck extends pier-like into the water and provides a romantic champagne and moonlight setting for the young at heart. Drink service is available from the Moby Deck Lounge.

Tale of the Whale is a modern wooden structure raised above potential storm tides by stilts. There are many window tables with water views. House specialties have changed over six seasons of opeation. Look for Seafood Crepes, Shrimp Kebob, Crab Meat and Shrimp Au Gratin, and Tenderloin Tips Saute.

The menu is extensive and includes all your seafood favorites, both fried and broiled, plus Prime Rib, Steaks, Fried Chicken, and four children's plates (including pizza!). A large salad bar is a part of your meal.

The Wanchese Style Clam Chowder, and the Peanut Pie (Carole will give you the recipe) should be sampled by at least one person at your table. The wine list here is also worth a special look. Service begins at 5 p.m. Thursday thru Sunday during April and May, and daily June thru September.

DANIELS' SEAFOOD RESTAURANT

Roanoke Island Causeway 441-5405
$$
Map, pg. 80

Daniels' was once a small unpretentious spot that received raves for its clam chowder, crab cakes, and hush puppies. House Beautiful Magazine even took notice, although the premisis were not plush. Then, several changes in ownership and a complete makeover of the building occurred. Cottage renters who had depended on Daniels' for no frills, and plenty of good food at reasonable prices probably feared that the new architecture, the broad porches equipped with rocking chairs overlooking the sound, and the cocktail bar meant that something terribly commercial had happened to their old mainstay. They had nothing to fear.

Although Daniels' has 150 seats now, and the booths along the back expanse of windows with the view of the sound that makes it appear that you are dining aboard a ship get snapped up, oh yes, and you can take a cocktail on the soundside porch if you want to... Daniels is still catering to families, and the same proven menu and friendly service still greets guests.

Seafood platters can come fried or broiled; the oyster and shrimp boats, and the open face sandwiches are still in demand, and a Child's Plate can still be had in eight combinations. Open for lunch and dinner. Sorry, no credit cards, or reservations.

THE DOCK

Roanoke Island Causeway   441-4077
$$

Map, pg. 80

Warren Jones, a former banking executive, and his wife, Sara, renamed and redecorated this prime restaurant location beside the Melvin R. Daniels Bridge on the Causeway to Manteo in 1981.

From one of the many soundfront tables (there really is a spectacular view!) diners look over a grassy knoll of yucca plants towards an expanse of water where the sun sets over a small island. Fishing boats pass nearby as they push up the sound toward Pirate Cove Marina.

The restaurant is divided into a cozy lounge where live fish swim beyond portholes in the wall, and the main window lined dining room. Tropical styled bar drinks are a specialty of the house.

The Dock's mainstays are the traditional Outer Banks seafood preparations, both fried and broiled. A choice of potato, slaw or salad, and hushpuppies come with the entrees. For appetizers, the She Crab Soup and Fresh Mushroom Caps sauteed in butter and sherry are extra good. Iowa Beef in Delmonico and Filet cuts, two steak and seafood combination platters, and a children's menu are also offered. For dessert there is Cheesecake, Key Lime Pie, and a daily surprise.

This is a casual, comfortable spot convenient to most resort accommodations and attractions. If you happen to have a boat, you might consider sailing or powering to the Dock and tying up at their pier. Locals do, and it seems like a great way to avoid traffic! The Dock is open every day during the season from 5:00 p.m. until....

THE SHIP'S WHEEL

Roanoke Island Causeway   441-2906
$$

Map, pg. 80

The Ship's Wheel is located in the building where Spencer's Restaurant used to hang their shingle, with a soundfront view that delights diners year after year. Seafood specials like Shrimp Scampi, Crab Imperial, and Lobster Tails are offered here as are all-you-can-eat specials (including steamed spiced shrimp!). All meals are served with a salad bar, choice of potatoe, french fries, or vegetable of the day. Steaks, ham, and chicken are also on the menu.

The atmosphere is nautical and casual so many vacationers who don't feel like dressing to the nines feel at home here. There are special provisions made for children and senior citizens who might not have as hearty of appetites as the rest of their party.

The Ship's Wheel also serves breakfast every morning and the menu is huge. One specialty is a crab omlette. Breakfast is served from 6 a.m. till noon. Dinner is served from 4 p.m. till 9 p.m.

ROANOKE ISLAND
RESTAURANTS

DUCHESS OF DARE

Downtown Manteo 473-2215
$

Map, pg. 289

The Duchess of Dare is Manteo's most enduring restaurant, and its position at the heart of the Island's civic, business, and municipal center makes it a popular year round meeting place. If you want to eat what the locals eat, and hear their native tongue, this is one place to have the experience.

Neighbors get special service here, but visitors are also welcomed. There are three dining areas with booths, and also counter service. The products from Doris Walker's kitchen focus on local seafoods. You can count on excellent sweet dough hush puppies here, too. Look for daily specials, and sample one of the homemade fruit pies.

The Duchess opens very early to serve breakfast to the fishing and boating crowd. Meal service continues until 9 p.m. Menu and price wise, this is a good choice for family dining. For private parties, dinners, and receptions the Duchess has a large, beamed ceiling functions room. It's one of the few facilities of its type on the Island, and the restaurant staff works hard to make catered events successful.

CAFE RENE

Downtown Manteo, in the Waterfront 473-1155
$$-$$$

Map, pg. 289

Cafe Rene is a newcomer to the Outer Banks restaurant scene but one that already is drawing a loyal crowd that loves its uptown, classy atmosphere. Located in the Waterfront in downtown Manteo, with a sweeping view of the sound, Cafe Rene provides candlelight dinners serenaded by a musician on a grand piano. Obviously well-trained waiters and waitresses give just the right amount of service.

The food is decidedly different from many Outer Banks restaurants - more on the gourmet side. Roast duck with special sauces and salmon wrapped in a light pastry shell are examples of the chef's determination to make this restaurant stand out from the crowd.

Although Manteo doesn't have liquor by the drink, the restaurant does offer an excellent wine and champagne list and the beer offerings are enough to satisfy.

Lunch is served here too. There are specials everyday, along with dressed up sandwiches, freshly made soups, and salads. We had a fruit and cheese plate that was especially good that contained, among other things, fresh raspberries and pineapple, and three different cheeses.

This is the place to come when you want that extra touch of romance as well as a well prepared meal. It's a surprising find in the middle of Manteo. Meals are served from 11 a.m. to 3 p.m.; dinner from 5 pm.m until 10 p.m.

THE ELIZABETHAN

Manteo   473-2101
$

Map, pg. 289

This roadside restaurant, resembling a Tudor styled inn, is popular locally. Marine science researchers, actors from the Lost Colony, and office workers frequent its convenient location especially during breakfast and lunch.

The Elizabethan opens early (6 a.m.) to serve a traditional country breakfast. Herring roe and eggs, pancakes with real bacon bits, made-from-scratch hash browns, country ham, grits, and "loaded" omelettes are featured.

There is always a daily special. A Boiled Dinner of ham, cabbage, potato and cornmeal dumplings is often on the menu. There are also sandwiches, soups, cold plates, fresh vegetables, and a salad bar, plus hot seafood and meat meals.

For dinner choose from traditional seafood preparations, plus steaks and a nightly special which reflects the southern style of cooking.

No alcoholic beverages. Dinner service until 9 p.m.

QUEEN ANNE'S REVENGE

Wanchese 473-5466
$$

Map, pg. 289

Two friends with a mutual interest in food, Donald Beach and Wayne Gray, conceived this restaurant in 1976. With family support, amid the doubting eyes of onlookers, they built a quality establishment far off the resort path on a dead end road in the woods of Wanchese. Despite the location, the delightful dining environment and the caliber of food service soon attracted patrons.

The attractive modern building has a wooded garden where seasonal flowers bloom in its front yard. Rose bushes and lawn chairs under the trees can be seen from tables inside the three dining rooms. A recently built addition contains a large fire place that creates a cozy atmosphere in the cold months. The walls are decorated with original art which can be purchased. Prices range from $75 to $1,000.

All dinners served at Queen Anne's come with cheese crock, large garden salad, a choice of potato, and house baked breads. Appetizers demonstrate the restaurant's flare with Imported Fresh Caviar on ice, and Smoked Shad with sour cream and chives. Calamari (fried squid), an unusual menu item for the Banks, is also served here.

Soups include French Onion, Wanchese Clam Chowder, and She Crab. The menu is balanced between 13 seafood selections, six cuts of beef (a huge Sirloin and a 32 oz. Chateaubriand for two), Smoked Ham, and Fried Chicken. Among the seafood entrees, the Crab Slough Select Oysters, the Wanchese Seafood Platter, and Blackbeard's Raving (mounds of crabmeat, large fantail shrimp, and chunks of lobster) always inspire table sighs.

Wanchese has no liquor-by-the-drink so "brown bag" and set-ups are the rule.

Queen Anne's Revenge continues to be one of the top dining experiences on the Outer Banks and worthy of the pleasant detour to the quiet woods of Wanchese. Dinner service only, 5:30 to 10 p.m.

FISHERMAN'S WHARF

Wanchese 473-5205
$

Map, pg. 289

Fisherman's Wharf is at the dirt road termination of Highway 345 at the south end of Roanoke Island. It is literally a restaurant amid the setting of a working commercial fishing port. The dining room is located above a wharf where fish are unloaded from the trawler fleet.

Once inside, you can view the water traffic and vistas over the sound in air conditioned comfort. The restaurant serves up to 600 persons a day for breakfast, lunch, and dinner.

Of course dining here is orientated toward fresh seafood. For starters there is Wanchese Clam Chowder, She Crab soup, Large Oyster Stew, and Louie, a combination of crab and shrimp Louie. Dinners include tossed salad or slaw, choice of potato, hushpuppies, and beverage.

The Wharf Seafood Platter, the Fried Whole Baby Flounder, and any Fried Fresh Local Fish will arrive in portions to satisfy a large appetite. Lobster, steak, chicken, and daily luncheon specials are on the menu, as are homemade pies and cakes.

Open 9 a.m., with service until 9 p.m. Closed Sunday. Now accepts major credit cards.

THE WEEPING RADISH

Manteo, at the Christmas Shop   473-1157
$$

Map, pg. 289

The first thing you'll notice about this new restaurant is the striking architecture. A working clock tower tops the impressive two story Bavarian inn, where arched doorways and windows overlook a pine wooded garden.

The food is authentically German, from a selection of sandwiches and salads for lunch to full course dinners during the evening hours. Entrees include local seafood prepared German style.

If we haven't piqued your interest so far, perhaps this will do it: there's a brewery at the restaurant producing beer for on-premises consumption. The entire operation can be observed from first and second floor viewing areas.

This restaurant is part of the popular Christmas Shop complex. Our guess is that reservations would be wise for dinner, especially during the summer.

Be sure to have your server tell you how the restaurant got its name. It's too long to tell here, but it's worth hearing.

THE SHIP'S GALLEY

Downtown Manteo, on the waterfront   473-3333
$

Map, pg. 289

Richard Brown owns and operates this cheery and convenient sandwich shop overlooking the sound and the ELIZABETH II. It has become a Manteo "thing" at lunch, when, it seems, every local within easy distance descends on the place between noon and 2 p.m. They come for good reason.

The Ship's Galley is a casual place where you stand in line to order your food then sit at any number of the indoor tables or sit outside on the porch to watch the Manteo scene.

Richard dishes up some of the best, freshly made soups anywhere in the area. If the Chicken Noodle is on the menu, get it. There's also broccoli and vegetable. Sandwiches, too, are a mainstay here, with selections ranging from grilled cheese to homemade turkey salad to saurekraut on rye. You can get them the way you like them. Salad plates and ice cream are also available.

Beer and wine are offered and the porch is often filled with thirsty vacationers enjoying a cool one. This is a great place to catch a bite before "The Lost Colony," or while you're in Manteo seeing the sights.

CHATTERAS ISLAND
RESTAURANTS

EMILY'S SOUNDSIDE RESTAURANT

Waves Village   987-2383
$$

Map, pg. 336

There are a lot of good things to tell about Emily and Jim Landrum's Soundside Restaurant. Near the historic Chicamacomico Lifesaving Station and adjacent to the K.O.A.

campground, they have been serving three meals a day for seven years (five at a previous location). Over the last year or so, the Landrums have totally revamped their menu, carefully selecting new dishes while making sure to keep their old favorites. Have no fear: the Hatteras-style use of fresh ingredients, original recipes, and old-fashioned seasonings apply to the entire menu.

Table service at the 85 restaurant seats is quick and courteous, and take-out and private party catering is also available. Breakfast is hardy here from 7 to 11 a.m. Lunch, from 11 a.m. to 3 p.m. includes a salad bar, soup, fried seafood platters, and appealing sandwiches. The Soundside Rollers, a dressed Hoagy roll topped with your choice of fried shrimp, oysters, or clam strips is a New Orleans Poboy by any other name. You will like the price, too.

Dinner (3 to 9 p.m.) is the major event. Everything is prepared and seasoned like it was going on a home table. Vegetables of the season, soups, and homemade salads are not slighted in the cornucopia of entrees. The offering goes beyond seafoods so that every member of the dinner party will be pleased. After you have sampled Lightly Battered Shrimp, Golden Fried Oysters, Crab Lumps sauteed with Country Ham, Alaskan Snow Crab Legs, Chicamacomico Crab Cakes, Fried Fresh Fish, Tender Clam Strips, Creamy Crabmeat Au Gratin, Atlantic Flounder Feast, Emily's Fried Chicken, Homemade Spaghetti, Prime Rib of Beef au jus, and Barbecue Pork or Beef with your hot bread, hot vegetables, three hot soups, salad bar, and other cold salads, don't forget to save room for the homemade pie. Item for item, with the large portions you get, this meal is one of the best values on the Outer Banks.

If you are day-tripping to Hatteras Village or Ocracoke from the Nags Head resort area, the Soundside is a wise dinner stop on that long return road to Oregon Inlet.

THE FROGGY DOG

Avon 995-4106

Map, pg. 344

$$

This Avon restaurant has made a major transformation in the last year with attractive additions to the building and decor. What used to be a very small, one-room restaurant is now three rooms, with pretty touches like stained glass and a screened porch dining area. The woodwork inside will be appreciated by anyone who knows the craft; it's extremely well done by someone who took no short cuts to get the job done.

The Froggy Dog is open for breakfast, lunch and dinner and they do a great job with all three. Breakfast offers the usual morning meal foods in hearty proportions. The biscuits are homemade and especially good. For lunch, the offerings center around sandwiches and salads. They have great onion rings, so if you've never tried them, or are an onion ring connoisseur, get them!

The dinner menu is varied and complete. You can get almost any of their seafood dinners fried, broiled, or sauteed, showing the chef's appreciation for the delicate flavor of his seafood treats. As alternatives to the fish, shrimp, and other dishes, you can order such meals as pork chops, broiled calves liver and onions, steaks, or honey dipped fried chicken.

All meals are served with a tossed salad with homemade dressings, a choice of the vegetable of the day or potatoe, and their specially made hushpuppies or rolls. The desserts are well worth saving room for, especially the home baked pie.

The Froggy Dog is open from 6:30 a.m. until 3:00 p.m., then from 5:00 p.m. till 9:00 p.m. during the week. On weekends, they stay open all day from 6:30 a.m. until 10:00 p.m.

Emily & Jim's Original

SOUNDSIDE RESTAURANT

Since 1972

Located on Highway 12, Waves Village on Hatteras Island. Beautiful sunsets. Holiday breakfast buffets. Emily's famous biscuits. Lunch specials, seafood salads and sandwiches. Salad bar, original soups and chowders. All you can eat Early Bird Specials (4 to 6 p.m.) from $6.95. Traditional Hatteras Island cuisine featuring fresh crabmeat and seafood dishes. Raw and steamed shellfish. Prime rib, handcut steaks, fried chicken and barbecue. Children's menu. Homemade pies. ABC license. Major credit cards accepted.

Jim & Emily Landrum
(919) 987-2383

Box 128
Rodanthe, NC 27968

THE LIGHTHOUSE

Buxton   995-5151

Map, pg. 344

$

    To meet the local people and fishing folk of Hatteras, the Lighthouse restaurant, hard by the Hatteras Light itself, is the place to hang your sea cap. From alligator emblem shirts to foul weather gear, you can come as you are to this traditional, simple eating house.

    Breakfast starts early here for fishermen at 5:30 a.m., and the menu is hardy with Eggs and Herring Roe, Hot Cakes, Omeletttes, and all the trimmings. Lunch stays mainly with soups (She Crab, Clam Chowder, Oyster Stew, plain or with milk, etc.) and sandwiches (Soft Crab, Crabcake, Burgers, Bar-b-que, hot sandwich of the day, etc.).

    Dinner offers traditional seafoods, steaks and chops, chicken, chef's salad, and hot vegetables of the day. Dinner service until 10:30 p.m. in season. No credit cards.

THE ORANGE BLOSSOM PASTRY SHOP

Buxton   995-4109

Map, pg. 344

$

    You know you've had it as soon as you walk in the front door and waves of freshly baked goodies' aroma grab you. Might as well give in, because it's just about impossible to get out of this shop without sampling at least one of their delights.

    All the usual bakery items are here, along with fresh coffee, and a wooden-floor, homey atmosphere. Their Apple Ugly is so good you'll think you're getting cuter by the bite. Everything, and we do mean everything, else is well worth tasting.

    Orange Blossom is open early in the morning for treats before hitting the beach or fishing, at 7:30. The shop stays open until 5 p.m. They stay open each year until a day or so before Christmas, then close until early March.

THE PILOT HOUSE

Buxton   995-5664

Map, pg. 344

$$

    Many people locally consider The Pilot House the premiere restaurant on Hatteras Island. Owners (Mr.) Bernice Ballance

and Edward Midgett have a beautiful 150-seat sem???
dining room with an unobstructed view of Par???
Every table has a view of memorable sunsets???
   The Pilot House opens Easter week thou???
9 dinner service. All the traditional ???
available, plus excellent Rib Eye st???
plates (barbecue, chicken, pork ???
to the off-menu specials
Mushrooms, a Shishka???
chowder have proven ???
   The seafood com???
and the Soft-S???
room for d???
Short C???
calo???

Ha???
Pam???
must???
deck s???
that tail???
table.

NOTE: In May of 1986, the Pilot House burned to the ground. Plans are already underway, however, to rebuild the restaurant and a completion date of late fall to early winter of 1986 is expected. The "talk around town" is that the new building will be even bigger and more impressive than the original one. We're looking forward to it!

...ountiful, ...a here. Save ...Pie, Strawberry ...House are worth the ...y on the southside of the ...eathered shingled oasis on the ...on is still a brown bag area so you ...rits and pay for set ups. An outdoor ...e restaurant leads us to believe, however, ...ails are consumed there while waiting for a

THE QUARTERDECK

Frisco   986-2425
              Map, pg. 344
$$

   Since 1963, the Quarterdeck has been pleasing patrons in its attractive, 125-seat restaurant. The Ochs have made their operation a family affair with their sons and daughter helping out. Just inside the entrance a cabinet full of fishing trophies won by family members attest to their Hatteras know-how.
   The menu does not at first appear extensive, but the 11 seafood entrees, five steaks, and five alternative items will please any dinner party. Five soups including Clam Chowder, Crab Bisque, Oyster Stew, and Hambone Vegetable are well made. The Quarterdeck Seafood Platter, broiled or fried, allows you to sample five seafood delicacies, and it is portioned for a big appetite. A Char-Broiled T-Bone, Prime Rib, and the Seafood Platter are the top priced menu items. You can expect good value from every entree on the list. A trip to the salad bar goes with the dinners, plus choice of potato, hushpuppies, and rolls.
   Fresh baked pies and cakes are part of the Quarterdeck tradition. Children's plates available. Serving daily 5 to 9 p.m.

GINGERBREAD HOUSE

Frisco 995-5204

Map, pg. 344

$

Since we first began reporting about the Gingerbread House it has expanded its service and hours to capture all the new customers who want to sample their treats.

It is still a genuine novelty: a chalet-styled road side house on a barrier island that has the quality of a Bavarian pastry shop. There are still only six tables inside, but now the famous Whole Wheat Pizzas are served all the time, and 15 sandwiches have been added, including pizza by the slice.

The venture began as a bakery with Carlos Caruso and his mother, Doris, making Croissants, Napoleons, Eclairs, Doughnuts, and, of course, Gingerbread in a variety of shapes. Now there are also breads, and a variety of cookies in the pastry showcase.

With success has come growth. Freshmade soups, chowders, and bisques, salads, quiches, the sandwiches, and pizza at all hours (it was once available only on Saturdays), plus all the bakery goods is a lot to produce from a small kitchen. Expansion is sure to come to the Gingerbread House unless the Caruso's elect not to follow the demands of success. We know, given their excellent reputation, that the charm and quality standards will not get lost in the process.

Nevertheless, if you find yourself on the road between Hatteras Village and Buxton, look to stop at the Gingerbread House for an unexpected treat. Now open daily 7 a.m. to 9 p.m. (Mon. - Sat.), 7 to 3 on Sun.

FRISCO DRIVE-IN

Frisco 995-5535

Map, pg. 344

$

For at least six seasons this small roadside take-out has enjoyed a big reputation for good food at a good price. It is amazing what this kitchen turns out between the hours of 7 a.m. to 8 p.m. daily.

The deli-type salads are all homemade, and there is a variety of bread and rolls for hot and cold overstuffed sandwiches. There are also Italian-styled hot plates, like spaghetti, to go, as well as burgers and dogs dressed the way you like them.

The Frisco Drive In is the place to stop for ice cream cones, sundaes, and shakes on the road from Buxton to Hatteras Village. Stanley Lawrence Jr.'s place accepts no credit cards.

BUBBA'S BAR-B-Q

Frisco 995-5421
Map, pg. 344
$

Larry Schauer (Bubba) and his wife (Mrs. Bubba) are former West Virginians who left their farm for the seaside. Bubba's Bar-B-Q is an extension of something they do best: cook.

Bubba's barbecue is the real thing. You can see the ribs, chicken, and pork shoulders cooking on the grill over a hickory-wood pit fire.

Ribs come by the slab, on a sandwich, or with a plate of homemade cole slaw, cornbread and french fries. The pork barbecue comes sliced, chopped, or on a plate. The chicken comes in quarters a la carte or with homemade side dishes on a plate.

Mrs. Bubba cooks several different pies everyday, and they are tried and proven winners. She does Paul Prudhomme's (K-Paul's of New Orleans) Sweet Potato-Pecan Pie, Feeling's (also New Orleans) Peanutbutter Pie, and her own heavenly Coconut Custard among others.

Everything is for take out, or you can enjoy your meal at one of the inside (air conditioned) picnic tables.

THE LIGHT SHIP

Hatteras 986-2630
$$ Map, pg. 344

Jack and Diane Quidley are your hosts at this truely charming restaurant across the street from the General Mitchell and Sea Gull Motels. The high ceiling, abundance of plants, and large picture window give the dining room a light, comfortable feeling.

The meals they serve give a comfortable feel too — as far as quantity and quality go. Here you can get an "all-you-can-eat" seafood dinner and salad bar! That's a good deal for hungry vacationers! They also serve breakfast and feature a bountiful breakfast special... you won't leave *this* restaurant unsatisfied.

One really special dish at the Light Ship is the Fried Hard Crabs, yes, hard crabs. This is their specialty; we know of no other restaurant in this area who does it, and word has it that people love them.

The Light Ship has one of the few private party and reception rooms in the Hatteras area. The room will seat 50 for dinner and has a brown bagging permit.

The Light Ship is open from 6 a.m. till 11 a.m. for breakfast and again from 5 p.m. till 10 p.m. for dinner, 7 days a week. MC and Visa are accepted.

THE CHANNEL BASS

Hatteras Village   986-2250
$$

Map, pg. 344

This restaurant beside the inlet bridge is a Harrison family affair. One daughter runs the kitchen while another manages the dining room. All the fishing trophies on the foyer walls belong to Shelby Harrison, the Mama!

You can meet Brenda and Debbie Harrison in their modern blond brick and brown shingle 178-seat restaurant when the dinner service begins at 5:30 p.m.

The fare, of course, features fresh Hatteras seafood with Seafood Platters, Broiled Scallops, and Crab Imperial as popular choices. For variety, see what the Channel Bass can do with Barbecue Beef Short Ribs, King Crab Legs, and Char-Broiled Steaks.

This has been a popular restaurant in Hatteras for over 16 years, and the tradition continues with a new generation. Some of the fish you may be served are caught aboard the Miss Channel Bass. The boat also landed the largest Blue Marlin caught in 1980 (591 lbs.), and also has a citation for a world record Red Drum. It is little wonder that sport fishermen hang out here.

OCRACOKE

RESTAURANTS

THE BACK PORCH

Ocracoke   928-6401
$$

Map, pg. 373

After creating the Pelican Restaurant on Ocracoke and operating it for an absentee owner for four seasons, John and Debbie Wells opened their own restaurant a block off Highway 12 in a pine grove across from Blackbeard's Lodge.

The Back Porch seats about 65 in a completely redecorated rustic wooden building. An Italian tile foyer, carpeting, upholstered banquettes, and a teal green, rose, and gray color scheme make for a comfortable, contemporary dining environment.

The successful duo of John hosting in the dining areas and Debbie overseeing the production of their popular desserts was added to for the 1986 season by Anna Bessillieu as head chef.

Dining here runs from 5 to 9. Anna carries through on the established gourmet menu with appetizers like Scallop Ceviche and Crabmeat Beignets. An outstanding soup or salad-of-the-day comes with the entree. The care in preparation and presentation of this course has done much to enhance the Back Porch's good reputation.

Entrees served here are always in good taste and done with flare. Look for Scallops cooked in lemon and wine and served in a puff pastry; or Shrimp with Tomatoes and Basil, or Roast Chicken with a Sauce of Orange and Brandy. Tournedos of Beef Basque, served with a spicy dark mushroom sauce, is a favorite with many.

To complement the dinner, there is fresh-baked bread and outstanding desserts, plus just-ground coffee and a wine list appropriate to the menu.

The Back Porch actually has a screened porch overlooking its wooded setting. We suspect that it will be crowded with loyal patrons who have followed the Wells.

ISLAND INN DINING ROOM

Ocracoke 928-4351
$$
Map, pg. 373

The atmosphere in this dining room captures the flavor of a bygone era of country inns. Service ladies are in Colonial period dresses with dust caps. The red terra cotta tile floor, rough hune columns supporting the ceiling, dark brown cane chairs, and antique paintings on the walls lend to the total effect.

Three meals, beginning with breakfast at 7 a.m. are served in season. The Inn is open all year, but the restaurant closes between two and five during the off-season. Dinners are served until 9 p.m.

The menu here includes Edna's Homemade Crabcakes, a locally celebrated creation, fresh seafoods of the day in generous portions, Oyster Stew (with milk), Ocracoke Clam Chowder, plus steaks, and chicken for variety. With advance notice, Larry (one of the Inn's owners) will prepare such special island delicacies as Chicken and Shrimp Ariosto, Stewed Shrimp and Corn Dumplings, Deviled Crab, etc.

Luncheons feature cold plates, creative salads, sandwiches, and selected seadood entrees. A "Light Appetite" section of the menu shows consideration for children and seniors who require less than the regular portions.

The Island Inn Dining room should not be missed on your visit to Ocracoke even if you can only pause briefly for coffee and a house dessert.

THE PELICAN

Ocracoke Village 928-6611
$$

Map, pg. 373

The Pelican, which has enjoyed a good reputation since the 1980 season, has new owner and a new staff. Ron Howard, who also owns Howard's Pub, runs the show now, serving gourmet lunches and dinners.

The Pelican is located in a hundred-year-old cottage nestled in a grove of willows across from the Post Office in Ocracoke Village. Meals can be taken in two small interior rooms seating a total of 26 persons, or on the 34-seat screened porch which provides views of village activity.

Lunch is served from 11:30 to 2 p.m. and consists of well conceived soups, salads, sandwiches and light, hot entrees. Several of our favorites are the Pelican Pasta Salad and the Seafood Salad Croissant.

Dinner in this country inn atmosphere shows imaginative preparations of local seafoods and the influence of continental recipes and preparations. Pasta, Veal, Steak, and Chicken dishes are also well represented on the menu. The wine list includes selected French and Spanish vintages to complement the menu. Service begins at 5 and continues until 9:30 p.m. from May through October, weather permitting. Ron also has a pleasant outside cafe from 2-5 p.m. during the summer.

Bird - a Louisiana heron in the marsh at Hatteras.

HOWARDS' PUB

Ocracoke 928-4441
$
Map, pg. 373

A plain weather board building near the airstrip at the edge of town houses Howards'. The exterior gives no clue to what is inside. Actually, being called a pub is appropriate to this establishment which offers a selection of domestic and imported beers, and wine by the glass or carafe, as well as plenty of friendliness. The place is not fancy but it's comfortable. There is a bar area, an addition of a breezy, screened porch, and a scattering of tables with red checked tablecloths.

The fare is light but with substance. Sandwiches such as the Pub Club, Howard's Pub Subs and luncheon platters like Fish and Chips are offered at midday along with salads. Dinner features full meals if steamed shrimp, bbq ribs, and pork chops just to name a few items. All dinners are served with salads, choice of potato, vegetable garnish and hot bread.

A great afternoon event is to sip wine spritzers on Howard's porch after a hot day in the sun. He encourages the fun. The Pub is open from 11:30 a.m. till midnight.

CAP'T. BEN'S

Ocracoke   928-9766
$$

Map, pg. 373

Ben Mugford's restaurant is on the edge of town near the airstrip. In dining and decor, he is offering a plush alternative to the traditional Outer Banks experience. He caters to serious diners rather than casual family groups, and thus Cap't. Ben's is perhaps not the place for small children who have not yet developed sophisticated tastes. It is perfect, however, for adults who enjoy spending the evening over rewarding things to eat and drink.

The dining room at Cap't. Ben's is beautifully appointed. Low wall dividers make semi-private alcoves where a tasteful painting or a stained glass window create a rich atmosphere. The restaurant seats 75 in comfort. Note the full size 1920's speed boat that serves as the salad bar.

Some of the delicacies you may not find on other menus locally are Crab Balls, Crab Stuffed Mushrooms, Shrimp Scampi, Baltimore Style Broiled Oysters, and Spaghetti and Clams. The house is also proud of its generous cut of Prime Rib at an excellent price. Sebastiani house wines, and a separate wine list chosen with care also indicate the style of eating here. The raw bar is open from 5 to 9 p.m.; dinners are served until 10 p.m. in season.

Cap't. Ben's also offers special platters, cold plates, and sandwiches for lunch. Open daily April through October. Sundays, 5 to 9 only.

PONY ISLAND RESTAURANT

Ocracoke   928-9776
$$

Map, pg. 373

The Pony Island Restaurant has long been a favorite with vacationers and locals alike in Ocracoke. Located right beside the Pony Island Motel off the main street coming into the village, the restaurant offers lots of special dishes in a relaxed atmosphere.

They're known for their steamed shrimp and their wonderful homemade desserts, but there are plenty of other great menu items. Seafood combinations in just about every combination, either fried or broiled are offered as are hand-cut rib eyes, large salads, and fried chicken. There's a children's menu, too, to satisfy the wee ones.

Another claim to fame for the Pony Island Restaurant is their nightly specials. Believe it or not, you can actually get Chinese food there on one of the special nights... a real popular thing with locals who welcome a diversion from all that fresh seafood! You can also bring them your own catch - cleaned - and they'll cook it for you.

Breakfast is served daily too, and the selection and protions are generous. Morning meals start at 6:30 a.m. and go until 11:00 a.m. Dinner runs from 5:00 p.m. until 9:00p.m.

OUTER BANKS
NIGHTSPOTS

The sun and surf seem to take the measure of the party people who come to the Outer Banks. After a day on the beach, and a satisfying evening meal, most of the family oriented resort visitors never see the clock hit midnight.

For those who want to dance and mingle late into the night, the entertainment scene has improved since the legalization of mixed beverage service on the Banks. There are now real watering holes serving all your favorite libations to the sights and sounds of live musical groups.

The following nightspot profiles are restricted to places that feature entertainment, and stay open late until the last legal drink can be served, generally until 2 a.m. Many restaurants in Kill Devil Hills and Nags Head have incorporated separate lounge operations into their food and beverage mix and schedule guitar singles and duos, piano stylists, and other small entertainments during the evening hours. These added attractions are noted in the restaurant profiles. They provide a relaxing environment for after dinner drinks and conversation.

# *SOUTHERN SHORES, DUCK, SANDERLING, COROLLA*
NIGHTSPOTS

BARRIER ISLAND INN

Duck   261-3901

Map, pg. 30

The Barrier Island Inn, located just above Duck village provides summer night entertainment Thursdays through Saturdays in their upstairs tavern. The shows usually start around 8:00 p.m. and last until 10:30 p.m. or so. Kevin Roughton, a popular local guitar player and singer frequently performs. The Inn adds an extra punch to the entertainment by featuring nightly food specials as well, such as Western Night or Potato Night.

Though current plans are only definitely set for summer entertainment, there is talk that they might extend it into fall at least for Monday Night Football events. If you're up that way during the off season, it's worth a phone call to see if anything is planned.

KITTY HAWK
NIGHTSPOTS

R.V.'S

Nags Head at the Causeway 441-4963
Kitty Hawk at the Traffic Light
Map, pg. 47

Between the stretch of the Bypass road known locally as French Fry Alley, R.V. Owens has positioned two fun loving restaurant-lounges of the same name: R.V.'s.

The original R.V.'s is located at the sound on the Causeway road to Manteo. It has been a well-patroned watering hole since it opened in 1982. After the dinner hours, it is the gathering place for the young and the restless who enjoy its lively atmosphere and party-inspired excitement. The people are the entertainment here whether they are stacked at the bar or lining the rail of the soundside porch. Service until midnight.

The R.V.'s in Kitty Hawk is twice as large as its namesake; and because of its location, size, and ambience, it attracts a fun-loving, exuberant crowd. There is plenty of room for live entertainment here, so check out the offering. Opened for the 1984 season, this R.V.'s has been the center of nightlife at the north end of the beach, and it draws heavily from the Southern Shores and Duck residential and rental populations. Service until 2 a.m.

Commercial fishing trawlers stand at ease in safe harbor.

KILL DEVIL HILLS

NIGHTSPOTS

SEA RANCH LOUNGE

Rt. 158 Business, MP 6   441-7126
Map, pg. 57

This large multi-level lounge looks more New York than Outer Banks. The pink decor, cozy shell booths, crystal chandeliers, and extra long bar where singles can observe the dancing marks the Sea Ranch Lounge as one of the most stylish on the beach. There are two dance floors, one on each of the major levels.

The groups that are booked here play for an audience that includes young married, singles, and more mature parties who do not want to be overpowered by the entertainment. You will thus hear current hits, plus old favorites that are easy to dance to. During the season there is nightly entertainment from 8:30 p.m. The Sea Ranch Lounge, and its highly rated restaurant within the motor inn complex are open all year.

MADELINE'S

Rt. 158 Business, MP 9.5   441-6333
Map, pg. 57

From Monday through Saturday beginning at 9 p.m., Madeline's roars past its 1920's decor into today's contemporary music for listening and dancing.

This lounge location in the Holiday Inn has always been popular with the summer working crowd of young adults. Since the 1983 complete makeover, the 70 lounge seats and the 80 restaurant seats are filled early when the music is hot.

The password at this facsimile speakeasy is "fun." In that spirit, the house specialty drinks invite you to drink your way through the Outer Banks experience. How about a Jockey Ridge Sling, a Lost Colony, a Hatteras Lighthouse, or a Duck Blind?

The music goes until 1 a.m., and the cover charge depends on the reputation of the specific group. Madeline's is open all year. The come-early nights are Wednesday, Friday, and Saturday.

PORT O'CALL GASLIGHT SALOON

Rt. 158 Business, MP 8.5   441-7484
Map, pg. 57

The 150-seat Gaslight Saloon, a major addition to the highly rated Port O'Call Restaurant, opened in 1983. In decor and concept, it is one of the most elaborate watering holes for a hundred miles.

The decor is Victorian with dark wood panels and gaslight effects throughout an open, two-story structure. The ascending staircase and the second-level gallery give the room a "great hall" appearance. The long mahogany bar looks as if it came out of a British mens' club. The antique accent furnishings contribute to the theme.

The Gaslight Saloon opens for libations at 5 p.m. daily and lasts until the 2 a.m. closing.

PAPAGAYO'S

Rt. 158 Business, MP 7 1/2   441-7232
Map, pg. 57

This nightspot has become one of the most popular ones on the beach for young adults. It attracts a nice crowd of folks who are there to have friendly conversations and listen to the nightly music.

One of the nicest things about Papagayo's upstairs lounge is the huge deck that overlooks the ocean. It's a perfect place to watch the moon on the water while sipping your favorite drink. The lounge opens with the restaurant at 5:30 p.m. and stays open until 2:00 a.m.

NAGS HEAD NORTH
NIGHTSPOTS

GANDALF'S

Rt. 158 Bypass, MP 11 1/2½   441-4773
Map, pg. 70

Bob and Jan Kannry had a dream for a long, long time to open a comfortable place where musicians, and people who would come to truly listen to them, could congregate. They have done just that at Gandalf's. It's probably one of the most ambiant places on the beach;locals and visitors in the know come here just to relax and enjoy the friendship that is always found.

The music that is offered here varies but usually centers around acoustic guitar. Outside, in back of the restaurant, they've built a performance area for concerts under the stars.

Word seems to be getting around the touring musicians wourld that Gangalf's is a great place to share their music, and bigger names are beginning to appear. We predict that, thanks to Bob and Jan's connections and their love of music, this will be a spot to see some fine music-makers with reputations to match.

FISHTAILS

Rt. 158 Bypass, MP 11.5   441-3001
Map, pg. 70

Up a winding carpeted staircase, just inside the front door at Fishtails, is a singles heaven seven nights a week.

The trendy restaurant and bar with the serious approach to food at Pirate's Quay turns into the dating game after 10 p.m. for those 21 years and over. A large contemporary bar, and a multi-level seating plan that makes sure that everyone sees everyone else, is second only to a mirrored dance floor with its dynamite sound system and light display.

If you are under 30, or wish that you were, this is one of the Outer Banks hot spots.

ATLANTIS

Rt. 158 Business, MP 12   441-6001
Map, pg. 70

This is the action scene for rock music or whatever is musically popular for the college singles crowd. There is a large dance floor, lots of tables, a couple of bars, and wall-to-wall people on the weekends.

Unless you come during an off night, or show up when the doors open, it may be difficult to get a table. The bands change frequently and the cover charge may also vary according to their respective reputations. The music starts at 9:30 p.m., and the dancing and drinking goes almost until 2 a.m. It's like a giant fraternity party everynight!

THE COMEDY CLUB

Rt. 158 Business, at the Carolinian Hotel   441-7171
Map, pg. 70

You might be used to seeing these live comedy shows in big cities, but did you know there was one on the Banks too? This is one fun, and certainly funny, place. Every week, a big name comedian entertains the crowds Monday through Thursday nights. Then, live bands take over the entertaining job on the weekends.

Showtime for the Comedy Club is 10 p.m. You should call to get reservations to assure a seat at this popular spot.

NAGS HEAD SOUTH
NIGHTSPOTS

STATION KEEPERS LOUNGE

Rt. 158 Business, MP 16.5 441-7309
Map, pg. 80

The second floor of the Life Saving Station structure which marks the entrance to Owens' Restaurant is the home of the Station Keepers Lounge.

Patrons ascend a free-standing, two-level polished natural wood staircase to a contemporary room of gleaming light wood panels, brass rails, and Tiffany-styled fixtures.

The bar specializes in frozen drinks with fruit daiquiris being the popular summertime request.

Entertainment is focused around a baby grand piano where showtunes, old favorites, pop and contemporary songs are played and sung for the patrons' enjoyment until midnight.

OUTER BANKS COLISEUM

Rt. 158 Bypass, MP 16 441-7080
Map, pg. 80

This large, tan building on the bypass behind the Ghost Ship has been transformed from a haven for roller skating pre-teens into a hangout for feet shuffling young adults. The Outer Banks Coliseum is now bringing in name bands playing everything from beach music to rock 'n roll so the young-at-heart can dance away the night. Doors open at 8:30 p.m. and the entertainment continues until 2 a.m. Admission varies depending on the popularity of the band.

During the spring and fall, special events such as the Nags Head fishing tournament banquet, an antique show, dinner theaters, and food shows are held.

DAREOLINA COVE LOUNGE

Rt. 158 Business, MP 16   441-7477
Map, pg. 80

Disco has arrived on the Outer Banks! This nightspot is the only one on the beach with that high-tech, high-volume, colorful appeal of city discos where couples come to dance the night away. Located adjacent to the Dareolina Cove Restaurant, this place usually attracts a young crowd ready for a night on the town. The action generally is strongest between 9 p.m. and 2 a.m.

OCRACOKE
NIGHTSPOTS

3/4 TIME LIVE MUSIC & SALOON

Ocracoke   Map, pg. 373   928-1221

Ocracoke has one of the best "get down and boogie" night spots on the whole Outer Banks. 3/4 Time, a real dance hall in the tradition of yesterday is located in the warehouse-like building near the edge of town. And it looks like a place for an old fashioned barn dance, though barn dancing isn't really what goes on here. But what does go on is fun and plenty of it... with some dancing on the side. There is a huge platform for bands and their amplifiers to set up. Groups come from the mainland for weekends, and a local band fills out the schedule. The tempo is Blues, Rock, and Country depending on the booking. The casual atmosphere makes for some fun cutting loose many nights on the large floor area. There are plenty of tables on two levels to accommodate the crowd. Bottle beer, sodas, and light snacks are available at the back bar.

Music usually starts around 9 p.m. and the fun goes on till around 1:00 or 2:00 a.m.

 # OUTER BANKS
SHOPPING

Shopping on the Outer Banks is a treat all to itself. We say this having known the Banks when there were only a few old standbys, and getting something other than staples or fishing gear was an occasion for a trip to the mainland.

How different things are now! Today the visitor will find over a dozen modern shopping malls, supplying every need and quite a few wants you never realized you had until confronting that piece of furniture, that handcrafted curio, that special dress. You'll find more than malls, though; the northern Banks have a wide variety of smaller specialty stores, carrying everything from abalone shells to zebra-striped bikinis. You'll find great bargains in things like handmade hammocks, jewelry, shell goods, candies and candles, photo and diving gear, sculpture, art, kites, tackle, brass, christening quilts, books, scrimshaw, gourmet delicacies, and a thousand other items.

This wealth of shopping will prove a godsend for you on rainy days, or when the sun just gets to be too much, but it does present Your Authors with a thorny problem. If we listed and described the shops north of Oregon Inlet in the detail we tried to do for Hatteras and Ocracoke, this book would be three times as thick. We can't be the Yellow Pages! In addition, each month new shops open, old ones close, owners change and so do stocks. This makes for adventures...just driving down Route 158, looking out of your window, you find something new and different every time. There's no way to keep up with shopping, unless the book came with a plug and a video monitor so that we could update it by computer!

What we've done is compromise.

To guide you straight to the concentrated shopping, we have researched, visited, and listed the major (roughly, over half a dozen stores in one location) malls. We've prepared a brief description of each, along with a few of the things that make it unique. We have shown their locations on the strip maps for these three towns, so that you can find them if you're in a hurry for something you really need.

You will also find, both here and in the rest of the book (Hatteras, Ocracoke, Roanoke Island, and the Duck area), that we have also done a few of the more interesting specialty shops — those we think will be of special interest to the visitor, either because of what they carry or because of their contribution to the atmosphere of the Outer Banks.

Don't think for a moment, though, that these are all the shops and stores you will find on the Beach. There are hundreds, and more appear every year. Also, be warned that many shops are still open during the warm months only, though we have noted a trend, especially for those carrying a varied line of goods, toward remaining open right through the year.

The trip

We hope these tips will help. From there on, though, the shopping safari will be all yours... which is the way we think you really wanted it anyway.

Enjoy!

SOUTHERN SHORES, DUCK, SANDERLING, COROLLA

SHOPPING

WINKS

Corolla 453-8166

Map, pg. 30

Like its counterpart in Duck, this Winks offers all the basic food supplies as well as souvenir items, magazines and newspapers, and beach supplies. It tends to stay well-stocked since it's the only game in town as far as groceries go. Open year round, it always begins business at 8:00 a.m. and stays open until 9:00 p.m. during the summer. In off season it closes earlier.

KELLOGG'S TRUE VALUE HOME CENTER

Duck 261-8121

Map, pg. 30

As you leave the center of Duck village and begin to round the curve heading north, you come upon a brick building that, if you just glanced, you might think it was a town hall. It seems so solid and official since most all the other buildings are wooden.

This is the newest home of Kellogg Supply company, with two other locations in Manteo and Kill Devil Hills. Within its sturdy walls are lawn and garden supplies, building materials, and home supplies — everything you'll need for fixing up that cottage or purchasing last-minute supplies you might have forgotten from home. Kelloggs is open all year.

THE LUCKY DUCK

Duck   261-7800

Map, pg. 30

Though their sign says "nautical gifts," you can really find more than that in this shop. Books, jewelry, crafts from North Carolina artisans, decorative accessories, stationery, bath and table accessories, and a boat full of seashells are just some of the gift items you'll find. Cards, Duck momentums, and t-shirts round it all out.

The shop is open year round with in season hours from 9:00 a.m. to 9:00 p.m. Off season hours are from 9:30 a.m. to 5:30 p.m.

WEE WINKS

Duck   261-2937

Map, pg. 30

There are four Winks stores on the Outer Banks, all supplying vacationers and locals alike with "essentials." This one in Duck village is always packed, especially around lunch time, when local builders come for their noon time break. You can find most all basic food supplies here, along with magazines, newspapers, and beach supplies.

Wee Winks is open year round with in season hours from 7:00 a.m. till 10:00 p.m. They generally close earlier in the off season.

LOBLOLLY PINES

Duck

Map, pg. 30

Another new shopping center located in the center of Duck, this one contains several women's clothing stores, The Phoenix and Victorian Lady, several souvenir-type shops, T.W.'s Bait and Tackle, a pizza place, an ice cream store, and a very nice seafood and vegetable market. Most the shops follow the 10:00 a.m. to 9:00 p.m. in season hours.

THE LION'S PAW

Duck   261-3803

Map, pg. 30

This women's clothing store specializes in resort clothing, but with an added flair. Cottons and silks abound, many batiked, many with cotton lace work. Also found in abundance are accessories — belts, pocketbooks, silk scarves, hats — along with handmade jewelry from Guatemala.

The shop is the second in a series, with the other located on Sanibel Island where one can find a scalloped shape shell appropriately named a Lion's Paw.

Hours are from 10:00 a.m. until 9:00 p.m. Monday through Saturday; until 6:00 p.m. on Sunday. Closed in the off season.

OSPREY LANDING

Duck

Map, pg. 30

This shopping area, opened in 1985, is a small, wooden structure located on the sound in the middle of downtown Duck. It contains a toy store, Things Papa Brings, a woman's clothing store, La Rive, Osprey Landing Gourmet, Birthday Suits (bathing suits!), a very nice gift store, Carolina Moon, as well as several other stores. Most shops are open in season from 10:00 a.m. till 9:00 p.m., seven days a week, with off season hours variable.

THE FARMER'S DAUGHTER

Duck   261-4828

Map, pg. 30

Imagine a country farmhouse filled with several generations worth of handcrafted accessories, furniture, quilts, etc., and you'll have a pretty good idea of what you're apt to find at this charming country store. In every nook and cranny you see what is properly called "folk art collectibles," but what's more descriptively called the following: needlepoint pillows, straw swan baskets, old tools restored to good condition, duck carvings, wooden hangings painted with country scenes, small reading lamps with decorative shades, wreathes made from apple slices, tin boxes, pegboards, brass items, wind-catchers, rugs, country prints... the list goes on and on. There's also a Christmas corner with trees decorated in a country motif. And for those who want to shop year round, no matter where they live, there's a Farmer's Daughter catalogue with delivery in three days.

The shop is open seven days a week in season and keeps hours from 10:00 a.m. until 9:00 p.m. There's also a shop on the bypass in Nags Head.

SCARBOROUGH FAIRE

Duck

Map, pg. 30

From the front of this attractive collection of shops, you would never think that, nestled back into the surrounding woods, there are over 21 stores. Scarborough Faire was designed to fit in to the environment, not overtake it, and that aspect makes it a very nice place to spend time, whether you're shopping or not. But you probably won't be able to resist most of the shops that are there. In several separate wooden buildings, all connected by wooden walkways and bridges, shoppers find a variety of tempting wares.

Ocean Annies is there (as well as several other locations on the Banks) with one of the best collections of pottery around. They also have great wines and coffees. M.B. Ritter, a woman's clothing store, offers clothes with an up-town feeling, many of them designer styles that the owner picks up on her travels to New York and beyond. Gray's Department Store occupies the front. An anchor store, it offers clothing, gifts, shoes and many other items. Morales Art Gallery features paintings by Jesse and Vivian Morales as well as custom framing, lithographs, and wildlife art. The Literary Duck is a complete bookstore, with books for every mood or need, and also carries cards. Jewelry By Gail is a showplace for intricate original designs by award-winning shop owner, Gail Kowalski. Other shops include Vitamin Sea Surf Shop, The Fudgery, Capt'n Franks, The Linen Closet, and Ocean Atlantic Rentals, the place to go for whatever you forgot to bring from home.

Suffice it to say that you'll probably find most all of what you're looking for at Scarborough Faire and enjoy the relaxed atmosphere as well.

DUCK BLIND LIMITED ART GALLERY
Duck 261-2009
Map, pg. 30

Too often you go into supposed "art galleries" and find reproduction prints and ceramics. Nothing could be further from that experience than this gallery, set into the curve as you come into the village. Here, quality contemporary fine arts and crafts are exhibited, with four or more shows a year featuring the works of individual artists.

The work you see is representative of all media. Mingled together in well-designed displays are handwoven baskets, delicate glassware and stained glass pieces, tapestries, pottery, etchings, handmade jewelry, paintings, handmade paper, and much more. The quality is as good as any we've seen in New York galleries.

Duck Blind Limited is open daily in season from 10:00 a.m. to 6:00 p.m. Off season hours vary, so the owners suggest you call before you come.

KITTY HAWK, KILL DEVIL HILLS, AND NAGS HEAD

SHOPPING

BEN FRANKLIN'S

Kitty Hawk	261-2010
Nags Head	441-7571
Manteo	473-2378

Map, pg. 47

Looking for a one-stop department store? Ben Franklin's is the Banks' answer to Macy's. It's a variety store in every sense of the word. Bathing suits, a tennis racket, stemware, coffee cups, towels, sheets, and a surprisingly great selection of clothing; whatever is on your shopping list, you'll find it here.

Ben Franklin's has three locations: Kitty Hawk, Nags Head and Manteo. The Manteo store recently changed its name to Moncies, but the dependable Ben Franklin quality merchandise is still found here.

THE DUNES SHOPS

Rt. 158 Bypass, MP 4½

Map, pg. 47

The Dunes is worth mention not so much for its size (a dozen shops) as for its mix. Along with essential services such as paint, carpeting, cleaners, glass work, hairdressing and a bakery, they have the original Chinese restaurant on the Banks (Trade Winds) and a very nice woman's clothing store (Libby's).

SEAGATE NORTH

Rt. 158 Bypass, MP 5

Map, pg. 47

This u-shaped collection of two dozen small-to-medium shops has something for everyone. There's a pottery shop, a bakery, book store, tackle shop, cards and gifts, and much more. It's an especially good mall for furniture. Anchored by the Seafare III restaurant, this is a convenient shopping place for those vacationing in the Kitty Hawk/Duck/Corolla area.

SHERLI SHOPPES

Rt. 158 Bypass, MP 6

Map, pg. 57

A small mall anchored by two fo the finer things in life: surfing and cheese. These seven shops include textiles, a glass service, cleaners, and sportswear. The two anchors are Vitamin Sea, one of the established surfing stores on the Beach, and Scandia. Scandia has been a lifesaver for Banks gourmets for a long time now, offering the finest cheeses, wines, and hot breads seven days a week, year-round.

OCEANSIDE PLAZA

Rt. 158 Business, MP 9

Map, pg. 57

Oceanside Plaza is another small mall. Its eight shops offering beach goods, kitchen designs, music, flowers, food and a video arcade that's open all year and very popular.

SEASHORE SHOPS

Rt. 158 Business, MP 9½

Map, pg. 57

The Seashore shops are a compact line of five stores, not large as malls go, but worth a visit. Convenient to Rt. 158 Business, west side of the road, with parking in front.

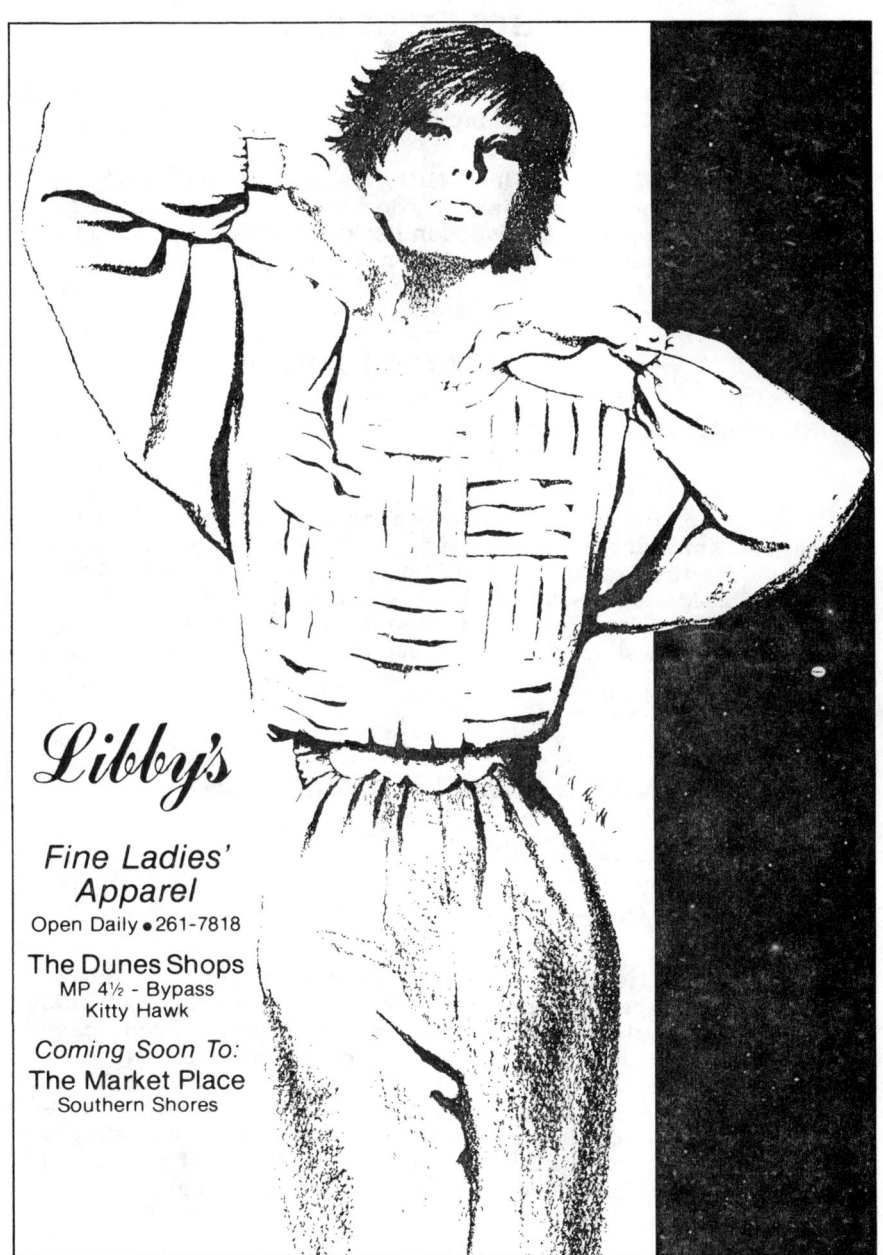

SEA HOLLY SQUARE

Rt. 158 Business, MP 9½

Map, pg. 57

Just north of the Kill Devil Hills/Nags Head line, Sea Holly Square is a shopping village. Its dozens of small shops are set close together on raised wooden decking, which is cool to the feet and pleasant just to wander on. Parking in front.

THE BEACH BARN

Rt. 158 Bypass, MP 10

Map, pg. 57

The Beach Barn, once one large shop, has been divided up into several smaller shops, most of which have been popular on the beach for the last few years. Here you'll find Birthday Suits, Carolina Moon, a wonderful gift shop, Bahama Bobs t-shirts, and the Shell Shop, selling just about every kind of shell there's ever been. The shops generally keep 10 a.m. to 9 p.m. hours in the summer.

NAGS HEAD HAMMOCKS

Rt. 158 Bypass, MP 10 1/2   441-6115

Map, pg. 70

Nags Head Hammocks are sold all over the country, but the claim to fame begins right here in Nags Head. The shop is in this new location next to the Pizza Hut and the expanded space allows for the displaying of the expanded product line. Not only do they make and sell hammocks, but you can also find a complete line of individually designed leisure furniture — porch swings, rocking chairs, foot stools and more. The shop is open from March till Christmas. They do plenty of mail order and will ship your purchase wherever it needs to go.

GRAY'S FAMILY DEPARTMENT STORE

Rt. 158 Business, MP 10½   Nags Head 441-5143
Scarborough Faire, Duck   Duck 261-3514
Map, pg. 70

Gray's has been an Outer Banks shopping place for over 35 years. Started by Mr. Gray (the father of this family owned and run business), the kids — Larry, Julie and Ronnie — now pretty much run the show. Here you'll find first quality clothing (namebrands such as Wrangler, Catalina, Keds, Portsider), shoes, beach supplies, toys, and gifts. You'll also find a homey atmosphere accented by the big band music that Mr. Gray loves and still promotes around the beach.

The Grays now have two stores: the original one on the beach road in Nags Head, open year-round, and a new one in the Scarborough Faire complex in Duck, open seasonally.

NAGS HEAD STATION

Rt. 158 Bypass, MP 11
Map, pg. 70

Located on the bypass, sound side, Nags Head Station is a painted pine, semi-indoor mall that is extremely pleasant on rainy or chilly days. Its multitude of small shops specialize in such goods as swimwear, jewelry, t-shirts, shoes, gifts, clothing, souvenirs, and snacks. One of our favorite stores here is the Southern Exposure Clothing Company, which specializes in fun, islandy-type clothes.

YE OLDE HAM SHOPPE

Rt. 158 Bypass, MP 9¾   441-6803
Map, pg. 57

This tiny shop is headquarters for an excellent selection of Smithfield and Country ham, slab bacon, hot ham biscuits and Virginia Diner peanuts.

The Ham Shoppe will bone and slice hams for party trays and will ships its merchandise anywhere. A catalog is available. The store is open year round. MC and Visa are honored.

GALLEON ESLANADE

Rt. 158 Business, MP 11   441-5505

Map, pg. 70

The Galleon is unmistakable — easily the least typecast shopping place on the beach. From far away it looks like Kublai Khan's pleasure dome, a gathering of white and pastel fairyland buildings that seem hardly to belong on the Banks. But they do. The Esplanade is built around a tastefully decorated courtyard that recalls the Arabian Nights. The shops specialize in clothing of outstanding quality and fine gift ideas. MC and Visa accepted throughout. A don't miss just north of the Esplanade is A Restaurant, by George, rated by many as one of the three or four finest on the beach (see our review in the Dining section).

SURFSIDE PLAZA

MP 13

Map, pg. 70

About half a mile south of Jockey's Ridge, between Rt. 158 Business and Bypass, this is a hard one to drive by. Twenty-five retail shops grouped like a British square around loads of parking. Jewelry, books, beach goods, ice cream, deli, fishing gear, toys, clothing, more.

OUTER BANKS MALL

Rt. 158 Bypass, MP 14

Map, pg. 80

Opened in 1983, with thirty-two retail stores, this vast new mall was immediately the largest on the Outer Banks — and it is still growing. This is an enclosed, extremely modern mall, with all the amenities like air conditioning, light wood, and attractive decorated atria among the shops. There are literally acres of parking out front. Anchored by Rose's, Peoples, and Safeway. Look for this one just south of Jockey's Ridge.

THE CHALET GIFT SHOP

Rt. 158 Business, MP 15½   441-6402
                        Map, pg. 80

A quick stop into the gift shop is impossible — there's simply too much to see to run in and out. Mrs. Johnson, the owner, has developed an impressive, wide-ranging collection of gifts, souvenirs, beach supplies, etc., in the years this shop has been around.

The shop has the largest collection of Raikes Bears in the area, music boxes of all kinds, jewelry, scrimshaw, Precious Moments figurines, pewter, clowns and carousels, and brass. They also carry collectible dolls and books.

The Chalet's summer hours are from 9 a.m. to 10 p.m. Off season hours are more limited.

NEWMAN'S

Rt. 158 Business, MP 13½   441-5791
                        Map, pg. 70

The bright pink building by the sea is all too easy to drive by for the first-timer. But generations of Beachgoers since 1939 have stopped here, making it one of the real old-time attractions of the Banks. The big draw, to us, was the exhibit of shells of the world, each marked with its scientific name and locale. (This is the best such display we have seen outside of a major metropolitan natural history museum.)

Newman's is also one of the best gift breaks in Nags Head. Along with thousands of Pacific, Indian Ocean, and Atlantic shells and shell items, they carry pewter, scrimshaw, beach clothing, jewelry, and lots of other gift items, many of which are locally made. Very few things, other than the shells, of course, are imported. Most are U.S.-made.

If you're on the Banks in mid-season, ask here about the annual Hermit Crab Race. It's sponsored by Newman's, and held the last Saturday in July. You can train up a champ yourself. It's great fun.

Newman's is open Easter to Thanksgiving. Off-season hours are 9 to 6 p.m., in-season open 9 a.m. to 10 p.m.

THE DISCOUNT STORE...
THAT DOESN'T DISCOUNT PEOPLE

In 1915, Mr. Paul Howard Rose opened a 5 & 10 Store with the dream of offering better quality merchandise at a lower price.

A lot has changed since Mr. Rose's time. From that one 5 & 10 Store in Henderson, N.C. grew a chain of over 214 Quality discount stores. Although our size has changed, some things will always remain the same at Roses.
— You can still find quality merchandise at affordable prices.
— We put our customers first because we appreciate your Business.
— Your satisfaction is always guaranteed or your money back.

Through the years, we have worked hard to meet your changing needs by;
— Buying in larger quantities, so your cost will be lower.
— We increased the sizes of our departments to bring you a wider selection of name brand merchandise. We now are 40,000 plus square feet.
— Each store is especially designed to meet the demands of your specific area.

All this plus fast and efficient service! Who could ask for more. Shop Roses and see that we live up to our motto... The discount store... that doesn't discount people...

Summer hours: 9 a.m.-10 p.m. Mon.-Sat.
9 a.m.-8 p.m. Sun.
7 days a week

R.V. CAHOON, INC.

Rt. 158 Business, MP 16½ 441-5358
Map, pg. 80

Cahoon's is one of the most general of general stores on the Banks. Located near Whalebone Junction, just north of Jennette's Pier, this store does a March through Thanksgiving business in convenience groceries, beer and wine, camping and fishing gear and supplies. Especially nice is their deli with custom-cut meats.

Open from 7 a.m. to 10 p.m. from Memorial Day to Labor Day; 7 a.m. to 8 p.m. during the fall and spring. Associated with the store are nine 2, 3 and 4-bedroom cottages nearby which can be reserved at the number above.

come make a discovery on roanoke island

Here on the isle of Roanoke, the spot chosen by Sir Walter Raleigh for the first colony in the new world... Here on our island in the sun, under swaying pines and live oaks... You'll find a special place. A sight to see. A world to discover if you haven't already. Room after room. 33 in all. Decorated with love and care. Chock full of all manner of gifts, crafts, fine art, jewelry and so much more. And Christmas things, of course. 25 beautifully decorated Christmas trees unlike anything you've ever seen before. Please come and experience it all.

Since 1967

island art gallery
and the
christmas shop

Highway 64 • Manteo   919 473-2838

a bavarian restaurant 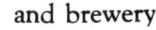 and brewery

the Weeping Radish

473-1157 at   The Christmas Shop

INSIDE

ROANOKE ISLAND

Few names in American history awaken echoes as "Roanoke" does. Roanoke Island...this is where, four centuries ago, the curtain began to rise on English colonization in the Americas...then dropped, never to lift again for that brave small first colony.

What happened to them? Where did they go, and why? To understand it all, to see the significance of this small, still-forested island, we'll have to go back—all the way to the 1580's.

In those days Spain, not England, ruled the waves, and the treasure lands in the New World as well. The Conquistadors had devastated South American Indian empires in their lust for gold. But they had left North America untouched, except for a settlement at St. Augustine, Florida. The French, too, were active, trying (and failing) to establish colonies in Canada and in South Carolina.

England was not in those days the daring seafaring nation she later became; but interest in the new lands was slowly building, fanned by Elizabeth's refusal to bow before Spanish might. It was Humphrey Gilbert, Sir Walter Raleigh's half-brother, who first advocated actual colonization of America, both as an advanced base for operations against the Spanish and to settle "...needie people of our Countrie, which now trouble the common wealth." Gilbert himself was lost on an expedition in 1583, but Raleigh caught the fever for colonization from him.

And fever it was. Raleigh, almost alone among his contemporaries, seemed to have some idea of the possibilities this vast, temperate, fertile land held for permanent settlers; and he was determined that they should be, not Spanish or French, but *English*.

In 1584 Raleigh dispatched his first exploring expedition. On July fourth—a date later to be commemorated throughout the land, but for different reasons—Captains Arthur Barlowe and Philip Amadas arrived off the Banks and began their explorations. They landed north of Kitty Hawk to take formal possession, and were astounded at the profusion of cedar, deer, wildfowl, and wild grapes (see 'Mother Vineyard'). They met the local Indians, who had a village on the northwest end of Roanoke Island, and found them friendly. They left after a month, taking along two Indians named Manteo and Wanchese, and their reports caused a stir in England. In fact, by the very next spring Raleigh had outfitted seven ships and 600 men, getting them to sea in April. Again, Raleigh himself could not go; Elizabeth wanted him in England in case of Spanish attack. Sir Richard Grenville was placed in charge of the fleet, with Ralph Lane as 'Lieutenant Governor'.

Grenville had a little trouble at Ocracoke Inlet—every one of his ships went aground, and his flagship was almost wrecked. But he pushed on, up the sound, to Roanoke.

Why did he choose Roanoke? There were better sites for a colony already known—the Chesapeake Bay area, farther north, had much better soil and also deep rivers. Grenville, Lane and Raleigh may have chosen Roanoke because it was inaccessible to large ships—*Spanish* ships. Or it may have been a simple miscalculation.

It was to have tragic effect.

The six hundred men spent the summer building a small earthwork fort, Fort Raleigh, and a few houses. In August, Grenville's ships sailed, leaving Lane in charge of 107 men.

The winter was not easy, but more ominous than the weather was the worsening of relations with the Roanoke Indians. A misunderstanding about an exchange of gifts led to a young Indian being accused of the theft of a cup. He was killed; the Indians retaliated; the English attacked their main village and killed many, including the chief. They tried to set up Manteo, who remained pro-English to the end, as the Indian king, but from then on Indian and white regarded each other as enemies. Perhaps that was why, when Grenville was late in returning, Lane decided to pull out when Sir Francis Drake stopped by in the spring. Grenville's relief fleet arrived just a few weeks later and he was surprised to find the island deserted. Unwilling to abandon the fort, Grenville left 15 soldiers there to winter over.

High dreams were dreamed that winter of 1586-7 in England, for Raleigh was pulling together, at long last, his colonizing expedition. Led by John White, three ships left Plymouth, carrying 120 men, women, and children.

The first mystery met them when they landed. The 15 men Grenville had left were gone; only one skeleton was found, moldering beside the demolished fort.

The new colonists shook their heads, doubtless prayed, but pitched in to clear land and build homes, guarding always against the hostile and shadowy figures in the forest. On August 18 a child was born, Virginia Dare, the first English child born in the New World (though let us not forget that the Spanish had been around, farther south, for almost a century). Governor White, her grandfather, left with the autumn for England to organize more supplies and colonists.

But war intervened, war with Spain, and, with Philip's Armada menacing England, Elizabeth had no ships to spare for Raleigh's dream colonies. It was not till 1590 that White was able to return, and when at last he landed again on Roanoke, the village had been evacuated, and the colonists had gone—where? On trees nearby were carved the words: CROATOAN; CRO. But on Croatan Island no traces have ever been found.

What happened to the Lost Colony?

Paul Green, in the last scene of his historical drama of the same name, suggests that they abandoned Roanoke because of a Spanish threat, hoping to stay with friendly Indians of Manteo's tribe. As to what happened after that, there are two theories current. One holds that the main body went north, arriving safely at Chesapeake Bay, but were later killed by Powhatan when the Jamestown expedition arrived in 1607. The other is that the main body did find friendly Indians at Croatan Island (now part of Hatteras) or elsewhere, intermarried with them as they wandered about North Carolina, and survive today in the blue eyes, curly hair, and English surnames of the Lumbee Indians of Robeson County.

No one will ever know for sure.

Roanoke was left to the Indians for a long time after, but eventually, circa 1655, the press of whites southward out of Tidewater Virginia reached the Northern Banks, and families still seen today on the island—names like Gallop, Baum, Meekins, Tillet, Daniels and Midgett—settled down to stay. The small population was supported by stock raising and small-scale farming through the 17th and 18th centuries.

The Civil War began the process of the island's awakening with a cannonade. At 10:30 a.m., February 7, 1862, a gigantic shallow-draft Federal fleet, with 12,000 troops aboard, began a bombardment of Confederate shore batteries on the northern end of the island (an overlook at Northwest Point today commemorates this battle). That evening 7500 Federals disembarked at Ashby's Landing (now Skyco). The next morning they moved north, opposed bitterly every step of the way up the island, till a final charge routed the Rebels, who surrendered. The War was marked also by the quartering, on the northern end of the island (west of where the Elizabethan Motel now stands) of some three thousand newly freed slaves, most of whom were relocated off the island when the war ended.

As population increased after 1865, homes clustered around the two harbors at Shallowbag Bay and at Mill Landing. These were referred to respectively as the 'Upper End' and 'Lower End' of the island. Around 1886 the 'Lower Enders' grew understandably tired of being called that and chose the name of Wanchese for their town; Manteo followed suit, incorporating in 1899, shortly after being named seat of newly formed Dare

County. Since then both towns have grown slowly, but steadily.

In 1902, Reginald Fessenden, a pioneer in the development of radio, transmitted signals from an apparatus on Roanoke Island to one on Hatteras.

In 1900-1903, the brothers Wright took a ship from Roanoke for Kitty Hawk.

In 1928, a privately-constructed bridge first connected the Island with the Beach at Nags Head, opening the outer islands to development.

In 1937, *The Lost Colony* was performed.

After World War II, the stabilization of the Banks and the construction of roads and bridges, along with the creation of the National Park, brought modern tourism and real-estate development to the Island.

Today Roanoke Island has two characters. For much of the year it is a quiet, low-key area, where most of the three thousand permanent residents know one another by name, and the principal commercial activity is fishing at Mill Landing. All this begins to change round about May, when the golden tide of tourists begins; and the months of summer are full of activity, especially at Fort Raleigh, *The Lost Colony,* and in the shops and stores of Downtown Manteo and along Route 64/264. Still, though activity is brisk, Roanokers have not yet succumbed to full-scale commercialism. Most of the island is still wild, with forests and marshes covering the land outside the town. The people are still friendly, and beauty still lies on the land during the long humming evenings of summer. As Amadas and Barlowe found in 1584, Roanoke might still be said to be "...the goodliest land under the cope of heaven."

THE QUADRICENTENNIAL

The years 1984-1987 are the quadricentennial of the Roanoke Voyages — the four hundredth anniversary of the first attempt at the explorations and colonizations that spread the English tongue from a small island on the coast of Europe to the farthest corners of the globe.

Preparations for a birthday party like that take a while. Fortunately, Great Britain, the U.S., North Carolina, and Dare County started early.

Canny as ever, the North Carolinians have decided against the kind of gaudy, hyped hoopla that is over in a day, leaving nothing behind but litter. Herbert Bliven, chairman of the county advisory committee and a well-known Manteo artist and printmaker, defined the careful objectives of the four-year-long celebration to us.

The first is educational: to bring the Roanoke story and the Elizabethan period to children and adults, to bring it to life again in the mind. The second was to build and beautify: to commemorate the anniversary with improvements that would add to the attractiveness of the island for years to come.

Of course, there will also be plenty of more participative celebrations, especially during the summer months. It won't be dull!

The educational goals of the celebration are being accomplished through the distribution of information on natural resources, history, Indian life, Elizabethan heraldry, and more. It is available at schools, tourist centers, and from the Dare County 400th Advisory Committee, P.O. Drawer 1000, Manteo, NC 27954.

Permanent improvements to the island are considerable, and continuing. We always considered Roanoke one of the garden spots of the country, but the new state-funded grading along Route 164, the 1500 live oak and crepe myrtle plantings, and the removal of billboards along the main highway have made it a kind of triumphal avenue in late spring and summer. The brilliant scarlets and violets of the myrtles set off the somber dark greens of forest, and the heraldic banners (representing local businesses, believe it or not) you will see along the roadway make four hundred years ago seem much closer to today than we ordinarily think.

The state has also funded major archaeological projects to clarify our understanding of the times. Eastern Carolina University teams are investigating Algonkian Indian sites, and the National Park Service is undertaking a new attempt to establish the location of the "Cittie of Ralegh."

Another island initiative is the establishment of a permanent fishing museum at Wanchese. You can visit the outdoor display, the opening phase of the museum, at the Seafood Industrial Park in Wanchese

Finally, the most ambitious and impressive permanent commemorative site is on Ice Plant Island, near Manteo: the Elizabeth II and the Visitor Center

ROANOKE ISLAND

ATTRACTIONS:
1. The Elizabethan Gardens, pg. 291
2. Fort Raleigh, pg. 292
3. The Lost Colony, pg. 293
4. N.C. Marine Resources Center, pg. 295
5. Weirs Point and Fort Hugar, pg. 296
6. Dare County Regional Airport, pg. 297
7. Mother Vineyard, pg. 299
8. Dare County Library, pg. 300
9. Dare County Tourist Bureau, pg. 300
10. The Island Gallery and Christmas Shop, pg. 301
11. Wanchese and Mill Landing, pg. 301
12. Downtown Manteo, pg. 303
13. Elizabeth II State Historic Site, pg. 304

RECREATION:
1. Salty Dawg Marina, pg. 312

HOTELS/MOTELS/CAMPGROUNDS
1. Elizabethan Inn, pg. 142
2. Dare Haven Motel, pg. 143
3. Duke of Dare, pg. 145
4. Scarborough House Inn, pg. 143
5. Sandpiper's Trace Campground, pg. 180

RESTAURANTS:
1. Queen Anne's Revenge, pg. 243
2. Fisherman's Wharf, pg. 243
3. The Elizabethan, pg. 242
4. Weeping Radish, pg. 244

SHOPPING:
1. Vista Florist and Garden Shop, pg. 313
2. Maria's Gift Corner/Wanchese Handicraft Center, pg. 313
3. Harbor Gifts and Crafts, pg. 314
4. Chesley Mall, pg. 314
5. Ace Hardware, pg. 314
6. RJ's Nursery, pg. 315
7. Second Time Around, pg. 315

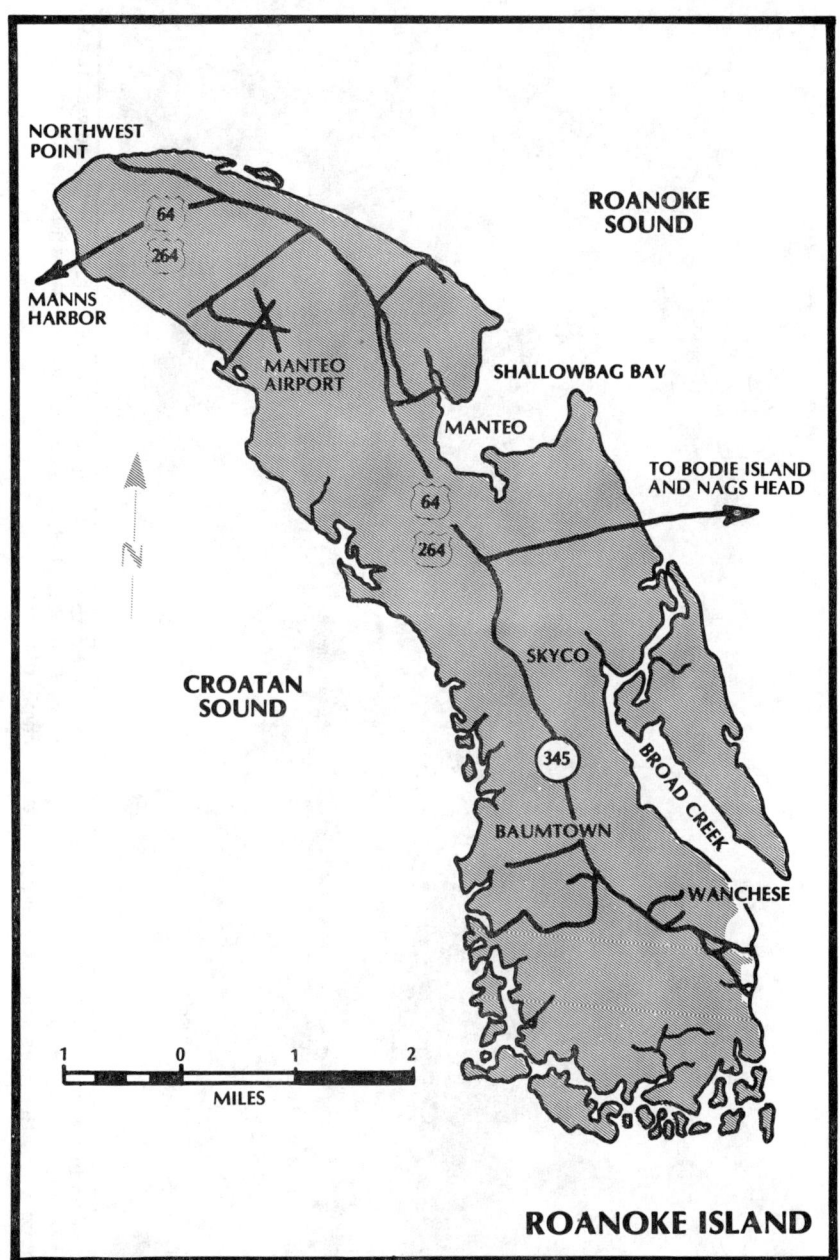

290 — ROANOKE ISLAND

Gardens in full bloom - the Elizabethan Gardens on the North end of Roanoke Island in full bloom. Those visiting the gardens are treated to a multi-colored show of nature's finest including the crepe myrtle shown in the formal garden above where the trees are at the height of their purple bloom.

ROANOKE ISLAND
ATTRACTIONS

THE ELIZABETHAN GARDEN

Manteo 473-3234
Map, pg. 294

    The Gardens are one of the 'must-see' attractions on Roanoke Island. Along with Fort Raleigh and *The Lost Colony*, the Elizabethan Gardens are located on Route 64 north of Manteo.
    And they are a sensual delight. From the moment of entry, through the ivy-covered Great Gate, a visitor begins to feel the hurry and anxiety of the twentieth century drop away. As in the formal gardens of the Governor's Palace at Williamsburg, each tree, each flower bed, each jewellike piece of statuary and each gently curving brick or sand path has been designed to a severe and classic discipline of beauty. Horticulturists, gardeners, and history buffs will all appreciate such touches as a replica of a 16th century orangery, an herb garden, an ancient live oak believed to have been living when Sir Richard Grenville first set foot on Roanoke Island. There is a great deal more to the Gardens than is evident from a quick glance, as Louis Midgett, the Superintendent there for more than 26 years, told us. For example, the bricks of the walks throughout were salvaged over the years from all over North Carolina, from churches and tobacco flues; they are all pre-Revolutionary. The famous Virginia Dare statue, which looks rather preciously and incongruously Graeco-Roman to the modern eye, was conceived after an Indian legend that said Virginia, far from dying, grew up amid them and became a beautiful woman. The statue itself was sculpted by Louise Lander in Italy in 1859, was lost at sea for some years, recovered, then stood in the North Carolina State House before being given to Paul Green to take back to Roanoke. But aside from all the history, the spot we like best was the Sunken Gardens. Its quiet beauty let us contemplate all the tumult of the past in bee-buzzing peace.
    The Elizabethan Gardens is open year round, though it's at its best in the months of April (azalea, dogwood, pansies, wisteria), May (rhododendron, marcrantha, hydrangea), July (gardenia, roses, magnolia, crepe myrtle, oriental lilies, all the summer annuals) and autumn (geraniums, hibiscus, impatiens,

camellias). Hours are from 9 to 5, except that, when *The Lost Colony* is playing during the summer months, the Gardens stay open till 8 p.m. Admission is $2.00 for adults; children under 12 free; call for group, senior citizen, and handicapped rates.

FORT RALEIGH

Rt. 64, north of Manteo   473-2111
Map, pg. 294

    The center, historically, of any Outer Banks trip is located some three miles north of Manteo, on Route 64, near the northwestern tip of Roanoke Island. Here are grouped a complex of activities, dramatic, historic, archaeological, horticultural, and just plain fun, all dedicated to those first efforts of the Elizabethan English who found a new nation in the West.
    The Fort Raleigh National Historic Site is the center and headquarters for the National Park Service on the Outer Banks. Designated as a National Historic Site in 1941, its 144-acre expanse of woods and beach includes the location of the settlement sites of 1585 and 1587, a Visitor Center, the (restored) fort that Ralph Lane built, and a nature trail. Nearby are located the Elizabethan Gardens, the Waterside Theatre, and National Park Service Headquarters.
    The visitor will enter the site by turning north (right, if you came from Manteo) off Route 64/264. A circular drive leads to parking lots located at the Visitor Center; admission and parking are free.
    The Visitor Center is a fun place. Probably it's best to start with the displays in the small museum to the right while waiting for the hourly movie to start. Between them, the museum and the 10-minute orientation movie will put you and the kids in the picture as to what you're about to see and experience. Ready for a musical interlude? Move into a 400-year-old Tudor room from Heronden Hall in Kent. Aficionados will delight in noting the Tudor rose in the mantlepiece, the large eyes and the masculinity of the carved women, the beautiful old oak panelling, the stone fireplace with facings of herringbone-laid brick, and the blown glass in the leaded window lights. The furniture, too, is period.
    Enter the musician in slops and doublets. For twenty or thirty minutes he'll entertain you with the lute, harpsichord, recorder, and psaltery, singing sweet madrigals and dancing.
    That complete, join one of the guided tours around the Fort area. Depending on the time of day and season of the year, you'll be treated to living history programs on such topics as "Food

and Farming in 16th Century America," "Life on Roanoke Island," or "Pikes, Powder Flasks and Petronels."

Sometime on your pregrinations, you will encounter the Fort. It is only partially a reconstruction, for it's on the exact site of the original, and is pretty much as it must have looked after the colonists disappeared and slowly, slowly, the pines and grasses began to take over the scarred earth again. It's a strange feeling standing inside the fort; it's so small, and the woods are so close. After the Indians turned hostile, the abandoned colonists must have felt themselves at the ends of the earth.

Just past the Fort, to your left, you'll find the Thomas Hariot Nature Trail. This is a short self-guided trail, with a soft fine pine-needle surface and gentle gradients. Plaques along the trail point out the native plants that the colonists encountered and tried to put to use. The lower part of the trail leads to the sandy shore of Roanoke Sound, quite near the spot where Sir Richard Grenville first stepped ashore on Roanoke. Swimming is permitted here, but it's quite shallow. There are no lifeguards.

Back at the Center, you might want to drop by the Lost Colony Craft Shop before you leave.

The Fort Raleigh National Historic Site is open on the following schedule:

Mid-June—Late-August: 9:00 a.m. to 8:00 p.m. Mon-Sat; Sundays, 9:00 a.m. to 6 p.m.

Remainder of year: 9:00 a.m. to 5 p.m., including Saturdays & Sundays.

THE LOST COLONY

Near Fort Raleigh, Manteo   473-3414
Map, pg. 294

The Lost Colony is, in a few words, a must-see.

It has been since 1937 — over forty years now. What is it? It's a marriage of drama, history, dance, choir, costume, and music, carried out in an expansive outdoor theatre on the shores of Roanoke Sound. Called 'historical drama', *The Lost Colony* was the first such work ever produced, the brainchild of Pulitzer Prize-winning author Paul Green.

The play is presented in two acts. Act I opens with a prologue by the Choir and the Historian, a sort of narrator who provides for unity in the drama. Subsequent scenes are set in an Indian village on Roanoke, 1584; in England, in the court of Elizabeth; again, on Roanoke, a year later; and on a street in Plymouth, England, as the colonists embark, filled with fear and hope. Act II is set, for the most part, in the 'Cittie of Raleigh' on Roanoke— which was somewhere within a quarter-mile of where the

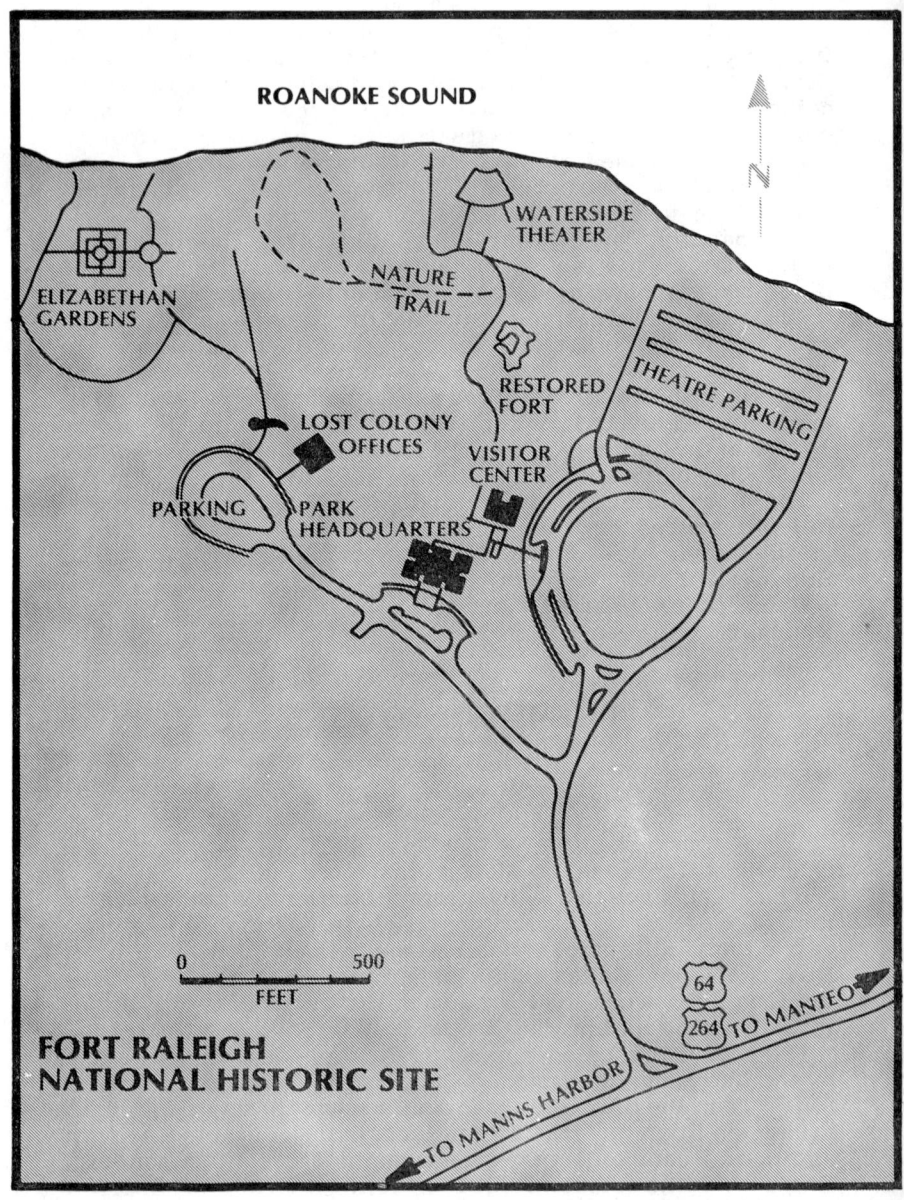

Waterside Theatre now stands—and follows the web of circumstance that led to the final tragedy: the disappearance of the colonists, into...legend.

It's great entertainment, but it's more. The ending is powerful, and sad. You may find yourself weeping.

The Waterside Theatre is the semicircular bowl where the play is presented. It's just north of Fort Raleigh; bear to the right as you enter from Route 64 to reach the large parking area. As you walk in you can see the waters of the sound over the backdrop. Things to be aware of at the Waterside are: the wooden seats are uncomfortable; bring blankets or pillows (pillows can be rented at the Theatre). It gets cold in the evenings, when the wind blows off the sound, so bring sweaters along even in July and August. Finally, mosquitoes can be vicious, especially when it has rained recently. The woods nearby are sprayed, but this is only partially effective; bring repellent. There are special accommodations available for the handicapped in the uppermost row at the entrance and in the first row.

And with all the creature comforts taken care of, settle back and enjoy a thoroughly professional, well-rehearsed, technically outstanding show. The leads are played by professional actors, and most of the backstage personnel are pros too; and it shows. Supporting actors are often local people, and some island residents pass from part to part as they grow up...but they are all good. The colorful costumes, the choir, the tension inherent in the play itself make it a combination of delights that you won't soon forget.

Now: tickets. All shows start at 8:30 p.m. The show season runs from June 11 to August 28 and is presented nightly, except Sunday. Adult tickets are $9.00 with lesser rates for children 12 and under, active military, senior citizens, and handicapped in wheelchairs. Groups of 15 or more can obtain a 10% discount.

This is probably the most popular event on the Banks in the summer, and we recommend you make reservations, though you can try your luck at the door if you care to. You can make paid mail reservations by writing *The Lost Colony*, Box 40, Manteo, NC 27954; or make phone reservations between June 7 and August 28 by calling (919) 473-3414. These unpaid reservations will be held at the box office for pickup until 7:30 p.m.

NORTH CAROLINA MARINE RESOURCES CENTER

Rt. 116   473-3493

Map, pg. 289

Tucked away northwest of Manteo on route 64, by Manteo

Airport, is a surprising place called the Marine Resources Center. Sounds dull, right? Sure it does — if we hadn't mentioned it you'd have driven right by. It isn't. It's one of the 'sleepers' of the Banks, a place you won't want to miss if you have the slightest interest in the sea, the Banks, or the life that thrives in this unique chain of barrier islands.

The Resources Center contains labs, for the use of marine scientists; and a reference library, on marine-related topics. But these aren't what attracts visitor. The display section and aquarium — that's what you'll want to see.

Admission is free. Once in the door, you'll walk among displays on underwater archaeology, cetacea, trawling, marine ecosystems; children love the touch table, with live marine creatures you can feel. The aquarium is surprisingly beautiful. Set like jewels in a long, darkened corridor, the lighted tanks display loggerhead turtles, longnosed gar, ugly burfish and sea robin, lobster, octopi, and a sharky-looking smooth dogfish. The aquaria start out with fresh water species, shading through brackish to salt water. The biggest is 3000 gallons, holding salt water. The fish are fed every day at 3:30 and you might want to make a special point to be there then.

And there's still more. Feature movies on marine and biological topics are shown at different times. During the summer, a lecture series runs on Thursday nights (7:30 p.m.; free). There's a schedule of daytime programs for all age groups, including field trips, bird walks through Pea Island, and more; check at the desk for a current schedule. The Center caters to groups of any kind, and can even supply meeting facilities in its conference room, seminar room, or 240-seat auditorium.

It's a surprising place. To reach it, drive north from Manteo on route 64. Turn left on Rt. 116, following signs to airport; the Center will be on your right. It's open from 9 a.m. to 5 p.m. Monday through Friday, 1 p.m. to 5 p.m. Saturdays and Sundays.

WEIRS POINT AND FORT HUGAR

N. end of Roanoke Island   Map, pg. 289

Another of the improvements for the 400th was the development of Weirs Point, at the northwest corner of the island, where the Route 64/264 bridge arrives from Manns Harbor. Empty shoreline as recently as fall of '83, it is now a pretty, easily accessible public beach. Parking is available at the first turnoff after the bridge.

About three hundred yards out (the island has migrated quite a bit in a hundred and twenty years), in six feet of water, lie the remains of Fort Hugar, the largest Confederate fort on the island during the Union invasion of 1862. Archaeological work is being undertaken there now.

A few years later, from a hut on this beach, one of the unsung geniuses of the electrical age began investigating what was then called "wireless telegraphy." Reginald Fessenden held hundreds of patents on radiotelephony and electronics, but died without credit for many of them.

For most people, though, swimming and fishing in the sound will take precedence over vanished forts and disappointed inventors. The beach is sandy and shallow, and shoals very gradually, except under the bridge, where currents scour a bit deeper. If you approach in a boat, watch carefully for stumps and old pilings. Picnic benches, a Dare County information kiosk, and restrooms are also available at Weirs.

DARE COUNTY REGIONAL AIRPORT

Rt. 116, next to the Marine Resources Center   473-2600
Map, pg. 289

Dare County (formerly Manteo) is the major airfield serving the Outer Banks, and the only one with fuel and services (the others, at Kitty Hawk, Hatteras, and Ocracoke, are paved strips only). Manteo has three runways, all asphalt-surfaced; orientation as shown in map. Runways 10-28 measure 3180, runways 16-34 measure 3290, and runways 4-22 measure 3800. Fuel: 100 octane low-lead and jet "A" fuel available. Equipment: VOR and DME, NDB, VASI, REILS, Unicom U-1 122.8. For runway lights key 123.0 five times in five seconds.

Dare County is the point of arrival of most of those who come to the Banks by air, including some VIPs, and it has the services to match. There are rental cars by B&R, a local company; a limo service; hot sandwiches and drinks from machines; and restrooms. There are also two taxi services (see Directory).

Dare County Airport is operated by the Dare County Airport Authority and managed by Mr. Clarence Skinner. It provides light aircraft rentals, flight instruction, sightseeing tours, and charter services out of Dare County. Call the number above to make arrangements.

In August of 1986 a brand new, Outer Banks style building will become the terminal, taking the place of the small, grey building presently serving this capacity.

Dare County Airport provides service and minor maintenance from 8 a.m. until 8 p.m. during the summer and from 8 a.m. until 6 p.m. during the off season.

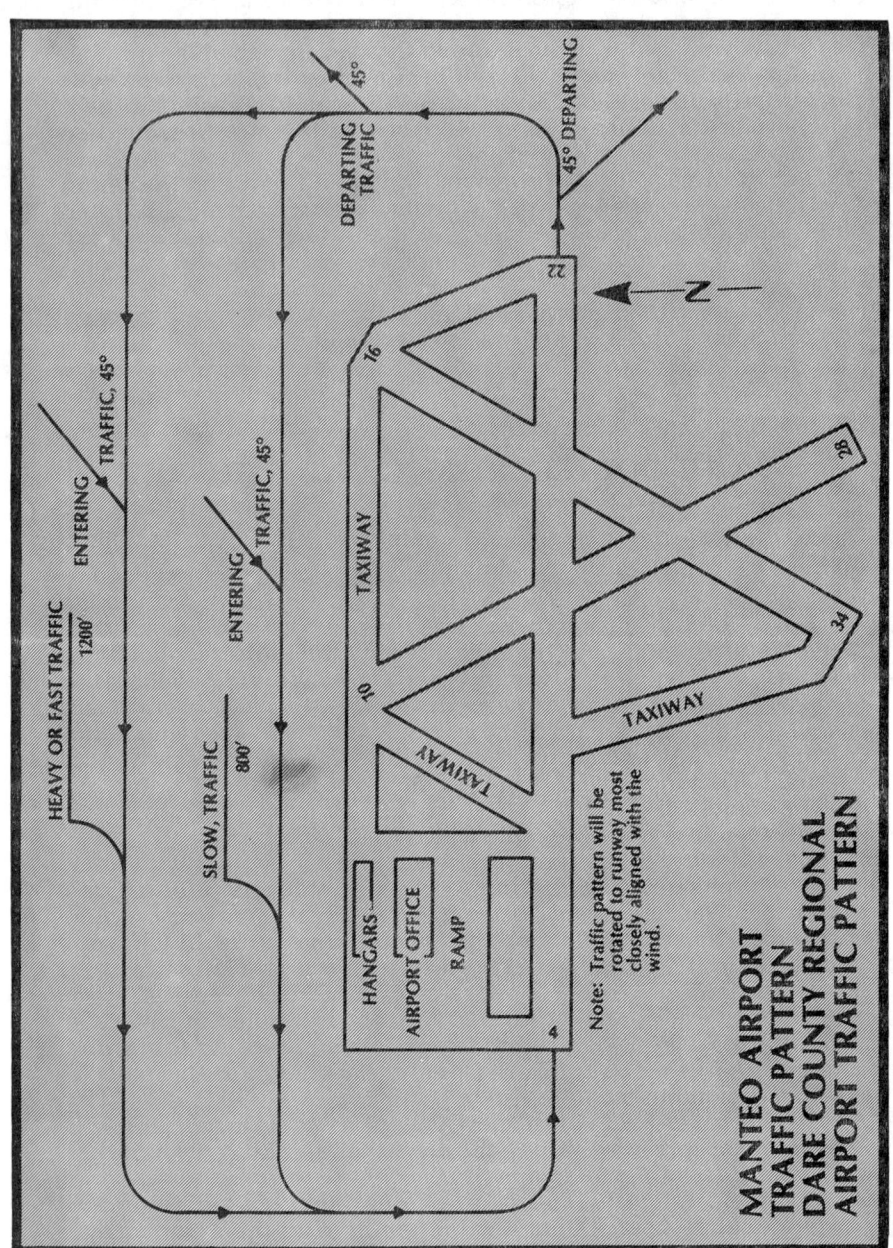

MOTHER VINEYARD

Manteo   Map, pg. 289

'Mother Vineyard Scuppernong, the Original American Wine' is still produced by a company in Petersburg, Virginia. Old-timers in town say the wine once produced in Manteo was far superior, but the Petersburg product did not taste bad when we sampled a couple of bottles. It is a pink wine, quite sweet. If you like white port or Mogen David you will take to scuppernong wine. You can find it in many of the Banks groceries.

All this is a roundabout way of getting to the fact that the oldest grapevine in the U.S. is in Manteo.

That's right: the oldest. You see, when the first settlers arrived here, the Banks were *covered* with wild grapes. Arthur Barlowe wrote to Sir Walter Raleigh in 1584:

> "...being where we first landed very sandy and low toward the water side, but so full of grapes as the very beating and surge of the sea overflowed them, of which we found such plenty, as well there as in all places else, both on the sand and on the green soil, on the hills as in the plains, as well on every little shrub, as also climbing toward the tops of high cedars, that I think in all the world the like abundance is not to be found."

The Mother Vine is one of those ancient grapevines, so old that it *may* have been planted even before whites arrived in the New World. Certainly it was already old in the 1750's, as records attest, and scuppernong grape vines do not grow swiftly. Another story is that this vine was transplanted to Roanoke Island by some among the Fort Raleigh settlers. Whichever story is true, whoever planted the Mother Vine, it is ancient— over three hundred years old, most likely. And still producing fine fat tasty grapes.

In fact, for many years a small winery, owned by the Etheridge family, cultivated the vine on Baum's Point, making the original Mother Vineyard wine until the late 50's.

Despite all its history, the Mother Vine doesn't offer much to the eye, nor is it easy to find. To try, drive north out of Manteo on Route 64. About 3/4 mile past the city limits, turn right on Mother Vineyard road. Go about half a mile, to where the road makes a sharp turn to the right at the bay. The patient old vine crouches beneath a canopy of leaves, twisted and gnarled, ancient and enduring, about three hundred feet on the left past the turn. It's private property — so please stay on the road.

DARE COUNTY LIBRARY

Manteo 473-2372
Map, pg. 289

Sometimes there's nothing for it but to curl up with a good book. One library building serves all the northern Outer Banks (there's also a branch in Hatteras Village). From a location on Highway 64, about half a mile north of Downtown Manteo, Librarian Amelia Frazer runs a 37,000-volume library with recordings, film strips and slides, meeting facilities, and a local history room that's invaluable for probing more deeply into the lore of the Banks. Hours: Monday, 9 a.m. - 7 pm.; Tuesday through Friday, 9 a.m. - 5:30 p.m.; Saturday, 10 a.m. - 2 p.m.; closed Sunday.

DARE COUNTY TOURIST BUREAU

Manteo 473-2138
Map, pg. 289

Got a question? The Dare County Tourist Bureau is set up to help, with a large collection of brochures, maps, and the latest data on hand and available to the visitor. They're located at the corner of Virginia Dare Road (Route 64/264) and Budleigh Street, in a low white stucco building. Parking is available in back; the information desk is through the right-hand door, fronting on Budleigh. Open year round Monday through Friday, 9 a.m. to 5 p.m., and open Saturdays and holidays as well during the summer season, 10 a.m. to 2 p.m.

In case you want to write ahead for specific information, Dare County's mailing address is P.O. Box 399, Manteo, N.C. 27954.

THE ISLAND GALLERY AND CHRISTMAS SHOP

Manteo 473-2838
Map, pg. 289

There is only one word for the Christmas Shop and Island Gallery: **fascinating.** From hundreds of miles away people travel to the Banks for the (nearly) sole purpose of visiting Edward Greene's burgeoning world of fantasy.

Basically, you might say that this establishment is a store...because things are sold here. There, all resemblance to conventional stores ends. There are seven rambling, multilevel buildings in the Shop, but there's not a single counter, display rack, or glass case. Instead there are rooms, room after room, furnished with antique furniture (*not* for sale), and each is filled with wonder.

"We stock a minimum of about 50,000 different items, from 200 companies, 150 artists and craftspeople, and 35 countries," says Greene, formerly an actor in New York City. "And there isn't a thing in the building anybody **needs** to have. So we have to let each product tell us how it wants to be displayed."

The result is mind-boggling...like a child's dream of everything you ever wanted in the world rolled into one. Whole walls are filled with toys, pottery, handcrafts. Whole rooms of porcelain eggs, others filled with baskets, with carvings, with miniatures, with handmade jewelry, with ornaments, with seashells, art, Christmas cards. 125 switches light innumerable atmosphere lights that give everything a magic glow. Imagine, added to all this, thirty-three decorated christmas trees. It sounds like quite a production...and it is. You'll have to see it before you realize what a fantastic place this is. Bring plenty of money or your credit cards.

The Shop and Gallery also contains a Garden Shop (thousands of house plants), an old-fashioned candy store, a card and stationery shop, a basket shop, an Edwardian portrait parlor, candles, ice cream, suncatchers, and an authentic Bavarian restaurant with its own brewery, The Weeping Radish...there's a lot of space, and it's crammed full.

The shop and Gallery is located about half a mile south of Manteo, on the sea (east) side of Route 64/264. Hours: mid-June through Labor Day, daily 9:30 a.m. - 9 p.m., Sundays 9:30 a.m. to 5:30 p.m.; Labor Day through mid-June, 9:30 a.m. to 6:00 p.m., Sundays 9:30 a.m. to 5:30 p.m. Closed Christmas and New Year's Day.

WANCHESE AND MILL LANDING

Wanchese   Map, pg. 289

Don't look for downtown Wanchese — you won't find any. This quintessential small town is miles of winding country roads, lined with white-clapboard 1920's-style homes, each with a boat in either the front or the back yard. Girls on horseback clop along the roads, and the people (almost all year round residents — Wanchese is no summer community, like Kitty Hawk or Kill Devil Hills) are North Carolina at its best, honest and uncomplicated and friendly. Small shell, curio, and handicraft shops are open in the summer, and if you're after sand-cast pewter, patchwork tablecloths, rusty old trawler anchors, or handmade shell goods, you can easily spend a day just wandering, looking, and buying.

At the very end of Route 345, you'll find one of the most picturesque, and also most overlooked, parts of the entire Outer Banks — Mill Landing. Painters, photographers, those who love the sea, and just plain tourists shouldn't miss it.

Mill Landing is a quarter-mile of crowded soundfront that is home port for a small fleet of oceangoing fishing trawlers. These sea-battered, rusty, but proud little ships spend most of their lives off Cape May and Hatteras, fifty miles out at sea, bringing in the seafood that appears in a day or two in restaurants all along the East Coast. Mill Landing is four fish companies, Wanchese Fish Co., Etheridge's, Randall Tillett's, and Moon Tillett's. In the middle of it all, perched above the booms and nets, it's the Fisherman's Wharf Restaurant. Mill Landing is hardly a "touristy" place, as you can tell while squeezing between refrigerator semis and breathing air thick enough to fertilize a cornfield, but it has its appeal. It's anything but quaint, but it's real, and if you want to lay in a stock of fresh fish, shrimp, or scallops, stop at the Wanchese Fish Company, halfway down the landing; they'll sell you some in retail lots. Fisherman's Wharf is the tall wooden building with the stairway.

Out beyond the inlet, you'll see the new concrete bulkhead recently built by the State of North Carolina as part of their effort to develop the fishing industry. It was designed to bring the really big companies in to pack fish right here in Wanchese. The current difficulty is the shoaling that Oregon Inlet (under the bridge to Hatteras Island) is experiencing; several trawlers have gone aground there, and many are avoiding it by using other, but less convenient, means of getting to the open sea. Large-scale dredging is necessary, and even this might not work. It has the local trawler operators worried (see "Oregon Inlet," pg. 106). Meanwhile, though, the visitor can enjoy the photo and painting opportunities. An especially interesting facility is a new four-hundred-ton marine railway at Wanchese Shiplift, Inc. (phone 473-2194). It's an interesting sight even if you don't have a hole in your hull!

The residents of Wanchese generally welcome visitors, but there *are* a few common-sense things to keep in mind. The trawlers are working boats, and are *not* enthusiastic about having uninvited visitors aboard. The fish processors and boatyards are also industrial enterprises, as well as presenting special hazards to the unwary, so don't go bumbling around; sketch and photograph as much as you like, but please don't interfere with work.

DOWNTOWN MANTEO

DOWNTOWN MANTEO

Roanoke Island   Map, pg. 308

Despite its indirect "Cittie of Ralegh" antecedents, Manteo, as a town, is not all that old. There were only a few houses on Shallowbag Bay, on the eastern coast of the island, when Dare County was formed in 1870 and the town designated as the county seat. ("Manteo" was one of the two Roanoke Indians who accompanied the explorers back to England after the first expedition.) Today, though, after over a century of slow growth, Manteo is the largest town on the Banks, and a year round, comfortable, diversified community.

The downtown area, fronting directly on the bay, has undergone intensive redevelopment in the last few years. "The Waterfront," a pleasingly styled shopping and residential project of Renaissance Development Corporation, is the main attraction of this new look to Manteo. Within its 3 story, courtyard design, 9 specialty shops, 34 condominiums and a first class restaurant, Cafe Rene, are located. With the breezeways and water views and the exceptional landscaping that surrounds the Waterfront, it provides a relaxing, cool alternative to the busier shopping available in the beach area. There are plans for expansion too. Within the next few years, the development should offer modern docks with 110 and 220 hook-ups and a comfort station with restrooms, showers, washers and dryers. Sales for the condominiums are handled by Hudgins Real Estate and an agent is usually on site in the model.

Across the street from the Waterfront, in the center of the downtown area, are other shops well worth your visit. Establishements such as Fearing's, the Green Dolphin pub, Manteo Booksellers, the Duchess of Dare Restaurant, the Pioneer Theatre, Tickled Pink, and almost forty other small-to-medium-sized businesses are packed into a four-square-block area, just like the center of every small town used to be before Henry Ford came up with his infernal carriage. (There's plenty of parking, though, by the Municipal Dock area — just drive toward the water.)

There's more to do than shop and eat. From anywhere on Queen Elizabeth Street you can look south and see R.K. Harniman's 15,000-lb., 24-foot statue of Sir Walter Raleigh. To its left, about 50 yards away on a point of land, stands the town's American Bicentennial Park. Read the inscription under the cross...and shudder at its relevenace today. There are picnic benches and comfortable places nearby to sit and enjoy the view.

Turning north, you will find the new docking of the waterfront a pleasant place to stroll, sit on weathered benches, and take pictures.

The Four Hundredth anniversary of the Roanoke Voyages brought the *Elizabeth II* to her mooring across Doughs Creek; more about her in a moment. A bit farther north is the municipal parking lot, a public boat ramp, and the Manteo post office.

The relaxed, small-town atmosphere typical of Manteo in the years we have known it has picked up quite a lot during Dare County's four-year-long commemoration of the Roanoke voyages (see "Roanoke Island"). During these celebration years visitors to the island, and to the town, will find a lot of new construction and a lot of things to do. Several downtown streets have been resurfaced with river rock. A boat construction way was built at the end of Sir Walter Street, and the *Elizabeth II*, a full-size reproduction of a 16-century English sailing ship, was launched there in 1983; it is permanently moored at The Elizabeth II State Historic Site (see "Elizabeth II"). Be sure and head across the new bridge and take in the Visitor's Center and new beach there.

If, as most visitors do, you reach the Banks via Route 158, you can find Manteo by continuing south till you reach Whalebone Junction. Turn right there on Route 64/264. Continue across both bridges and the causeway and turn right again at the T at its end. Turn right at either of the town's first two stoplights to go downtown.

We think you'll like Manteo, and make friends there. We certainly have.

THE ELIZABETH II

Elizabeth II State Historic Site   473-5522
Map, pg. 308

The centerpiece of the quadricentennial, moored permanently in the harbor of downtown Manteo, is one of the most characteristic artifacts of English preindustrial civilization — a wooden sailing ship.

And a beautiful one. Unexpectedly colorful in bright blue, red, and yellow, her hull of nut-brown, gradually weathering wood, she lifts her foremast, mainmast, and lateen mizzen sharply toward the sky. Her rigging is a hempen web of tackle, so complex as to confuse the eye. Her high-sided hull and sloped stern and foredeck lend her the awkward grace of a newly hatched duckling.

Elizabeth II's story properly begins in 1584, when Thomas Cavendish mortgaged his estates to build the Elizabeth for the second expedition to Roanoke Island. With five other vessels, she took the first colonizing expedition to the New World.

Four hundred years later, galvanized by the approaching quadricentennial of that faraway beginning, private and governmental entities in North Carolina began planning for an ambitious commemorative project: an authentic reproduction of an Elizabethan ship, a living and sailing link to the past.

After thorough research of available plans and histories, the American Quadricentennial Corporation, the organization funding and directing the construction, concluded that there wasn't enough information today to faithfully reconstruct one of Sir Walter's original vessels. But there was, fortunately, some data available for one of the ships in Sir Richard Grenville's 1585 expedition. With this as guidance, William Avery Baker and Stanley Potter, probably America's foremost experts on Elizabethan-era sailing ships, designed the Elizabeth II.

The construction contract was let in June 1982 to O. Lie-Nielsen, a shipbuilder in Rockland, Maine, and construction began at a for-the-purpose boatyard on the Manteo waterfront. The completed fifty-foot, twin-decked ship — all seventy feet of her — slid smoothly down hand-greased ways into Manteo Harbor in late 1983. She is as authentic as love and research could make her. Built largely by hand, her frames, keel, planking, and decks are fastened with seven thousand trunnels (pegs) of locust wood. Every baulk and spar, every block and lift are as close as achievable to the original, with only two exceptions: a wider upper-deck hatch, for easier visitor access, and a vertical hatch in the afterdeck to make steering easier for the helmsman.

In July, 1984, the official opening of the quadricentennial, Elizabeth II was turned over to the state of North Carolina for berthing and display at a brand-new visitor's center and dock, across a bridge east of downtown Manteo. Currently, she leaves the island in spring and fall for trips to nearby towns, making her the only traveling historic site in the state.

To reach the ship, you can park in downtown Manteo and walk across, or drive over the new arched bridge and park on the island (on the whole, we recommend the latter). Once there, you'll find a new Visitor's Center, picnic area, and a shallow, sandy beach.

The Visitor's Center is built after the style of the classic old Nags Head cottages, with cedar shake roofing and wide porches. Inside, you'll find an exhibit area, a gift shop, auditorium, and restrooms.

Admission to the ship is three dollars for adults; $2.00 for senior citizens; $1.50 for children 6 to 12; free for children under 6. Group rates are available; call 473-5522. The price of admission includes the twenty-minute presentation, held every half hour in the auditorium, and a tour of the ship. Costumed sailors and soldiers will be there to explain how the ships of Elizabethan England were built and sailed. Hours of operation: Memorial to Labor Days, 9 a.m. to 7 p.m. Monday through Saturday, 9 a.m. to 5 p.m. Sunday. Rest of the year, open 9 a.m. to 5 p.m. Monday through Saturday and 1 p.m. Sunday.

DOWNTOWN MANTEO

ATTRACTIONS:
1. Elizabeth II State Historic Site, pg. 304
2. Sir Walter Raleigh Statue, pg. 308
3. Bicentennial Park, pg. 308
4. The Waterfront Dock, pg. 308

 RECREATION:
1. Boat Ramp, pg. 304

 RESTAURANTS:
1. Cafe Rene, pg. 241
2. Ship's Galley, pg. 245
3. Duchess of Dare, pg. 241

 SHOPPING:
1. Manteo Booksellers, pg. 310
2. The Waterfront, pg. 310
3. Fearing's, pg. 311
4. Tickled Pink, pg. 311
5. Splash, pg. 312

308 — ROANOKE ISLAND

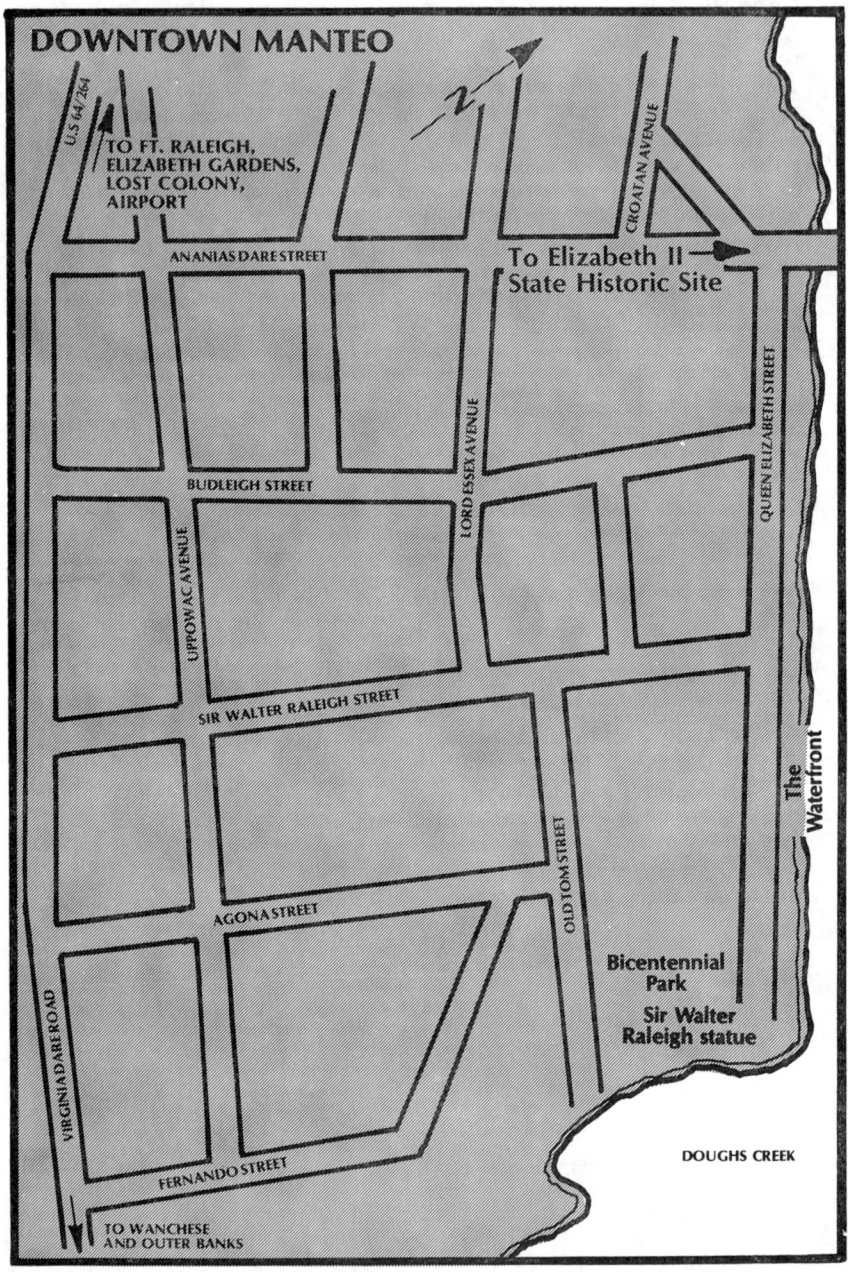

ROANOKE ISLAND — 309

MANTEO BOOKSELLERS

Sir Walter Raleigh St.   473-1221
               Map, pg. 308

This is one of the most incredible bookstores we have ever been in, and believe us, we've been in a bunch of them. Owned by The Christmas Shop's Eddie Green and managed by Steve Brumfield, the shop offers a huge selection of about every kind of book in print. There is an especially complete selection of short stories as well as a complete line of cookbooks, children's books, popular bestsellers in both hard and soft covers, regional selections, and fine art books. Anything they don't have in the store, they will happily order for you. You can also get your books gift wrapped or mailed.

The interior design of the store is quiet and beautiful, with specially made Tiffany style lamps, soft, muted carpeting, low lighting, classical music, and big easy chairs placed stratigically to encourage thorough browsing. This is one bookstore where you honestly feel like you could stay all day just looking at all the books and reveling in the cool serenity that surrounds everything. Puppy, the store cat, is always there to make you feel welcomed too.

Along with the books, you'll find a carefully chosen selection of cards and a selection of magazines that will please even the choosiest reader.

The shop is open each day during the summer from 10 a.m. until at least 6 p.m. During the off season, the hours are from 10 a.m. until 6 p.m. and closed on Sunday.

THE WATERFRONT

Manteo Dock   261-4646
               Map, pg. 308

The Waterfront is a 34-unit condominium and marketplace at the head of downtown Manteo overlooking Shallowbag Bay. It was completed early in 1985. The four story architectual style is Old World, and its scale compliments the small town feel of Manteo. With it's festive shops, opening onto a breezy courtyard, it is promising to become one of the cornerstones of the revitilized downtown area.

The first level of the development is reserved for private parking. Level two contains some 20,000 sq. ft. of retail space. The third and fourth levels are entirely residential. Two and three bedroom units with decks were originally priced from

$90,000 to $150,000. Residents get to keep their "yachts" at the backdoor docks on the Manteo harbor. A ship's store, shower facilities, and washer and dryers are on the way.

Visitors enjoy the public areas of The Waterfront which include a dockside walkway, Cafe Rene, a lovely restaurant specializing in Continental cuisine, and a variety of shops, including a bathing suit shop and a gourmet wine and coffee store.

FEARING'S, INC.

111 Budleigh St.,   Dress Shop-473-5465
Downtown Manteo   Gifts & Interior Design-473-2149
Map, pg. 308

Fearing's is an institution. It's been serving the needs of local islanders for over 56 years. After several moves over the last couple of years (due to a fire), the popular downtown department store has now settled into its beautifully presented new space near the Manteo waterfront. You'll find find women's and children's clothing, cosmetics and accessories downstairs. There's also a nice gift shop with such things as candles and Russell Stover Candies. And upstairs, Suzanne Scott, a talented interior designer (she does boat interiors as well) displays home furnishing and decorative accessories.

Fearing's is well worth a leisurely visit. Hours are Monday through Saturday, 9 a.m. to 5:30 p.m.

TICKLED PINK

Downtown Manteo   473-5951
Map, pg. 308

You're drawn into this store by the displays of wicker in the windows - there seems to be an endless supply of it in all forms. There's also a lot of pink things, as you might have guessed by the name of the shop, including an assortment of flamingos. The collection of gifts is very nice and a bit different from other shops in the area. One specialty of the house is individually designed gift baskets that you can order. The owner, Joyce Brown-Tickle, will put together a collection of interesting items especially chosen for your occasion. There are honeymooner baskets, thank-you baskets, and even Over-the-Hill baskets for people reaching significant birthdays done completely in black. You can also find a wine and champagne section with a very good variety.

This is a fun shop to browse. Open in the summer from 10 a.m. until 8 p.m. (though sometimes later), and in the off season from 10 a.m. until 6 p.m.

SPLASH

The Waterfront shops 473-2354

Map, pg. 308

There isn't a chance that you won't find at least one bathing suit to fit your body or mood here. There are hundreds to choose from in every color and style. There's also a good line of casual, sportswear. Name brands include Catalina, Roxanne, Sandcastle, Bay Club, Harbor Casuals, Seat Covers, and more. There's a Splash II shop in Sea Holly Square, too.

The shop is open 11 a.m. until 7 p.m. Monday through Saturday and from 11 a.m. until 5 p.m. on Sundays during the summer. Off season hours are shortened slightly.

ROANOKE ISLAND
RECREATION

SALTY DAWG MARINA

Manteo 473-3406

Map, pg. 308

Harry Schiffman, owner and manager of the Salty Dawg, says "We're oriented to fishing, and to people just bein' pleasurable to each other." Salty Dawg is south of Manteo proper on Route 64, about a thousand meters north of the Christmas Shop, on the eastern side of Roanoke Island. From seaward, you can find it northwest of the last day marker in Shallowbag Bay, as if you were entering downtown Manteo harbor.

This is mainly a dry storage marina, with 280 dry slips, but it is currently in the midst of expansion. Thirty-five new wet slips are scheduled soon, in addition to the present eighteen, which can take boats up to 55 feet long, with water and power available. There's a full marine supply store, restrooms and shower, fishing accessories, ice, and bait. Dealer and services for

Mercruiser, Mercury Outboard, Volvo, OMC, Chrysler, and Pleasurecraft. Boat dealers in Blackfin and Shamrock. Harry also acts as a boat broker, and has contacts all along the coast.

Salty Dawg is home base for the *Li-jo*, a 32-foot diesel charter that runs Gulf Stream, inlet and sound fishing trips out of Shallowbag Bay for $500 per day. Call for reservations.

ROANOKE ISLAND
SHOPPING

VISTA FLORIST AND GARDEN SHOP

Rt. 64, Manteo   473-3491

Map, pg. 289

Vista's business is growing things; it's a florist and nursery shop. Out back is a 3000-square-foot greenhouse for tropical plants. Most of the shrubbery that Vista deals in is native, or at least viable on the Beach. If you're buying a home in the area they can help you with those green things that grow in the yard—yuccas, yaupon (a native Japanese holly), or myrtle bushes (pronounced 'merkle' by Bankers). Out front is a small gift shop, carrying specially handcrafted gifts—cards, planters, dried flowers.

Something out of the ordinary is dried sea oats. It is illegal to pick sea oats on the Banks (a $500 federal offense), but Vista imports it from the Caribbean and sells it for a ridiculously low price. Vista is on the west side of Route 64/264 south of Manteo, about one block north of the Christmas Shop. Hours: 9-5 p.m., year round.

MARIA'S GIFT CORNER/
WANCHESE HANDICRAFT CENTER

Wanchese, Rt. 345   473-3393

Map, pg. 289

This white Neo-Georgian classic house, now a North Carolina

historic landmark, played a large part in Wanchese's history. Built in 1892, it was the Wanchese Academy, the Masonic Lodge, and the home of the Bethany Methodist Church, and not unnaturally the town's social life revolved around it.

Today, Maria's/The Center specializes in needlepoint, hooked rugs, and other traditional and modern handicrafts. Unimpressive from the road, it's actually one of the largest handicraft suppliers on the Outer Banks. Especially interesting are the handmade christening gowns, as well as a large collection of the highest quality sand-cast hand-polished pewter, which has won several *House Beautiful* awards. Open weekends during the off season, and daily during the season from 10 a.m. to 4:30 p.m. Accepts MC and Visa; closed Tuesdays.

HARBOR GIFTS AND CRAFTS

Wanchese   473-2976
Map, pg. 289

This is a crammed-full gift shop specializing in suncatchers, handicrafts, and especially shells, many of them from exotic lands. Lucretia and Woodrow Stetson run a seashell importing and exporting business next door to the shop, wholesaling all along the East Coast, so if you're in the business, ask about it. Winter hours are 10 a.m. to 5 p.m. Monday to Saturday; Summer hours 10 a.m. to 9 p.m. Monday to Saturday. Closed Sundays.

CHESLEY MALL

Manteo   Map, pg.
Map, pg. 289

Chesley mall is where Manteo goes to shop. Just north of the Christmas Shop, it's anchored by Revco Discount Drugs on one end and Davis clothing store on the other. In between are a pizza shop, Moncie's, photo services, a book and card shop, a convenient coin laundry, and a fine Foodarama Supermarket. More shops are on the way; this is a growing mall. Open all year.

ACE HARDWARE

Manteo   473-1444
Map, pg. 289

Ace Hardware, open year round, carries an impressive

assortment of items for every project. In addition to a full line of hardware, they handle garden supplies, plumbing supplies, electrical supplies, paint, and fish tackle. We were impressed by the boating supply line and the farming supplies. Where else can you buy pig rings?

Ace Hardware is located on Virginia Dare Road (Highway 64). Look for the impressive, new white stucco building at the first stoplight in Manteo. Open: Mon. through Sat., 8 a.m. to 5:30 p.m.

RJ'S NURSERY

U.S. Highway 64, in Manteo   473-3889
Map, pg. 289

This nursery, located right across the street from the Elizabethan Inn in Manteo, offers one of the most complete selections of plants in the whole area, supplied from one of the owners own five greenhouses. Flowering baskets, Poinsettias, pampas grass, all kinds of shrubs, bedding plants, trees, Christmas trees, and soil products are all sold. Open 8 a.m. to 6 p.m. daily.

SECOND TIME AROUND

U.S. Highway 64, Manteo   473-3127
Map, pg. 289

Second Time Around is one of the fund raising arms of the Outer Banks Hotline, a crisis intervention service provding free telephone peer counseling and a shelter for battered women. The shop is a thrift store that sells donated items, everything from clothes to beds to household goods. The quality of the merchandise is surprisingly good. It seems the shop gets so many donations from the supportive Dare County residents, they can afford to be choosy about the things they put out for sale. We were told it's not unusual for the shop to even get items such as estate jewelry!

The building that houses Second Time Around is huge and filled to the brim. You could take a full hour or more going through it. If you have time, or are one of the many people who have a penchant for good merchandise at extra great prices, stop on by. The money you spend will do others more good than it even does you. The shop is open from 10 a.m. to 5 p.m. Monday through Friday and from 12 noon until 5 p.m. on Saturday, year round.

The Hatteras Lighthouse stands over 200 feet above the surf. Its 800,000 candlepower light is visible more than 20 miles out to sea.

INSIDE
HATTERAS ISLAND

THIS IS HATTERAS

Hatteras Island, in many ways, *is* the Outer Banks. In its over fifty-mile length is wrapped up everything for which the Banks are famous. Solitutde. Unspoiled nature. In the Pea Island National Wildlife Refuge, comprising the northern end of the island, you can drive for miles, hearing only the sea and the call of the wild geese, seeing only the dunes.

Farther south, you roll through the very stuff of Banks legend: tiny communities whose whole livelihood came from the sea. From Rodanthe, Waves, and Salvo the Bankers of the Life Saving Service battled storm and surf to save strangers' lives. Today's visitor finds wrecks still on the beaches—and the best pier fishing on the Banks.

Some forty miles south of Oregon Inlet, the island takes a sharp westward turn, leaving Cape Point jutting out into the Atlantic. Here, at its 'elbow', is Cape Hatteras, feared for centuries by mariners as the Graveyard of the Atlantic. Here the century-old Lighthouse still sends its warning beam seaward, and here surfers and surf fishermen find the acme of their sports.

Inland of the Cape, at the widest part of the Banks, small communities have established themselves, nestled in the depths of a unique maritime forest. Buxton and Frisco offer camping, shopping, and a chance to stock up on gas and food before continuing south.

Hatteras Village, close to the western end of the island at the ferry terminus for Ocracoke, is a mecca for sport fishermen—and for shoppers.

Most of Hatteras Island is part of the Cape Hatteras National Seashore, and is administered by the National Park Service (Pea Island: U.S. Fish and Wildlife Service). This provides for the preservation of most of the island. A well-kept series of campgrounds (3), swimming beaches (4), and fishing piers (3), as well as the Visitor Center at Cape Point, provide for the convenience of visitors. These are supplemented by numerous private campgrounds and motels listed in previous chapters.

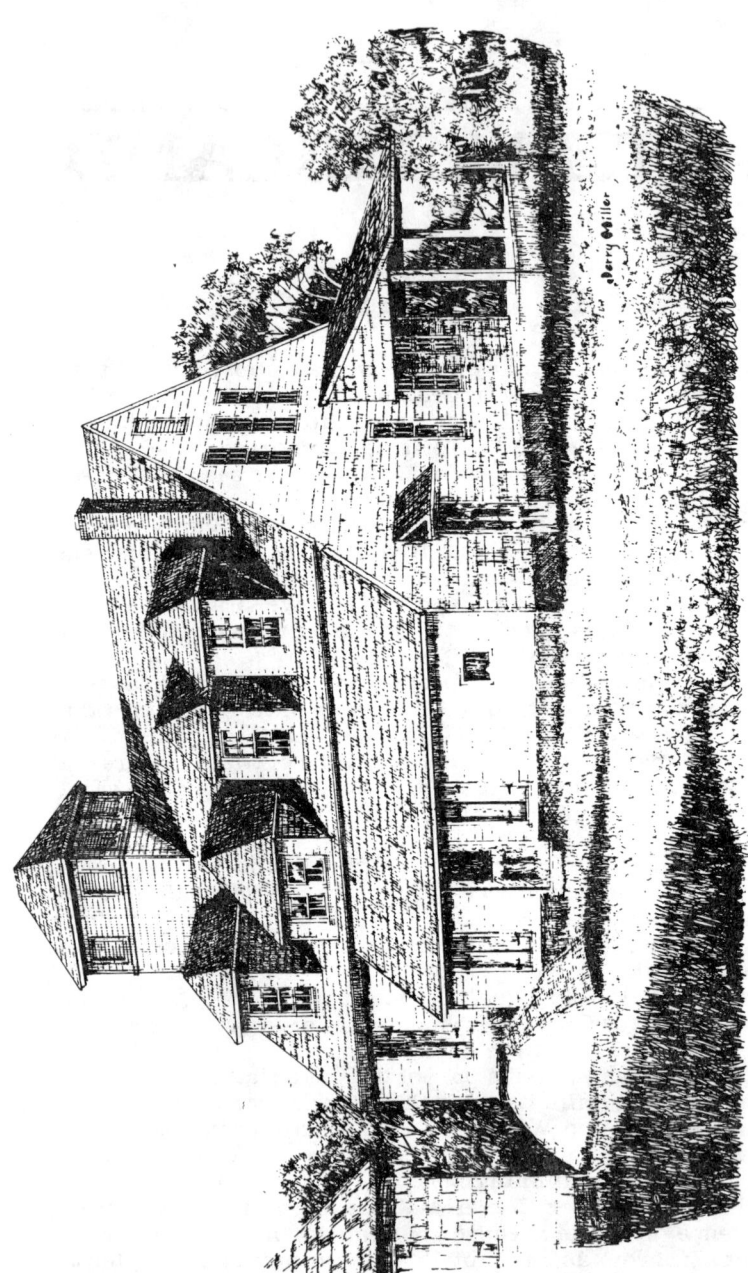

Chicamacomico Life Saving Station est 1874 Outer Banks near Waves, NC

Drawing by Jerry Miller

In the early years, the Islanders lived cut off from others, evolving their own microculture, preserving old ways of speech and suspicion of authority. Since 1964, the Oregon Inlet Bridge has largely ended that isolation. Yet traces of it linger, and you will find Hatteras *different* from Kitty Hawk and Nags Head. There are no fast food outlets... no bars... no discos... and only one movie theatre. The Hatteras people are friendly, but... they don't accept outsiders immediately. Their villages, their economy, is geared to the summer visitor trade, but still with reservations, as if this, too, may be a passing thing. Living on shifting sand, alone and isolated all winter, and knowing that any summer the hurricanes can change everything, even the shape of the land, the Hatteras people learn to trust only themselves, and the eternal sea.

No visitor to the Outer Banks should miss the southern islands, Hatteras and Ocracoke. There you will find, still strong, something increasingly rare in the modern world.

Independence.

RODANTHE, WAVES, SALVO

Rodanthe, Waves, and Salvo are small communities of perhaps two or three hundred people each... during the winter. In summer they blossom with tackle shops, stores, gift shops, campgrounds and small restaurants, all to tempt and serve the thousands of visitors streaming south on Highway 12. Many visitors stop, and discover these tiny towns...but too many drive by, intent on getting to storied Hatteras Village or Ocracoke. But if you like fishing, Rodanthe has the Hatteras Island Pier. If you like wrecks, the LST #471 lies near the pier. History buffs should stop at the Chicamacomico Lifesaving Station. And if you're a camper, there are half a dozen places to stay, probably the biggest concentration of camping sites in the Banks. This is a beautiful, relatively undeveloped area, and the Insiders predict a real estate boom here soon.

AVON

Avon, the last town on the northern arm of the Island before the run through Park-owned territory to the Cape, is thirty miles south of Oregon Inlet. Once remote, it has become much more accessible since the opening of the Herbert Bonner Bridge, and now sees a modest but growing stream of tourists. It's still primarily a summer community, though, with lots of single-family cottages. One quiet summer evening, looking west over a mirrorlike sound toward the setting sun, we understood why; there was at that moment no more beautiful place on the Banks. The winter population is still small but growing. Avon boasts one of the primary social centers of the southern Banks, the Colony movie theatre; the Avon Fishing Pier; and some convenient groceries, shops and campgrounds. In previous editions of the Guide we predicted real estate development in this area, and it is finally happening. Large oceanfront developments are being paralleled by increased cottage construction, following the pattern previously established farther north.

BUXTON, FRISCO, AND HATTERAS VILLAGE

The southern "arm" of Hatteras Island — from the "elbow" at the Cape west and south, toward Ocracoke — is more populated and more habitable than the open land to the north. More of it is privately owned, in contrast to the overwhelming proportion of National Seashore land on the rest of the Island. Higher and more stable geologically, the southern arm is primarily a maritime forest habitat, often thick with live oak and red bay, dogwood and pine. It offers more shelter from wind and storm, and has borne a small and hardy population from the earliest Indian times. Historically, they made their livings from the sea; and although tourism and commercial ventures are supplanting this, many local people are still part-time commercial fishermen.

Buxton, just inland from Cape Hatteras itself, is a small and growing town of motels, campgrounds, and permanent residents. The fishing flavor is strong here during the spring and fall seasons. Buxton is a Mecca for sport fishermen and Atlantic Coast surfers. (See the "Fishing Guide" section and "Surfing along the Banks").

A winding, pleasant road winds west from Buxton, through the forest, toward Frisco. On the way you will pass several attractive campgrounds and many roads leading back into new real estate developments, both on the ocean side and on the higher land overlooking the sound.

Hatteras Village, at the western tip of the island, is second only to Wanchese as the Banks' center of commercial fishing activity. We have seen upwards of sixty drop-netters (gill netters) run out from here during the late fall and early spring. At the docks, during this time of year, you can see tons of trout coming in under the watchful eyes of wharf cats, gill nets being dried, all the activity of a busy fishing port. (See "Nedo's") Trout, croakers, big blues, and king mackerel from Oden's and Hatteras Harbor are packed in shaved ice, trucked out in five-thousand pound lots, and end up in Fulton's Fish Market in New York City within twenty-four hours. Most of these boats come from other towns, and spend the season out of Hatteras, fishing in the neighborhood of the Light. Feel like a different kind of vacation? Sometimes, if you're young and hearty, you can talk yourself into a billet aboard one of these hard-working craft.

Sport fishing, for marlin and other big sport fish, is another Hatteras specialty. The Hatteras Marlin Tournament is perhaps the biggest single week in Hatteras Village. Fifty or sixty private boats, carrying some of the East Coast's leading politicians and businessmen, attend this invitation-only championship, one of the most prestigious in the country. The Tournament is hosted by the Hatteras Marlin Club, in the Village, and takes place the second week in June.

OWNERSHIP ON HATTERAS ISLAND

Though still important to the island's economy, fishing has been overshadowed in recent years by the increase in tourism and the growth of residences and cottages. For many years this lagged behind the northern towns, but in the mid-eighties bids fair to rival it. Tim Midgett, a Hatteras resident who is knowledgeable in real estate, summed it up in an interview for this book: "In the next two years we'll see a lot more development. Many of the larger parcels that have been held by families in the past will be selling due to tax increases in 1984." Midgett sees developable land running short in much of the Banks, with Frisco and Avon as the prime areas still to come on the market. (If you're a seasoned Insider, you'll remember that we predicted the land boom in Hatteras some years back.) Development in Hatteras is still primarily single-family, in contrast to the multi-family dwellings going up to the north. "We don't have the bright lights and the boardwalks down here," Midgett said. "It's more of a family area, with spring and fall fishing and the beaches."

For more information on renting or owning in Hatteras, see our sections on "Rentals,"; "Condominiums,"; and "Buying Real Estate." The following brokers are among those active on Hatteras itself:

Austin Realty	987-2208
Colony Realty	995-5891
H. Curtis Gray and Associates	995-5779
Midgett Realty Avon (995-5333), Hatteras (986-2141)	
Sea Gull Realty	987-2258
Williams Realty	995-5211

HATTERAS ISLAND
ATTRACTIONS

PEA ISLAND
NATIONAL WILDLIFE REFUGE

N. end of Hatteras Island   987-2394
Map, pg. 323

Once you cross Oregon Inlet, leaving the Herbert C. Bonner bridge behind, you're in Pea Island. On your left is the surf, on your right the marsh. And everywhere, everywhere—are birds.

Pea Island was founded on April 12, 1938, when Congress provided that Pea Island be preserved as a haven for wildlife, specifically as a wintering area for the Greater Snow Goose. Roosevelt's CCC was put to work stabilizing the dunes with bulldozers and sea oats, sand fences were built, dikes were constructed to form ponds, and freshwater marshes and fields planted to provide food for wildfowl. The refuge was seldom visited by tourists until the Oregon Inlet bridge was constructed in 1964. Now Pea Island is one of the most popular spots on the island with naturalists, bird-watchers, and just plain lovers of wildlife.

Both bird watchers and wreck lovers will want to stop at the Rest Area some 4½ miles south of the Bonner Bridge. To the surf side, if you walk over the dunes to your left, you will be able to glimpse the remains of the Federal transport *Oriental*. The tall black mass is thought to be her steel boiler, all that remains of the ship that went ashore in May, 1862. To the sound side, a short walk leads to an overlook of North Pond and New Field, where special crops are sown each year for the use of the waterfowl that winter over in the milder climate of the Banks.

While there, you may see some of the Refuge's guests. The 5,915 acres of the Refuge are an important wintering ground for whistling swans, snow geese, Canada geese, and 25 species of ducks. Many other interesting species, such as the Savannah (Ipswich) sparrow, migrant warblers, shorebirds, gulls, terns, herons and egrets can be found here during the winter months and the spring and fall migrations. During the summer months several species of herons, egrets, and terns, along with

HATTERAS ISLAND — 323

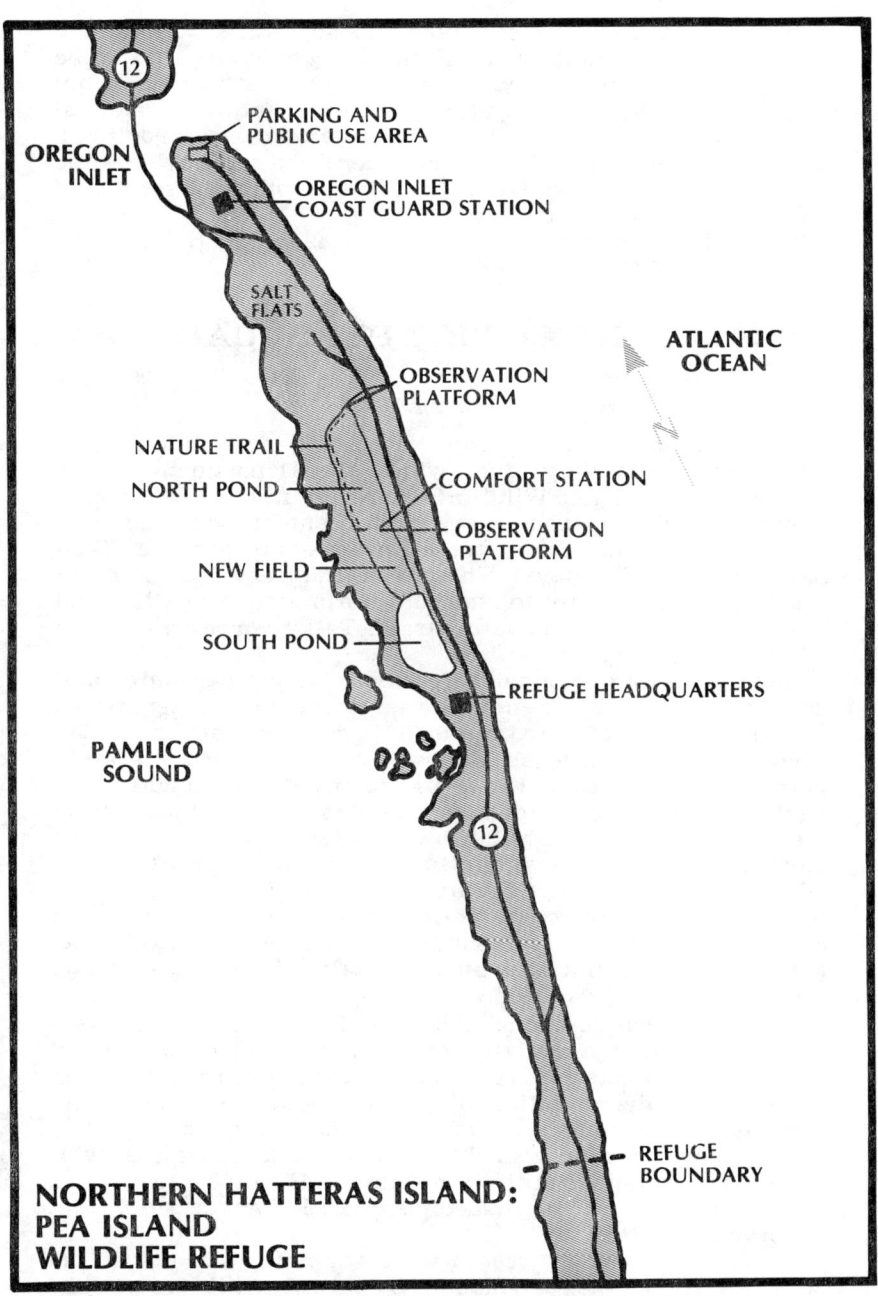

American avocets, willets, black-necked stilts, and a few species of ducks nest at the Refuge. Oceanic species can be expected during most any season but are most common from late summer through fall into late winter. Following storms, many species unusual for this area have been observed. In all, over 265 species of bird have been identified repeatedly at the Refuge or over the ocean nearby, with another 50 species of accidental or rare occurrence.

The Refuge is controlled from the Headquarters, some 7½ miles south of Oregon Inlet.

PEA ISLAND REFUGE HEADQUARTERS

Highway 12   987-2394

Map, pg. 323

On the sound side, 7¼ miles south of Oregon Inlet, is the headquarters building from which the Department of the Interior, U.S. Fish and Wildlife Service administers Pea Island. There's a small parking area and visitor center (open 8 a.m. - 4:30 p.m. every day, though duty personnel may not be at the HQ on Saturdays and Sundays). Though visitor services there are limited, you may want to stop in. Information is available on bird watching and use of nature trails. Talks can be arranged in advance for groups.

We talked with personnel there about what you can and cannot do on the Refuge. You're not allowed to hunt, of course; that's a $500 fine maximum. No camping ($25), no open fires (again $25). Dogs must be on a leash. Four wheel drive vehicles are not permitted on the beach. Firearms are not permitted within the confines of the Refuge. Headquarters personnel say that even on the road, driving straight through, shotguns and such must be stowed out of sight. Those hunting farther south on Hatteras are advised not to flaunt their equipment on the Refuge. Only those with a special collection permit, which is available upon application to Refuge Manager, Pea Island, Box 150, Rodanthe, N.C. 27968, are permitted to pick up or take vegetation, eggs, etc. Beach fishing is permitted.

We might suggest one side trip from the headquarters building. It's only a few hundred feet, the last ten on sand, but it takes you back many years in time. Just east of the headquarters building, in the direction of the surf, you will find a few remnants of the foundation of an old life saving station.

Pea Island Station was the only U.S. Life Saving Service station to be manned entirely by blacks. How it came to be so, and what they accomplished, is a little-known story that deserves to be told.

Established with the rest of the stations in 1879, Pea Island was at first, like the rest, manned by entirely white crews. Like the others, it had black personnel, but they were confined to such menial tasks as caring for the tough little ponies tht dragged the surfboats through the sand.

But this first crew let the Service down. They were dismissed in 1880, one year later, for negligence in the Henderson disaster. The authorities then collected the black personnel from other stations, placed them in the charge of Richard Etheridge, who was part Black and part Indian, and set them to their duty.

They fulfilled it magnificently. In dozens of disasters, the Pea Island crew risked life and health in rescuing the crews and passengers of the vessels that came driving ashore in storm and hurricane. Etheridge became known as one of the best-prepared, most professional, and most daring men in a Service where daring and selflessness were a matter of course.

The Station closed in 1947, but the story of the Pea Island Crew lives on in Coast Guard lore.

CHICAMACOMICO LIFE SAVING STATION

Rodanthe Map, pg. 336 Map, pg.

The buildings, once boarded up, with broken windows, and rusted padlocks, are now being restored to their once stately beauty, thanks to a group of dedicated citizens who refused to see the historic buildings fade into oblivion. For, Chicamacomico was one of the most famous Life Saving Stations on the Outer Banks.

In 1874, Chicamacomico Station was part of a daring new concept in lifesaving. In that year the U.S. Life Saving Service was building a chain of seven stations along the Banks, at the points of greatest danger for oceangoing vessels. Each station was supervised by a Keeper, and had permanent winter crews of six skilled, strong, and brave surfmen.

They quickly proved their worth in an area known to all seamen as the "Graveyard of the Atlantic". Ships had a habit of coming ashore on the Banks in storms; the strong northeast winds and seas that developed during winter storms drove sailing ships into shoal waters, where pounding surf soon broke them up. Those who tried to swim ashore or row in life boats usually perished, battered to death in the icy water, or freezing slowly on a deserted coast.

The mission of the Life Saving Service was to rescue those on grounded ships...and a demanding, often suicidal mission it was, too. The surfmen stood watch all along the coast, in the foulest winter weather. Once a wreck was spotted, they had to return to the station, get boats, rescue gear, and the rest of the crew, and then drag everything in heavy carts through the soft sand to the point where the stricken vessel lay. There they might go out to her by boat, driven not by engines but by strong arms on the oars; might attempt to swim out; might fire a line with a Lyle gun and pull the shipwrecked mariners and passengers to safety one by one by breeches buoy high above the deadly surf. In the wrecks of the *Metropolis* (1878), *A.B. Goodman* (1881), and dozens of others, these hardy men, for the most part Banksmen, distinguished themselves in courage and seamanship.

And Chicamacomico Station at Rodanthe, Number 179, was foremost. Under three Keepers—Captain Ben Midgett III, Captain John Allan Midgett, Jr., and Captain Levene Westcott Midgett — it guarded the sea along the northern coast of Hatteras for 78 years. Number 179 and the Midgetts are still legends in the Coast Guard, with which the Life Saving Service was merged in 1915. Since 1876 seven Midgetts have been awarded the Gold Life Saving Award and three the silver; most worked or lived at Chicamacomico.

The Station was active through World War II, until it was closed down by the Coast Guard in 1954. It languished unused for some years threafter. Today, like so many newly appreciated reminders of the Banks' seagoing heritage, it is being restored. The Chicamacomico Historical Association, Inc., a nonprofit organization established for its preservtaion, has begun work to clean up the interior and restore the exterior, and has opened displays in the main station building; but they, like so many other good causes, can't depend solely on government funds. You can help with a check to the Association at P.O. Box 140, Rodanthe, N.C. 27968. Be a lifesaver!

During the summer, Chicamacomico is the site of commemorative life saving drills held by the National Park Service, which still owns the boat house. Check at any Park Service facility for dates and times. Admission free.

LST #471 WRECK

Rodanthe Map, pg. 336 Map, pg. -

In February, 1948, while being towed with several sister ships to Charleston, LST #471 parted her lines and drifted ashore on Hatteras Island. Personnel from the then-active Chicamacomico Coast Guard Station rescued three of the crew with beach apparatus (see Chicamacomico Life Saving Station). The LST remained there and has since been gradually covered by the moving sands. To reach it turn left at Spur Road 1247 at Rodanthe (same direction as to the Hatteras Island fishing pier). There's parking next to the pier. Five minute's brisk walk to the north along the beach will bring you to a small point, where the pilothouse, still unburied, remains in view.

OREGON INLET COAST GUARD STATION

North end of Hatteras Is.   987-2311
Map, pg. 336

Just east of the south end of Oregon Inlet Bridge, this small U.S. Coast Guard station and dock services a cutter, several motor lifeboats and other small craft, and the Army corps of Engineers dredges *Sweitzer* and *Merrit*, which take turns keeping the Oregon Inlet channel open. Search and rescue is the primary job of the Station and the eighty-two-foot cutter *Point Brown*, though they also run law enforcement and antidrug patrols out of the inlet. Most interesting to the visitor may be the three-story cedar-shingled "old building," built in 1874, along with Chicamacomico and the other stations along the coast. This, though, is the only one still in service, and its fresh paint and air of daily use contrast sharply with the others. Along with the smaller stations at Hatteras Village and Ocracoke, it is all that today remains of the once pervasive Coast Guard influence among the Bankers.

As an operating base, Oregon Inlet isn't really set up to handle your basic tourist, but *ad hoc* tours of the whole station are available on request from 1 to 4 P.M. weekdays and 8 to 5 on weekends. Cameras and sketchbooks are welcome, but try not to intrude too much on operations.

Oregon Inlet monitors 2182 (International Distress) and Channel 16 FM.

U.S. COAST GUARD FACILITY, BUXTON

Buxton   Map, pg. 344

Formerly the Naval facility at Buxton, the grounds and buildings were turned over to the Coast Guard in June of 1982. It's not normally open for visitors, but retired military, dependents, and military personnel may use the few remaining facilities. There's a limited commissary, a small exchange, recreational facilities (tennis, bowling, basketball, and swimming) and a small dispensary. The hours, at all military bases and stations, are subject to change, but don't plan on anything being open after 5 p.m.

THE ALTOONA WRECK

Cape Point   Map, pg. 344

Driving to the end of the Cape Point road, you will see Ramp 44 straight ahead. Don't try to drive over, or even to, this ramp in a regular car. A four-wheel-drive vehicle will make it over the soft sand between the road and the ramp; a two-wheel-drive one will not. We speak from experience, as we tried to and lost... and towing fees in Buxton are, to say the least, uncompetitive. Instead leave your car on the solid ground near the road and walk over the ramp, continuing straight ahead for about 1/3 of a mile.

The *Altoona* was a cargo ship, a two-masted, 100-foot-long schooner out of Boston. She was built in Maine in 1869. In 1878 she left Haiti with a load of dyewood bound for New York. She was driven ashore on the Cape by stormy season on October 22, 1878. Her crew of seven was rescued, the deck cargo lost, but the cargo in the hold was salvaged. A few years sufficed for the shifting sands to bury her, as they are doing right now to the LST #471, at Rodanthe. She reemerged in 1962 in a storm, and was quickly broken apart by the sea. The bow and part of the hull, still with greenish copper teredo sheathing on it, lie pointing south. A few odd pieces of her ribs and beams lie scattered between her and the Atlantic.

DIAMOND SHOALS LIGHT

Off Cape Point   Map, pg. 344

From the lighthouse, or even from the eastern shore of Cape Point, you may be able to see on a clear night a sudden white flash of light from far out at sea. Time it; if the flashes come every two and half seconds, you are looking at the Diamond Shoals Light, some thirteen miles out at sea southeast of the lighthouse, marking the very end of the Shoals that have claimed so many ships.

Through the years, there have been numerous attempts to build lighthouses out there, on the shifting sandbars; all have failed. Three lightships have been on station there since 1824. The first was sunk in a gale, in 1827; the second lasted from 1897 until 1918, when it was sunk by the German submarine U-140; and the third remained in service until 1967, when it was replaced with the present steel structure.

How long will it last?

THE MONITOR

Off Cape Hatteras   Map, pg. 344

Every American knows the story of the Monitor from schoolbooks. How, during the Civil War, the Confederates built the first ironclad warship from the hulk of the Union frigate Merrimack, renaming it the Virginia. How, in the early hours of March 8, 1862, the tent-shaped ship steamed out of Norfolk to challenge a Union blockading force of six wooden ships — and how, by the end of the day, she had sunk two of them and damaged another. Broken the blockade, and written a new chapter in naval history.

The Monitor was an even more daring innovation. Built by John Ericsson, a Swedish-American engineer, the "Cheesebox on a raft" was a low-slung ironclad whose main battery was carried in a futuristic revolving turret. Arriving in Norfolk in the nick of time — the next day — the Monitor battled her adversary throughout the ninth, and finally, the fight at a draw, the Virginia retreated back under the guns of Norfolk.

Neither of these first ironclads lived very long. The Virginia was destroyed by retreating Confederates; the Monitor, ordered south, foundered off Cape Hatteras during a New Years' Eve storm in 1862. And there she lay for a hundred and twenty years, unseen by human eye, even her location unknown.

She was rediscovered in the late seventies, resting quietly

Photo courtesy Sea Technology Magazine and Harbor Branch Foundation, Inc.

upside down, just as she sank, in two hundred feet of water 25 kilometers south-southeast of Cape Hatteras.

Since then, the Monitor has been designated the first National Underwater Marine Sanctuary, and has been the object of repeated dives and evaluations by government agencies and underwater archaeologists. A few small artifacts — bottles, silverware, that sort of thing — have been recovered, and in 1983 the ship's distinctive four-bladed anchor was located and raised by a NOAA/East Carolina University expedition.

So far, aside from a touring collection of artifacts, there's nothing to actually see of the Monitor. But someday there might be. NOAA is considering the feasibility of raising the turret, which is relatively complete, and possibly other parts of the ship's hull for preservation and eventual display.

BILLY MITCHELL AIR FIELD

Frisco   Map, pg. 344

This is a small no-frills landing strip located about a mile south of Highway 12 just west of Frisco. Named after the controversial Army aviator who conducted some of his bombing tests near here in 1921, the strip is 3,000 feet long, 75 feet wide, oriented NE/SW, and asphalt paved.

Stu Membel's Outer Banks Airways operates out of Billy Mitchell Field. The service includes sky diving, lifts, charters, photography, sightseeing, fish spotting and just about anything else you and Stu can dream up. Call toll free: 800-824-7888 Ext. M-712 or on the Banks 986-2383.

CAPE POINT, CAPE HATTERAS NATIONAL SEASHORE

Buxton

Map, pg. 344

As you continue that leisurely drive south along the length of Hatteras Island, you will come to th sharp elbow in the road that leads into Buxton. To your left, beyond a small cluster of motels, you can hear the surf booming; to the right are the trees of a small forest — here, on the Banks! As highway 12 curves to the right, signs point to the left, toward the Lighthouse and the Coast Guard Facility. Resist your first impulse to turn, continue about 200 yards past the turn for the Facility, and turn left there to the Cape Point area of the Cape Hatteras National Seashore.

The approach is beautiful in and of itself. It is a winding drive between brush-covered dunes, with the white and black striped Lighthouse looming on your left. There's a nice photograph on your left, about halfway there, where the lighthouse is reflected in the water of a pond.

Cape Point contains a number of attractions and recreational opportunities: the Visitor Center, the Lighthouse, a shipwreck, a nature trail, and a campground. Surfing and surf-fishing are permitted year round, and a protected (lifeguarded) beach is available for swimming near the campground in the summer.

HATTERAS ISLAND VISITOR CENTER

Near Hatteras Lighthouse   995-4474
                    Map, pg. 344

Built in 1854, this two-story frame house was for many years the home of the assistant keepers of the light (the smaller home just to the east was the quarters of the Keeper himself). Today it's a National Park Service Visitor Center, the central one for the island of Hatteras, and extensive historical renovation has just been completed to restore the building to its original condition. The Principle Keepers Quarters is now being restored too.

Along with a helpful ranger at the information desk, it now houses a well-kept museum devoted to Man and the Sea at Hatteras. The exhibits and displays center around shipping, the Cape at War, Making the Cape Safe, the lighthouses themselves, and the heroism of the Life Saving Service, later to become the Coast Guard. There's fancy ropework, information on the rescue of passengers from stranded ships in storms, and a small but well-stocked bookstore carries related books. Last but not least there are clean restrooms.

In addition to its own exhibits, the Center is where you can obtain a schedule for the activities the Park Service conducts on Hatteras Island during the summer. They change each season, of course, but here are samples of what's offered:

SEASHORE ARTS—What you can create with things you pick up by the sea.
HATTERAS HISTORY—What it was like at Cape Point a hundred or more years ago.
FISH WITH A RANGER—Free tackle and pier admission, or surf-fishing...how to do it.
CATCH A SAFE WAVE—How to surf.
MORNING BIRD WALK—Bird-watching with an expert around the Point.

Most of these programs, as well as others, are conducted weekly. Pick up a schedule at the Center, or call the number above, for exact times and dates.

The Center is open from 9 to 5 daily September through May, and 9 a.m. to 6 p.m. in June, July and August (hours subject to change).

CAPE HATTERAS LIGHTHOUSE

Cape Point   Map, pg. 344

For over a hundred and seventy-five years, mariners rounding stormy, dangerous Cape Hatteras have searched for the glimmer of Cape Hatteras Light to assure them of safety. Sometimes they found it in time; sometimes, as the bare-boned wrecks on the point testify, they didn't.

Hatteras has been a place of danger for ships since the Europeans first began crossing the Atlantic. Its typically turbulent weather is caused by the confluence of two currents: the warm, northward-flowing Gulf Stream, and the southbound, inshore Virginia Coastal Drift. A ten-mile finger of shoal water, the Diamond Shoals, and the low, featureless nature of the Banks coastline conspired to lure hundreds of ships to rest in the "Graveyard of the Atlantic."

The first lighthouse at Hatteras Point was raised in 1802. When we first began to write about the Outer Banks, not that many years ago, its sandstone ruin was still visible about three hudnred yards south of the present lighthouse. A blizzard in March, 1980 finally took it, so utterly that you can now search the beach for a single piece of crumbling sandstone. It was ninety feet high, with a feeble whale oil light, and proved inadequate. Also, as the century progressed, it became evident that erosion would soon overtake it. It was heightened and improved, but as the years went by, erosion weakened it, and by the late 1860's it had to be replaced. The War between the States had left its mark, too; the Confederates, retreating 1861, took the light's lens with them.

The new lighthouse was built in 1869-70, of 1¼ million Philadelphia-baked bricks, at a cost of $150,000. It's built on a crisscross of heavy pine beams, with its foundation thirteen feet deep in the sand. A granite base sits atop that, and then the brick begins, carrying the lighthouse up to the light at 180 feet, and from there to the very tip of the lightning rod two hundred and eight feet above the ground. The first light installed was kerosene, with a special Fresnel lens to flash its beam far out to sea. The eye-catching spiral paint job was added to make the lighthouse visible far out at sea during the day, so that ships could determine their position by taking bearings from a known point. When it was completed, the old lighthouse was dynamited. The new lighthouse was in service from 1870 to 1935, when it was abandoned, due to beach erosion. The erosion was controlled, and in 1950 the lighthouse was reactiviated by the Coast Guard. Today its 800,000 candlepower electric light flashes every 7½ seconds, reaching out more than 20 miles to sea.

From the Visitor Center, you can walk across to the lighthouse. As you can see, the beach migration that destroyed the first lighthouse here has recently begun to seriously threaten the second. This threat from the sea (as if in revenge for all the ships this old light had cheated it of) became critical in December of 1981, when the high tide came within fifty feet of the structure's base! Emergency protection (dumping of rubble, sandbags, beach nourishment) fought the sea back a few feet, but any winter now it could come roaring over, sweeping away the sand and toppling the graceful height of the lighthouse into the waves.

Currently, the National Park Service, the state of North Carolina, and interested local citizens (notably the "Save Our Lighthouse" campaigners) are exploring permanent answers to the problem. Various experts have proposed options ranging from moving the lighthouse bodily to letting it go to the sea. The best answer seems to be emerging as a combination of short-term breakwaters, or rip rap revetments, and perhaps a longer-term project costing upwards of two million dollars, permanently preserving the Cape Hatteras Lighthouse on its own island as the point recedes around it. The debate is still in progress, but one thing is certain: this striking structure is one of the quintessential symbols of the Banks, and of the men who for centuries have battled the seas of Hatteras. We should make every effort to save it.

BUXTON WOODS NATURE TRAIL

Cape Point   Map, pg. 344

The Nature Trail is ¾ mile long, leading from the road through the wooded dunes, vine jungles, and fresh-water marshes of Buxton Woods. It's the best nature trail on the Banks. It is a must...don't miss it.

Beginning on the right side of the road south from the lighthouse to the Point, the trail winds at first among low sand hills, then into the maritime microforest that has gradually established itself on this broadest part of the island. Its natural beauty is enhanced by small plaques, masterfully written, explaining the changing surroundings in terms of the closed, fragile ecosystems of the Banks; the water table, the role of beach grass and sea oats in stabilizing dunes, the beach microforest and its stages of development, and the harshness of the Banks environment of wind, sand, and salt.

There are cottonmouths on this trail, unmistakably fat-bodied rough-scaled snakes in various dull colors (brownish, yellowish, grayish, varying almost to black), though they are rare. Don't stick your hands or feet where you can't see. If you encounter a snake, allow it time to get away; generally it will retreat. The local people advise extra caution when encountering a cottonmouth during chill weather, in spring or fall. During this period, they say, the snakes are less confident of their ability to get away from you, since they're rather sluggish in cool weather, and they're more likely to attack. In midsummer they will generally scurry off quickly.

We don't recommend this trail for handicapped or very small children, but for everyone else, it's a must.

Picnic tables and charcoal grills are located just south of it for lunch.

HATTERAS ISLAND NORTH

ATTRACTIONS:
1. Pea Island National Wildlife Refuge, pg. 322
2. Pea Island Refuge Headquarters, pg. 324
3. Chicamacomico Lifesaving Station, pg. 325
4. LST #471 Wreck, pg. 326
5. Oregon Inlet Coast Guard Station, pg. 327

RECREATION:
1. Waterfall Water Slide/Cape Hatteras Speedway, pg. 338
2. Hatteras Island Fishing Pier, pg. 338
3. Oregon Inlet Fishing Pier, pg. 100

HOTELS/MOTELS/CAMPGROUNDS
1. Hatteras Island Motel, pg. 146
2. Ocean Aire, pg. 146
3. Pea Island Resort, pg. 182
4. Cape Hatteras KOA, pg. 182
5. KOA Holiday Campground, pg. 182
6. North Beach Campground, pg. 182

RESTAURANTS:
1. Emily's Soundside, pg. 245

SHOPPING:
1. Island Convenience Store, pg. 352

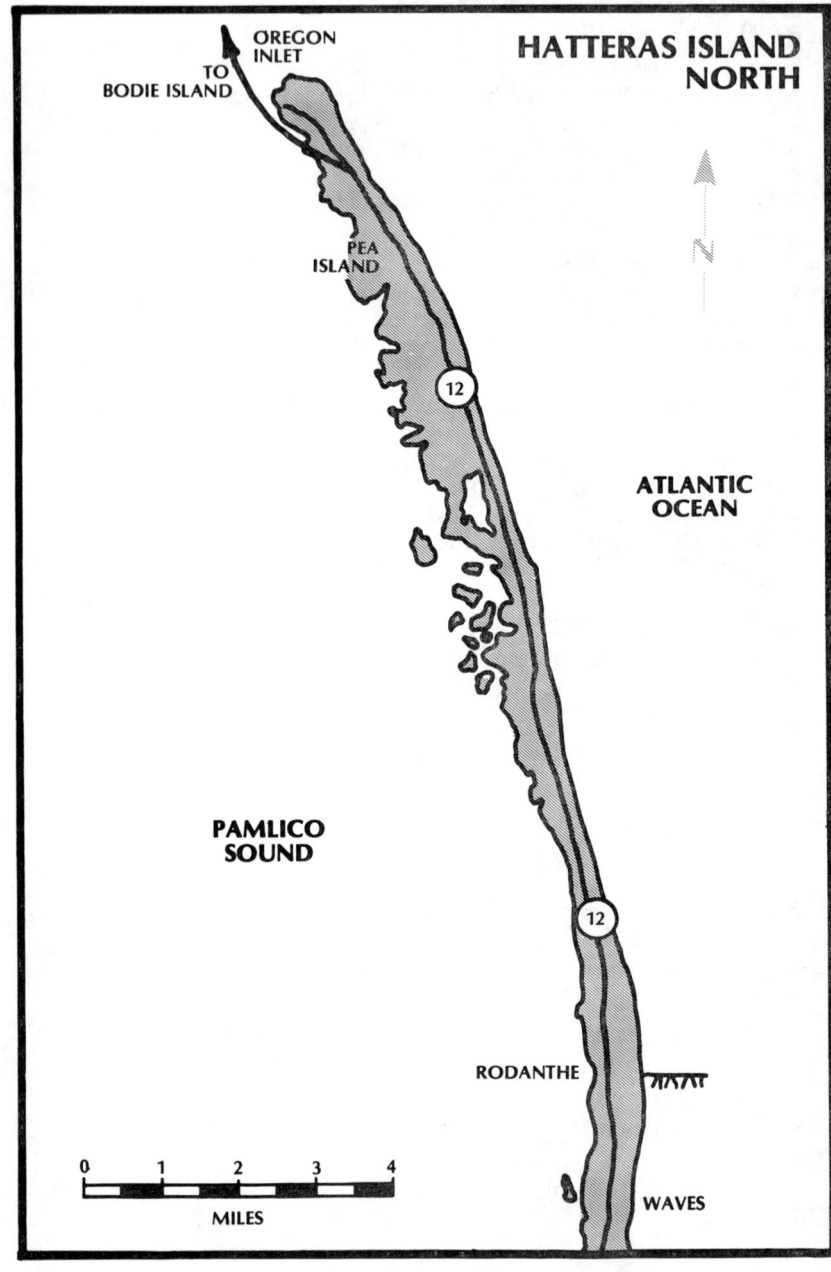

Net mender - commercial fishing is a way of life at Hatteras village.

HATTERAS ISLAND
RECREATION

HATTERAS ISLAND FISHING PIER

Spur Rd. 1247, E. of Hwy. 12   987-2323
Map, pg. 344

   The National Park Service has leased three piers to concessionaires along the fish-rich shores of Hatteras Island. Hatteras Island, in the small village of Rodanthe, is the northernmost. As you drive south on 12 from Oregon Inlet you'll find it on your left, well advertised by signs, as you pass through Rodanthe.
   Hatteras Island Pier, which also includes a motel, a restaurant, and a recreation center, is 1100 feet long, in about twenty feet of water at its head. During the open season (April 1 to November 30), Claude Howard, the pier manager, provides bait, tackle, ice, tackle rental, and "all sorts of fishing paraphernalia." The pier is accessible to handicapped. Prices: $4.00 daily; $15.00 weekly; or $45.00 for a pass good all season.
   Local fisherfolk recommend this pier for large channel bass, and as a matter of fact the world's record of *ninety pounds* was caught here by Elvin Hooper in 1973. It is mounted here for view, and it's quite an inspiration.
   Plenty of parking.

WATERFALL WATER SLIDE
CAPE HATTERAS SPEEDWAY

Rodanthe   987-2213
Map, pg. 336

   This is the first, and so far the only, water slide and go-kart track south of Oregon Inlet, and there are eight different rides here, including Bumper Boats, Quad Runners, Can Am Races, and Honda Odyssey. You'll find it just south of Spur Road 1247, on Highway 12, sea side. The slide is an impressive structure, both from an engineering and a fun point of view. Four corkscrew turns provide a ride that the more common slides built on hills just can't match.

We liked the go-karts. Five-horse Honda engines propel these miniscule speedsters around an oval track. If you haven't tried go-karts yet, they operate just like a full-sized car, with gas pedal, brakes, and a centrifugal clutch, but everything happens *a lot faster*, especially with several other drivers competing for the road. This fun spot is open from 9 a.m. until 9 p.m. Memorial Day through Labor Day. The prices begin at $3.00, with 11 different ticket combinations to choose from.

AVON FISHING PIER

Avon   995-5049

Map, pg. 344

The second Park Service concession pier on Hatteras Island, Avon was built in 1964 and is 930 feet long. It's a large, modern pier, lighted, with the usual services: tackle, bait, ice, and a snack bar. Large channel bass, gray trout, and huge bluefish haunt the often-stormy waters off Hatteras Cape, and this pier is where you can catch them. Open April 1 to November 30. Just off Highway 12 at the south end of Avon.

COLONY HOUSE AVON

Avon   995-5323

Map, pg. 344

Television has only partially come to the Southern Outer Banks, and reception is often poor. There are no roller rinks, bowling alleys or other recreational centers in the small towns on Hatteras and Ocracoke. That leaves the inhabitants with few things to do at night. But one of them is to go to the Colony House Avon, a part of the Colony Cinemas from the Northern Banks. It's not a big theatre, but it runs both first-runs and popular oldies. Come early on weekends if you want a seat. Closed for part of the winter; open the rest of the year.

SURFING ALONG THE BANKS

Surfing has been around on the Banks since Bob Holland first began coming down from Virginia Beach in the late 50's. Word of the good surf here has spread; the East Coast Surfing Championships started here in the late 70's, and in 1978 and 1982 the U.S. Championships were held here.

"The best spot is at the lighthouse," says Scott Busbey, a resident pro and owner of the Natural Art surf shop. "Waves there usually break from the left, and the three jetties they built for erosion control formed a good sand bar."

Local surfers look forward to the hurricane season, from about the first of June to the end of November. This is when they begin to watch weather reports, hoping for the big northern swells. Waves get up to eight feet, and sometimes larger, but over about eight feet it tends to be "victory at sea."

Cape Hatteras (not just Cape Point) is always a popular spot. It has the advantage of having two beaches, facing in different directions; one faces south, the other east by southeast, so that when wind and swells are unsuitable at one, the other may be surfable. But when the wind comes from the southeast, which it often does in mid-summer, be prepared to go swimming; surfing is poor. Two to three feet tends to be summer average. There's no channel at the Cape, which means you've got to muscle your way out there in heavy weather. Beware of the current when the waves come up; it's often two knots or more to the south along the beach, faster than you can swim, though on a board you might fight it. Wet suits a must until about the first of June; after that skin is OK till late October, or even later, depending on the lateness of the summer.

The lighthouse is usually the best, but not the only good break. The sandbars off the Banks are constantly shifting and changing, and there's a continual migration of surfers along them to find the best spots, which are then kept more or less secret. Surf along the Banks is where you find it. Places to check: Ramp 22; Frisco pier (off Billy Mitchell airport—stay at least 400 feet from the pier itself); Kitty Hawk Pier, south of Coquina Beach. But you can always find a crowd at the Lighthouse.

LEARNING TO SURF

A lot of people, many of them from far inland, have learned to surf at Hatteras. If you've never done it, but you suspect that riding those big Atlantic waves in to the Cape Point break might be your kind of thrill, here are some tips to help you get started.

First, a bit of traditional surfer lore: the younger you are, the easier it is to start. If you're old enough to swim, and feel confident a hundred yards off the beach, you can surf. Here's how.

You can't surf without a board (body surfing doesn't count). You can rent one, or borrow one — if you can convince a surfer to let go of his custom-made. Fortunately, any of the surf shops will rent you one for around ten dollars or so a day, a reasonable price, we think. (There will also be a deposit.) If you rent yours, be sure to ask if it's been waxed; if it hasn't, you'll be sliding all over the wave.

Second, you've got to find a break. We suggest not starting off where all the others are surfing. Get off by yourself, so that you won't be in the way of the more skilled. The break won't be as good, but then, neither are you. Right?

Item number three. To surf, you've got to learn to paddle the board. Find your balance position. Your chest should go about at the thickest part of the surfboard. This is important, so try paddling about till you feel comfortable. Watch how the others do it, up the beach.

Now paddle out to sea.

To surf, you must realize that the wave is moving toward the beach at some speed, while the shallowing water forces it to crest. You won't be picked up by it unless you're moving in the same direction at almost the same speed (this is why paddling is so important). This is the hardest part of learning — getting your timing down, learning to watch and catch the wave at that exactly correct fraction of a second.

Once the wave has you, you'll know it. You'll be carried forward fast and effortlessly, part of the sea in motion. It's a thrill.

Finally, to get up: just stand up, just as if you were doing a pushup from the speeding board. Don't get to your knees first. Just stand up naturally. Place one or the other foot forward (most people do it left foot forward, but there's no shame in being a "goofy-foot"), about a shoulder-width apart.

If you can stand up, and ride a wave into the beach that way once, you've done pretty well for your first day; don't stay out forever and agonize with sunburn tomorrow. The rest — the turning, and the other advanced maneuvers you see the more experience people doing — will come with practice.

When you feel more confident, when you want to try the good breaks with the others, remember your manners. Stay out of the way if someone's already on a wave. That's about the only point of etiquette that's really important. You'll find, after hanging around for a while, that most surfers are friendly, and with time you'll fit in with the others just fine.

"A*woo!*"

SURF SHOPS

There are several surf shops on the Banks, scattered north and south, including:
Fox Water Sports, Buxton, 995-4102
Natural Art, Buxton, 995-5682
For a 24-Hour surf report, call 995-4646
Hatteras Island Surf Shop, Waves, 987-2296
Resin Craft Surf Shop, Whalbone Junction, 441-6747
Wave Riding Vehicles, Kitty Hawk, 261-7952
For a 24-Hour surf report, call 261-3332
Secret Spot Surf Shop, Nags Head, 441-4030
Vitamin Sea Surf Shop, Kill Devil Hills (MP5), 441-7512

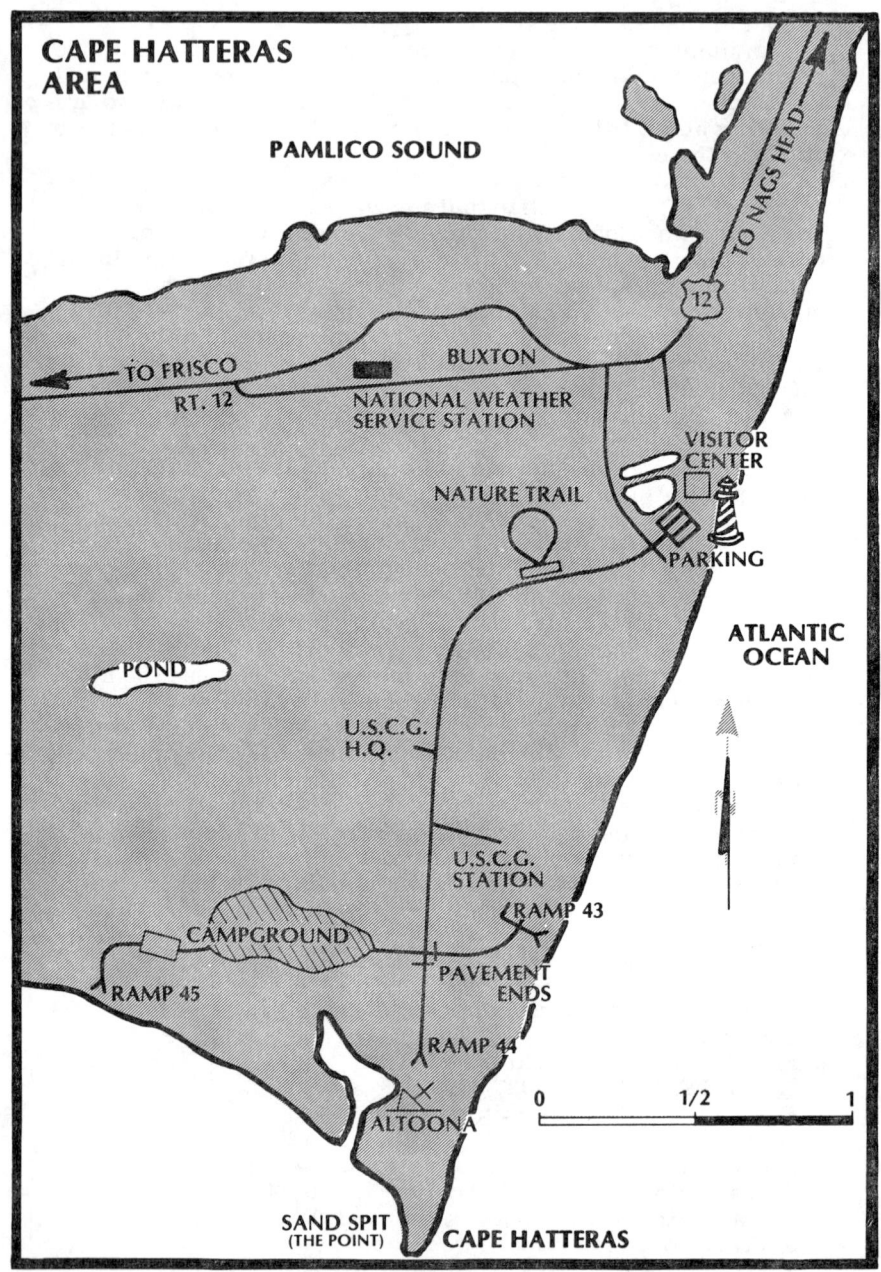

HATTERAS ISLAND SOUTH

ATTRACTIONS:
1. U.S. Coast Guard Facility, pg. 327
2. Altoona Wreck, pg. 327
3. Diamond Shoals Light, pg. 328
4. The Monitor, pg. 328
5. Billy Mitchell Air Field, pg. 330
6. Cape Point, Cape Hatteras National Seashore, pg. 330
7. Hatteras Island Visitor Center, pg. 331
8. Cape Hatteras Lighthouse pg. 332
9. Buxton Woods Nature Trail, pg. 333

RECREATION:
1. Avon Fishing Pier, pg. 339
2. Colony House Cinema, pg. 339
3. Cape Hatteras Pier (Frisco Pier), pg. 345
4. Hatteras Fishing Center, pg. 345
5. Hatteras Harbor Marina, pg. 345
6. Miss Hatteras, pg. 346
7. Surfing, pg. 340

HOTELS/MOTELS/CAMPGROUNDS
1. Avon Motel, pg. 148
2. Tower Circle, pg. 149
3. General Mitchell, pg. 149
4. Cape Hatteras, pg. 150
5. Cape Sandbox, pg. 150
6. Outer Banks, pg. 151
7. Lighthouse View, pg. 151
8. Falcon, pg. 152
9. Kona Kai, pg. 152
10. Durant Station, pg. 153
11. Seagull, pg. 153
12. Hatteras Harbor, pg. 153
13. Hatteras Marlin, pg. 154
14. Burrus Motor Court, pg. 154

SHOPPING:
1. Nedo's Dock and General Store, pg. 351
2. Kinnakeet Shopping Center, pg. 351
3. Avon Shopping Center, pg. 352
4. Pirate's Chest, pg. 352
5. Natural Art Surf Shop, pg. 353
6. Fox Water Sports, pg. 353
7. Sea Bear Country Store, pg. 353
8. Pelican's Roost, pg. 354
9. Lee Robinson General Store, pg. 354
10. Burrus' Red & White Supermarket, pg. 354
11. Buxton Village Books, pg. 355
12. Scotch Bonnet, pg. 355
13. Cape Point Tackle, pg. 355
14. Daydreams, pg. 356
15. Dillon's Corner, pg. 356
16. Browning Art Works, pg. 357
17. Fishin' Stuff/Summer Stuff, pg. 357

RESTAURANTS:
1. The Froggy Dog, pg. 246
2. The Lighthouse, pg. 248
3. Orange Blossom Pastry Shop, pg. 248
4. Pilot House, pg. 248
5. The Quarterdeck, pg. 249
6. Gingerbread House, pg. 250
7. Frisco Drive-In, pg. 250
8. Bubba's Bar-B-Q, pg. 261
9. The Light Ship, pg. 251

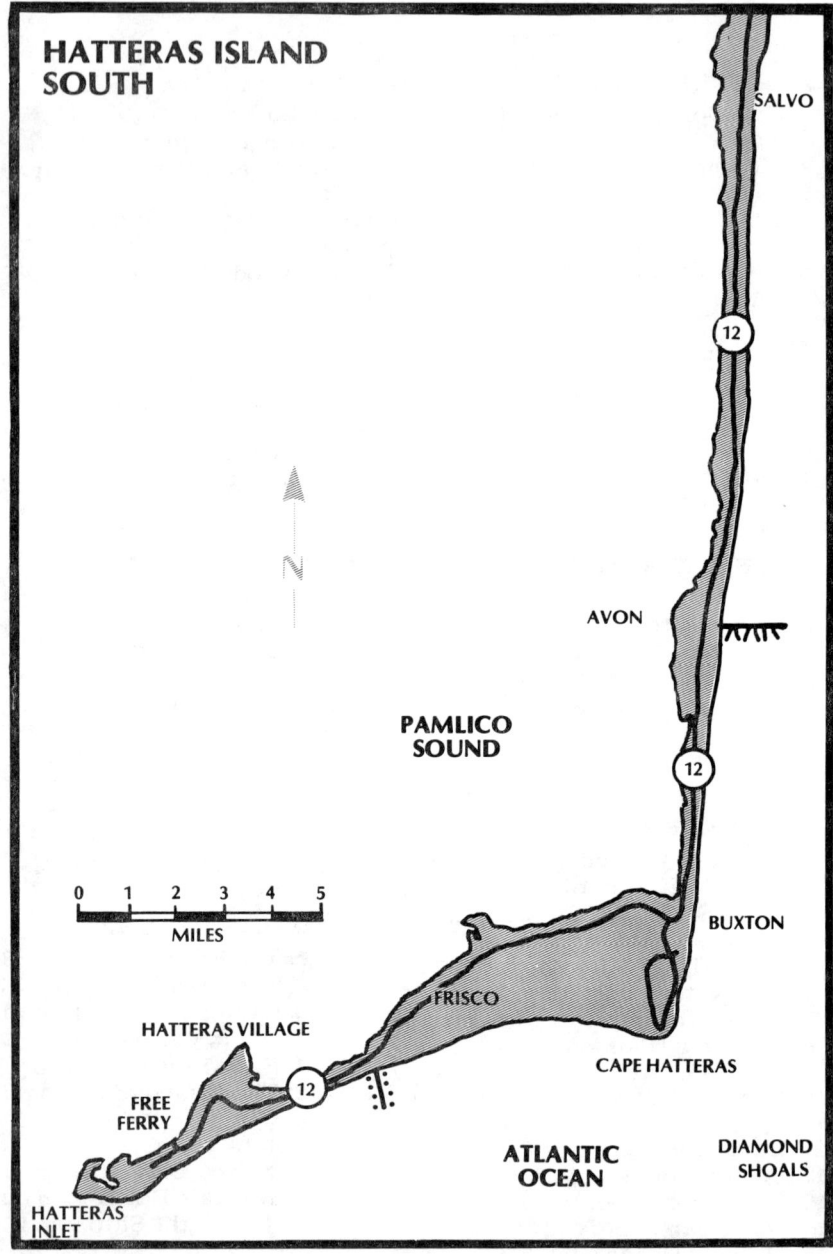

CAPE HATTERAS PIER
(Frisco Pier)

Frisco 986-2533

Map, pg. 344

The third National Park Service concession pier on Hatteras, "Frisco," as it's called locally, is about two miles west of the village of Frisco. Built in 1960, the wooden pier is 600 feet long, with about 24 feet depth at its end. Same species as the other piers, perhaps with more king mackerel. It's lighted, of course, and stocks bait, tackle, ice, and rental rods. There's a snack bar. Rates: basic fee $4.00 per day, $21.00 weekly, $80 for a season pass for an individual, and $120 for a husband and wife team for the season. Open from about April 1 to the end of November.

HATTERAS FISHING CENTER, INC.
(formerly Teach's Lair Marina)

Hatteras Village 986-2532

Map, pg. 344

This is the largest marina in a village full of marinas. Its eighty-six slips accommodate everything from ten feet long up to 42 feet, all with full hookups (no sewage). The owner, Frank B. Nelms, bills it as a "complete marine facility." The Fishing Center's services include a boat ramp (charge $2.00); a medium-sized tackle shop with a good range of fishing gear, all kinds of bait, and ice; and dry storage for boats and campers. Several charter boats operate from here, with the thirty-foot *Zola Fay* as flagship; she'll take you out in the Gulf Stream for about $350 a day. Finally, there's a campground next door, with 33 full hookup drive-through sites at $7.00 a night. A lot of services, conveniently located a stone's throw from the Ocracoke ferry terminal. Lenwood Quidley, the manager, is a great conversationalist, and he invites fishermen and wildfowl hunters especially to stop by for information.

HATTERAS HARBOR MARINA, INC.
(formerly Hatteras Holiday Harbor)

Hatteras village 986-2166

Map, pg. 344

HHM is located on the sound side of Highway 12, about 1½

miles northeast of the Ocracoke ferry landing. There's been a lot of effort and construction going on here in the last few years, and the result is the most modern marina on Hatteras, in our judgment. It's the center of operations for eighteen deep-sea charter fishing boats, making it pretty much the home of the Hatteras Village charter fleet.

Facilities: 46 slips, accommodating boats up to sixty feet long, with water and 110/220V power at each slip. Exxon petroleum products are also available. The basin was dredged in 1978 to seven feet at mean low water, so if you've got a really big one this is the place to put it. The new office complex contains a lounge, restroom with hot showers, washers and dryers, ice, soft drinks, and bait, along with a nice big freezer. The new marina store carries some fishing supplies, but is primarily a yacht chandler, with a nice selection of marine hardware, instruments, and clothing. Store hours: 6 a.m. to 9 p.m. summer, 7 a.m. to 7 p.m. winter.

MISS HATTERAS

Hatteras Village   986-2365

Map, pg. 344

Miss Hatteras, a sixty-foot twin diesel, runs out of Hatteras Harbor Marina. Owner and captain Spurgeon Stowe plans two cruises per day, of up to 47 people, during the season. But, on Fridays, there is an evening cruise too. The 7:30-12 morning and 1-5:30 afternoon cruises are devoted to fishing. The evening cruise, from 7 p.m. to 8:30 p.m., will be primarily sightseeing with light snacks. Prices are $20 per head per half day for adults and $16 for kids under 12, with evening cruises a bargain at $5.00. Special parties and charters as well as dive trips can be arranged in advance.

HATTERAS INLET (OCRACOKE) FERRY

Hatteras Village   Map, pg. 344

This free state-run ferry service links Hatteras with Ocracoke Island with an enjoyable 40-minute trip. The ferries accommodate cars and even large camping vehicles and are scheduled often enough during the summer so that your wait will not be long. Reservations are not required, as they are for the Cedar Island and Swan Quarter ferries from Ocracoke Village.

The summer schedule is as follows:

SUMMER SCHEDULE
APRIL 15th thru OCT. 31st

Leave HATTERAS	Leave OCRACOKE
5:00 AM	6:00 AM
6:10 AM	7:10 AM
6:50 AM	7:50 AM
7:30 AM	8:30 AM
8:10 AM	9:10 AM
8:50 AM	9:50 AM
9:30 AM	10:30 AM
10:10 AM	11:10 AM
10:50 AM	11:50 AM
11:30 AM	12:30 PM
12:10 PM	1:10 PM
12:50 PM	1:50 PM
1:30 PM	2:30 PM
2:10 PM	3:10 PM
2:50 PM	3:50 PM
3:30 PM	4:30 PM
4:10 PM	5:10 PM
4:50 PM	5:50 PM
5:30 PM	6:30 PM
6:10 PM	7:10 PM
7:00 PM	8:00 PM
9:00 PM	10:00 PM
11:00 PM	

WINTER SCHEDULE
NOV. 1st thru APRIL 14th

Leave Hatteras every hour on the hour from 5:00 AM to 5 PM, and at 7:00 PM, 9:00 PM, and 11:00 PM.
Leave Ocracoke every hour on the hour from 6:00 AM to 6:00 PM; 8:00 PM and 10:00 PM.

HATTERAS VILLAGE

 ATTRACTIONS:
1. Ocracoke Ferry Terminal, pg. 346

 RECREATION:
1. Hatteras Fishing Center, pg. 345
2. Hatteras Harbor Marina, pg. 345
3. Miss Hatteras, pg. 346

 HOTELS/MOTELS/CAMPGROUNDS:
1. General Mitchell, pg. 149
2. Durant Station, pg. 153
3. Sea Gull, pg. 153
4. Hatteras Harbor, pg. 153
5. Hatteras Marlin, pg. 154
6. Burrus Motor Court, pg. 154
7. Cape Point Campground (NPS), pg. 184
8. Hatteras Sands Campground, pg. 185

 RESTAURANTS:
1. The Light Ship, pg. 251
2. Channel Bass, pg. 252

 SHOPPING:
1. Nedo's, pg. 351
2. Sea Bear Country Store, pg. 353
3. Pelican's Roost, pg. 354
 4. Lee Robinson General Store, pg. 354
5. Burrus' Red & White Supermarket, pg. 354

HATTERAS ISLAND — 349

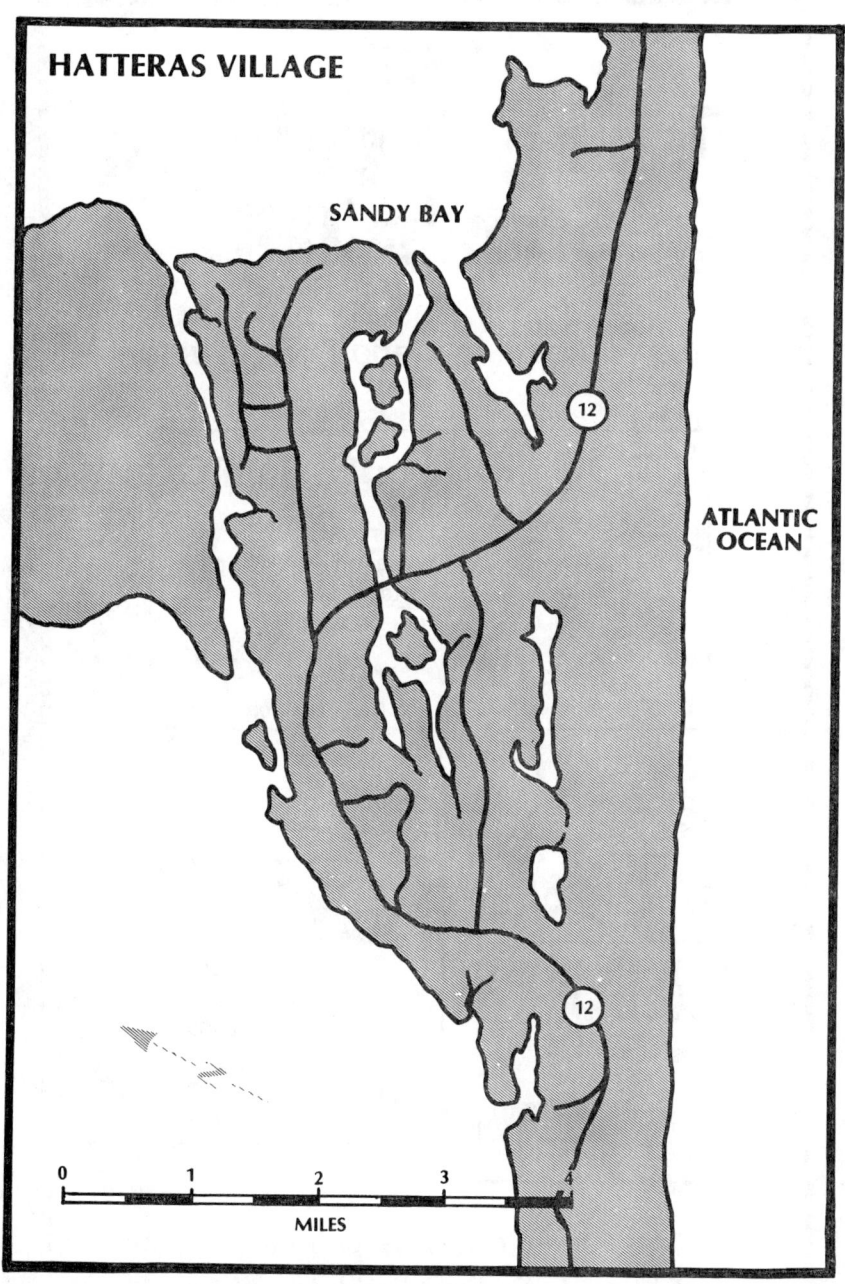

Our Fishing Reputation Stands Tall

Join the action on Cape Hatteras at Cape Point-Buxton

cape hatteras motel

Fishing and Vacation Complex

- Rooms
- Efficiencies
- Cottages
- Swimming Pool & Spa
- Lighted Tennis
- Right on Ocean

(919) 995-5611

Your Hosts — Dave & Carol Dawson

CAPE POINT TACKLE

Professional Tackle
Latest Fishing Info.
Expert Guide Service

(919) 995-5815

Daydreams

Beachwear
Activewear
Aerobics

(919) 995-5548

For more information write:
P.O. Box 339 G, Buxton, NC 27920

HATTERAS ISLAND
SHOPPING

NEDO'S DOCK AND GENERAL STORE

Hatteras Village   986-2545
                 Map, pg. 349

Remember Oden's General Store? That old, fishy building that sat just off the road in the village? Well, Oden's has been transformed into a new entity now, called Nedo's... notice anything about the name? The interior of the shop, at least in terms of the supplies carried, is still the same. But you sure won't find any old fish smell now or the feeling of the Hatteras of old gathering place. We guess all things - even our favorite Oden's store - must change.

The new Nedo's has the same general store supplies but they've added on a lot more clothing, hardware and houseware items, camping supplies, and beach supplies. You'll find most anything you might need here, and the folks who run the store are very friendly.

The dock behind Nedo's is the center of activity for a lot of fish packing after the boats come in every day. Though not really a spectator sport, it might be interesting to wander back to take a look at the process. But be sure to stay well out of the way. These folks do this for a living and don't have time to be answering a lot of questions or worrying about your safety.

Though we will certainly miss the old Oden's, the new store is sure to be a success. Open during the summer from 8 a.m. until 10 p.m., seven days a week. Open in the off season from 8 a.m. until 5 p.m. and closed on Sundays.

KINNAKEET SHOPPING CENTER

Avon   Map, pg. 344

This attractive, wooden-decked shopping center houses one of the best gift shops — The Village Gift Shop — in the southern beaches area. You'll also find Outer Beaches Realty here, as well as Dairy Queen, a t-shirt shop, and a hair boutique.

ISLAND CONVENIENCE STORE

Rodanthe 987-2239

Map, pg. 336

As you come into Rodanthe from the north, you find this store on your right. Owned and operated by Mac and Marilyn Midgett, Island Convenience truly lines up to its name. In one-stop shopping you can find a good stock of grocery items, souvenirs, tackle, bait, and even an AAA garage. Summer hours run from an early 6 a.m. to midnight; off-season hours from 7 a.m. to 7 p.m.

AVON SHOPPING CENTER

Avon 995-5362

Map, pg. 344

One of the best places in the northern half of the island to replenish staples (be they grocery staples or hardware staples). The Shopping Center, a low building on the sound side of Highway 12, is one of the largest hardware and building needs suppliers on the southern Banks, carrying a complete Sentry line. There's also a good selection of basic auto needs, books and magazines, ice cream treats, a fine selection of fishing tackle, and Exxon gas out front. Open 7 a.m. to 9 p.m. summer, 7 a.m. to 7 p.m. winter, both weekdays and weekends. Accepts MC and Visa.

PIRATE'S CHEST

Frisco 995-5118

Map, pg. 344

There are new owners in this small shop that was one of the first gift stores on the island, and it has been given a fresh facelift. Still featured are local woodcarvings, art supplies, antiques, specimen shells, driftwood, paintings, and other items reminiscent of the Banks. Demonstrations are often given in pottery making, shellcraft, and macrame.

Summer hours are 7 a.m. to 10 a.m. Open Easter to Thanksgiving in their location on the sound side of Highway 12.

NATURAL ART SURF SHOP

Buxton   995-5682
                    Map, pg. 344

Scott and Carol Busbey own and run this two-story, natural-wood-finished, duodecagonal, ramped building on the sea side of Route 12, about a quarter of a mile east of the Cape Pines Motel. "This is a surfer's surf shop," Scott says. "We have one of the best selections on the Banks of wet suits, boards, and bathing suits." He has rental boards available and is generous with advice to beginners. A noteworthy sideline is a nice selection of *handmade* beachwear, made by Carol in the little room behind the showroom. Shorts go for about $20, shirts for around $22, and no two of them are the same. Natural Art also sells the manufactured beachwear, and a lot of t-shirts. Hours are usually 8 a.m. to sunset "Except when the surf is up — then we'll be gone." Closed January.

FOX WATER SPORTS

Buxton   Map, pg. 344

The Fox name is a popular one among surfers. Ted James, one of the company's owners, builds about half the boards they sell right here in Buxton, importing the rest from the main factory down in Florida. A low, brown-sided building with a "pier" porch in front, this shop carries swimming and beach gear, wet suits, sandals, and a *lot* of t-shirts. And, of course, Fox boards!

SEA BEAR COUNTRY STORE

Hatteras   986-2695
                    Map, pg. 349

Just across from the library in Hatteras Village is a wonderful place, the Sea Bear. At this establishment, natural foods, gourmet coffees, teas, nuts, dried fruits and mixes, gourmet wines and fine imported beers, and a huge variety of cheeses take the spotlight. The easygoing atmosphere and the marvelous juniper fragrance set the backdrop. Most natural items are displayed in tubs and sold by the pound. If you are going to take the ferry to Ocracoke and your plans include a picnic, Sea Bear has just the mouth-watering, no mess treats your whole family will enjoy. Open daily, 9 a.m. to 9 p.m.

PELICANS ROOST

Hatteras 986-2213
Map, pg. 349

Pelicans Roost is a well-equipped one stop shop, but is more specialized than a Seven-Eleven. Pelicans Roost has facilities for selling gasoline and making minor auto repairs, in addition to weighing fish. The store has ice, tackle, bait, refreshments, and an adequate supply of groceries. For daily necessities, Pelicans Roost carries toilet articles and beach items such as sun glasses, sun tan lotion, post cards, and magazines. Hours: daily, 7 a.m. to 11 p.m. MC and Visa are honored.

LEE ROBINSON GENERAL STORE

Hatteras Village 986-2381
Map, pg. 349

Lee Robinson's amazingly complete store is located half a mile northeast of the Ocracoke ferry terminal, on the sound side. It's been here for over thirty-three years, and behind that big old porch you'll find everything you'll need — groceries, fine wines and beer, beach needs, sport clothing, books, magazines, camping supplies — a little of everything, just what a general store ought to have. Open all year, from 7 a.m. to 11 p.m. during the summer, and 9 a.m. to 9 p.m. during the winter.

BURRUS' RED & WHITE SUPERMARKET

Hatteras Village 986-2333
Map, pg. 349

Located right in the center of Hatteras Village, this store, now an independently-owned member of the Red & White chain, has to hold the longevity record... it's been here since 1865, operating in the same place for more than a hundred years. You only last that long when you deal fairly with people. The present owner, Bill Burrus, specializes in fresh meats, produce, and groceries, but also carries housewares, cold beer and wines, and a large book and magazine section. Traveler's checks accepted, but no credit cards or out-of-state personal checks. Open all year, 7 a.m. to 9 p.m. daily, Sundays 2 to 9 p.m.

BUXTON VILLAGE BOOKS

Buxton   995-4240
                    Map, pg. 344

Gigi Rozelle operates this comfortably small and well-stocked bookshop in the heart of Buxton village. She carries a full line of fiction and nonfiction, children's books, and regional guides. The back wall is full of quality collectible blank cards. She also stocks office supplies, rents VCRs, TVs and movies, and provides 4-day film processing. Buddy, the bookstore cat, usually demands a back scratch before you check out.

SCOTCH BONNET

Frisco   995-4242
                    Map, pg. 344

This two-story white frame house on the sound side of the highway was first opened in 1965. We've watched it grow steadily into one of the more complete collections of shells and gifts on Hatteras Island. The local crafts are very good. The local art, prints by Ruth Ann Burgess and other well-known Banks' artists, is worth investigation. Janet O'Brien also stocks lots of tackle and bait and a line of truly *custom* (i.e., *individual* — she can arrange special art) t-shirts. Recently added during this steady growth is a sound boat rental service, providing jon boats, sailboards, snarks, jet skis, and surfjets. Open Easter to October, 9 a.m. to 5 p.m.; tackle shop, 6 a.m. to 5 p.m.

CAPE POINT TACKLE

Buxton   995-5815
                    Map, pg. 344

Cape Point Tackle might look unpretentious from the outside, but inside it offers about as complete a line of fishing supplies that you'll find anywhere. They sell custom, made to order rods, and a large selection of reels, waders, line, tackle, coolers, slickers, and bait. There's also a good amount of beach supplies: t-shirts, toys, sunglasses, towels, suntanning products. And, not to be left out, there are also cold beers and soft drinks. Ben Doerr runs his surf guiding out of here too.

DAYDREAMS

Buxton
Map, pg. 344
995-5548

Carol Dawson decided the time had come for a truly great clothing store in the Hatteras area. So, with a background in retailing, she set out to open Daydreams. And, let us tell you, she sure hit her mark. This shop has great clothing! It's not the run of the mill lines that are found in most other places. She has managed to get the exclusive on certain lines, like Surf Fetish, and her others are well chosen and fun. There's a large selection of Jams and Jimmy Z's, women's clothing by Gottex and Ann Cole, a collection of swim suits in styles we hadn't run across in other stores, body wear for workouts, cotton sweaters, jewelry and other neat accessories, and a whole lot more. There's also a children's section.

We predict that as word spreads about the clothes in this store, they'll have shoppers from the upper beaches too. Daydreams is open March through November at the present time, with in season hours of 9 a.m. to 9 p.m., and off season hours from 9 a.m. till 6 p.m.

DILLON'S CORNER

Buxton
Map, pg. 344
995-5083

Dillon's Corner is the attractive, wooden building up on stilts with the long ramp leading to the front door, caddy-corner to the road that leads to the lighthouse. It's as attractive inside as out, with some real friendly folks running it, Ollie and Kathy Jarvis. Here you'll find everything you might need for a day on the beach along with a complete line of fishing supplies. They sell custom made rods here that are amazingly light... but strong. And they are the headquarters for the well known Outer Banks Safaris Guiding Service, led by Ken Lauer, who gives instructions in long distance surf casting and leads surf, sound, and inshore trips.

Dillon's Corner is open from 6 a.m. till 11 p.m. during the summer, from 5 a.m. till 11 p.m. during the drum fishing season, and from 7 a.m. during the off season.

BROWNING ART WORKS

Frisco

Map, pg. 344

Don't miss this place. It offers first rate, North Carolina arts and crafts that are obviously chosen by someone who knows art... you won't find "souvenirs" here. There are beautiful porcelins, handmade jewelry, unique basketry, oven proof stoneware, decorative decoys by George Fulcher, wood crafts, and a limited number of working decoys from the 1940s. The arrangement of the shop is quiet and tasteful and it offers a cool, interesting hiatus from the sun and bustle.

The shop is owned and operated by Linda and Lou Browning and his parents, Dixie and Lee. Dixie, as some might recognize, is the well known water color artist turned Silhouette Romance writer.

Browning's is open during the summer from 10 a.m. until 6 p.m., Monday through Saturday. Off season hours vary.

FISHIN' STUFF/SUMMER STUFF

Hatteras Village   986-2111

Map, pg. 294

Just to the left as you slide into the village, Fishin' Stuff/Summer Stuff has more than fishing tackle — but we'll start with that: they have over four hundred square feet of it, specializing in offshore tackle and surf gear, too. You can get fish mounts here, and there's a nice collection of locally available fish mounted around the walls of the store. And then there's clothing: t-shirts, a full line of sportswear, beach clothing, boat shoes. Adjoining rooms hold an above-average collection of gift items, especially brass, glass, carefully selected nautical memorabilia, local books, and a toy gallery. Shoppers will find a well selected, tasteful inventory on display. Summer hours: 7 a.m. to 10 p.m. daily; winter hours: variable.

358 — OCRACOKE ISLAND

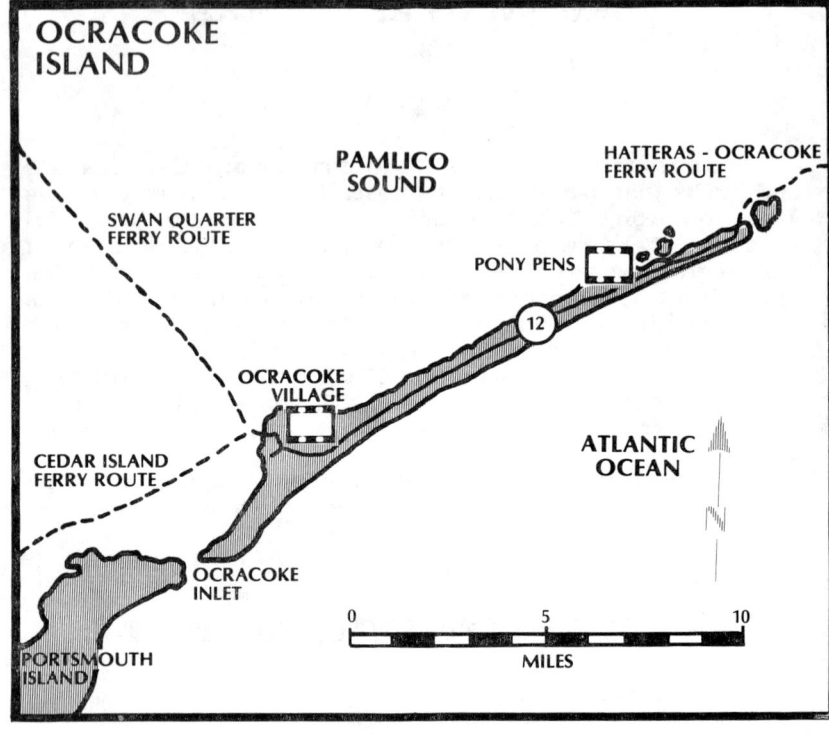

INSIDE
OCRACOKE

Ocracoke Island is the most remote inhabited island of the Banks, and Ocracoke is the southernmost town within the limits of the National Park.

It's reached by ferry from Hatteras Village (see previous chapter). The trip across is fast, free, and scenic, following a winding course west of Hatteras Inlet, in the calm waters of the sound. Even when the surf breaks whitely on the bar the ferry hardly rolls. Feeding the gulls that hover over the moving ferry and dive for tidbits is part of the fun of the crossing.

Bring binoculars, if you own a pair. To your left as the ferry hums along you can see the distinctive vegetation and wildlife of the Sound side of the banks. Low, sandy islets slip by on either side as the ferry approaches the pier on the northeastern end of Ocracoke Island, and Highway 12 resumes.

Most of the island is still just as uninhabited as you drive down it as it was on a spring day in 1585, when seven English ships appeared off Ocracoke Inlet.

Sir Richard Grenville was in command, a seasoned, experienced soldier. He had about three hundred troops aboard his fleet. His mission, entrusted to him by Sir Walter Raleigh and the Queen, was to establish a permanent English base in the New World. He was to fail at Roanoke Island; but that summer no one yet suspected the fate that awaited those first colonists.

The Banks welcomed him in characteristic fashion, leaving his flagship, *Tiger*, hard aground on the bar. He and Ralph Lane took advantage of the delay to explore north and west in smaller vessels (see 'Ocracoke Pony Pens', in this chapter — these hardy ponies may stem from stock lost from the *Tiger*). When the ship was floated and repaired, he headed to Roanoke, leaving the island sleeping and deserted once again.

It's thought that the name 'Woccocon,' which was applied to the island at first, was derived from the neighboring Indian tribe the 'Woccons.' But its precise derivation, like that of so many Outer Banks names, is unclear, as is its subsequent degeneration through 'Wococock,' 'Occocock,' 'Ocreecock,' and other variations to the present 'Ocracoke.' Spelling held a low priority in those days, a state to which the English tongue seems to be reverting.

Most of the island remained in its wild state, with sheep, cattle, and horses released by the early owners to graze freely. But the gradual increase in colonial trade in the early 18th century saw more and more ships using the Inlet, in those days deeper than it is now (too, ships, were of shallow draft). In 1715 the colony of North Carolina established Ocracoke as a port, setting aside land on the western tip of the island for the homes of pilots (for midwesterners, and other non-seagoing types, a 'pilot' meets incoming ships at sea and guides them safely in. Pilots are generally older men, brine-encrusted, who know the configurations of sand bars and channels from painful experience).

A new problem also arose: pirates. They interfered with the pilots, terrorized the inhabitants of the islands, boarded and robbed ships at sea, murdered crews and passengers, and made themselves generally unwelcome. John Cole, Robert Deal, Anne Bonny, and dozens of others operated along the Caribbean and Southern Atlantic coasts in the early eighteenth century.

But it was the notorious Blackbeard, standing out as the worst of a bad lot, who left his name stamped on the Outer Banks, and, on Ocracoke, one of his lairs. Much of his early career lies somewhere between conjecture and legend. It is thought that he started as an honest English tar named Edward Drummond, born, perhaps, in Bristol.

He may have started, like many pirates, as a privateer — a sort of seagoing guerrilla. But by 1716 he had turned pirate, calling himself Edward Teach. He had found his metier, and his rise was rapid. He seems to have been a man of organizational ability, for in short order he was in command of a sizeable fleet of ships, and some hundreds of men.

He also understood advertising. An evil reputation is a great thing to a terrorist, for it weakens the other side's morale and leads to quick capitulations. Blackbeard was a master in dressing for success and winning through intimidation. Tall, broad, and with a bushy coal-black beard, he festooned himself with cutlasses, dirks, and loaded pistols. In battle his beard was plaited, with little ribbons to add a festive air. Lighted cannon fuses dangled from under his hat, an affectation of dubious safety with primed flintlocks in his belt, but unquestionably effective in giving him the air of the very devil.

And a devil with political clout. He bought Governor Eden, of North Carolina, and was able to move ashore to Bath with his booty in 1718. Like many men, he became bored with retirement, and before the year was up he was out raiding again part-time. Eden stayed bought and did nothing, so a few citizens went north to ask a favor of Governor Spotswood, of Virginia.

Spotswood sent the Royal Navy. In November of 1718, Lt. Robert Maynard left the James River, heading south in two sloops manned with sailors from British men-o'-war. Maynard must have had confidence in himself; his two small sloops had no cannon, only small arms. The shallow-draft boats were able to penetrate where larger warships could not go, and Maynard was able to track Blackbeard's *Adventure* to Ocracoke Inlet.

Dawn, November 22. Ocracoke Inlet resounded to the boom of pirate guns and the crackle of British musketry fire. The *Adventure* grounded, but her well-laid cannon took heavy toll of the Royal Navy men. Maynard ordered them below, then stood ready on deck as his sloop drifted down on the larger ship.

They met. Teach's men launched a volley of grenades and swarmed aboard. The sailors came up from below to begin a merciless hand-to-hand struggle. The pirate chief and the lieutenant faced each other. An exchange of pistol balls wounded the pirate, but in the next moment he had broken the officer's sword with his cutlass. Another sailor sliced the massive buccaneer in the neck, but he fought on...then collapsed. The battle was over. The pirate's head was cut off and hung from the rigging for the trip back, that all might see he was dead. The body was thrown overboard, where, island legend has it, it swam seven times round the ship before sinking. Most of the rest of his crew were taken to Williamsburg and given a fair trial before they were hanged. His treasure? Probably there was none—he spent what little money the coasting trade yielded. But legends persist....

With the pirates cleaned out, trade flourished. Most of the seaborne commerce of North Carolina, and much of that of Virginia, came through the inlet, and gradually families settled there to service the ships. There were sporadic Spanish incursions and raids in the 1740's and 50's, and at one time they even had a camp on the island. Eventually peace came between England and Spain and they went home.

It was in 1753 that the village became a recognized town, and then there were only about a hundred inhabitants. Most of the island remained in a wild state. The inlet was fortified in 1757. Across the water, the town of Portsmouth was also growing up, and the little port of Beacon Island Roads, as the two towns were commonly called, was doing well when the Revolution arrived. Much of Washington's army was supplied through Ocracoke, and coastal North Carolina trade remained intact although the British patrolled outside, landed troops, and engaged in various futile retaliations.

After the war, the lighthouses were built by the new government, the first in 1798 on Shell Castle Rock, the second (the present one) in 1823. But even as they went up the golden age of Ocracoke was drawing to an end. Hatteras and Oregon inlets opened during a storm in September of 1846, and as these were deepened by outflow, Ocracoke Inlet began to shoal. The fort was abandoned by the Confederates in 1861 and the Government sank several ships loaded with rock in the channel to seal it. Such seagoing traffic as remained to the Banks—for by now oceangoing ships had grown much larger and deeper — shifted to Hatteras Inlet. After the war the village declined to a hundred or so inhabitants, who subsisted as fishermen, boatmen, or lifesavers. Many went to sea, and not all of them returned.

It took a war to bring new life. Silver Lake Harbor (formerly Cockle Creek) had been dredged out in 1931, and in 1942 a naval base was established there. As cargo ships burned offshore, as oil and debris and dead bodies drifted ashore, telephones and paved roads were brought to the villagers. The base was closed in 1945, but in the mid-50's the National Seashore and the highway brought a new source of revenue: the tourist.

Today tourism has taken the lead over fishing as the town's major livelihood, although the same increased access that has brought visitors has made crabbing commercially productive.

But a walk, or a bike ride, will show you that Ocracoke hasn't been spoiled yet. There are no tourist traps, traffic lights, or movie theaters. There's now (one) ABC store; only one doctor. Many of the streets are really only sandy paths, still unpaved, and unlikely ever to be. Some of the paved roads are so narrow and winding that two Caddies will scarce pass abreast. A handful of gift shops, a few restaurants, a few motels...and that's it. Commercialization has as yet hardly reached the island.

And to the north and east...Ocracoke Island is still virgin. The sea roars against the long rows of dunes; the road, silent and empty, shimmers amid the beachgrass and yaupon. Toward the sound, the wild ponies graze warily, and Ocracoke is quiet by the jealous sea.

OCRACOKE
ATTRACTIONS

OCRACOKE PONY PENS

Soundside

Map, pg. 358

'Ponies?' The word conjures up a picture of something small, shaggy, and friendly. None of these adjectives, however, exactly fits the semiwild Ocracoke ponies.

They're not really that small, perhaps thirteen or fourteen hands high. They are shaggy, in the winter. But they are definitely not friendly.

History, economics, and even anatomy have been used to try to explain the derivation of these hardy russet-colored animals that, in former days, roamed wild on the length of the island, as well as on Hatteras Island. The accepted version goes as follows. In 1585, the vessels carrying the first colonists to Roanoke made their first landing at Ocracoke Inlet, where the flagship, *Tiger*, grounded. Sir Richard Grenville ordered the ship unloaded, and its cargo, which included a brace of horses purchased in the West Indies (then under Spanish rule), was put ashore while the *Tiger* was taken off the shoal. The usual method of getting horses ashore in those days was to let them swim; and it is thought that some escaped, and began their wild existence on the Banks. Other theories say they came from Spanish shipwrecks, or, more prosaically, were introduced by the early Bankers as a ready source of horseflesh. The rugged, wild ponies *have* been proven to be of Spanish mustang descent by the number of lumbar vertebrae and number of ribs.

At one time there were more than a thousand of them, roaming free, subsisting on marsh grass. As civilization came to the Banks they were penned and sold off. When the Cape Hatteras National Seashore was established they were taken over by the Park Service. There are now about nineteen ponies in the herd.

The Pony Pen is located some four miles southwest of the Hatteras-Ocracoke ferry landing, on the sound side. Park Service signs will direct you to a wooden observation platform overlooking the mile-long fenced pasture. Don't count on seeing

OCRACOKE LIGHTHOUSE
Drawing by Jerry Miller

the ponies, especially in rough weather; they have shelters down near the southwest end that they retreat to. *Don't* cross the fence into the pasture. These are wild ponies, and they can bite and kick.

OCRACOKE VISITOR CENTER

Near Cedar Island and 928-4531
Swan Quarter Ferry Slips
        Map, pg. 358

    The Silver Lake Visitor Center, run by the National Park Service as part of the Cape Hatteras National Seashore, is located right on Silver Lake, at the southwest end of Highway 12. To reach it from 12, remain on the highway past the Island Inn until you reach the Lake and a T. Turn right and continue around the shore of the Lake for about half a mile. The Center is located in a new building constructed in 1979-80.
    The Center itself contains an information booth, a small book sales shop, and exhibits on local shells, the ponies, piracy, and other aspects of local history. It's also the place for arrangements for the Silver Lake Marina and for use of the picnic area just across the road.
    Things are about as quiet at the Center during the winter as they are in the rest of the village, but during the warm months activity picks up considerably. The Rangers offer a couple of dozen 'Discovery Adventures,' all free, presented several times each week (a schedule of times and locations can be obtained at the information desk). There are such programs as beach and sound walks, surfing lessons, interpretations of the life and times of a pirate, both day and night walking tours of the village, bird lectures, history lectures, knot-tying... and quite a few more. Once you've looked around the village you will appreciate the Park Service's thoughfulness in arranging things for you to do.

OCRACOKE COAST GUARD STATION

Silver Lake 928-3711
        Map, pg. 358

    The southernmost of the chain of Coast Guard stations along the Banks is Ocracoke. Its complement of twenty-one men maintain a 44-foot motor lifeboat and several other, smaller vessels for search and rescue, law enforcement, and servicing aids to navigation. In an average year, they respond to 250 calls for assistance from fishermen and boaters. Visitors may enjoy looking around the station building, built in 1938 to replace an older building on the same site, and strolling down the two piers to see the Coast Guard's pride — its boats. You're welcome for an accompanied tour from 2 to 4 p.m. daily; check in at the communications station on the wide front porch.

OCRACOKE VILLAGE

West end of Highway 12   Map, pg. 373

The little village of Ocracoke is a world of its own. Reclusive, hidden, romantic... these are words used by those who know her. A haunt of writers, artists, and lovers, this small lost hamlet at the world's end (or at least at the end of the highway, a phrase that has a touch of the mysterious itself) is unlike any of the other towns on the Banks.

Things have changed since WWII and the coming of paved roads, but not all that much. The map of the village shows you nearly all that's there. The roads are still narrow, the people friendly but a touch reticent, with manners and a speech of their own distinct from mainland North Carolina. We love Ocracoke, and you will too.

For a short walking tour of the village, park in the lot opposite the Visitor's Center. Turn left out of the lot and walk down Route 12, along the shores of the Lake, toward the Post Office. Notice the large house just opposite the Visitor's Center. The railed platform atop it is called a 'widow's walk,' a fairly typical feature of architecture in English seaside towns; from it the womenfolk watched for returning sails.

Opposite the little post office, on your right, a sandy, narrow street angles to the left. This is Howard Street, one of the oldest and least changed parts of the village. Note the smallness of the old homes, the cisterns attached to them for collection of rain water, and the detached kitchens. If you've been to Colonial Williamsburg you will recall seeing these detached kitchens under somewhat more monumental circumstances.

After some four hundred yards Howard Street debouches by the Methodist Church and public school. The church is usually open for visitors, but use discretion; there may be services in progress.

If you enter, note the cross displayed behind the altar. Thereby hangs a tale, and not so very ancient a one. The cross was carved from a wooden spar from an American freighter, the *Caribsea*, sunk offshore by U-boats in the dark early months of 1942. By the strange workings of circumstance, the *Caribsea's* engineer was James Baugham Gaskill, who had been born in Ocracoke. He was killed in the sinking; and local residents will tell you a further strange fact; that several days later a display case, holding, among other things, Gaskill's mate's license, washed ashore not far from his family home.

If you'd like to walk to the lighthouse on the tour — it adds about another half mile — turn right (west) and follow the road past the Island Inn about five hundred yards. You will see the lighthouse towering on your right. After inspecting it (see 'Ocracoke Inlet Lighthouse') return to the church and school.

The next leg of the tour takes you across the grounds of the public school and out onto the paved road beyond it to the east. Turn left. This was the first paved road on the island, and was constructed by Seabees during WW II. Turn right after a third of a mile (first stop sign). A few minutes' walk along this narrow, tree-shaded road will bring you to the British Cemetery. You have to watch for it; it's on your right, set back a bit from the road, and shaded by live oak and yaupon. The big British flag makes it a bit easier to spot. It's not an impressive site; very small, very understated; entirely appropriate. The *Bedfordshire* was a trawler, one of a small fleet of twenty-four antisubmarine vessels that Churchill loaned to the United States in April 1942 to help us against the U-boats. She was a small ship, only 170 feet long, displacing 900 tons and armed with a single 4-inch deck gun, but full of fight. She had no chance; she was torpedoed off Cape Hatteras during the night of 11 May by U-558. Six bodies washed ashore. Four were interred here by the Navy and Coast Guard, and the little cemetery is maintained by the USCG.

To return to the Visitor Center, walk west till you reach the lakeshore, then turn right.

OCRACOKE LIGHTHOUSE

NW corner of Ocracoke Village

Map, pg. 358

This, the southernmost of the three famous lighthouses of the Banks, is also the oldest and the shortest. It's the second oldest operational lighthouse in the United States as well. Yes, it's still flashing away, still warning mariners away from the ever-changing shoals offshore.

When it was built, in 1823, this was a busy port. The present lighthouse replaced a still older one, the Shell Castle Rock

Open from 5:30-10 p.m.
(919) 928-6401
Look for our directional sign on Highway 12
in Ocracoke village.

lighthouse, which had been built in 1798 but which was rather left behind when the inlet moved south.

The Ocracoke Inlet Lighthouse houses a 360° non-rotating light with a range of 14 miles. Focal plane height is 65', overall height of the structure is about 75'. The brick walls are five feet thick at the base. That pretty, textured white surface is mortar, hand-spread over the bricks. The two-story white house you will find nearby was orginally meant for the lighthouse keeper; now, with an electric instead of an oil lamp in operation, it is a Ranger residence. The light itself is operated by the Coast Guard and cannot be entered.

To reach the light, turn left off Route 12 at the Island Inn, and make the next left. A white picketed turnoff on the right after about ¼ mile allows you to park your auto and walk the last few yards to the base of the structure.

SILVER LAKE MARINA

At Visitor's Center   928-4531
Map, pg. 358

Silver Lake is the Park Service-run marina in Ocracoke, and is the only large one there. It is run differently from a commercial marina in that there are no dockage fees and no reservations. The marina has no slips, only four hundred feet of frontage on Silver Lake with tie-up facilities. Water is available, and so are power hookups ($1/night). The basin has been dredged to eighteen feet.

Basically, the way to get a slip is to arrive at the right time. If there's one open just pull in and tie up. There's a fourteen-day limit in the summertime. Actually, the rangers tell us that it's possible to get a slip there even in the summer, although it gets crowded on weekends.

If the marina should be full when you arrive, don't panic. Just anchor out in the lake, staying out of the channelway and out of the way of ferry operations.

OCRACOKE TROLLEY

Trolley Stop One, Highway 12   928-4811
Map, pg. 358

It's one thing to see Ocracoke Island through your own eyes, and another thing altogether to see it through the eyes of a local,

Beach people - A grassy dune edged with sea oats provided this setting for these vacationers on a summer evening as they enjoyed a stretch of undeveloped shoreline on the Outer Banks of North Carolina.

someone who knows every nook and cranny of the island. That's why you should definitely plan to take this one-hour tour, besides the fact that it's just plain fun. The Trolley runs three times a day during the week and twice on the weekends and takes you past some of Ocracoke's history you'd never know was there on your own.

The narrated tour includes the Coast Guard Station, the WW II Naval Base, several Sam Jones homes, the British Cemetary and Howard Grave Yard, a WW II Mine Control Tower, Blackbeard's Hideaway, the Civil War headquarters for the Union Forces, and lots more. Not only do you get an enjoyable lesson in the area's history, but you also get a cool, relaxing trip around the island.

It's lots of fun and we highly recommend it. Reservations are required for busses or groups numbering over 25, but for others, you should just show up at the Trolley Stop One (you can grab a quick bite there too while you're waiting). Tours leave at 10:30 a.m., 2:30 p.m., and 6:00 p.m. Mondays through Saturdays, and at 1:00 p.m. and 6:00 p.m. on Sundays. Tours, of course, are lessened during the off season and end altogether after Labor Day, but you can call to make special arrangements. Rates are $3.00 for adults, $1.50 for kids under 12, and 15% off for senior citizens.

Located on Hwy. 12 in the heart of Ocracoke Village

Lunch
11:30 a.m.-2 p.m.
Dinner
5-9:30 p.m.

Outside Cafe
2-5 p.m.
Open May through October weather permitting
(919) 928-6611

OCRACOKE VILLAGE

 ATTRACTIONS:

1. Ocracoke Visitor Center, pg. 365
2. Ferry Landing, pg. 347
3. Ocracoke Coast Guard Station, pg. 365
4. Ocracoke Lighthouse, pg. 367
5. Ocracoke Pony Pens, pg. 363

 RECREATION:

1. Silver Lake Marina, pg. 369
2. Ocracoke Trolley, pg. 369

 HOTELS/MOTELS/CAMPGROUNDS:

1. Berkley Center, p. 155
2. Bluff Shoal, pg. 155
3. Silver Lake, pg. 157
4. Island Inn, pg. 157
5. Pony Island, pg. 159
6. Oscar's House, pg. 159
7. Boyette House, pg. 160
8. Harborside, pg. 160
9. Sand Dollar, pg. 161
10. Ship's Timbers, pg. 161
11. Crew's Inn, pg. 161
12. Blackbeard's Lodge, pg. 162
13. Ocracoke Campground (NPS), pg. 186

 RESTAURANTS:

1. The Back Porch, pg. 252
2. Island Inn Dining Room, pg. 253
3. The Pelican, pg. 254
4. Howard's Pub, pg. 256
5. Cap't. Ben's, pg. 256
6. Pony Island Restaurant, pg. 257

SHOPPING:

1. Community Store, pg. 374
2. The Gathering Place, pg. 375
3. O'Neal's Dockside, pg. 375
4. The Merchant Mariner, pg. 377
5. The Old Post Office Shop B.W.'s Surf Shop, pg. 377
6. Harborside Gifts, pg. 378
7. Ride the Wind, pg. 378
8. Ragpicker Rugs, pg. 379
9. Village Craftsmen, pg. 379
10. Ocracoke Variety Shop, pg. 379
11. Ocracoke Art Co-op, pg. 380
12. Tradewinds Tackle Shop, pg. 380

 **NIGHTSPOTS:**

3/4 Time, pg. 266

OCRACOKE ISALND — 373

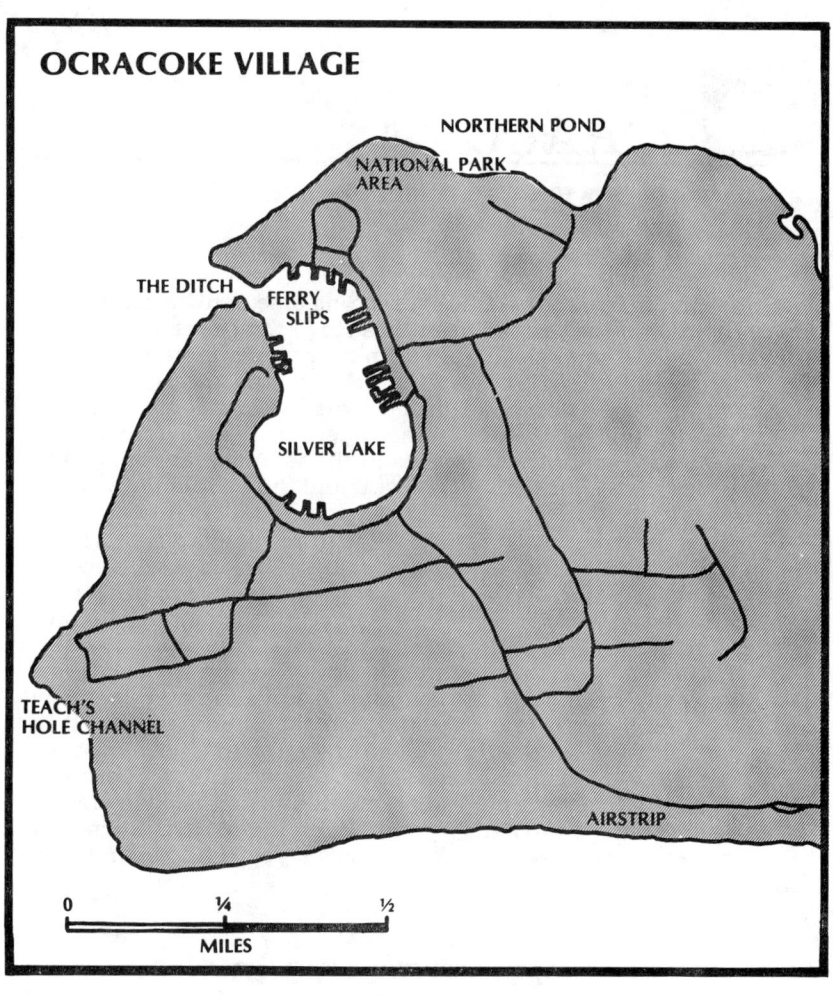

OCRACOKE
SHOPPING

Shopping in Ocracoke, like everything else, is different than it is in the rest of the Outer Banks. It's slower, more relaxing, and possibly a little cheaper. There aren't the vast numbers of shops you'll find in Nags Head or Kitty Hawk, and the selection of some of the basic items is limited. This is balanced by the fine local crafts and art, and by the selectivity and care of the shopkeepers, most of whom live on the island year round, and who really care about what they sell and the people they buy it from.

The best bargains on Ocracoke seem to be objects d'art (simple ones, not Fifth Avenue-style) and crafts. Carved toys, decoys, and other handicrafts are popular and well-made. North Carolina pottery and household items in glass and brass are attractive and priced well.

Perhaps the best thing, though, about shopping Ocracoke Village is the pace. It's a walking pace, not a driving one. You can walk or bicycle to every shop on the island, stopping in between for a look at the lighthouse or the Coast Guard Station, or for a meal at one of the excellent local restaurants. The sun is warm and the breeze is cool in summer, and on the back streets the trees lean over the sandy paths. Even if you don't normally like to shop, try it just this once. We think you'll find something nice.

COMMUNITY STORE

Ocracoke   928-3321

Map, pg. 373

The Community Store's motto is too good not to share. Here it is: "We have almost everything you need, some things you don't need, and a few things you couldn't use if you had!"

This is one of the places where Ocracoke residents shop all winter, and it has all the staples. Considering money shipping must cost, the prices aren't that different from the mainland. It's a country style store, bare wood, people just hanging around outside on the benches, a community bulletin board where you can find out who's renting a cottage and where the Historical Society is meeting this month, beer, popsicles, and everything else you're likely to need, including hardware and housewares. During the winter the Community Store is open Monday through Saturday, 9 a.m. to 6 p.m.; summers, open an hour later in the evenings.

THE GATHERING PLACE

Ocracoke   928-3321
Map, pg. 373

David and Sherril Senseney, the proprietors of The Community Store, have another unique stores located on the Ocracoke Harbor. The Gathering Place was formerly a turn-of-the-century island residence which was moved and restored to save it from demolition. It is now a craft and antique shop featuring bird carvings, paintings, prints, photographs, frames, pottery toys, and needlework. Many of the items for sale were made by local craftsmen and artists.

There is also a constantly changing collection of primitive and country antiques ranging from pie safes and victrolas to old hats and kitchen ware. Don't fail to go upstairs and catch a view of the harbor from the second-story windows of the Gathering Place - the dock has been redone there so there are often nice sailboats secured in front of the store.

O'NEAL'S DOCKSIDE

Ocracoke   928-3361
Map, pg. 373

O'Neal's is the place to go when you need boat and fishing supplies. Located directly across from the Community Store, it supplies a full line of fishing gear and bait, nautical gear, as well as ice and gas. This is also where you can charter boats for offshore fishing adventures. The Sand Dollar, Rascal, and Southwind are three of the boats. Call for details and reservations.

PONY ISLAND RESTAURANT

- **Nightly Specials**
- **"Bring Your Own" Fish Dinners**
- **Famous Homemade Desserts**
- **Steamed Shrimp Specialty**
- **Children's Plate**
- **Beer and Wine**
- **Breakfast and Dinner Served Daily**

Located next to Pony Island Motel.
Breakfast served from 6:30 a.m.-11 a.m.
Dinner served from 5 p.m.-9 p.m.
Call 928-5701.

THE MERCHANT MARINER

Next to the post office   928-6141
Map, pg. 373

You can't miss this interesting shop if you're wandering down the "main street" in the village; it practically sits right on the road. Gifts are the name of the game here, and you'll find plenty of them. There's nautical glassware, antique and new decoys, seafood kitchen gadgets, puzzles, gift wrap and stationary, games, sea shells, taffy, books, pirate flags, nautical napkins, note cards, baskets, etc., etc., etc. They even offer children's t-shirts that they design.

The shop is breezy and cheerful and the owners, Guy and Sally Newell, are usually around to welcome you. Open 9 a.m. till 9 p.m. in season, with shortened off season hours.

THE OLD POST OFFICE SHOP AND B.W.'S SURF SHOP

Behind the Merchant Mariner   928-6141
Map, pg. 373

Used to be that this was just a little, one room shop offering a nice but limited supply of clothing and accessories, cards, and sun supplies. Now, after some extensive additions in the winter of 1985, the shop has metamorphasized into a full-line surf shop and clothing store. Ladies' casual wear, lingerie, and swim wear are sold alongside sandals, perfumes, soaps, sun supplies, and jewelry. It's a nice selection of wearables!

In the surf shop side, wet suits, Morey Boogie Boards, beach umbrellas, chairs and towels, clam rakes, skim boards, all weather gear, "Surfer Magazine," and a complete line of surf boards and Hobies are sold. Name brands on boards are Alpha and Hotline. You can also rent boards and boogies. Lessons are also offered, ask for Eric.

With its perfect location right on the shore of Silver Lake, the owners - Guy and Sally (they're busy folks) - decided a waterfront "fun spot" would be a good idea. So, right out the back door, you can enjoy tetherball, picnicing, windsurfing or sailing. They say it's an excellent location for beginners to learn since it's protected and shallow with a good bottom.

With all the activity from the shops and the waterfront, this will probably become a popular place to just hang out and have some fun. Hours in season are from 9 am.m till 9 p.m.

HARBORSIDE GIFTS

Ocracoke Village 928-3111
Map, pg. 373

Lots of folks who have been to Ocracoke before and know some of the shopkeepers make it a point to go by Harborside just to visit with the owners, Sue and Corky Pentz. Their packed-full gift shop, across from their hotel of the same name, is one of the friendliest places in the village, and the selection of gifts isn't bad either.

Jewelry, clothing, cards, books, shells, carvings, brass, and Ocracoke memorabilia are just some of the items you'll find at Harborside. It will take some time to see everything they offer! Summer hours run from 9 a.m. until 9 p.m., seven days a week. Winter hours are from 9 a.m. till 7 p.m. They generally close around mid November and open back up in early spring.

RIDE THE WIND

Behind the Ocracoke school 928-7451
Map, pg. 373

Three friends who were all in to water sports, especially windsurfing, decided that a shop was needed on the island that supplied the gear and clothing they needed to enjoy their sports. So, by golly, they opened one. Ride the Wind, opened in May of 1986, carries island-like clothing, swimwear, jewelry, sunglasses, in both men's and women's wear. Then there's sailboards and skateboards with all the necessary accessories.

The three partners all teach lessons in sailboarding and they encourage an easy, confident attitude about the sport. "Anyone can learn to sailboard," says Daphne Bennink, one of the owners. "You don't have to be a super athlete to enjoy the sport. We work with anyone and everyone." They must mean what they say because they even offer rigs for children.

If you already know how to surf, rentals are offered from the shop. All the equipment is new and well maintained.

Ride the Wind is open from 11 a.m. till 10 p.m. during the summer and from 11 a.m. till 7 p.m. during the off season...but, it's always good to call, especially if there's some great sailing weather!

RAGPICKER RUGS

Corner of N.C. Hwy. 12 & Silver Lake928-7571
Map, pg. 373

Mickey Baker and Carmie Prete opened shop in this spot to sell, among other things, their beautiful, handmade rugs. Created in any color you could ever think of wanting, the rugs seem more like woven art than something you'd put on the floor and walk on. Nonetheless, you probably won't be able to resist at least one of them, if, that is, you can decide which one you want. Along with the rugs, good quality gifts are offered. Suntiles, carved birds, wooden boxes, pottery, tapestry bags, post cards and blank cards, prints, books, and intriguing iron puzzles (we worked on one for a long time and still couldn't figure it out!) are to be found.

Ragpicker is open year round. Summer hours are from 10 a.m. to 8 p.m. Monday - Saturday and 10 a.m. to 5 p.m. on Sunday. The winter hours vary but are always posted, so take a stroll by to find out what they are. You'll find the friendliness of the island certainly rules here.

VILLAGE CRAFTSMEN

Howard Street928-5541
Map, pg. 373

A hundred yards down Howard Street (see "Ocracoke Village"), Philip and Julia Howard run one of the best local craft shops. Yes, they're the Howards the street is named after; eight generations ago, William Howard owned all the island, and Philip suspects he is the same man who was listed as Blackbeard's quartermaster. The Howards stock handmade items like ring boxes, potteries, hand-dipped candles, and country toys. All made in the U.S.; nothing foreign. We especially liked the hand-carved railroad whistles; blow hard and they sound just like a steam locomotive! Open from mid-March through December, 10 a.m. till...? Closed Sundays.

CCRACOKE VARIETY SHOP

Highway 12928-4911
Map, pg. 373

The Ocracoke Variety Shop, which stays open year round, contains one of the largest stock of groceries and the other things travelers need on the island. Owners Cecil and Julia Hutcherson carry magazines, beachware, camping necessities, wine and beer. Winter hours: 8 a.m. to 6 p.m. Summer: 8 a.m. to 10 p.m.

OCRACOKE ART CO-OP

Next to the Variety Store   928-1451
Map, pg. 373

One of the things that is nicest about Ocracoke and the folks who choose to live here year round is the quality of life that is protected. This is evident in their operation of this art co-op that provides studio and show space for many of the island's resident artists. We're not talking cutsey, amateurish stuff here. What you'll find is art and crafts done by artisans dedicated to their work, and justifiably proud of it.

Prints, photography, oil and water color paintings, and weavings are just some of the items displayed for your enjoyment. The Co-op is open April through November from 10 a.m. till around 9 p.m. Swing by. You'll be glad you did.

TRADEWINDS TACKLE SHOP

Ocracoke   928-5491
Map, pg. 373

Tradewinds, on the main road just before it reaches Ocracoke Village proper, is the place to stop for fishing supplies as well as basic grocery and camping needs. The general-store array of merchandise also includes food, snacks, wine and beer, hardware and electrical repair parts, boating supplies, and a good selection of line. Open 7 a.m. to 9 p.m. daily.

SCUBA DIVING ON THE OUTER BANKS

"Most divers who arrive on the Banks as tourists don't realize what we have down here," says Art LePage, dean of the Banks' sport and commercial divers. "What we have is nothing less than the finest wreck diving on the Atlantic Coast."

Amen. The more than 600 wrecks that have made Hatteras and the Banks area dreaded by mariners for centuries have also made the area a paradise for the hard-case wreck diver. Hard-case, because the waters offshore are often cold and have variable visibility and strong currents, as well as a sizeable shark population. The changeable weather of Hatteras itself is another hazzard. The shifting sands cover and uncover new wrecks almost every year, and the divers of the area are busy discovering them, so any list of good spots can be only partial; check at local shops for the up-to-the-minute information that will assure you a safe and enjoyable dive. With that in mind, here is a partial list of Banks diving opportunities, to whet your appetite for salt water:

LST 471—sunk in 1949. About ¼ mile north of the Rodanthe Fishing pier, 100 yds. offshore in 15 feet of water. Partially visible from the beach at low tide.

Oriental (Boiler Wreck)—thought to be a Federal transport that sank in 1862. About four miles south of Oregon Inlet; the boiler of the ship is visible in the surf.

Triangle Wrecks—Josephine (lost 1915), **Kyzickes** (1927), **Carl Gerhard** (1929). Off 7-mile post at Kill Devil Hills, about 100 yds. out and 200 yds. south of the Sea Ranch. Depth about 20 feet.

USS **Huron**—Federal screw steamer lost off Nags Head in 1877. Now in 26 feet of water. Many artifacts.

Liberty Ship (Zane Grey)—About one mile south of Oregon Inlet at eighty feet.

U-85—German sub sunk in 1942. Northeast of Oregon Inlet in 100 feet of water. Boat needed (see Bodie Island section).

York, Benson, Buarque—Freighters and tankers sunk by U-boats during Operation Paukenschlag in 1942. They lie offshore, but within dive boat range, in from 100-120 feet. Good challenging dives.

Beach Diving—There are over 12 wrecks in shallow water between Duck and Hatteras. Great for free diving (without scuba gear) and spear fishing. Ask local divers for locations.

Sound diving—if you don't mind shallow, murky water, you may enjoy groping around north and west of Roanoke Island, where old Civil War forts lie submerged. Local divers have found cannonballs, bottles, relics, etc. with metal detectors.

Numbers to keep handy:
  Oregon Inlet USCG station—987-2311
  Ocean Rescue Squad (helicopter available)—911

Decomp Chamber U.S. Amphibious Base, Norfolk — (804) 464-7404 or 680-7404

Shops and Facilities: Three full-service dive shops serve the Banks, Outer Banks Dive Shop, Atlantic Divers, and Nags Head Divers.

NAGS HEAD PRO DIVE CENTER

Rt. 158 Busines, MP 13½   441-7594
Kitty Hawk Connection shops

Map, pg. 70

This is the oldest dive facility on the Outer Banks offering a full line of services — equipment sales and rentals, airfills to 5,000 psi, service, and PADI and NAUI instruction. The Nags Head Divers also run their 50 dive boat, the Sea Fox, out of Pirate's Cove Yacht Basin to all the historic wrecks off the Outer Banks coast including the York, U-85, and U.S.S. Zane Grey and Dionysus. Open seven days a week, 9 a.m. to 9 p.m. from Memorial Day to Labor Day; open off-season on a regular schedule, hours were not set by this writing. Call for information.

ATLANTIC DIVERS

Bayside Water Sports, MP 16   441-1111

Map, pg. 80

The newest dive service on the Banks. Atlantic, located at Bayside Water Sports, offers equipment sales, rentals, tank charges, PADI instruction — full service. Its brand new charter boat is a thirty foot diesel, handling up to six divers at a time. Atlantic runs trips to the Liberty ships, the U-85, Benson, York, Ciltivaira, and other local wrecks. Call. Open seven days a week from March to October, weekends during the rest of the year. Call for information.

OUTER BANKS DIVE SHOP

Rt 345   473-5269

Map, pg. 289

Melody and Art LePage's Outer Banks Dive Shop, along with

the 35 Fathom Shop, is the center of SCUBA diving activity on the Banks (Art is also a skilled commercial diver). Their small but well-stocked shop half a mile south of the 345-64 intersection on Roanoke Island offers air, rental, repair and sales (U.S. Divers, Dacor, Sherwood, other major manufacturers). Art and Melody have a newly-overhauled thirty-foot inboard that will carry six divers at 25 knots to the best spots on the Banks: daily trips to the Liberty Ship, Boiler Wreck, Huron, Tug Boat, for $25 per diver: charter trips to U-85, York, Benson, City of Atlantis, and the Buarque for $40.00 per diver (minimum party of 6). Hours: from mid-November to May 1. 12 - 5 p.m. Tuesday through Sunday; Summer hours, 10 a.m. - 7 p.m. Closed Mondays.

THE OUTER BANKS
FISHING GUIDE

Fishing is, beyond any doubt, the number one participant and spectator sport of the Outer Banks. In its various forms — surf fishing, sound fishing, pier fishing, and full-scale Gulf Stream billfishing — it is available for most of the year, with temporary but fierce booms when the season arrives and the big ones begin to bite.

It's available right through the Banks, from Corolla down to Portsmouth, and on to Cape Lookout, but Hatteras Island is the true mecca of fishermen. Off Cape Point, beyond the lighthouse and Diamond Shoals, is the point where the warm blue waters of the Gulf Stream collide with the cooler, food-rich Virginia Coastal Drift. The combination provides a long fishing season and a variety of species matched by few if any other places in the world. Kitty Hawk and Nags Head have their piers and charter boats, but this special fishing guide will concentrate on Hatteras... because the fish seem to!

The island's heavy dependence on, and concentration on, sport fishing, along with its relative isolation, have made it the testing ground for many of the rigs and ideas that are now common in salt water fishing. Probably 60 to 65% of the terminal gear used in North Carolina is made by various small subcontractors on the Outer Banks, who sit around in the off season and manufacture instead of fish. This has, in turn, led to the development of specialized rigs for the different types of fishing found on the Banks.

"We basically get two kinds of fishermen here on the Banks," says Ken Lauer. "The first are the tourists, who like to 'play' on a pier, or in the surf. They're happy with a six or twelve-inch fish. We see them between May and Labor Day. After that, the serious fishermen start to arrive."

Though the techniques overlap at places, there are basically three ways to fish on the Banks. These are from the surf (or a pier); from a boat, in the sounds; or from a larger boat, out in the Stream.

SURF AND PIER FISHING

Surf fishing is a sport and an art form all its own. It involves, much of the time, the use of four-wheel-drive vehicles and guides. Armed with specialized gear and up to seven rods apiece, the hard-core surf fisherman spends September and December roving the Hatteras beaches at low tide to read the configuration of the sand bars. Where is it shallow? he asks himself, his guide, and every other fisherman he meets. Where are the bars? Where are there offshore holes at high water, where the fish will lurk?

On the Banks, the surf fisherman will find distinct species of fish around at different times of the year. Surf fishing really begins in early to mid-March, for those migratory fish (such as croakers and trout) that 'hibernate' offshore in winter and then move inshore and head north in the spring.

The next class is perhaps the most sought after: the drum family, or channel bass, as the largest are called (to clarify: a *Sciaenops ocellata* weighing, say, one pound, is known on the Banks as a 'puppy drum'. A little older, a little bigger, and it becomes a 'yearling drum'. One from 35 to about 70 lbs. will be called a red drum, or sometimes an 'old drum'. The really big ones, and it takes from forty to sixty *years* out there for them to attain this seniority, are 'channel bass', for which the world's record is 90 pounds, caught off Rodanthe in 1973). The drum and channel bass have two seasons: mid-March to mid-May, as they move north, and then again mid-October to early December, as they move south again.

Another popular surf and pier fish is the blue, or bluefish, a vicious, toothy little fellow who's found at his best around here from mid-October to late November. There's a spring run for blues, too, but they tend to be emaciated. These, along with flounder, are the most popular fish available to the serious surf or pier fisherman. By the end of May surf fishing begins to taper off. In May to July about all the surf holds is one-pound blues, and Spanish mackerel in about the same size range. There are some summer fish, available mainly from the piers, and good for fun; spot, croaker, grey trout — nice pan fish, but nothing to write home about. And then there are the miscellanea: skate, blowfish, dogfish, rays, tarpon in late summer, and assorted sharks — none all that common, but don't be surprised if one shows up on your hook.

Most fishing from piers and in the surf is done with casting lures or rigs using a sinker that will anchor in the sand and one or two hooks arranged to keep the bait away from the bottom. Hooks are usually size 4 to 6 for the smaller species and 6/0 to 9/0 for the larger. Bait is generally cutbait, sea mullet heads, shrimp, minnows, bloodworms, squid, or flounder and shark belly. Trout are commonly caught on a medium to large plastic lure; mackerel and large bluefish on metal casting lures; channel bass on mullet heads or whole spot or whiting. As far as tide and time, low and incoming tides are often more productive than high water. Trout are best taken near dawn in clear water, while smaller drum are most likely found in the morning or evening in rough, murky water.

To try for the really big fish, you've got to haunt the ends of the piers, with a long rod (most often custom made), live-lining bluefish or spot with a heavy cork float and a four-foot wire leader.

Sounds too complex for you? The novice **can** catch fish on the Banks, if he uses his head. The tackle shops listed at the end of this section are stocked up not only with equipment but with information. All too often the visiting fisherman brings equipment that is too light and not suited to unique Banks conditions. It can make sense to leave your stuff at home and buy equipment here—it will certainly be better suited to conditions, and may (since it's made here) be cheaper as well. A second option is renting. Most Banks tackle shops and piers rent rod, reel, terminal gear, and sometimes even foul weather gear and waders.

HEAD BOATS

An excellent intermediate choice between pier fishing and chartering a big boat yourself is the head boat, so called because it takes all comers on a regular schedule and charges X dollars "a head" (usually from ten to fifteen dollars per person for a half-day, morning or afternoon). A lot of experienced fishermen enjoy head boating, but beginners especially love them. There's no pressure to bring home a big one, though certainly you can, and there's lots of fun and cameraderie for a small amount of cash.

Banks head boats generally cruise the sounds and inlets. In the spring and fall, however, they often head out to sea. Croaker, flounder, spot, and sea trout are the mainstays, depending of course on the season and your luck. Head boats generally provide fishing tackle, ice, bait, snack facilities, restrooms, and soft drinks, and the crew will help you bait your hook and deal with the fish once it's aboard, if you really aren't sure how it's done.

Oregon Inlet Marina, Oden's Dock, Pirate's Cove, and several other locations on the Banks run head boats, especially during the season. See entries on individual marinas for more information on times, prices, and itineraries.

FRESH WATER FISHING

The fresh water fishing on the Outer Banks isn't nearly as well known as the salt water fishing, but it's there, as Dick Baker told us, and it's good. Kitty Hawk Bay and Currituck Sound offer "super bass fishing," and there are white and yellow perch and some nice catfish in the brackish sounds too. Numerous bass clubs fish this area, and the Master's Bass Classic has been held at Kitty Hawk. In early spring, Baker recommends crank and spinner baits, and worms in the summer, of course; go back to spinner and crank baits in the fall. For Kitty Hawk Bay, the public boat ramp west of the bypass opposite Avalon Pier offers the easiest access.

Don't say we didn't warn you, though, that fresh water licenses are required. North Carolina has carefully drawn lines between prominent points, and state fish and wildlife commission patrols will take *you* if you fish inside them or north of the Wright Memorial Bridge. Licenses are available at Tatum's, The Tackle Box, The Fishing Hook, Buck's Seafood, Virginia Dare Hardware (Kitty Hawk), and Colington Creek Marina, among other agents.

BOAT FISHING: THE SOUNDS

Pamlico, Albemarle, Roanoke Sounds — the small boater excels in these broad, shallow, brackish waters between the Banks and the mainland. The sounds in summer are crammed with fourteen-to-twenty-fourfooters after the hordes of gray trout, croakers, spot, flounder, tarpon, and at night even channel bass. Another popular fish in the sounds is cobia, which seems to hit its peak about the third week in May; this is a dramatic fish, a hard fighter, and good eating as well.

But in general, sound fishing is a more relaxed, family type of recreation than either surf or ocean fishing. You can hire a guide and a boat; or just set out on your own from a handy ramp in your own rig. A long, carefree day of summer fishing in the calm sound, maybe a case of beer... who needs to fight a marlin?

OCEAN FISHING

The ocean fisherman, that's who. He (and a lot of shes) revels in the Hemingwayesque challenge of a big, fighting billfish. And they're out there... **big** ones; in 1974 the IGFA all-tackle record blue marlin, 1,142 lbs., was taken off Oregon Inlet, and this was no fluke... hundreds are regularly taken off Hatteras during the summer months.

Most of the Gulf Stream charter boats operate out of Oregon and Hatteras Inlets, plus a couple from Ocracoke and Roanoke Island. The Stream lies about an hour out, some 25 to 40 miles offshore. Black and white marlin, dolphin, tuna, and wahoo are taken primarily by trolling. The blue marlin begin to show in mid-April, and peak in June; during July and August they taper off, but they're still there. By then the white marlin is getting plentiful, with a normal catch being one per boat per day. August is a good month for sailfish. Just beginning to catch on is the technique of long-lining for swordfish at night. There is a little wreck fishing off the Banks coast, but not as much as elsewhere along the Atlantic coast; skippers seem to prefer trolling to wreck-fishing. Certainly there are enough wrecks.

AUTUMN AND WINTER FISHING

Most Banks fishermen look forward to autumn. As the water cools in September, the larger fish begin to come inshore once again. The bluefish reappear, in larger sizes; Spanish mackerel show from four up to possibly nine pounds; puppy drum arrive n the surf. In October begins the return of the bluefish, now fat at ten and fifteen pounds. There is generally a terrific run of spot in September and October, averaging around a pound apiece, but copious, easy to catch, and tasty. As autumn goes on, the 'pier jockeys' begin to pull in channel bass again, especially from the two piers on the east face of the island (Hatteras Island and Avon).

November is the most looked-for month in terms of both quality and quantity of fishing, with Thanksgiving traditionally the peak (channel bass, bluefish, loads of two to five-pound flounder, and gray trout). This may continue on into December if the weather is warm.

The winter is a lull, it's very cold, there is little fishing from mid-December to mid-March. But the fish are there; big trout and croakers, bluefish and striped bass. As it gets colder they move offshore, to 80-100 feet of water. The commercial fishermen take them there, and many of the charter captains of Hatteras are commercial fishermen in the winter. Few sport fishermen can muster much enthusiasm for the Hatteras winter weather.

All in all, the Banks, especially Hatteras, offer the best year-round salt-water fishing to be found for a long way up or down the Atlantic coast.

OFF-ROAD VEHICLES—
THE CONTROVERSY

The use of Off-Road Vehicles (ORVs) on the beaches of Hatteras, Ocracoke, and Bodie Island has been limited by the National Park Service, on the grounds that they cause damage to beach flora and fauna and accelerate beach erosion. Surf fishermen, who use the vehicles to transport themselves and their gear from place to place along the beach, have protested the plan, contending that charges of erosion have not yet been proven and that simple staking-off of ecologically sensitive areas would be sufficient. Both sides have valid points. A 'zone' concept governs beach driving now, with these zones being opened or closed by Park Service officials depending on erosion, hatching season, etc.

Though no permit is required to drive on the beach in the Park area, it is smartest to check with a ranger before you venture out to make sure you understand their guidelines and assure you are not entering a closed zone. Not knowing is no excuse, especially if you've wound up in some ecologically sensitive area.

Once you're safely and legally on the beach, having reached it only by using one of the clearly marked and numbered ramps, you should remain on the portion of the beach between the water and the foot of the dunes, in other words, DO NOT drive on the dunes. The same goes for soundside driving: you should stay on the marked routes only. Your speed should be resonable and prudent.

For current information on open zones and guidelines, you may contact the Headquarters, Pea Island National Wildlife Refuge, any National Park Service visitor contact facility, or you may write to: Cape Hatteras National Seashore, Route 1, Box 675, Manteo, N.C. 27954.

Each township on the Banks have their own requirements for permits to allow beach driving during certain times of the year. To get information or permits, contact the town administrative offices individually.

CITATIONS AND TOURNAMENTS

The Official North Carolina Saltwater Fishing Tournament is held annually to recognize outstanding angling achievement. The Department of Commerce, Travel and Tourism Division, awards citations for eligible species caught at or over certain minimum weights. Regulations on eligibility and boundaries may be obtained at these locations, which are also weighing stations for fish presented for citation:

>The Fishin' Hole, Salvo
>Hatteras Fishing Center
>Hatteras Harbor Marina, Hatteras
>Hatteras Island Fishing Pier, Rodanthe
>Hatteras Marlin Club, Hatteras
>Hatteras Tackle Shop, Hatteras
>Island Marina, Manteo
>Jennette's Pier, Nags Head
>Nags Head Fishing Pier, Nags Head
>Nags Head Ice & Cold Storage, Nags Head
>Oregon Inlet Fishing Center, Manteo
>Outer Banks Pier and Fishing Center, Nags Head
>Outer Banks Fishing Unlimited, Buxton
>Pelican's Roost, Hatteras
>Cape Point Tackle, Buxton
>The Red Drum Tackle Shop, Buxton
>Salty Dawg Marina, Manteo
>Sportsman's Center, Buxton
>Tatem's Tackle Box, Nags Head
>Village Marina, Hatteras
>Whalebone Tackle, Nags Head
>Willis Boat Landing, Hatteras

ELIGIBLE SPECIES AND MINIMUM WEIGHTS FOR CITATIONS, 1985:

Amberjack	50 lbs.
Barracuda	20 lbs.
Bass, Black Sea	3 lbs.
Bass, Channel	40 lbs.
Bass, Striped	18 lbs.
Bluefish	16 lbs.
Cobia	40 lbs.
Croaker	3 lbs.
Dolphin	30 lbs.
Flounder	6 lbs.
Grouper (any)	20 lbs.
Mackerel, King	30 lbs.
Mackerel, Spanish	4 lbs.
Marlin, Blue	300 lbs.

Marlin, White .... 50 lbs.
Sailfish .... 30 lbs.
Shark (any) .... 100 lbs.
Snapper, Red .... 10 lbs.
Snapper, Silver (porgy) .... 4 lbs.
Spot .... 1 lbs.
Tarpon .... 30 lbs.
Trout, Gray .... 6 lbs.
Trout, Speckled .... 4 lbs.
Tuna (any) .... 60 lbs.
Wahoo .... 35 lbs.

*Citation for release regardless of size
**Citation for fish 46" in length.

CURRENT ALL-TACKLE N.C. SALTWATER GAME FISH RECORDS

Fish	Weight	Location	Date
Amberjack	125	Off Cape Lookout	1973
Barracuda	57½	Off Hatteras	1982
Bass, Black Sea	8¾	Off Oregon Inlet	1979
Bass, Channel	90*	Hatteras Island	1973
Bass, Striped	60	Hatteras Island	1972
Bluefish	31-12*	Off Hatteras Island	1972
Cobia	97	Off Oregon Inlet	1952
Croaker	5	Oregon Inlet	1981
Dolphin	77	Off Hatteras Island	1973
Flounder	20½	Carolina Beach	1980
Grouper, Warsaw	245	Off Wrightsville Beach	1967
Mackerel, King	69	Cape Lookout	1978
Mackerel, Spanish	12¾	Off Hatteras Island	1980
Marlin, Blue	1142	Off Oregon Inlet	1974
Marlin, White	118½	Off Oregon Inlet	1976
Sailfish	80	Off Oregon Inlet	1974
Shark, Tiger	1150	Yaupon Beach	1966
Snapper, Red	40	Off Cape Lookout	1970
Snapper, Silver	11½	Off Hatteras Inlet	1978
Spot	1-11	Oregon Inlet	1978
Tarpon	164	Indian Beach	1978
Trout, Gray	14-14	Nags Head	1980
Trout, Speckled	12-4	Wrightsville Beach	1961
Tuna, Bluefin	732½	Off Cape Hatteras	1979
Tuna, Yellowfin	237	Off Cape Lookout	1979
Wahoo	127	Off Oregon Inlet	1973

*World All-tackle record

To make application for all-tackle record recognition, write Outdoor Editor, N.C. Travel and Tourism Division, 430 N. Salisbury St., Raleigh, N.C. 27611.

Information current as of date of publication. Check at a tackle shop for latest update.

FISH MARKETS

If your day on the water hasn't been productive the Outer Banks houses a number of seafood markets that can provide you with fresh fish. Most seafood markets will store your catch for a reasonable period of time for a small fee, and clean and filet your fish, too.

Carawan and Son, Kitty Hawk	261-2827
Colington Seafood, Colington	441-6155
Crab Slough Seafood, Wanchese	473-2804
Nunemakers Fish Co., Nags Head	441-1670
Nunemakers Fish Co., Colington	441-7344
Wanchese Seafood Shanty	441-7818
South Point Seafood, Ocracoke	928-5601
Austin Seafood, Nags Head	441-7412
Carolina Seafood, Kill Devil Hills	441-6700
Mid-Atlantic Smokehouse and Seafood, Kitty Hawk	261-4221
Village Seafood, Duck	261-8344

TATEM'S TACKLE BOX, INC.

Between Beach Road & Bypass at Jockey's Ridge   441-7346
Map, pg. 70

Tatem's is one of the oldest tackle shops in the area. You'll find just about everything you need here to catch that big one: custom rods, all types of bait, hunting, fishing and commercial licenses. They also repair rods and reels and are an official weighing station. Open year round.

TW'S BAIT AND TACKLE

Seagate North Shopping Center   441-7140
Kill Devil Hills, NC
        Map, pg. 57

Terry Stewart runs this shop offering a complete supply of fresh and salt water fishing gear. He also carries live bait. Rod and reel rentals are available here too.

TACKLE EXPRESS

Rt. 158 Bypass, MP 9½   441-4807
Avon, NC   995-5829
        Map, pg. 344

The two Tackle Express locations offer a complete selection of salt and fresh water fishing supplies. You'll also find beach supplies, grocery items, t-shirts, health and beauty aids, cold drinks and beer.

WHALEBONE TACKLE SHOP

Nags Head-Manteo Causeway   441-7413
        Map, pg. 289

Bill McCaskill's Whalebone is a small building on the south side of the causeway and in his own way, Bill is an artist too; see his painstaking mountings of waterfowl (not for sale, he says). He stocks custom rods for surf fishing, bait, tackle, ice, beer, and soft drinks. He's the person to see to contact Outer Banks Fishfinders Guide Service. Fishfinders provides four-wheel-drive vehicles, tackle and guides for full-day and half-day surf fishing adventures.

FISHING UNLIMITED DISCOUNT TACKLE

Causeway 441-5028

Map, pg. 80

The Nags Head location of the Banks-wide Outer Banks Fishing Unlimited organization is on the south side of the Nags Head-Manteo causeway, just before the Washington Baum Bridge. Like the Hatteras shop, it has a large selection of specialized fishing tackle, for sale or rent; camping equipment, bait, beer, and ice. Surf and Sound fishing guides are available here as well (for more details on fishing, see Hatteras Island section). And out back is a 300-foot lighted pier on the sound. There's fourteen feet of water at the end, and excellent crabbing. Open 5 a.m. to 9 p.m. the summer season; hours vary the rest of the year.

RED DRUM TACKLE SHOP

Buxton 995-5414

Map, pg. 344

Just to the left as you enter Buxton is the Red Drum complex, consisting in full of an Exxon station, a food market, and the Red Drum Tackle Shop, well known among those who fish Hatteras. There's a nice big beer cooler, housewares, wine, and cold drinks, along with gas and groceries; but the spotlight has to stay on the tackle shop, which carries a vast collection of surf fishing equipment, custom rods, bait, ice, and tackle. See Bob Eakes for special advice on how and where to surf fish in Hatteras. The Red Drum also offers fish mount service, guiding services, booking for the 35' charter boat *Bullfrog* (about $240 for a day offshore, everything included), and free and up-to-the-minute advice on offshore, inshore, and shark fishing. Hours: 6 a.m. to 9 p.m. Sunday through Thursday, and Friday and Saturday till 10 p.m. Closed in January and February.

PORTSMOUTH ISLAND — 395

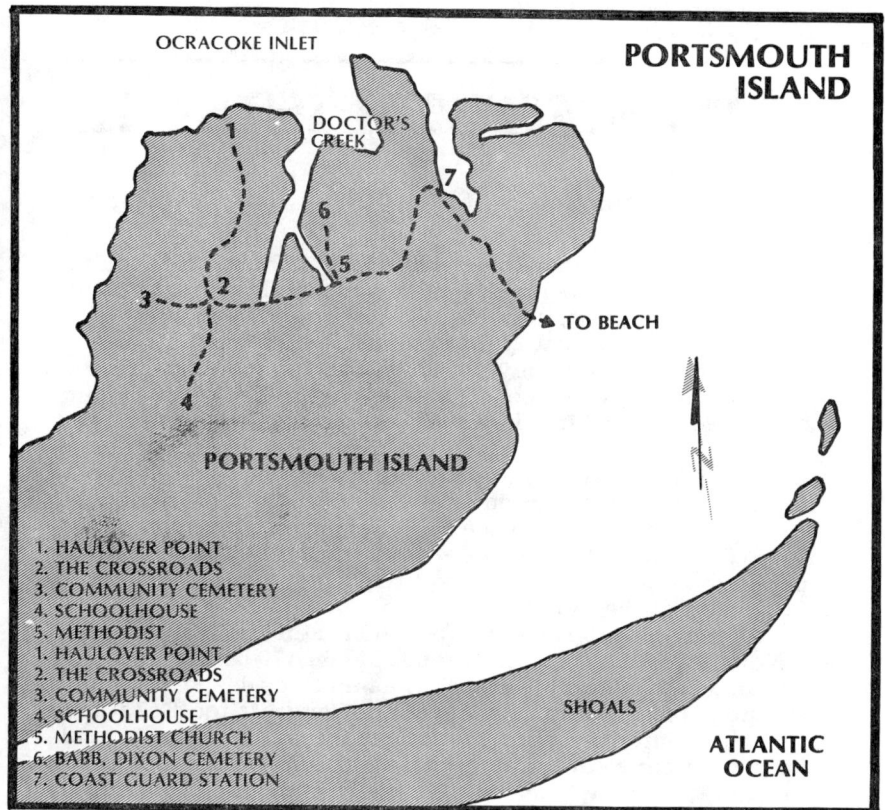

INSIDE

PORTSMOUTH ISLAND

Southwest of Ocracoke   Map, pg. 395

It's deserted now, abandoned, empty. A ghost town. If you've never had that eerie feeling...then maybe you'll want to take the trip to quiet, roadless, unpopulated Portsmouth Island.

It wasn't always that way. Portsmouth, which was authorized by the Colonial Assembly in 1753, was for many years the largest town on the Banks. The slow changes of geology and trade have left it behind, however, and now it is deserted.

There is no bridge to Portsmouth from Ocracoke; there isn't even a ferry. The only way to get there, unless you brought a boat with you is to make arrangements with one of the local residents to take you over. Check at the Park Service Visitor Center for advice. Charge will be negotiable, around $20-$30 per party, depending on size and duration of trip.

As you cross the inlet (if you decide to go), reflect on the fact that this was once the channel for much of the trade of Virginia and North Carolina. You see, throughout the 1700's, and up to the mid-nineteenth century, Ocracoke channel was deeper than it is now, and of course ships were of shallower draft, too. Seagoing ships could enter the inlet, moor near the southwest side, and offload their cargo into smaller coasters, which then took it up the sound to such early ports as New Bern and Bath. Portsmouth Village was established to facilitate this trade by providing piers, warehouses, and other port facilities.

The newly-established town grew rapidly. The British raided the town during the Revolutionary War; a steady flow of supplies moved through it to General Washington's embattled armies. At its peak, just before the Civil War (War between the States) began, it had a total population of almost 600—no Boston or New York, but definitely the largest town on the islands.

Two things doomed Portsmouth: war and weather. In September of 1846, a terrific storm had opened two new inlets (named Hatteras and Oregon), and these gradually deepened as Ocracoke Inlet began to shoal. War merely hastened Portsmouth's end. Seagoing traffic, such as was left to the Banks, shifted to Hatteras Inlet. After that it was a question of time. Few villagers returned after the War, and the population steadily declined. Its last male resident, Henry Piggot, died in 1971.

Now only the mosquitoes inhabit it. Portsmouth Island now

belongs to the Cape Lookout National Seashore, and plans are underway to preserve parts of the town; but so far, it's a lonely and deserted place.

As you debark, at Haulover Point (1), (see map) you will be standing where wharves, warehouses, and small craft once serviced the larger ships lying in the Inlet. For a short tour, proceed up the road. The first two houses you come to on the right are more recent buildings and are now sometimes leased. Down the main road, you will see a fence on the right and then a collapsed house. This house, perhaps the oldest structure on the island belonged to a Henry Babb.

The small white building at the crossroads (2) is the former U.S. Post Office. This was more or less the center of the village in its day. About forty yards west of the Post Office is the community cemetery (3), the largest in the village with about 40 graves.

From the crossroads, follow the footpath south across the marsh to the former schoolhouse (4). Classes were taught in this one-room building until 1947.

Proceed down the main road to the east. If you stop on the first bridge and look to the north you will see a pink cottage formerly owned by the last resident of the town, Henry Piggott. Continue across the second bridge. To your left you will see the Methodist Church (5). This church is kept in repair by local residents from Ocracoke. Inside, the bell still operates. Please don't play the organ. Behind the church is the Babb, Dixon plot (6). Piggott is buried here.

Going east from the church, beyond the last houses you will enter a long stretch of open road. Beyond this lies the landing strip, the old Coast Guard station, watch tower, and outbuildings (7). Surf rescue boats were kept in the large building, as at Chicamacomico. The station was closed in 1947.

About a hundred yards south of the station, now covered by overgrowth, is the cistern of the old marine hospital that served quarantined seamen. It burned down in 1894 and was not replaced.

To reach the beach, walk on past the station; it's about another mile.

A few notes of caution: prepare for mosquitoes and sun exposure if visiting in the summer. There's no mosquito control any more on Portsmouth Island and they get fierce. Don't try to enter any of the buildings, other than the church; they all belong to the Park Service and they are off-limits.

A note to fishermen: Portsmouth Island offers good fishing, and you don't have to share it with a million other people. Don Morris, in Atlantic, N.C., has a car ferry that can take a limited number of four wheel drive vehicles over. Park Service permits are required for vehicles, but Morris can sell them to you. He's at (919) 225-4261.

FERRY CONNECTIONS FROM OCRACOKE: SWAN QUARTER AND CEDAR ISLAND

RESERVATIONS

To avoid possible delay in boarding the Cedar Island-Ocracoke Ferry and the Swan Quarter-Ocracoke Ferry, reservations are recommended. These may be made in person at the departure terminal or by telephone. For departures from Ocracoke, call (919) 928-3841; for departures from Cedar Island, call (919) 225-3551; and for reservations for departures from Swan Quarter, call (919) 926-1111. (Office hours 6 a.m.- 6 p.m.) Reservations may be made up to 30 days in advance of departure date and are not transferable. These reservations must be claimed at least 30 minutes prior to departure time. The name of the driver and the vehicle license number are required when making reservations.

GROSS LOAD LIMITS

Currituck Sound
- Any axle — 13,000 lbs.
- Two or more axles — 24,000 lbs.

All Other Crossings:
- Any axle — 13,000 lbs.
- Two axles (single vehicle) — 24,000 lbs.
- Three or more axles — 36,000 lbs.
- (single or combination vehicle)

More information may be obtained from Director, Ferry Division, Morehead City, NC 28557, or by calling (919) 726-6446 or 726-6413.

OCRACOKE-SWAN QUARTER TOLL FERRY

Crossing Time Approx. 2½ hrs.
Capacity Approx. 35 Cars
YEAR-ROUND

Leave Ocracoke	Leave Swan Quarter
6:30 AM	9:30 AM
12:30 PM	4:00 PM

FARES AND RATES APPLICABLE (ONE WAY) Same as Cedar Island - Ocracoke Ferry Rates.

CEDAR ISLAND—OCRACOKE TOLL FERRY
Crossing Time Approx. 2¼ hrs.
SUMMER SCHEDULE

Leave Cedar Island		Leave Ocracoke
	April 15 thru Sept.15	
7:00 AM		7:00 AM
9:30 AM		9:30 AM
12:00 Noon		12:00 Noon PM
3:00 PM		3:00 PM
6:00 PM		6:00 PM
8:30 PM		8:30 PM
	Sept. 16 thru Oct. 31	
7:00 AM		7:00 AM
10:00 AM		10:00 AM
1:00 PM		1:00 PM
4:00 PM		4:00 PM

WINTER SCHEDULE
Nov. 1 thru April 14

7:00 AM	10:00 AM
1:00 PM	4:00 PM

FARES AND RATES APPLICABLE (ONE WAY)

A. Pedestrian   1.00
B. Bicycle and Rider   2.00
C. Single Vehicle or Combination 20' or less in length and motorcycles (minimum fare for licensed vehicle   10.00)
D. Vehicles or Combinations from 20' up to 40' in length   20.00
E. All Vehicles or Combinations 40-55 feet in length having maximum width of 8 feet and height of 13'6"   30.00
*(Vehicles in excess of 50' (55' maximum) M/V Sea Level Only).

SERVICE & INFORMATION
DIRECTORY

MEDICAL CARE

Basic and emergency medical care is available on the Outer Banks although there are no hospitals or secondary care facilities. The nearest general hospital is Albemarle Hospital in Elizabeth City. Air evacuation is available to the Eastern Virginia Medical Center in Norfolk.

To call for an Ambulance:
North of Oregon Inlet 911
(Sanderling, Duck, Southern Shores, Kitty Hawk, Kill Devil Hills, Nags Head, Roanoke Island)

South of Oregon Inlet 986-2144
(Rodanthe, Salvo, Avon, Buxton, Frisco, Hatteras)

Ocracoke 928-4831
For less serious emergencies, and routine care, the following clinics may be consulted.

Outer Banks Medical Center 441-7111
Nags Head, MP 11-12 Bypass
Clinic Hours: 8 a.m. to 8 p.m.
Open 24 hrs. on emergency basis.

Beach Medical Care 441-2174
Kill Devil Hills, MP 10½ Bypass-next to Beach Pharmacy
In Buxton, next to Beach Pharmacy 995-4455
Minor emergencies and routine health care.

Dare Medical Associates 473-3478
Manteo, North Main Highway
Mon. - Fri. 8:00 a.m. to 5 p.m.

A member of the cast of the Lost Colony outdoor drama.

Virginia Dare Women's Center 441-2144
Nags Head, Bypass, MP 11, next to Beach Pharmacy
Routine women's health care, OB/GYN
Open year round 9:00 am to 5:00 pm Mon.-Fri.

Kitty Hawk Medical Center 261-3848
Kitty Hawk, MP 2¾, Bypass
Hours: In Season: 8:00 - 5:00, Weds. 8:00 to 9:00, Sats. 8:00-5:00; Off Season: 8:30-5:00, Weds. 8:30-8:00, Sats. 9:00-1:00
Full service and emergencies.

Medical Associates of Hatteras 986-2388
Community Center, Hatteras Village
Daily 9 a.m. to 4 p.m. except Sunday.

Ocracoke Health Center 928-1511
Minor emergencies and health care.

EMERGENCY NUMBERS

For all police, fire, and beach emergencies north of Oregon Inlet including Roanoke Island 911

OCRACOKE DIRECTORY

EMERGENCY NUMBERS

Fire and Rescue	928-4831
Park Ranger (day)	928-5111
Park Ranger (night)	928-5431

HANDY NUMBERS TO HAVE

Coast Guard	928-3711
Ferry Information	928-5311
National Park Visitors Center	928-4531
Ocracoke Trolley Information	928-4041
Western Union Telegraph	1-800-257-2241

CHURCHES

Assembly of God Parsonage   928-4091
    Services: Sunday: 11 a.m., 7:30 p.m.

Ocracoke Methodist Parsonage   928-4211
    Services: Sunday: 6:15 a.m., 11 a.m., 7 p.m.

COAST GUARD

Buxton Village	995-5881
Hatteras Village	986-2175
Hatteras Island	987-2311
Nags Head, Kill Devil Hills, Kitty Hawk	Dial 911

FIRE DEPARTMENT

Avon Village	995-5021
Buxton Village	986-2500
Hatteras Village	986-2500
Kill Devil Hills	911
Kitty Hawk	911
Manteo	911
Nags Head	911
Salvo Village	987-2411
Ocracoke	928-4831

POLICE DEPARTMENTS

Hatteras Village	986-2144
Kill Devil Hills	911
Manteo	911
Nags Head	911
Ocracoke	928-7301

PHARMACIES

Jacock's, Kitty Hawk	261-3333
Miller's, Nags Head	441-7228
Beach Pharmacy, Nags Head	441-4430
In Buxton	995-4450
Revco, Manteo	473-5056
Peoples Drug, Outer Banks Mall	441-3434
Bear Drugs, Kitty Hawk	261-7999

CHIROPRACTIC SERVICES

Outer Banks Chiropractic Clinic 441-1585
Nags Head Professional Building
Mon. Wed. Fri 9 to 6, Thurs Sat. 9 to 1.
Available for 24 hr. emergency.

ANIMAL SERVICES

Outer Banks Animal Hospital 441-2776
Outer Banks Mall annex
(Night time emergency) 473-3991
Mon. - Fri. 8:30 to 6:30 p.m., 9 a.m. to 4 p.m. Sat, 12:30 to 2:00 p.m. Sun

Coastal Animal Hospital, Kitty Hawk 261-3960
Mon.-Fri. 9 a.m.-12, 3 p.m.-6 p.m.; Sat. 9 a.m.-12 noon

Airdrie Animal Clinic, Manteo 473-3117

KENNELS

Water Oak Kennel, Buxton Village 995-5663
Salty Dog Grooming and Boarding, Colington 441-6501

Lost & Found Animals (9 to 5) 473-2143

EMOTIONAL CRISIS

Outer Banks Hotline (Confidential counseling and
information for any problem, and shelter for battered women.)
North of Oregon Inlet 473-3366
South of Oregon Inlet 995-5104
All calls are free.

EYE CARE

Dare Vision Center Manteo 473-2155
Kill Devil Hills 441-4872
William J. Adams, OD
Rt. 158 Bypass, MP 9. Hours: 9:30-12:00, 1:30-5:00 year round.

Professional Opticians 441-6353
J.H. Goldschmidt, MD and William Blakemore, MD 441-5911
Nags Head, Outer Banks Mall, MP 14. Hours: convenient hours, open Saturdays.

Albemarle Opticians 441-3373
Wed.-Fri. Ophthalmologist available: Marshall S. Redding, MD and Robin F. Beran, MD.
Mon.-Wed.-Fri. Optician available: Ted Pepper
Kill Devil Hills, Rt. 158 Bypass, MP 8½. Hours: 9-5 five days a week. Half-day on Saturdays.

THE MEDIA

Newspapers:

The Banks' two local papers are *The Coastland Times*, a semiweekly tabloid format published in Manteo, carrying mostly local news; and the *Outer Banks Current*, which made its appearance in mid-1980. Published in Kill Devil Hills and owned by Atlantic Publications, it is a weekly full size format that focuses on Dare County news. Also published by Atlantic Publications: The Beachcomber, Surf Side Magazine, and Sea Shelters.

The Coastland Times - 473-2105
The Outer Banks Current - 441-3411

Newspapers from nearby cities and major metropolitan papers are carried in a variety of locations throughout the Outer Banks.

Television:

Outer Banks Cablevision, in Kill Devil Hills, supplies cable television service to sections of Sanderling-to-Hatteras area, plus Roanoke Island. Most motels and hotels are subscribers. Stations received are:

Channel	Call	Network
2	WUND	PBS
3	WTKR	CBS
4	CBN	CBN
7	WITN	NBC
8	WYAH	Independent
9	WNCT	CBS
10	WAVY	NBC
13	WVEC	ABC
12	FM music, weather, time	

Television reception on Ocracoke is facilitated by a satellite dish, so it's usually good, with many channels received.

OUTER BANKS PANORAMA

Presented on Channel 12 (the cable station) many times per day, these informative, entertaining programs give Outer Banks visitors an overview of the many things to see and do around the area.

Radio:

The Banks' first native radio station is WOBR, Wanchese, AM 1530, FM 95 stereo. It plays basic top-40 music on its FM station and country music on the AM frequency.

WWOK began broadcasting in 1983 at FM 105.7. The format here is also top-40.

WVOD, Manteo, 99.3 began broadcasting in the spring of 1986. The station offers an interesting mix of classical, jazz, big band, "golden oldies," and popular.

Reception is also good for a wide choice of stations in southeastern Virginia and eastern North Carolina.

CATERING

If you are at a cottage or planning a small party in your room, chances are you will want something nice to snack on. Here are a few recommendations for places that can turn out party platters that are ideal for most any occasion.

Cafe Rene	473-1155
Station Six	261-7337

FLORISTS

Vista Florist & Garden Center, So. Main Highway, Manteo	473-3491
Nags Head Florist, Rt. 158 Bypass, Nags Head	441-4861
Moonshine Florist, Buxton	995-5536
Island Florist, Wanchese	473-2165
Flower Barn, Wanchese	473-5283
Petal Pushers, Kill Devil Hills	441-4593

AUTOMOTIVE SERVICES

The Banks have adequate service and parts outlets to keep standard American makes going and most imports. But, if you break down in a vintage 1952 MGTD, you might have a bit of a wait till parts arrive.

There are three full-service dealerships on the Banks:

R.D. Sawyer Ford, Manteo	473-2141
McLeod Chevrolet - Buick, Manteo	473-2125
Outer Banks Chrysler, Plymouth, Dodge, Kill Devil Hills	441-1146

Other recommended auto services and towing:

Kitty Hawk Exxon, Kitty Hawk	261-2720
Murray Auto Supply	
Manteo	473-3466
Kill Devil Hills	441-7163
Kitty Hawk	261-7855
Hatteras	986-2115
Jackson Auto, Manteo	473-5990
Car Care Center, Colington	441-6517
Farrow Brothers Automotive, Avon	995-5944
Frisco Auto Repair, Frisco	995-5660
Autotech, Nags Head	441-5293

TAXI SERVICE

There are now 4 taxi/limousine services on the Banks.

Roy's Taxi, which uses the slogan, "Call Roy, He's Your Boy," gives you three ways to contact them: Daytime, call 473-2716; Night time, call 473-3208; and, to reach the pager, call 473-7087.

Dare Cab Company can be reached during the day at 473-5562; night and weekends at 473-3865.

Outer Banks Transit will pick you up or take you to the Norfolk International Airport, or anywhere else in the Norfolk area. Call 441-7090.

Outer Banks Limousine Service offers 24-hour taxi and limo service and also will pick up or deliver to the Norfolk International Airport. Call 261-3133.

WESTERN UNION

Outer Banks Transit supplies the Outer Banks area with Western Union services, sending or receiving. Money orders, telegrams, and telex service available. They can also handle your UPS or next day air service. Call 441-7090 or go by their office on Rt. 158 Bypass, MP 9.

CATCH THE EXCITEMENT OF THE OUTER BANKS.

Catch "Outer Banks Panorama," a lively television show that presents a TV tour of all the best there is to do on your vacation. "Outer Banks Panorama" features informative profiles of area attractions, events, shops, restaurants and much more.

WATCH TV CHANNEL 12.

Catch a wave, catch a breeze, or catch the sights. Everything you'll want to see and do while on the Outer Banks is previewed on a television program that is presented throughout each day — watch it at your convenience.

Catch the excitement ... watch "Outer Banks Panorama" on TV Channel 12. Tune in and turn on to the Banks.

A Production of Metro Communications, Inc.,
Kill Devil Hills, NC 27948

NATIONAL CAR RENTAL

Rt. 158 Bypass, MP 5   (919) 441-5488

Car rental agencies are scarce on the Banks, but National has a small office just south of the Kitty Hawk - Kill Devil Hills line, on the sea side of Route 158 Bypass. Open 9:00 a.m. to 5:00 p.m., Closed Wednesdays. Toll free reservation number is (800) CAR-RENT. Handy to First Flight airstrip.

LIQUOR LAWS & ABC STORES

After a long dry spell, mixed drinks are now being served in most restaurants along the upper Outer Banks. Manteo, Wanchese, and the beaches south of Oregon inlet do not have liquor by the drink, only beer and wine. Beer and wine are available in most convenience stores and supermarkets, but bottle liquor is available only in package stores market ABC for the Alcohol Beverage Control Board of North Carolina.

There are three ABC package stores on the resort strip, and one on Ocracoke Island.

Kitty Hawk ABC Store
Located near MP 1 on RT. 158 in the Three Winks Shoppes between the Wright Memorial Bridge and the Visitors Center.

Nags Head ABC Store
Located near MP 10 on the Bypass, north of the Galleon.

Manteo ABC Store
Located on RT. 64 and 264 across the Washington Baum Bridge (causeway) on the road to Manteo.

Ocracoke ABC Store
Located on the road to the Ferry Slip in Ocracoke Village near the Variety Store.

ABC stores are generally open 10 a.m. to 9 p.m., Mon. - Sat. No personal checks, or credit cards accepted. You must be 21 years old to enter the store. The legal purchase is one gallon.

In Manteo and Wanchese and on Hatteras Island the "brown bag" law is still in effect. Restaurants with a brown bag license will allow you to bring your own bottle into the establishment where you surrender it at the table and have the house mix the drinks. You will be charged for mixes and setups.

DIRECTORY — 411

Canoes and Cordgrass - Beached on the edge of a whispering prairie of marsh grass at the edge of Roanoke Sound, a fleet of aluminum canoes gleam in the morning sun. A party of vacationers exploring the terrain on the reverse side of the sandy beaches on North Carolina's Outer Banks find these canoes an ideal way to explore the many winding creeks and observe the abundant wildlife found along the shallow sound front shore.

STORM AND HURRICANE PROCEDURES

June through November is hurricane season on the Outer Banks. All of the southeastern U.S. is prone to hurricanes — but the Banks, due to their low elevation, frontage on the ocean, and lack of shelter, are particularly vulnerable. A hurricane strikes the Banks about every nine years; a major one every 42 years; a tropical cyclone about every five years. The Dare County Civil Preparedness Agency promulgates the following Hurricane Safety Rules:

1. Enter each hurricane season prepared. Every June through November, recheck your supply of boards, tools, batteries, nonperishable foods, and the other equipment you will need when a hurricane strikes your area.

2. When you hear the first tropical cyclone advisory, listen for future messages; this will prepare you for a hurricane emergency well in advance of the issuance of watches and warnings.

3. When your area is covered by a hurricane watch, continue normal activities, but stay tuned to WOBR radio (1530 AM; 95.3 FM), WWOK radio (105.7), WVOD (99.3), or the National Weather Service Station at Buxton for advisories. Remember, a hurricane watch means possible danger within 24 hours; if the danger materializes a hurricane warning will be issued. Meanwhile, keep alert. Ignore rumors.

4. When your area receives a hurricane warning:

    Plan your time before the storm arrives and avoid the last-minute hurry which might leave you marooned, or unprepared.

    Keep calm until the emergency has ended.

    Leave low lying areas that may be swept by high tides or storm waves.

    Leave mobile homes for more substantial shelter. They are particularly vulnerable to overturning during strong winds. Damage can be minimized by securing mobile homes with heavy cables anchored in concrete footing.

Moor your boat securely before the storm arrives, or evacuate it to a designated safe area. When your boat is moored, leave it, and don't return once the wind and waves are up.

Board up windows or protect them with storm shutters or tape. Danger to small windows is mainly from wind-driven debris. Larger windows may be broken by wind pressure.

Secure outdoor objects that might be blown away or uprooted. Garbage cans, garden tools, toys, signs, porch furniture, and a number of other harmless items become missiles of destruction in hurricane winds. Anchor them or store them inside before the storm strikes.

Store drinking water in clean bathtubs, jugs, bottles, and cooking utensils; your water supply may be contaminated by flooding or damaged by hurricane floods.

Check your battery-powered equipment. Your radio may be your only link with the world outside the hurricane, and emergency cooking facilities, lights, and flashlights will be essential if utilities are interrupted.

Keep your car fueled. Service stations may be inoperable for several days after the storm strikes, due to flooding or interrupted electrical power.

Remain indoors during the hurricane. Travel is extremely dangerous when winds and tides are whipping through your area.

Monitor the storm's position through National Weather Service advisories.

5. When the hurricane has passed:

    Seek necessary medical care at the nearest Red Cross disaster station or health center.

    Stay out of disaster areas. Unless you are qualified to help, your presence might hamper first-aid and rescue work.

    Do not travel until advised by the proper authorities.

    If you must drive, do so carefully along debris-filled streets and highways. Roads may be undermined and may collapse under the weight of a car. Slides along cuts are also a hazard.

Avoid loose or dangling wires, and report them immediately to your power company or the nearest law enforcement officer.

Report broken sewer or water mains to the water department.

Prevent fires. Lowered water pressure may make firefighting difficult.

Check refrigerated food for spoilage if power has been off during the storm.

Remember that hurricanes moving inland can cause severe flooding. Stay away from river banks and streams.

Tornadoes spawned by hurricanes are among the storm's worst killers. When a hurricane approaches, listen for tornado watches and warnings. A tornado watch means tornadoes are expected to develop. A tornado warning means a tornado has actually been sighted. When your area receives a tornado warning, seek inside shelter immediately, preferably below ground level. If a tornado catches you outside, move away from its path at a right angle. If there is no time to escape, lie flat in the nearest depression, such as a ditch or ravine.

During the summer season visitors may be notified of hurricane watches or hurricane warnings. The hurricane watch means that a hurricane could threaten the area within 24 hours. Evacuation is not necessary at that point, but you should be alert and check on the storm's progress from time to time via radio. If a hurricane **warning** is promulgated, visitors should leave the Banks and head inland using Rt. 64/264 or U.S. 158, following instructions of local authorities.

OUTER BANKS
PLACES OF WORSHIP

DENOMINATION   **SUNDAY SERVICES**

ASSEMBLY OF GOD
Worship Center Ark, Nags Head MP 13   8:30 a.m., 11:00 a.m. 7:30 p.m.
Wanchese Assembly of God   11:00 a.m., 7:30 p.m.
Manteo Assembly of God 10:00 a.m., 7:00 p.m.

BAPTIST
First Baptist Church, Kitty Hawk   8:30 a.m., 11:00 a.m., 7:00 p.m.
Nags Head Baptist Church, MP 13½   10:00 a.m., 7:30 p.m.
Manteo Baptist Church   8:30 a.m., 11:00 a.m., 7:30 p.m.
Roanoke Island Baptist Church   11:00 a.m., 7:30 p.m.

CATHOLIC
Holy Redeemer, Kill Devil Hills, MP 7   8:00 a.m., 10:30 a.m., 12:30 p.m., and Sat. 5 p.m. and 7 p.m.
Our Lady by the Sea, Buxton   3:30 and 5:00 p.m.
Holy Trinity Mission, Whalebone Junction   9 and 11:00 a.m., and Sat., 4 and 6:00 p.m.
Ocracoke Catholic   Sun., 4 p.m.

CHURCH OF CHRIST
Roanoke Acres, 1 mile N. Rt. 64/264   11:00 a.m.

CHURCH OF GOD
Manns Harbor   11:00 a.m., 6:00 p.m.

EPISCOPAL
St. Andrews by the Sea, Nags Head, MP 13   8:00 and 11:00 a.m.

LIBERTY CHRISTIAN   10:30 a.m., 7:30 p.m.

LUTHERAN
Grace by the Sea (Meets in St. Andrews)   9:15 a.m.

METHODIST
Duck United Methodist   10:00 a.m.
Colington Island   8:30 a.m.
Kitty Hawk United   8:30 a.m., 11:00 a.m.
Bethany, Wanchese   11:00 a.m., 8:00 p.m.
Mt. Olivet United   10:55 a.m., 7:30 p.m.
Buxton United   9:30 a.m.

PRESBYTERIAN
Outer Banks Chapel,
Kill Devil Hills, MP 8   8:30 a.m., 11:00 a.m.

INDEPENDENT
Rock Church of the Outer Banks   11:00 a.m., 7:30 p.m.

UNITARIAN
Universalist Fellowship, first and third Sun.,   10:00 a.m.
Nags Head Woods Visitors Center
Circus Tent Ministries,   July and Aug. activities.
Kill Devil Hills, MP 9

OUTER BANKS
ANNUAL EVENTS

Jan.	Old Christmas celebration at Rodanthe. Dancing, oyster roast, appearance of "Old Buck," the Christmas bull. Sponsored by local residents.
February	Frank Stick Invitational Art Show
Mid-April	Wilbur Wright Fly-In, First Flight Airstrip, Kill Devil Hills, 441-6094.
Late April	Annual Cape Hatteras Lighthouse 10K Run and Fun Run
Early May	Ocracoke Crab Festival, 928-6141.
Early May	Hatteras Island Spring Festival, Hatteras Island.
Mid-May	Hang Gliding Spectacular at Jockey's Ridge. Sponsored by Dare County Jaycees and Kitty Hawk Kites, 441-7575.
1st Sat. in June	Dare Days Celebration, Manteo. Crafts, street dances, entertainment, parade. Sponsored by Dare County Bicentennial Commission.
Early June	Annual Rogallo Kite Festival, Nags Head, 441-4124.
Mid-June	Annual Blue Marlin Tournament, Hatteras. Sponsored by Hatteras Marlin Club. Call Gae Zindel, 995-3401.
Mid-June	*The Lost Colony* season opens, running through Aug. 25. Sponsored by Roanoke Island Historical Association, 473-2127.
Mid-late June	Annual Seafood Festival, Wanchese, 261-3801.
Late June	Annual Blue Water Open Billfish Tournament, Hatteras, 986-2166

418 — ANNUAL EVENTS

July 4	Fourth of July celebration at Cape Hatteras Lighthouse. Sponsored by local civic organizations.
Mid-July	Youth Fishing Tournament, Nags Head. Sponsored by N.C. Beach Buggy Association, Call Jim Lee, 441-6528.
Late July	Annual Wright Kite Festival, Kill Devil Hills, 441-6235.
August 18	Virginia Dare Day. Celebration of first English child born in America at Fort Raleigh National Historic Site, 473-5772.
Mid-Aug.	New World Festival of the Arts in downtown Manteo, 261-3165.
Late-Aug.	Marine Arts, Photography, and Crafts Contest, Manteo, 473-3493.
Early-Sept.	East Coast Surfing Association Championship, Buxton, 995-5785.
Mid-Sept.	Outer Banks Sailing Regatta. Sponsored by Outer Banks Sailing Association.
Mid-Sept.	Oregon Inlet Billfish Release Tournament, Oregon Inlet, 441-6301
End of Sept.	Annual NC Waterfowl Weekend, Kitty Hawk, 261-3801
Early Oct.	Annual Nags Head Surf Fishing Tournament. Sponsored by Nags Head Surf Fishing Club. Jim Lee, 441-6528.
Mid-Oct.	Marlin Club Invitational Tournament, Hatteras.
Early Nov.	Annual Cape Hatteras Surf Fishing Tournament, sponsored by Cape Hatteras Anglers Club, Buxton, 995-4253.
Dec. 17	Anniversary of First Flight. At Wright Brothers National Memorial, sponsored by The First Flight Society, 441-7430.

PERFORMING ARTS

The Banks have no resident opera, ballet, or professional theatre, of course. But the performing arts are slowly evolving, especially in Manteo, the county seat of Dare County.

THE LOST COLONY

Manteo 473-3414

A continuing outdoor historical drama, written by Paul Green and performed during the summer season at the Waterside Theatre, near Fort Raleigh. Season from mid-June to late August. For more details see entry in Roanoke Island section.

SEA AND SOUND ARTS COUNCIL

Manteo 473-2138

The Dare County cultural organization, the Council fosters development of visual and performing arts within the Banks. Symphonies, concerts, showing of artists' works, musicals, and dramatic works are presented at varying times throughout the year. Season tickets available. Call for schedules and information.

Several Outer Banks marinas feature a fleet of charter boats standing ready to take parties offshore for a day of sports fishing.

 NEARBY ATTRACTIONS

THE DISMAL SWAMP

The Great Dismal is one of the least known wonders of northeastern North Carolina and southeastern Virginia. Over two hundred thousand acres of it sprawl midway between the two states. This vast landscape of peat beds, vine and briar thickets, pines and hardwoods, cedar and cypress, canebrakes and canals hides in its heart a mysterious, deserted amber jewel of a lake. And it all lies only an hour's drive from Kitty Hawk.

The Indians knew and thinly inhabited what is now the Dismal long before the coming of the white and black men. The English, who were quick to snap up all the available real estate in the area, avoided the Dismal, and Lake Drummond itself remained undiscovered until 1650, when it was found by a hunter who had lost his way. Little more was known about it until 1763, when one George Washington decided to survey the area.

And herein is the strangest tale of all. He discovered that the storied Dismal Swamp was not a swamp at all.

A 'swamp' is a low-lying area where surface water collects and cannot escape. The water stagnates and becomes polluted and noisome. Life teems, but it is a parasitic, unhealthy life feeding on decay.

At first glance, the Dismal seems to be a swamp, simply because the ground is wet and there is lots of vegetation. But it is not a low-lying area. In fact, it is some twenty feet above sea level at the center of the lake. Washington said, "The Dismal Swamp is neither a plain nor a hollow, but a hillside with its lake at the top of the slope." The water in the Dismal is not salt, like a marsh, but fresh; not stagnant, but drinkable. What the Swamp is, in fact, is the only live peat bog in North America.

Now a few words about peat.

Peat is dead, preserved vegetable matter. You may know it as 'peat moss,' one of the best garden fertilizers around. Well, give peat a few million years and it is apt to turn up as coal. Peat itself burns well, as the Irish have known for quite a while. And the Swamp produces peat. How? The lush plant life, as it dies, falls into the dark water. The tannic acid in the water (from the cypress roots) preserves this matter; it cannot rot, and peat is gradually formed.

Water is thus essential to peat formation. And unless the water table remains high, the peat will dry out and may catch fire. Where, then, does the water come from? Not from the sea, not from runoff (water doesn't go uphill). Instead, deep springs feed Lake Drummond from underneath. Five rivers flow out of this 'swamp;' none flow in. All the water is fresh, and the tannic acid, though it gives the water a dark color and flavor, keeps it clinically sterile and quite drinkable (much like tea, which is also rich in tannic acid). In sailing ship days, in fact, this water was highly prized, as it stayed 'sweet' in wooden casks for months longer than rain water.

All of this, plus a variety of wildlife (even black bears), makes the Swamp and its lake a different proposition than Okefenokee or the Everglades. It is one of the undiscovered fun spots, and is sure to see much greater promotion in the future. But you can see it before it's spoiled! The Dismal Swamp Canal is administered by the U.S. Army Corps of Engineers, and the Wildlife Refuge by the Department of the Interior, so it's not a National Park or anything like one. In fact, it's still pretty wooly, and not at all for the camp-in-homelike-comfort set, although these latter will enjoy a boat tour before camping elsewhere.

The best route to take to reach the Swamp from Kitty Hawk is to cross the Wright Memorial Bridge and stay on Rt. 158 past Belcross. Turn right on Rt. 343 through South Mills and on to Rt. 17, which parallels the dismal Swamp Canal, a little-used but still officially open side route of the Intracoastal Waterway.

Lake Drummond lies exactly in the center of the Dismal and is accessible only through a 3½-mile-long feeder ditch (the ditch, incidentally, supplies the water for the Dismal Swamp Canal portion of the Intracoastal). You have to go in by boat; building any sort of road on a peat bog is hopeless. If you have your own boat, there's a ramp into the Canal half a mile north of where the feeder ditch joins it. If not, you can rent a canoe or take a boat tour from Alvah Duke.

Alvah Duke is a story in himself. If you take the tour you'll meet him. He's 'Mr. Dismal;' his books, talks, and appearances before Congress have almost single-handedly saved the Dismal from drainage, destruction, and development at the hands of rapacious real estate sharpers. Listen to every word he says. He is a prophet.

Duke's tour boat is the best way to see the swamp for the first time. Stop at the Dismal Swamp Boat Tours, Information Center, and Restaurant at 4107 George Washington Highway

(Route 17), just at the Feeder Ditch intersection with the Canal. The tours last for 2½ hours and leave at 10:00 a.m., 12:30 p.m., and 3 p.m. May through August. Rates: adults $5, children under 12, $3, call for group, student, and senior citizen rates. Tours run pretty much regardless of weather (but not in thunderstorms), and the boat is covered. Call 421-3991 for more information.

The trip is great. *Emma K II* is a 30-passenger diesel-driven boat that just about fills the feeder ditch. "The African Queen" springs to mind as she rumbles through walls of jungle over water dark as chocolate syrup. Water moccasins, heads craned above the water, cross the blunt bow.

Grapevines and overhanging trees brush the boat as Duke tells hair-raising snake stories. Half a mile from the lake is a Corps of Engineers dam where you must change boats. (If you have your own, there's a railway, but it is limited to 1000 pounds weight and is not equipped for B-bottoms).

Drummond is a wide, shallow lake of amber water, dotted with ancient twisted cypresses. The dark water is a perfect mirror. It's potable, but only six feet deep even in the center, and full of underwater stumps and logs. Canoes can explore the edges and probe up the drainage ditches, but we advise poor boaters to (a) stay away from the edges of the lake, and (b) bring a spare prop just in case.

Drummond is open from sunrise to sunset for boating and fishing. It is very seldom visited, and is entirely unpopulated. For that reason alone, if not for its lonely beauty, it is a treat.

CAMPING: About 10 primitive camping spots are available on a first-come basis at the Corps dam. There are toilet facilities, picnic tables and grills. The water, from wells, is safe to drink but tastes awful — better bring something in bottles. Call 421-7401 to see if it's full before you plan on staying there.

MUSEUM OF THE ALBEMARLE

Elizabeth City   335-1453

This small regional museum is devoted to the history of northeastern North Carolina. Area geography, Indian history, lumbering, farming, hunting, lifesaving, nautical history, wildfowl hunting — this one-story brick building is crammed. Hours: 10 a.m. to 5 p.m. Tuesday through Saturday, 2 to 5 p.m. Sunday. Closed Monday. Small charge; special rates available for groups. To reach it, drive north from Kitty Hawk on Rt. 158, through Camden, across the Pasquotank River, and through Elizabeth City; it's on the right side of the road, a few miles west of the city. Total distance from Kitty Hawk about 47 miles.

SOMERSET PLACE

If you like mansions and plantations, you'll like Somerset Place. The mansion itself, a 2½-story white frame building with 14 rooms, was built in 1830, in Greek Revival style. It has been fully restored, with period furnishings. The plantation was once enormous, one of the four biggest in North Carolina, with over 300 slaves growing corn and rice. Of the twenty original outbuildings, six are being restored, and four others have been reconstructed. The lawns and gardens alongside nearby Phelps Lake are especially beautiful in summer. Open 9 a.m. to 5 p.m. Monday through Saturday, 1-5 p.m. Sunday, year round. No admission charge. To reach it take Rt. 64/264 west across the Croatan Sound from Manteo and follow it west for about 40 miles. Turn left at the little town of Creswell and another five miles will bring you to Pettigrew State Park and Somerset.

HISTORIC EDENTON

Edenton, N.C. was settled about 1660, and was a center of colonial-era commerce and government. Joseph Hewes, a signer of the Declaration of Independence, lived here, as did Dr. Hugh Williamson, who signed the Constitution. Edenton had its own Tea Party in 1774, with the exception that the protesters were women—one of the first female political actions on the continent. Later, Edenton became a backwater, like Williamsburg was for many years. And, like Williamsburg, this preserved it, and the old houses and buildings were still standing years later when historians 'rediscovered' the town. Today you can see such showpieces of colonial architecture as the Barker House, the Cupola House, the Chowan County Courthouse, the James Iredell House, and St. Paul's Episcopal Church. Guided tours around the town begin at the Barker House on South Broad Street, at the edge of Albemarle Sound, Open 10 a.m. to 4:30 p.m. Tuesday through Saturday, 2-5 p.m. Sunday; closed Monday. Open year round. Edenton is most easily reached by crossing the Croatan Sound from Manteo on Rt. 64/264 and continuing forty miles west until turning right on Rt. 32 to cross the Albemarle; turn left after you cross the bridge and drive about another five miles toward Edenton; Historic Edenton will be on your left.

We made a tasty find in Edenton that you should discover, too. Right off Broad Street, in Gaslight Square (you should look for the baker man pointing the way to the Square) is a place called the Edenton Bake Shop. You could easily follow your nose to find it because out of this shop comes some really incredible food. Elizabeth and Bo Cleveland, the owners, open up at 6 a.m. to begin selling their just-made breads, pastries, doughnuts, rolls, and most any other type of tempting treat, to hungry locals and visitors. They also serve traditional breakfast food to those who might resist the bakery items... but we sure didn't, and we wouldn't advise you to either! Then, as the lunch hour nears, lucky diners get to experience "the owners' creative outbursts," as Elizabeth describes them, which translates into lunch specials ranging from lasagne to Chinese food in the wok to spinach salad with fried tofu and herb dressing. Lunch winds down around 3 p.m. and, if the specials every day are anything like ours were. we bet they never have any leftovers.

The shop is open Monday through Saturday. One note of interest: if you have a large group and would like to get lunches to go, you can call them at (919)482-2711 in advance and they'll get them made and have them waiting for you. It's a great bake shop, and you'll be sorry if you miss it.

CAPE LOOKOUT NATIONAL SEASHORE

Low, unpopulated, almost forgotten even by North Carolinians, more barrier islands stretch southwestward for 58 miles from Ocracoke Inlet. Portsmouth Island, Core Banks, Cape Lookout, and Shackleford Banks were incorporated in the Cape Lookout National Seashore in 1966.

These low, sandy barrier islands have been untouched by either development or by stabilization. Neither public nor private facilities are available for the visitor; no motels, no restaurants, no roads, no campgrounds. But if you don't mind really roughing it, they're a great place for camping, fishing, boating, and birdwatching. Always stay alert for storms, for there is little shelter on most of the islands, and a good storm will actually change their conformations.

At Cape Lookout itself are located the lighthouse, erected in 1859, and a small Coast Guard Station.

Access: if you have your own boat, you will find launching ramps at marinas throughout Carteret County, though the easiest access to Cape Point is from Shell Point on Harkers Island. Concessionaire ferry services, available from Harkers Island to the Cape Lookout Light are, from Davis to Shingle Point, and from Atlantic to an area north of Drum Inlet. Private charter services are also available. For more information write or call the National Park Service, Cape Lookout National Seashore, P.O. Box 690, Beaufort, N.C. 28516. Telephone for Park Headquarters: (919) 728-2121.

426 — NEARBY ATTRACTIONS

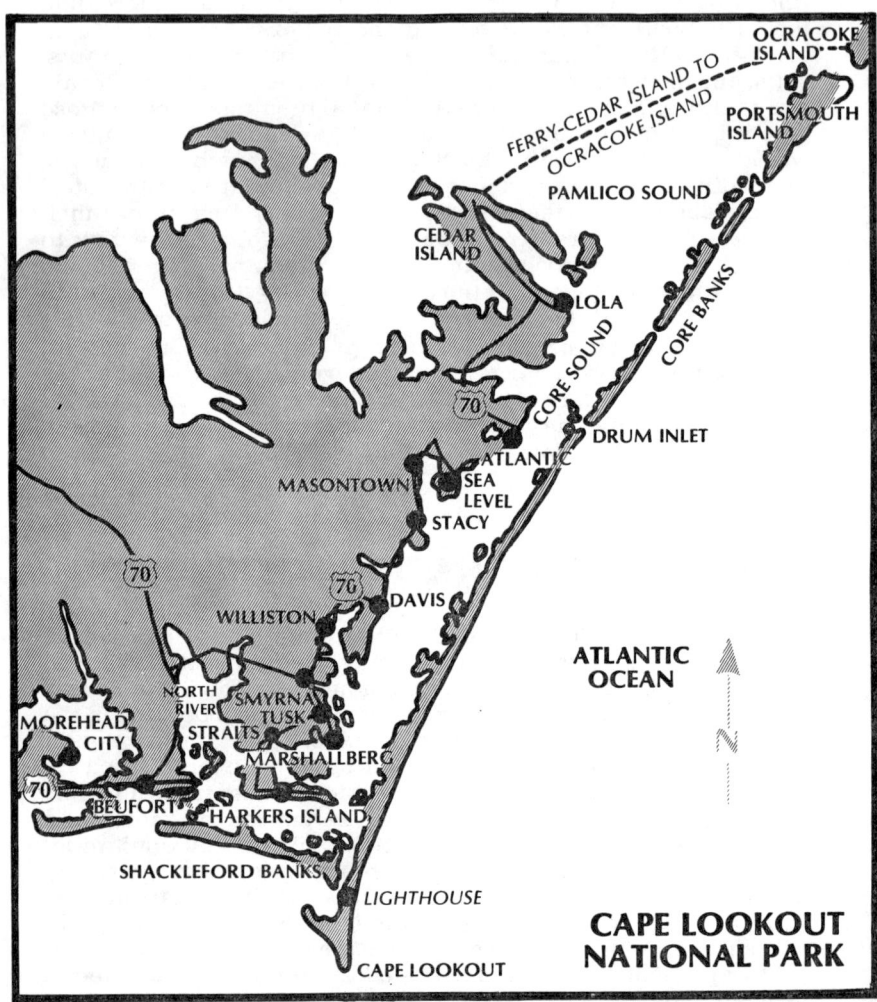

ALSO FROM STORIE/McOWEN PUBLISHERS, INC.

THE GUIDE TO DINING ON THE OUTER BANKS:
With almost a hundred restaurants and eateries on the Outer Banks, finding the right place to dine can be confusing. This helpful volume includes menus, location maps and other information for over 35 of the finest Outer Banks eating establishments. There's even a selection of local recipes and a page of valuable coupons. *The Guide to Dining* is a must for any Outer Banks vacationer. $2.95

THE INSIDERS' GUIDE TO WILLIAMSBURG
Written by Susan Bruno and Donna Quaresima
Another great Insiders' book that helps visitors to this colonial capital city get the most out of their stay. Written by two insiders, it gives information on accommodations, restaurants, attractions, campgrounds, shopping and more on Williamsburg, Jamestown, and Yorktown. $4.95

AMERICA'S 400TH ANNIVERSARY HANDBOOK
Written by Doug Barger, Nick Hodsdon, Phil Evans
Edited by H.B. Rogers
Anyone who visits the Outer Banks during America's 400th Anniversary Celebration (1984-1987) will want the Handbook. It's the Official Guide and Souvenir Program for the festivities, and includes maps, schedule of events, messages from the Governor and the Secretary of the Department of Cultural Resources and information about Celebration guest, Princess Anne from Britain's Royal Family. The Handbook also provides an informative, easy to read and enjoyable history of the colonization of the New World by the English settlers, written to appeal to young people and adults alike. Well-designed, and full of colorful photos and illustrations, America's 400th Anniversary Handbook will be a keepsake of the Celebration for years to come. $4.95

THE INSIDERS' GUIDE TO THE TRIANGLE
The quickly growing central area of North Carolina — Raleigh, Cary, Durham, Chapel Hill, and surrounding towns — is the subject of this highly informative book. Included is information on relocating to the area, with realtors, relocation companies, builders, designers, landscapers and other "home helpers" highlighted, as well as complete information on restaurants, accommodations, parks, sports, hospitals, services,

schools, neighborhoods, attractions, maps, and much more. It's the only total guide to the Triangle. New in September 1986. Approximately 600 pages. $7.95

To order, send check or money order for cost of book plus $1.00 for postage to: SMP, Box 308, Manteo, NC 27954. (NC residents add 4½% sales tax.)

BOOKS BY DAVE POYER
THE RETURN OF PHILO T. McGIFFIN
A Novel of Annapolis

If you enjoyed *The Insiders' Guide to the Outer Banks,* be warned: Dave Poyer, who wrote the historical and recreation section, is hitting the streets with his fourth novel, a comedy about the Naval Academy. Roger Staubach (Class of '65) says: "*The Return of Philo T. McGiffin* is a book worth reading. Funny, touching, completely true to life, this tale will have every reader rooting for its memorable hero." Published by St. Martin's Press in May 1983; $13.95 in hardcover at fine bookstores everywhere.

BOOKS BY MONTY JOYNES
THE INSIDERS' GUIDE TO NEW ORLEANS

By St. leger "Monty" Joynes and Jack Duarte

Praised by the *Times Picayune, Bon Appetit Magazine* and many other critics, this is the one book to have about New Orleans if you could have only one. It covers the top restaurants, hotels, historic attractions, legends, and the Mardi Gras city's food and beverage traditions in over 330 pages with 50 full-page maps and photographs. Paperback. $4.95

THE INSIDERS' GUIDE TO NEW ORLEANS RESTAURANTS & ACCOMMODATIONS

By St. Leger "Monty" Joynes and Jack Duarte

New for the 1984 New Orleans World's Fair summer, this book is the standard reference for the traveling public on the hotels and restaurants of the Crescent City. The four-star rating system critiques over 110 restaurants, and names 20 others as The Most Overrated. Over 85 accommodations are described in detail and categorized by price. Includes 35 nightspot recommendations, food traditions, and many photographs. Paperback. $4.95

Both New Orleans books can be ordered from Insiders' Publishing Group, 3711 Saratoga Drive, Metairie, LA 70002. Include cover price plus $1 for each book ordered.

BE AN INSIDER

You can become one of the Insiders by sharing your Outer Banks travel experience. What you tell the authors of this guidebook will be weighed seriously in the editing of a revised edition.

Tell us about the good and the bad as you follow our recommendations. If enough of you are disappointed in a restaurant or motel, and our investigation confirms your experiences, we promise to drop the offending place out of our book. Your opinion has power.

On the positive side, share the happy times with your fellow vacationers. What places provided exceptional service, or helped you in an unusual way? Let's use *The Insiders' Guide* to recognize and reward excellence on The Outer Banks.

What about the organization of the book, itself? If you discovered a defect, or have a suggestion to improve its usefulness, write us about it.

The authors of *The Insiders' Guide* intended that this book should save you time, money, and a lot of exasperation and frustration. We travel a great deal ourselves, and in making this book, we tried to put in it all the things that we would want to know if we came to your city or town. Now that you'e used our book, help us to refine it and make it serve you better on your return visit.

Share your experiences with us and become one of the Insiders. Write us collectively, or as individuals. We'll be grateful to hear from you. Send your letters to: Storie/McOwen Publishers, Inc., P.O. Box 308, Manteo, NC 27954.

Storie/McOwen Publishers, Inc.

ORDER FORM

Use this convenient form
to place your order for any of Storie/McOwen's
books — fast and simple!

STORIE/McOWEN PUBLISHERS

P.O. Box 308, Highway 64
Manteo, North Carolina • (919) 473-5881

Send to: _____
(please print) Name

Address (Box, Route, Street) _____

City _____ State _____ Zip _____

Quantity	Title	Unit Price	Post. & Hndlng.	Total
	Insiders' Guide to Williamsburg @ $4.95		$1.00	
	Guide to Dining @ $2.95		$1.00	
	America's 400th Anniversary Handbook @ $4.95		$1.00	
	Insiders' Guide to the Outer Banks @ $5.95		$1.00	
	Insiders' Guide to the Triangle @ $7.95		$1.00	
NC residents add 4½% sales tax.			Grand Total	

Check, cash, or money order accepted.

INDEX

A

Accommodations, See "Cottages"
Adventure, The, 361
Airplane Rides: See "Flying"
Airstrips, 59, 297, 330
Albemarle, Museum of, 420
Algonkian Indians, 15, 287
Alston, Theodosia Burr, 66
Altoona Wreck, 327
Amadas, Philip, 283
Amusement Park, 74
Annual Events, 414
Antiques, 270
Apartments, 163
Aquaria, 295
Armada, Spanish, 285
Arts, Performing, 416
Art, 272, 357, 379, 380
Auto Services, 404
Avon, 319

B

Back Bay Wildlife Refuge, 24
Barlowe, Arthur, 283
Barrier Islands, 13
Bars: See "Nightspots"
Beaches, Coquina, 86
   Guarded, 116
Bedfordshire, The, 367
Bicycling, 21
Birds, 195, 322
Black History, 285, 324
Blackbeard, 17, 360, 361
Bluefish, 197
Boats, Rental, 35, 77, 83, 346, 377, 378
Bodie Island, 86, 88
Bridges, Herbert Bonner, 14, 106
   Oregon Inlet, 14, 106, 318
British, 361, 367
Burr, Aaron, 66
Buxton, 320
Buxton Books, 355
Buxton Woods, 333
Buxton Woods Nature Trail, 333

C

Caffeys Inlet Station, 205
Campgrounds, Bill & Barb's, 183
   Cape Point, 184
   Cape Woods, 183
   Colington Park, 179
   Cozy Cove, 179
   Frisco, 185
   Frisco Woods, 184
   George's, 186
   Hatteras Sands, 185
   Kitty Hawk Camping Park, 178
   KOA Holiday, 182
   Cape Hatteras KOA, 182
   North Beach, 183
   Ocean Beach, 178
   Ocracoke, 186
   Oregon Inlet, 179
   Sandpiper's Trace, 180
   Surf and Sound, 185
   Teeter's, 186
Camping, on Hatteras Island, 181
Cape Hatteras National Seashore, 17, 86, 317
Cape Lookout, 422
Cape Point, 317, 328, 384
Car Rental, 405
Caribsea, The, 367
Catering, 403
Cavendish, Thomas, 305
Chamber of Commerce, 45
Chicamacomico, 319, 325
Children, First English in America, 284
   in Motels, 113
Chinese Restaurants: See "Restaurants"
Chowder, 199
Christian Fellowship Activities, 63
Churches, 412
Churchill, Winston, 367
Cinema: see "Movies"
Circus Tent, The, 63
Cittie of Ralegh, 286, 303
Civil War, 17, 67, 89, 285, 296, 329, 332, 362
Civilian Conservation Corps, 18, 322
Clams, 199
Clubs, Hunting, 23
Coast Guard, 89, 325, 327, 365
Cockle Creek, 362
Colington, 62
Colleton, Sir John, 62
Condominium Developments, 36, 163, 188
Condominium Rentals, 163
Condominiums, 163
Coquina Beach, 86
Coquinas, 88
Corolla Light, 37
Corolla, 27
   Academy, 24
   Lighthouse, 32
Corps of Engineers, USA, 28
Cottage, History, 19
Cottage Rental Booklets, 163
Cottages, Locations, 165

Pets in, 167
Rates for, 165
Rental Firms for, 169
Rental Periods for, 167
Rentals, 169
Reservations for, 166
Seasons, 164
Crabs, 198
Croatoan, 285
CSS Virginia, 329
Cuisine, 198
Currituck Sound, 27

D
Dare, Virginia 284
  Statue, 291
Dare County, 400th, 286
  History, 303
  Incorporation of, 285
  Information Center, 45
  Libraries, 300
Dare County Tourist Bureau, 45, 300
De Ayllon, Vasquez, 15
Diamond Shoals, 384
Diamond Shoals Light, 328
Dining on the Outer Banks, Book, 202
Dismal Swamp, 418
Doctors, 400
Doenitz, Karl, 90
Downtown Manteo, 303
Drummond, Edward: see "Pirates"
Duck, Village of, 28
Duck Road, 28
Ducks, Hunting of, 23
Dune Stabilization, 322
Dunes, walking, 71

E
Ecological Habitats, 14
Edenton, 421
Elizabeth, Queen, 283
Elizabeth II, 304
Elizabethan Gardens, 291
Elizabethan Heraldry, 287
Elizabethan Period, 286
Emergency Care, 400
Emergency Numbers, 400
English Colonization, 283
Ericsson, John, 329

F
Ferries, 21, 347, 358, 398
Fessenden, Reginald, 286, 297
Films: See "Movies"
Fire, 403
Fish Markets, 392
Fishing, 312, 320, 338, 339, 345, 384
  Commercial, 301, 320, 345
  Marlin, 100

Oregon Inlet, 100
Shark, 83
Fishing Piers,
  Avalon, 63
  Avon, 339
  Cape Hatteras Pier,
    (Frisco Pier), 345
  Hatteras Island, 338
  Jennette's, 83
  Kitty Hawk, 49
  Nags Head, 74
  Outer Banks, 82
Fishing Piers in General, 385
Fishing: Records/Citations, 390
Fishing: Weighing Stations, 390
Florists, 406
Flowers, Seasonal, 291
Flying, Tours, 60, 62
Food, Distinctive Banks Food, 198
Footsball, 74
Fort Hugar, 296
Fort Raleigh, 17, 284, 292
French, 283
Frisco, 320

G
Gardens, Elizabethan, 291
Geology, 13
Gilbert, Humphrey, 283
Go-Karts, 338
Gold and Silver Seasons, 195
Golf, 49, 50, 116
Golf (Miniature): See
  "Miniature Golf"
Grapes, Wild, 299
Graveyard of the Atlantic:
  See "Hatteras"
Green, Paul, 293
Grenville, Sir Richard, 283, 305
  359, 366
Gun Clubs, 23, 86

H
Habitats, Ecological, 14
Hang Gliding, 71, 77
Harniman, R.K., 303
Hatteras, and Development of
  Radio, 286
Hatteras Island, History, 317
Hatteras Lighthouse, 332
Hatteras Village, 320
Head Boats, General, 386
Head Boats: See "Fishing"
Herbert Bonner Bridge, 14, 100
Hitchhiking, 21
Hitler, Adolf, 18, 90
Hotels: See "Motels"
Hunting, 23
  Commercial, 44

Gun Clubs, 23, 86
Huron Disaster, 67
Hurricanes, 412
Hushpuppies, 200

I
Ice Age, 13
Ice Plant Island, 286
Indians, Algonkian, 15, 286
  Croatoan, 15
  Lumbee, 285
  Poteskeet, 15, 43
  Roanoak, 15, 284
  Woccons, 359
Information, Dare County, 45, 300,
  Dare County Chamber of Commerce, 45
  National Parks, 82
Inns: See "Motels"

J
Jamestown, 285
Jeeps, 389
Jockey's Ridge State Park, 71

K
Kill Devil Hills, History, 51, 58
Kitty Hawk, History, 43, 283

L
Laura A. Barnes, Wreck of, 88
Libraries, 300
Life Saving Service, 24, 29, 317, 325, 331
Lifeguards, 116, 403
Lighthouse, Bodie Island, 86, 88
  Cape Lookout, 425
  Corolla, 27
  Hatteras, 332
  Ocracoke, 367
Liquor Laws, 410
Lost Colony, 285, 293, 419
Lounges: See "Nightspots"
LST, 319, 326
Lumbee Indians, 285

M
Manteo, 284, 303
  History, 303
Marinas, 85, 312, 345, 365, 369, 375, 386
  Oregon Inlet, 100
Marine Resources Center, 295
Marlin, 100, 321
Maynard, Robert, 366
Media, 405
Medical Care, 400

Midgetts, and Lifesaving, 326
Mill Landing, 285, 301
Minature Golf, 73, 75, 78
Monitor, The, 328
Monkey Island, 23
Motels,
  Armada, 139
  Avon, 148
  Bel-Air, 120
  Berkley Center, 155
  Blacksbeard's Lodge, 162
  Bluff Shoal, 155
  Boyette House, 160
  Burrus, Motor Court, 154
  Cabana East, 132
  Cape Hatteras, 150
  Cape Sandbox, 150
  Carolinian, The, 131
  Cavalier, 125
  Chart House, 123
  Checkout Times, 113
  Children In, 113
  Colony IV, 126
  Dare Haven, 143
  Deposits for, 113
  Duke of Dare, 145
  Durant Station, 153
  Elizabethan, 142
  Extra Persons in, 113
  First Colony Inn, 133
  General Mitchell, 149
  Harborside, 160
  Hatteras Harbor, 153
  Hatteras Island, 146
  Hatteras Marlin, 154
  Holiday Inn, 127
  In Outer Banks, 108
  Island Inn, 157
  Islander, 137
  Koni Kai, 152
  John Yancey, 128
  Lighthouse View, 151
  Mariner, 122
  Minimum Stays, 114
  Nags Head Beacon, 131
  Ocean Aire, 146
  Ocean Veranda, 132
  Off Season, 115
  Old London Inn, 133
  Oscar's House, 159
  Outer Banks Motel, 151
  Outer Banks Motor Lodge, 126
  Owen's, 138
  Paying Bills, 114
  Pebble Beach, 136
  Pets, 113
  Pony Island, 159
  Rates, 110
  Rating Periods, 111
  Sandpiper Court, 141
  Scarborough House, 143

Sea Foam, 138
Sea Gull, 153
Sea Oatel, 137
Sea Ranch, 122
Sea Spray, 135
Seasons, 115
Silver Lake, 573
Silver Sands, 136
Tan-A-Rama, 120
Tanglewood, 125
Tanya's, 127
Tower Circle, 149
Weekly Rates, 115
Mother Vineyard, 283, 299
Movies, 50, 73, 83, 339
Museum of the Albemarle, 423

N
Nags Head, History, 18, 66, 71
   Old, 71
   South, 79, 136, 231
Narrows Island, 23
National Park Service, 82, 287, 292
   Campgrounds, 179, 184, 185, 186
   Fort Raleigh, 292
   Hatteras, 331
   Information Center, 82
   Marinas, 100
   Ocracoke, 331
   Wright Memorial, 58
Nature Trails, Buxton, 333
Newspapers, 405
Nightspots, 258
   Atlantis, 264
   Barrier Island Inn, 258
   Comedy Club, 264
   Dareolina Cove, 266
   Fishtails, 263
   Gandalf's, 263
   Madeline's, 261
   Outer Banks Coliseum, 265
   Papagayo's, 262
   Port O'Call, 262
   R.V.'s, 259
   Sea Ranch, 261
   Station Keepers, 265
   Three-Quarters Time, 266
North Carolina Marine Resources Center, 295
Northwest Point, 285

O
Ocracoke, History, 359
Ocracoke Lighthouse, 367
Ocracoke Ponies, 363
Ocracoke Village, 366
Off Season, 115, 195
Off-Road Vehicles, 389
Oregon Inlet, 14, 106
Oregon Inlet Bridge, 106
Oregon Inlet USCG Station, 327
Oriental Wreck, 322, 381
Oysters, 198

P
Pea Island Station, 322
Pea Island Wildlife Refuge, 324
Performing Arts, 419
Pets, in Cottages, 167
   in Motels, 113
Pilots, 60, 62, 297, 330
Pine Island Sanctuary, 32
Pirates, 17, 66, 359
   Female, 360
Plymouth (England), 284
Police, 403
Ponies, Ocracoke, 363
Portsmouth, NC, 361
Portsmouth Island, 396
Powhatan, 285

Q
Quadricentennial, 286

R
Radio, Development of, 285, 297
Radio Stations on Banks, 406
Raleigh, Sir Walter, 283, 303, 359
Real Estate on Hatteras, 321
Real Estate: Buying, Advice on, 192
Rearview Mirror, 68
Rentals, Cars, 410
   Cottage: See "Cottage Rentals"
   Cottages, 163
Restaurant Prices, 201
Restaurants, 198
   A Restaurant By George, 227
   Avalon Pier, 209
   Back Porch, 252
   Barrier Island Inn, 204
   Bubba's Bar-B-Q, 251
   Cafe Rene, 231
   Capt'n Dave's, 219
   Capt. Ben's, 256
   Carolinian, 225
   Channel Bass, 252
   Daniels', 238
   Dareolina Cove, 232
   Dock, 239
   Duchess of Dare, 241
   Duck Deli, 206
   Dunes, 233
   Elegant Pelican, 231
   Elizabethan, 242
   Ella's, 208
   Emily's Soundside, 245
   Etheridge, 220
   Evans' Crabhouse, 223
   Fish Market, 221

Fisherman's Wharf, 243
Fishtails, 229
Frisco, Drive-In, 250
Froggy Dog, 246
Gandalf & Co., 229
Gingerbread House, 250
Howards' Pub, 255
Island Inn, 253
JK's, 218
Jolly Roger, 215
Kelly's, 226
Krause's, 213
Light Ship, 251
Lighthouse, 248
Madeline's, 220
Midgett's, 215
Miller's Seafood & Steak House, 222
Miller's Waterfront, 232
Newby's, 211
Orange Blossom, 248
The Pelican, 254
Peppercorns, 221
Pilot House, 248
Plantation, 228
Pony Island, 256
Port O'Call, 217
Quarterdeck, 249
Queen Anne's Revenge, 243
R.V.'s, 207, 237
Sam & Omie's, 235
Sanderling, 205
Sands Family, 224
Seafare III, 213
Ship's Galley, 245
Ship's Wheel,239
Sinbad's, 226
Sportsman's, 211
Stack 'Em High, 219
Starkey's Pizza, 222
Station Six, 209
Sweetwaters, 225
Tale of the Whale, 237
Top of the Dunes, 214
Trade Winds, 208
Weeping Radish,244
Whaling Station, 216
Windmill Point, 236

Roanoke Indians, 15, 283
Roanoke Island
 History, 17, 283
 In Winter, 196
Roanoke Voyages, 285, 304
Robeson County, 285
Rodanthe, 319
Rogallo, Francis M., 75
Roosevelt, Franklin, 322
Rosepock, 51

S

Sailing, 35, 77, 82, 83
Saloons, see "Nightspots"
Salvo, 319
Sand, 71
Sanderling, 227
Scallops, 198
Schedules, Ferries, 347, 398
Scuba Diving, 381
Scuppernong, 299
Sea and Sound Art ing, 227
Scallops, 198
Schedules, Ferries, 347, 398
Scuba Diving, 381
Scuppernong, 299
Sea and Sound Art Council, 419
Seafood Industrial Park, 301
Shallowbag Bay, 285, 304
Shell Castle Rock, 361, 367
Shiplifts, 301
Shipwrecks, 88, 318, 326, 327, 328, 381
Shoaling, 106, 301
Shopping, 267
 Ace Hardware, 314
 Avon Shopping Center, 352
 B.W.'s Surf, 377
 Beach Barn, 276
 Ben Franklin's, 273
 Browning, 357
 Burrus' Red & White, 354
 Cape Point, 355
 Chalet, 279
 Chesley Mall, 314
 Community Store, 374
 Daydreams, 356
 Dillon's Corner, 356
 Duck Blind, 272
 Dunes Shops, 273
 Farmer's Daughter, 270
 Fearing's, 311
 Fishin' Stuff/Summer Stuff, 357
 Forbes, 75
 Fox Water Sports, 353
 Galleon Esplanade, 278
 Gathering Place, 375
 Gray's, 277
 Harbor Gifts and Crafts, 314
 Harborside, 378
 Island Convenience 352
 Island Gallery/Christ- mas Shop, 300
 Kellogg's, 268
 Kinnakeet, 351
 Kitty Hawk Sports/Kites, 77
 Lee Robinson, 354
 Lion's Paw, 270
 Loblolly Pines, 269
 Lucky Duck, 216
 Manteo Bookseller, 310
 Maria's Gift Corner, 313

Merchant Mariner, 377
Nags Head Hammocks, 276
Nags Head Station, 277
Natural Art Surf Shop, 353
Nedo's, 351
Newman's, 279
Oceanside Plaza, 275
Ocracoke Art Co-op, 380
Ocracoke Variety Store, 379
Oden's, 298
Old Post Office, 377
O'Neal's, 375
Osprey Landing, 270
Outer Banks Mall, 278
Pelicans Roost, 354
Pirates Chest, 352
Ragpicker Rugs, 379
Ride the Wind, 378
RJ's Nursery, 315
R.V. Cahoon's, 281
Scarborough Faire, 271
Scotch Bonnet, 355
Sea Bear, 353
Sea Holly Square, 276
Seagate North, 275
Seashore Shops, 275
Second Time Around, 315
Sherli Shoppes, 275
Splash, 312
Surf Shops, 341
Surfside Plaza, 278
Tackle Shops, 390
Tickled Pink, 311
Tradewinds, 380
Village Craftsmen, 379
Vista Florist, 313
Waterfront, 310
Wee Winks, 269
Winks, 268
Ye Olde Ham Shoppe, 277
Shrimp, 198
Silver Lake, 361
Skyco, 285
Slaves, 285
Smith, John, 17
Snakes, 334
Somerset Place, 424
Soup, 198
South Nags Head, 79
Southern Shores, 27
  Town of, 27
Spain, 283, 361, 363
State Parks, Jockey's Ridge, 71
Storm Procedures, 412
Storms, 21, 412
Surfing, 340
  Learning to, 340
Swan Island, 23
Swimming, 86, 116, 292
  Coquina Beach, 86

Guarded Beaches, 86, 116

T
Teach, Edward, 17, 360
Television, 405
Tennis, 65, 116
Tiger, The, 359, 363
Time-Sharing, 188
Tornadoes, 414
Treasure, 361

U
U-Boats, 18, 89, 366
U.S. Army Coastal Research Facility, 28
U.S. Life Saving Service, 18, 325, 331
  Blacks in, 324
USS Huron, Wreck of, 67
USS Monitor, 328, 381
USS Oriental, 322, 381

V
Verrazano, Giovanni, 15
Virginia, Tidewater, 285
Visitors Center, Elizabeth II, 304

W
Wanchese,
  (Indian), 284
  Community, 301
  Effect of Shoaling on, 106
Wanchese Shiplift, 301
Washington, George, 361, 396
Waterfront, Manteo, 303
Watersports, 73, 77, 82, 338
Waves, 319
Weirs Point, 296
Welcome Center, 45
Whalebone Junction, 86
Whalehead, 23, 32
White, John, 17, 284
Wine, 299
Winter, 195
Woccon Indians, 359
World War II, 18, 88, 286, 366
Worship, 415
Wrecks, see "Shipwrecks"
Wright Brothers, 18, 43, 53, 58, 76
Wright Memorial, 58

X

Y

Z

Wright Memorial

Drawing by Jerry Miller

NOTES

NOTES

NOTES — 445